KGB Today
The Hidden Hand

John Barron

CORONET BOOKS
Hodder and Stoughton

Copyright © 1983 by The Reader's Digest
Association, Inc.

First published in Great Britain 1984 by
Hodder & Stoughton Ltd

Coronet edition 1985
Second impression 1985

British Library C.I.P.

Barron, John, *1930–*
   KGB today.
   1. Soviet Union. *Komitet gosudarstvennoĭ
   bezopasnosti*
   I. Title
   327.1'2'0947   HV8224

   ISBN 0–340–35212–4

This book is sold subject to the condition that
it shall not, by way of trade or otherwise, be
lent, re-sold, hired out or otherwise circulated
without the publisher's prior consent in any
form of binding or cover other than that in
which this is published and without a similar
condition including this condition being
imposed on the subsequent purchaser.

Printed and bound in Great Britain for
Hodder and Stoughton Paperbacks, a
division of Hodder and Stoughton Ltd.,
Mill Road, Dunton Green, Sevenoaks,
Kent (Editorial Office: 47 Bedford
Square, London, WC1 3DP) by
Cox & Wyman Ltd., Reading

TABLE OF CONTENTS

Author's Preface

ANYONE WHO WRITES ABOUT secret subjects and asks to be taken seriously is obligated to explain the origin, methods and purpose of his or her work, and above all to cite sources.

This book had its beginnings on a gloomy, rainy evening in November 1979, when Major Stanislav Aleksandrovich Levchenko came to my home. Not many days before, Levchenko had escaped to the United States from Tokyo where for nearly five years he had been at the core of great KGB operations.* He was still experiencing the traumas of flight, of the loss of his family, of permanent severance from his culture, and of entry into an alien society he had been taught to despise.

Yet, from the outset, Levchenko behaved as an officer and gentleman, a Russian patriot, who, though he had come to hate the KGB and the Soviet system, still revered his native Russia

---

*The letters KGB stand for the Russian words *Komitet Gosudarstvennoy Bezopasnosti*, which mean Committee for State Security. The KGB is an apparatus that functions as a secret political police force within the Soviet Union, and abroad as an instrument of clandestine action. Founded December 20, 1917, as the Cheka, the apparatus has undergone numerous titular changes, being known successively as the GPU, OGPU, GUGB, NKVD, NKGB, MGB and, since March 13, 1954, the KGB. Always it has been the "Sword and Shield of the Party"—the shield which protects the Soviet Communist Party oligarchy, the sword by which the oligarchy attempts to impose its will within and without the Soviet Union.

and his countrymen. I liked him instantly. We talked by the fire and listened to recorded music, most of it unfamiliar to him. He asked that some melodies be played again and again—"Plaisir d'Amour," "Parlez Moi d'Amour," "A Mighty Fortress Is Our God," "The Battle Hymn of the Republic."

Levchenko had asked to see me because he had read an earlier book I wrote about the KGB. Around 2 a.m. he picked the book from the shelf and called my attention to a passage that reproduces a letter written from a Soviet mental institution by a young college instructor, V. I. Chernyshov. It says:

"Having been buried, it is hard to prove that you're alive—except perhaps if a miracle should happen and someone dug up your grave before you died for good. It is hard to prove one's soundness of mind from within the walls of a psychiatric hospital.

"I finished the mechanics-mathematics course at LSU (Leningrad State University), then worked as an instructor of math with the title of assistant in the Leningrad branch of the Moscow Institute. I got carried away with collecting books and records, wrote poems for myself, short stories and philosophical essays. I typed up all my writings and bound them in three notebooks: poems and aphorisms, short stories and abstract dissertations, philosophical essays and statements of my ideas, of an anti-communist nature. During my five years of writing philosophical studies, I gave them to only two people. In March 1970 I was arrested for 'anti-Soviet propaganda.' One of the readers of my writings repented at once and was given his freedom. The other, a graduate of the Art Academy, V. Popov, whose guilt was in having drawn a bookplate in my notebook, was arrested.

"In prison I was examined for 30 minutes, and a diagnosis was reached: chronic schizophrenia of a paranoid type. I didn't see a lawyer, was not present at the trial and wasn't even told of the diagnosis or about the trial for a month and a half. My wife told me about it during a visit after the trial. The same diagnosis was reached for Popov. . . .

"In America Angela Davis was arrested. The whole world up to now knows about her fate, she has lawyers, people protest in her favor. But I, I have no rights, not once did I meet a lawyer, I wasn't present at the trial, I have no right to complain, I have no right to go on a hunger strike. I myself have seen how in psychiatric hospitals they tie protesting political prisoners, who refuse to take food or 'medicine,' give them a shot after which they cannot move, and forcibly feed and 'treat' them. A man called V. Borisov has protested for the past two years— they treat him with aminazin, which results in a loss of individuality, his intellect gets blunt, his emotions are destroyed and his memory disappears. This is the death of creativity: those given aminazin cannot even read afterward.

"Even though I am afraid of death, let them rather shoot me. How vile, how repulsive is the thought that they will defile, crush my soul! I appeal to believers. N.I. Broslavsky, a Christian, has languished here for over 25 years. And Timonin, whose guilt consists solely of having poured ink in a voting urn. They jeer at Timonin's religious feelings, they demand that he repudiate his faith, otherwise they won't let him out. Christians! Your brothers in Christ are suffering. Stand up for their souls! Christians! . . .

"I am afraid of death, but I'll accept it. I'm terribly afraid of torture. But there is a worse torture, and it awaits me—the introduction of chemicals into my mind. The vivisectors of the twentieth century will not hesitate to seize my soul; maybe I will remain alive, but after this I won't be able to write even one poem. I won't be able to think. I have already been informed of the decision for my 'treatment.' Farewell."

Levchenko said, "You see, I am a Christian." He also confided that his mother was Jewish, a fact he had always hidden from the KGB and everyone else.

Although he had been a secret Christian for 15 years, Levchenko was not a pacifist. He wanted to combat the KGB by revealing to the world his life within the KGB. He asked for no money, or anything else for himself; only that his story be narrated accurately.

Beginning in April 1980, Levchenko and I spent three weeks on the island of Maui, reconstructing his entire life; and we talked often during the next two years. These interviews form the basis of Chapters II, III and IV.

Levchenko contributed much more than his own story. He had worked at KGB headquarters in Moscow, and in Soviet fronts endeavoring to manipulate peace movements around the world. So he knew which types of espionage the Soviets currently emphasize, the clues that distinguish a KGB officer from a bona fide diplomat, and the signs that betray Soviet inroads into legitimate organizations. Enlightened by his briefings, I and my associates investigated, mainly through overt sources, KGB theft of advanced technology and efforts to influence peace groups. These investigations yielded most of the data for Chapters V and VI.

In March 1980 the FBI disclosed the defection of Colonel Rudolf Herrmann, who had served as an illegal KGB agent in North America for 17 years. I wrote to Herrmann through the FBI, and in November 1980, at Williamsburg, Virginia, he shared with me the full story of his life. Chapters VII and VIII recount that story.

One of the most important confederates of Colonel Herrmann was Professor Hugh George Hambleton, a Canadian economist who served as a KGB agent for 23 years. Having learned much about him from Herrmann, I approached him, and he consented to interviews, which were conducted in Quebec during December 1980. Chapter IX tells his story.

Reader's Digest, in its October 1982 issue, published a condensation of Chapter VI, concerning the nuclear-freeze movement. The condensation attracted abnormal attention and caused some controversy after President Ronald Reagan cited it as one basis for his judgment that the Soviets are trying to influence the movement. Subsequently, various Soviet spokesmen vitriolically condemned the condensation. However, to my knowledge, no one has adduced the least evidence demonstrating that there is a single error of fact in what The *Digest* published.

That is so because of the extraordinarily exhaustive and skillful research of *Digest* Associate Editor G. William Gunn and Research Associate David Pacholczyk. For almost a year, they labored six and seven days a week verifying facts, reading obscure literature and dreary communist polemics, and interviewing diverse people, some of whom have been hostile. They made many original discoveries. On a sweltering Sunday afternoon, for example, Bill Gunn came into my office with an old issue of the Communist *Daily World* and said, "I may have found something." A story on an inside page reported that one Radomir Bogdanov had spoken on Capitol Hill to members of Congress. From past research, I knew Radomir Bogdanov to be a veteran KGB colonel. This was our first evidence of KGB involvement with U.S. Congressmen in support of the nuclear-freeze movement.

The House Permanent Select Committee on Intelligence in December 1982 released the record of hearings it conducted regarding Soviet Active Measures. Along with testimony heard, the published record contains exhibits comprised of studies or documents submitted by the CIA and the FBI. Making a final check of a few points, David Pacholczyk studied this Exhibit XI in my office late at night. Suddenly, he exclaimed, "My God! They've doctored the document!" In preparing Exhibit XI, the House committee artfully deleted significant sections of an original document. The portions excised revealed names of Congressmen who had joined Soviet agents in meetings at the Capitol advocating disarmament. (Some of the data this Congressional committee curiously withheld from the public is reproduced at the end of Chapter VI.)

Gunn and Pacholczyk, with help from *Digest* researchers Nancy Tafoya and Katharine Clark, compiled the extensive Chapter Notes that detail the sources of information and enable readers to assess the factual validity of the book's content. In so doing, they detected and saved me from a number of errors.

I am indebted to others. Specialists in Soviet, East European and Japanese studies at the Library of Congress generously have shared their expertise and pointed out much source data. Konstantin Simis, a former Soviet lawyer, granted me permission to quote from his important new book, *U.S.S.R.: The Corrupt Society*. J. Fred Bucy, president of Texas Instruments in Dallas, instructed me at length about technological subjects and pointed us to significant findings about KGB activities in the United States. John L. Martin, chief of the Internal Security Section, Criminal Division, Department of Justice, provided invaluable guidance and criticism.

Digest Editor-in-Chief Edward T. Thompson authorized this project, put the magazine's resources at my disposal, granted me all the time needed and complete liberty to proceed as I judged best. Executive Editor Kenneth Gilmore and Washington Editor William Schulz enhanced the manuscript with ideas and editing. Their counsel and support sustained me throughout the research and writing. Patricia McLamara patiently and expertly typed the numerous drafts of the manuscript and protected me from many distractions.

I gratefully acknowledge the help of others, in America and abroad, whom I am not at liberty to identify. All share the credo Winston S. Churchill expressed when he declared: "We fight not for glory, not for riches, not for honor; we fight only and alone for *freedom*, which no good man surrenders, save with his life."

It is impossible to understand the Soviet Union without understanding the KGB and its transcendent role in Soviet policy and society. I hope this book may in some measure contribute to such understanding. For understanding is the first requisite to remaining free of all that is symbolized by the KGB.

John Barron
Washington, D.C.
March 5, 1983

I

A TYRANNY IN TROUBLE

THE RUSSIAN, a tall, dignified man in his 60s, entered the Moscow apartment about 6 p.m., followed by three aides who kept a respectful distance. His thick, gray hair was brushed straight back above an ashen face that expressed deep fatigue. Behind rimless glasses, his hazel eyes seemed thoughtful and searching, but they too bespoke weariness.

Without introducing himself or being introduced, he said in halting, formal English, "Professor Hambleton, I am pleased to welcome you to Moscow. I hope you have found the arrangements here satisfactory and your work productive."

Professor Hambleton was Hugh George Hambleton of Laval University, in Quebec, Canada. A handsome, debonair economist of some note, Hambleton had been a KGB agent for nearly 20 years, during which he had slipped the Soviets more than 1200 classified NATO documents. More significantly, he had supplied the KGB with its first authentic intelligence disclosing that both Israel and South Africa were producing nuclear weapons. Now the KGB hoped that he could emplace himself in some secret research center in the United States.

A KGB housekeeper had set out a cold supper, along with carafes of wine, on a dining table, and the Russian invited Hambleton to be seated. While one aide stood behind to assist him with his English, the other two braced themselves against the wall, and Hambleton realized they were bodyguards.

As they dined, the Russian posed a series of questions: Is not military spending becoming too onerous for the United States? Are Jews persecuted in America? What is the attitude of American youths toward the Soviet Union? Will not the European Common Market eventually fail? When the conversation turned to China, he remarked sadly, "Our relations with them are a tragedy."

After surveying the world, the Russian discussed future KGB assignments with Hambleton, including one in the United States. "In any case," the Russian concluded, "it is clear we can continue to use you in denied areas, like Israel, in trouble spots all over the world."

Almost exactly an hour after his arrival, the visitor rose from the table, and Hambleton stood also. Shaking hands, the Russian said, "I hope our collaboration will be even more fruitful in the future, and I wish you personally health and good fortune."

As soon as the visitor left, the KGB officer staying with Hambleton in the apartment filled two glasses with vodka, his hands trembling, and slumped into a chair.

"Who was that guy?" Hambleton asked.

"You mean you didn't know?" exclaimed the officer. "That was Yuri Vladimirovich Andropov, chairman of the KGB."

As KGB chairman and a full member of the Politburo, Andropov was one of the busiest men in the Soviet oligarchy. Yet that evening in July 1975, he took time from his weighty duties to personally attend to someone really important, a visiting spy.

That spy is now in a British jail. The spymaster now rules the Soviet Union.

The Politburo itself periodically sits down to ponder details of espionage, deceptions and sometimes more sinister subterfuges. In the autumn of 1979 the Soviet rulers assembled to meditate upon a particularly delicate question. Should the KGB assassinate the president of Afghanistan, Hafizullah Amin, and replace him with a Soviet agent? After studying the plan, conceived by Andropov's underlings and approved by him, the Politburo voted *da*.

The KGB chose a well-qualified officer, Lieutenant Colonel Mikhail Talebov, to be the assassin. As a member of Directorate S, which illegally infiltrates disguised KGB officers and agents into other nations, Talebov was highly versed in clandestine tradecraft and accustomed to perilous assignments. Having grown up among Muslims in the Soviet republic of Azerbaijan, on the Iranian border, he spoke Farsi as well as any Afghan. And with identification papers forged by the KGB, he had lived several years in Kabul, passing as a native Afghan.

Talebov entered Afghanistan in late October or early November 1979, posing as an Afghan chef; and, through arrangements made by the KGB network in Kabul, he obtained a job as a cook at the presidential palace. In the palace kitchen the lieutenant colonel awaited his opportunity. Always he had with him a colorless, odorless poison brewed by the Technical Operations Directorate in Moscow specially for President Amin. And according to his reports to the Kabul Residency, at least twice he dropped poison into fruit juice ordered by Amin.

However, while aware of Amin's fondness for fruit juice, the KGB did not appreciate how wary and wily he was. Fearful of poison, he always filled his glass with small portions of juice from many different containers. By mixing the juice, he reduced the poison ingested from any one batch to a non-fatal level, and apparently did not even become ill, for there was no investigation of the kitchen staff.

Dubious about whether Talebov would ever succeed in

poisoning the president, Andropov and the Politburo ordered
more forceful action. On the night of December 27, 1979, a
KGB assassination team, led by a Colonel Bayerenov and
backed by Soviet commandos, stormed the palace. In an up-
stairs salon they found Amin and killed him, along with a
lovely female companion. But the palace guards fought so
ferociously that Colonel Bayerenov dashed outside to call in
reinforcements. Because the Soviets wanted no living witnesses to the assassination, the attacking troops were under
orders to allow no one to leave the palace alive, and in the
darkness they shot their commander, mistaking him for an
Afghan.

Ultimately, the Soviets did kill nearly everyone inside the
palace. Among the few survivors was Lieutenant Colonel
Talebov. Though no one had told him of the raid, and no one
had told the raiders about him, he managed in the confusion of
the slaughter to escape.

Politburo members personally concern themselves with
forgeries, as well as assassinations. In the fall of 1981 the KGB
forged the signature of Ronald Reagan on a bogus letter to
King Juan Carlos of Spain. The fabrication stated that representatives of the military, the political parties and the Catholic
church close to the king were conniving to obstruct Spanish
entry into NATO. It asserted that there were "good grounds"
for the king to destroy "left-wing opposition," and hinted that
if he did so the United States might support the return of
Gibraltar to Spain. In sum, the letter depicted the President of
the United States dictating to the king of Spain and interfering
in Spanish internal affairs.

Evidently, this seemed like a good idea to the Politburo,
and with its authorization KGB agents in Madrid mailed
copies of the letter to Spanish newspapers and numerous
European diplomats. But this little operation served no purpose except to envenom U.S.-Soviet relations. Spanish journalists promptly branded the letter a forgery, and several
suggested it was Soviet-inspired. The White House interpret-

ed the forgery as an unprecedented and taunting personal affront to an American President in the early months of his Administration.

The spectacle of the most exalted leaders of the Soviet Union taking time from critical matters of state to plot murders and petty forgeries, to fete and consort with itinerant spies, may strike foreigners as odd, if not unseemly. Yet the intimate personal involvement of the leadership in such intrigues is the natural consequence of inordinate Soviet dependence upon clandestine action, a dependence inextricably rooted in both past and contemporary realities of the Soviet Union. This dependence does much to explain why the Soviet Union is ruled as it is, why the Soviet oligarchy behaves as it does, and why future Soviet oligarchs, in the near term at least, are unlikely to behave much differently. It also explains why the KGB, as the principal instrument of clandestine action, so pervades Soviet internal and external affairs alike—and why in 1982 the aging conspirators of the Politburo in desperation turned over the Soviet dictatorship to men from the KGB.

By early 1982, Brezhnev's health had so deteriorated that he was largely incapacitated and not expected to live much longer. In retrospect, it seems clear that by the spring of 1982 the oligarchy had settled upon Yuri Vladimirovich Andropov as his successor. In May, Andropov moved from the chairmanship of the KGB to replace the Party's principal ideologue, Mikhail Suslov, who had died. Andropov had only to wait days, weeks, a few months at the most, to become the fifth ruler in the history of the Soviet Union.

A spate of remarkable stories flattering Andropov surfaced in the Western press in the months before his ascension. They variously portrayed him as a pragmatic, flexible, humane, cosmopolitan intellectual, who spoke English fluently and understood the United States; as a compassionate reformer, who privately sympathized with dissidents; and as a dedicated devotee of détente. He danced the tango, drank good Scotch and cognac, favored American jazz and read Jacqueline

Susann, dressed elegantly and was "the perfect host." Some evenings he whiled away the hours listening to the Voice of America or drinking with dissidents, whom he invited to his apartment to broaden his vistas. Andropov might even be, suggested a Washington *Post* story, a "closet liberal."

Many of these adulatory characterizations were attributed to unnamed sources, and almost none can be independently corroborated. Andropov has shrouded his personal life in secrecy and, aside from spies, few if any Westerners have had opportunity to observe him privately during the past 25 years. Given the lack of firsthand data from credible witnesses, Andropov must be assessed on the basis of his recorded words and deeds. The portrait that emerges from the documented record is not that of a Kremlin swinger or a "closet liberal," but that of a quite different man.

Andropov was born June 15, 1914, in Nagutskaya Station, a tiny railroad settlement located in southwest Russia near the foothills of the Caucasus. He worked as a telegraph operator, movie projectionist and Volga sailor, before completing vocational training at the Technical School of Water Transportation in Rybinsk. Rather than languish on the rivers of Russia, he joined the Komsomol in 1936 and, as a political agitator, began making his way upward through the youth branch of the Party.

His first career break came in 1940 with transfer to Karelia, part of which the Soviets had seized from Finland the year before. The assignment entailed helping integrate the occupied territory into the Soviet Union, but that was not overly difficult because most of the Finns had fled. After open warfare erupted, Andropov participated in partisan operations against the Finns and became a protégé of Finnish Communist Party leader Otto Kuusinen. A longtime agent of the Communist International, Kuusinen was among the first to advocate creation of disguised Soviet fronts to subvert other nations. As early as 1926, he declared: "We must create a whole solar system of organizations and smaller committees around the Communist Party, so to speak; smaller organizations working actually under the influence of our Party (not under mechanical leadership)." Decades later, with Andropov as its chief, the KGB re-emphasized development and maintenance of just such a subversive "solar system" both in the West and Third World.

Probably at the behest of Kuusinen, the Party in 1951 promoted Andropov to an administrative post with its Central Committee. Stalin had renewed the purges, and an atmosphere of paranoia, plots, and rigid orthodoxy prevailed in Moscow. Yet Andropov so flourished that he gained a diplomatic appointment to Hungary in 1953, and the next year, at age 40, he attained the rank of full ambassador.

In Budapest, many foreigners did observe Andropov. The respected British journalist Noel Barber characterized him as a "humorless, narrow-minded Stalinist with an inscrutable expression." One Hungarian official considered him "absolutely ruthless." But others perceived him as an intelligent, poised and polite diplomat, keen to learn and understand.

However differently Andropov impressed diverse people in Budapest, there is no ground for dispute about his crucial intervention during the Hungarian Revolution. For a few days in the autumn of 1956, it appeared that the Hungarian people had achieved the impossible—independence under a new nationalist government, led by Imre Nagy. On November 1, Ambassador Andropov earnestly assured Nagy that the Soviets were prepared to negotiate withdrawal of all their forces from Hungary. That afternoon Nagy telephoned in alarm about reports that new columns of Soviet armor were advancing into Hungary. Andropov solaced the Hungarian Cabinet with more assurances—the reports were an "exaggeration." That same night, at the Soviet embassy, Andropov began plotting with Janos Kadar to overthrow Nagy and re-establish a puppet regime backed by massive Soviet reinforcements, which in fact were on their way.

The next day, Andropov called Nagy to complain that rioters were besetting the Soviet embassy. A Hungarian general hurried to the embassy, found all quiet, and reported so to Andropov. Thanking him, Andropov remarked, "We Russians don't want to mix in your business. We understand your troubles and are on your side."

The night of November 3, Andropov enticed Defense Minister Pal Maleter, a hero of the uprising, to a dinner, ostensibly to discuss details of the Soviet withdrawal. During the dinner, KGB toughs stormed in and dragged Maleter away to be shot.

After Soviet tanks crushed Hungarian resistance and imposed Kadar's regime, Nagy and aides took refuge in the Yugoslav embassy. In collusion with Andropov, Kadar sent them a pledge of amnesty. They were free, he wrote, to return to their homes and normal lives without fear of reprisal. The night of November 22, Nagy and the other Hungarians stepped out of the embassy and boarded a bus waiting to take them home. The bus transported them instead to the Soviet embassy and Andropov. The Soviets grabbed Nagy and deported him to Romania, and later he too was murdered.

The Party in 1957 rewarded Andropov for this distinguished performance by appointing him chief of the Central Committee department charged with controlling the Communist Parties of Eastern Europe, China and, later, Cuba. The position made him a regular participant in Politburo meetings and required frequent travel within the Soviet empire. But his duties, which he evidently discharged well, were essentially those of staff officer and administrator, rather than leader and innovator.

Once Andropov became chairman of the KGB in 1967, however, he was totally in command. By objective measurements, his stewardship must be rated as a singular success. He could not have succeeded as well as he did for 15 years without immersing himself deeply in the workings of the KGB and ratifying, if not originating, all of its principal policies and actions. These actions thus afford clear insight into his character, mentality and outlook.

Under Andropov, the KGB established an entire new Directorate, the Fifth, to hound Jews, persecute religious believers, eradicate the self-expression of underground publishing and silence dissidence. And the rooting out of ideological heresy became much more systematic, scientific and effective than at any time since the death of Stalin. As Andropov said in a 1977 tribute to the first chieftain of the secret political police, "We try to help those who are confused and try to get them to change their minds, and dispel their confusion."

Under Andropov, the KGB institutionalized the perversion of psychiatry for purposes of political repression. Since 1967, it has established or taken over numerous mental institutions. Without a normal trial or evidence, without transgressing the bounds of "socialist legality," the KGB psychiatrists can incarcerate a citizen for as long as they choose. They need only say that the intellectual deviant suffers "paranoid delusions of reforming society" or "moralizes" or "overestimates his own personality" or exhibits "poor understanding of reality." In these mental wards, the KGB can torture victims as it pleases, degrading them into zombies with drugs that destroy mind and spirit. This perversion of psychiatry, abundantly documented by honest Soviet and foreign psychiatrists alike, is one of the "reforms" with which Andropov must be credited.*

Under Andropov, the KGB has increasingly involved itself in international terrorism. About 15 miles east of the Moscow circumferential highway, just off Gofkovskoye Shosse, stands a forbidden complex known within the KGB simply as Balashikha. It is administered by the most sinister division of the First Chief Directorate—Department 8 of Directorate S, which is responsible for sabotage, abduction and assassination. A school in one area of the grounds provides training in terrorism to students imported directly from Third World countries or from Patrice Lumumba University in Moscow. The KGB regularly recruits some of the more able and amena-

*Because of the malpractices, members of the World Psychiatric Association resolved to propose ouster of the Soviets at the international organization's 1983 convention. The Soviets in February 1983 abruptly quit the Association. The president of the British Royal College of Psychiatry, Kenneth Rawnsley, told the Associated Press he believed they did so to avoid "the possibility of a humiliating defeat in the full glare of public debate."

ble pupils to serve as its agents inside terrorist movements abroad. Obviously, the KGB would not bring people from all around the world and school them to kill and destroy unless it wanted and expected them to kill and destroy.

Since 1980, ever larger numbers of KGB officers themselves have undergone training at Balashĭkha in sabotage and terrorist tactics. Again, the KGB would not teach officers such tactics unless it anticipated using them.

While ardently advocating détente, Andropov vastly increased the scope and tempo of the clandestine Soviet assault upon the West, especially the United States. The KGB currently is stealing technology from the industrialized democracies on an unprecedented scale. And it has orchestrated to a new crescendo a worldwide campaign to disintegrate NATO and disarm the United States in the name of peace.

Andropov's publicly reported exhortations to the KGB are also revealing. At various times, he told his men:

"Peaceful coexistence is a form of class struggle. It implies a bitter and stubborn struggle on all fronts—economic, political and ideological."

"The arena of the historic confrontation between socialism and capitalism is the whole world, all spheres of social life—economics, ideology, politics."

"Cheka authorities (the KGB) operate in an area where there are no, nor can there be, truces and breathing spaces."

Soon after his investiture in November 1982 as General Secretary of the Party,* Andropov turned over the Ministry of Internal Affairs, which controls the civilian police, to a ruthless KGB general, Vitali Fedorchuk. He appointed another KGB veteran of internal repression, Geidar Ali Rza Ogly Aliev, First Deputy Premier and positioned him to take charge of the economy. And to guarantee his own continuing mastery of the KGB, Andropov chose a trusted deputy, Viktor Chebrikov, to be its new Chairman. Never before in Soviet

---

*Andropov's official title is General Secretary of the Central Committee of the Communist Party of the Soviet Union. From this position, he rules the Party, and whoever rules the Party rules the nation.

history has so much power been concentrated into the hands of KGB alumni.

The willingness of the oligarchy to entrust its fate and that of the Soviet state to these men reflects recognition of a dominant reality.

Basically, the plight of Soviet rulers in the 1980s differs little from that of the early Bolsheviks. Better than anyone else, they understand that they have yet to attain the legitimacy of popular support from their own people. Their rule still depends upon force, and that force still is ultimately supplied by the secret political police, known today as the KGB. In other respects, the straits of contemporary Soviet oligarchs are bleaker and more desperate than those of their predecessors. For they can no longer reasonably believe that time is on their side, or that their most acute internal problems can be solved by the existing Soviet political and economic system.

A comparison of past Soviet promises with the realities of today dramatizes the severity of current problems. At the Twenty-Second Congress in 1961, the Communist Party solemnly proclaimed that by the year 1980 the Soviet Union would achieve the utopia of True Communism. As the Party officially promised and explained through all available media, at countless assemblies in schools, factories, farms and offices, True Communism would flood the land with a super-abundance of goods and services, all material things anyone could desire. The cornucopia of quality food, housing, clothing, appliances, automobiles, taxis and other transport, medicine and medical care, educational, cultural and recreational facilities would enable all citizens, irrespective of status, occupation, age, sex, ethnic origin or locale, to partake of whatever they wanted in any quantities desired. And everything would be free!

Better still, True Communism would reform human nature and bring about the final stage in human evolution by creating the New Communist Man, the perfect being. Daily gratification of all material needs and wants would permanently purge human beings of imperfections such as greed, avarice, duplicity, jealousy, selfishness, miserliness, infidelity and indolence. The resultant New Communist Man would be noble, altruistic, honest, courageous, strong, compassionate and comradely. Obviously and inevitably, with the advent of True Communism and the New Communist Man, crime, alcoholism and all other social ills inherited from capitalism would forever vanish.

Endlessly repeated in all seriousness during the 1960s, these Party promises of the millennium were heard less and less in the 1970s, then not at all as 1980 approached. In light of the actual conditions prevailing in the 1980s, their repetition would constitute a kind of black comedy.

Between 1964 and 1980 the mortality rate in the Soviet Union increased almost 50 percent, from 6.9 to 10.3 deaths annually per 1000 people. "This rise is more than can be accounted for by the increasing proportion of elderly persons in the population and is due to sharp increases in death rates for infants and males aged 20–44 in particular," writes Murray Feshbach of the Center for Population Research at Georgetown University. "Barring times of war, this trend is unique in the history of developed countries."

From available data, Feshbach and demographer Christopher Davis estimate that between 1971 and 1979, infant mortality soared from 22.9 deaths to 35 or 36 deaths per 1000 births. (The U.S. infant mortality rate in 1979 was 12.9; in 1981 it was 11.7.)

A Soviet male born in the mid-1960s could expect to live 66 years. Geoffrey Baldwin of the U.S. Census Bureau's Foreign Demographic Analysis branch deduces that by 1980, the year True Communism was due, the life expectancy of a newborn Soviet male had slipped to 62 years.

"Already at the beginning of the 1970s, a male child born in the Soviet Union could be expected to live ten years less than a newborn girl," Feshbach notes. "Now the difference is 11.6 years. No other developed country has such a gap."

The unprecedented increase in infant mortality and decrease in life expectancy result in part from the inadequacies of the Soviet medical system, which Brezhnev, in February 1981, admitted is deficient. Feshbach reports: "Physicians, mostly low-paid women,* work short hours (28 hours a week), crowded clinics are open only part of the day, the waits are long, diagnostic work is haphazard, and doctor-patient relations are often unsatisfactory. Medical equipment is in short supply and often out of date, and even such rudimentary medicines as aspirin are often unavailable, especially in rural areas." Sophisticated emergency treatment, which in North America annually saves countless lives, especially those of coronary patients, is unavailable to most citizens. Public confidence in the standard medical care is so low that people who can afford it are willing to pay 200 rubles for a "black-market" appendectomy, i.e., surgery privately performed in a physician's office under relatively sterile conditions and with the assistance of a qualified anesthetist and nurse.

A leading American authority on Soviet medicine, Dr. William A. Knaus of the George Washington University Medical Center, reports: "From 1960 to 1978, Soviet death rates from all cardiovascular diseases increased from 247 deaths for every 100,000 citizens to over 500—the reverse of what happened in the United States. Here an aggressive program aimed at detecting and treating hypertension, improving diet and exercise, and developing new drugs dropped heart disease-related deaths by 23 percent and the number of strokes even further. Few of these advances, including an organized program of detecting and then modifying risk factors, exist in the U.S.S.R. Hypertension is frequently not detected and often undertreated."

Despite these ominous demographic developments, despite public admission that Soviet medical care is inadequate, the

---

*The Central Statistical Directorate of the U.S.S.R. groups wages of physicians with those of all persons employed in health-care fields. In 1981 the average wage of persons in the health-care grouping was 128.5 rubles a month. This was roughly 40 percent less than the average wage of Soviet construction workers and nearly a third less than the average wage of industrial workers.

Party between 1965 and 1978 decreased the portion of the national budget allotted to health services by more than 20 percent (from 6.6 to 5.2 percent).

Alcoholism is another cause of the soaring Soviet death rate, in the judgment of such eminent scholars as Feshbach and Vladimir Treml of Duke University. "Alcoholism, now pandemic in the U.S.S.R., is undoubtedly a leading factor behind the mortality rise among working-age Soviet men, although heavy drinking is also increasing among women and teenagers," Feshbach says. "Urban families in the Soviet Union devote nearly the same proportion of their weekly budgets to alcohol as U.S. families do to food."

Alcoholism and poor medical care are intertwined with, and probably the consequences of, more profound Soviet problems, all of which are worsening. In November 1981 Brezhnev stated that, of all Soviet problems, the problem of agriculture is the greatest, both "economically and politically." While unfavorable weather doubtless has exacerbated the shortcomings of Soviet agriculture since 1979, its failures are endemic and chronic.

Roughly a fourth of the whole Soviet labor force is employed in agriculture. Factories disgorge tractors and other agricultural implements in the quantities, if not always in the quality, needed. Agriculture commands priority attention from the oligarchy and the supporting bureaucracy.

Yet in most of the Soviet Union, sometimes even in Moscow, shops periodically are empty of meat, dairy products, fruits and many vegetables. Relative to average income, the cost of food is extremely high in state stores and far higher on the black market. A detailed, authoritative study conducted during March 1982 found that the typical Moscow worker must labor 53.5 hours to provide a family of four with basic groceries needed for a week. (The same study showed the comparable work times to be 18.6 hours in Washington, 22.2 hours in Paris, 23.3 hours in Munich, and 24.7 hours in London.) Moreover, Soviet consumers complain widely that they must often buy in quantities larger than desired because much of the meat and produce sold to them is spoiled or decayed beyond use. Repeatedly the Soviets have staved off disaster only by massive importations of grain, primarily from the United States.

There is no mystery why Soviet agriculture habitually fails, just as there is none why American agriculture, which engages 3.4 percent of the U.S. labor force, produces enough to feed much of the world. Efficient modern agriculture requires that the farmer possess practical knowledge about not only agronomy but also cost accounting, marketing, animal husbandry, veterinary medicine, mechanics, carpentry, meteorology, botany, chemistry, personnel management, and capital investment. It requires an infrastructure that swiftly delivers produce from farm to market, as well as seed, fertilizer and spare parts from factory to farm, and the latest data from laboratories and universities to a farmer who comprehends the advantages of adapting new technology. Above all, it requires that the farmer-entrepreneur make and accept responsibility for the decisions governing his business, and that he be rewarded materially and socially in proportion to his productivity.

These requirements are not met by the Soviet agricultural system, which is based upon state and collective farms administered by rigid dogma and decrees issuing from a remote, centralized bureaucracy in Moscow. Responsibility for what happens on any given Soviet farm is so diffused that it is difficult to fix responsibility. For years, the lure of urban life and higher-paying industrial jobs has drained the farms of younger, more vigorous people and left a work force containing disproportionate numbers of elderly and lesser skilled people. Still living in hovels without plumbing, veritable serfs of the state, given subsistence wages and few cultural or recreational opportunities, farm workers are not concerned if a combine breaks down in the midst of a harvest, or if machinery rusts and crops rot in open fields because the state has not built barns. It does not matter to them whether the fields are properly seeded and fertilized, because neither the fields nor the fruits of their labors belong to them.

Each year, as harvest time nears, a national emergency arises in the Soviet Union. It is as if the harvest is a unique phenomenon, never before experienced. Soldiers, students, office and factory workers are hauled en masse into the countryside to fight the desperate battle of the harvest. A sizable percentage of the crops brought in by their mighty efforts will spoil because someone in the Ministry of Transportation has neglected to arrange for freight cars to arrive on time; more will be lost through spoilage and seepage in transit.

Many former Soviet nationals of diverse backgrounds, now in the West, bear witness to these agricultural conditions. But official Soviet statistics themselves provide the most damning indictment of the agricultural system. In certain circumstances, agricultural workers are allowed to farm private plots, to sell their produce and keep the earnings. The private plots may be no more than 1.25 acres in size, and in aggregate they compose only 1.3 percent of the land under cultivation in the Soviet Union. Yet, according to official data, this miniscule percentage of privately tilled land in 1980 yielded two-thirds of the potatoes and eggs and one-third of the vegetables and meat produced in the entire Soviet Union!

Another fundamental Soviet problem destined to worsen grows out of the composition of the population, which consists of 15 nationalities and more than 100 ethnic groups, speaking 127 languages. Lenin pledged that communism would guarantee equality and cultural autonomy to all. However, the Soviet Union is ruled by Russians who, while comprising slightly more than half the population, occupy the most preferred and influential positions in the Party, bureaucracy and economy. Most Soviet military pilots, as well as officers in the missile and submarine forces, are Russians or Slavs. Additionally, the Party methodically has tried to smother nationalism and individual cultures among the minorities, especially among the country's Muslims, estimated to number 44 million. Geoffrey Wheeler, a student of the Central Asian republics, where the Muslims are concentrated, observes that the Party is resolved to rip apart the "whole fabric of Islamic culture and society" by destroying religious, educational and family traditions.

"Rather than waning, however, Muslim and ethnic consciousness and assertiveness have grown in recent years in Central Asia," Murray Feshbach says. "Traditional Muslims have gained more self-confidence with the drive for Pan-Turkism, which has involved the Turkic Muslims in the Soviet Union, and Iran's rise as a model of a Muslim society. . . . Soviet authorities are aware that if the Muslims of the U.S.S.R. were to form a cohesive ethnic bloc, this could be a threat to the central authorities in the event of any future conflagration in the area."

Among the 50 million people of the Ukraine, where armed resistance to the central regime was not finally quelled until several years after World War II, nationalism and anti-Russian animus persist. The Baltic republics of Lithuania, Estonia and Latvia, forcibly annexed by the Soviet Union in 1940, seethe with hostility toward Russians; and Russians are regarded as occupying colonialists by many Armenians and Georgians.

Muslims, because of traditions encouraging large families, taboos against divorce and abortion, and infrequency of alcoholism, have the highest birth rate in the Soviet Union. They are multiplying four to five times faster than Russians, and will double in number during the next three decades. The Russian birth rate is one of the lowest of any Soviet nationality. According to latest Soviet projections, Russians by the year 2000 will form less than 47 percent of the total population, and that percentage may well be lower unless present mortality trends are arrested. In any case, the number of Russians of working age will actually shrink during the next 15 years. Muslims are much less acclimated to urban and industrial life than Russians, and many speak and understand the Russian language poorly. Yet increases in the industrial labor force can only come from Muslims, and the Soviets will have to draw from them ever more extensively in conscripting for the military.

While the Soviets clearly recognize all the potential perils inherent in these demographic shifts, they are confronted by a more imminent and momentous problem, whose portent perhaps is fully understood by scientists and officers in the Scientific and Technical Directorate of the KGB.

As a result of the Soviet system, the Soviet Union is ill-prepared to join and absorb the benefit of the oncoming second industrial revolution. Soviet industry is mired in inertia and reflexively resistant to change. The Soviet press abounds with reproving reports of industrial managers who, rather than install new equipment, have allowed it to rust in warehouses or factory yards. But these chastised managers are not fools. They are judged by how well they fulfill production quotas arbitrarily set by central planners in Moscow. If they interrupt production to install new equipment, if the new equipment does not function as intended, or if workers cannot quickly master its functions, the manager will fail to meet the quota and be punished. If new equipment is installed and productivity increases, he will only be rewarded with higher quotas.* Soviet scientific and research centers usually are isolated from industry and not attuned to its problems and needs. And when a Soviet scientist does conceive a new idea or process useful to industry, there is no assurance that it will be accepted or even communicated.

Consequently, the Soviet Union always has lagged behind the West technologically, except in some areas of military technology, to which the largest share of its scientific and industrial resources is devoted. In the past it has been able to muddle along and keep within sight, stealing or copying the inventions of others; or, as in the notorious case of the Kama

*Andropov, in a speech to the Central Committee on November 22, 1982, urged the "large-scale and speedy introduction of scientific and technological achievements and advanced experience in production." He summed up the problem thus: "This question is not new, of course. It has been raised more than once at the Party's congresses and at the Central Committee's plenary meetings. Nevertheless, progress is slow. Why so? The answer, too, is long known: To introduce a new method or new technology, production has to be reorganized in one way or another, and this affects fulfillment of plan targets. Moreover, you may be taken to task for failing production plans but only scolded at the most for poor introduction of new technology."

River truck plant,* enticing Western concerns to build factories for Soviet use. In the future, that will be much more difficult.

The advent of semi-conductor technology, conceived by Bell Laboratories in New Jersey, and the silicon chip, first manufactured by Texas Instruments in Dallas, Texas, inaugurated a new era for mankind. The semi-conductor chip is a thin piece of silicon about the size of a match head, onto which presently tens of thousands of memory or logic functions can be impressed. There are many different kinds of silicon chips. For instance, the combination of memory and logic functions on a single chip form what is in effect a tiny computer.

These chips, which typically sell for a few dollars each, can be utilized individually to regulate a hand-held calculator, an internal combustion engine, the navigational and avionics systems of aircraft, or the guidance systems of missiles, and can be used for endless other purposes. Or the chips can be integrated in almost infinite numbers to form computers of heretofore unimagined capacity. Ever more powerful, smaller and less expensive computers will be employed in myriad ways, including the design and management of error-free robots and completely automated assembly lines.

Already the chip is changing scientific research, industrial production and daily life. But what has begun to happen is the merest of beginnings. As Texas Instruments President J. Fred Bucy said in 1978: "The explosion of computer technology will expand knowledge exponentially. Mankind will be able to consider and solve theoretical problems of which we now cannot even conceive. The world has entered the second industrial revolution, and we can no more foresee all the benefits it will bring than 19th-century man could foresee the consequences of the first industrial revolution."

*The Kama River plant, the largest truck factory in the world, was built in the 1970s with the aid of $1.5 billion worth of U.S. and West European equipment. Many of the military trucks that carried Soviet forces into Afghanistan as well as many poised on West European borders come from the Kama River plant.

Today the Soviets lag five to ten years behind the United States in the technology of computers, semi-conductors, micro-circuitry and computer-aided design. Because of the accelerating, geometric progress in the West, the gap will almost certainly widen. For example, several Japanese and American companies soon will be producing chips with 256,000 bits of memory. Bucy predicts that before the end of the decade, there will be developed the four-megabit chip with four million bits of memory on one tiny sliver of silicon. As technology advances into ever more arcane realms, the Soviets are likely to fall further behind, unless they fundamentally reform their system so they can innovate for themselves.

Additionally, low productivity, born of worker indifference and lethargy, increasingly blights the controlled Soviet economy. Soviet labor productivity is only about 40 percent of that in the United States, and many workers care nothing about the quality of their output. In 1980 Andropov said: "It must be confessed that we all know that alongside the shock workers of socialist competition you still encounter people with a negligent attitude toward matters, absentees and drunkards. We still encounter cases of pilfering, eyewash and bureaucratism, attempts to deceive the state, to do as little as possible." In Andropov's judgment, such behavior persists because the Soviets have not yet created the New Man, whose formation, he concedes, "is a complex and protracted process."

However, Richard Pipes, one of the foremost American students of the Soviet Union, believes there are other causes. "In essence, the mass of Russians, descendants of bonded peasants, treat the Soviet state, their current master, much as their enserfed ancestors have treated their landlords," Pipes says. "Like them, they have developed myriad subterfuges to evade their responsibilities, to steal the master's property, to squeeze him out of the land and factory. The Soviet regime seems helpless to cope with this nationwide passive resistance and grudgingly has to acquiesce to it. The fall in productivity observable in the Soviet Union, in the final analysis, is the revenge of the modern serf on his master, the State."

Soviet capacity to cope with critical national problems is seriously diminished by pervasive corruption, which has assumed such proportions that it must now be regarded as a basic problem unto itself. Growing numbers of Soviet émigrés in recent years have cited examples of corruption that would have seemed incredible had not the witnesses proven reliable about other matters, and had not their accounts been paralleled by those in the Soviet press itself.

New buildings rapidly deteriorate or actually fall apart because of substandard construction, resulting from diversion of building materials to the black market. The output of factories, hours flown by aircraft squadrons, reports of inspection commissions, and sales figures are often flagrantly falsified. Black-market entrepreneurs have become millionaires by maintaining underground factories, replete with illegal nationwide distribution systems. The necessity of paying bribes or tribute to obtain meat, clothing, housing, quality medical care, admission to a university, or a fair judgment in court has become a reality of daily life accepted by many, if not most, Soviet citizens.

The most authoritative and comprehensive revelations of why corruption has swollen into such an economic and social malignancy come from a former Soviet lawyer, Konstantin Simis. As an attorney and professor of law, Simis often traveled from Moscow into the provinces to defend people charged with corruption. From clients, court cases, and colleagues in the legal profession, he became intimately familiar with the forms and practices of corruption. After the KGB discovered and confiscated a manuscript he had written, it gave him and his wife, an attorney who defended dissidents, a choice: concentration camp or deportation. He rewrote his manuscript in the United States, and it was published late in 1982 under the title *U.S.S.R.: The Corrupt Society.**

The book details and authenticates what many others have alleged. Corruption in the Soviet Union begins atop the Party

*Simis, Konstantin, *U.S.S.R.: The Corrupt Society*, Simon and Schuster, 1230 Avenue of the Americas, New York, N.Y. 10020, 1982.

hierarchy in Moscow and spreads down through the provinces into virtually all eddies of society. Bidders gladly pay more than 100,000 rubles for key administrative positions in the Party, knowing they will recover many times their investment through receipt of bribes and sale of subordinate positions. Simis shows that even when culprits in the Party are exposed by honest investigators, prosecutors or journalists, the defendants usually escape serious punishment because they have protected themselves through bribes or the influence of patrons who also are on the take.

To entertain officials and inspectors, a state construction organization built a fine little resort hotel on the Volga and hired skilled wrestlers to guard the well-kept grounds. Ordered by management to procure women for the guests, the guards lured schoolgirls and young women to the hotel, raped them and photographed their defilement. Told that the photographs would be shown to parents, teachers or employers, a number of the traumatized victims agreed in effect to be staff prostitutes, rather than be publicly disgraced. Some schoolchildren, though, reported to their parents, who complained to the public prosecutor. Simis writes: "These complaints contained hard facts, dates and names, but in response came the unvarying reply: 'Upon checking your statement, it has been impossible to corroborate the facts. It has not been deemed that grounds exist for the institution of criminal proceedings against X under Article 117 of the Criminal Code of the RSFSR (rape).' "

The hotel sponsors had taken the precaution of including among their guests leaders from the Party, the police, and the prosecutor's office. However, despite resistance from the regional Party establishment, *Literaturnaya Gazeta*, which has political influence of its own, ultimately publicized the scandal and forced prosecution. Only some of the guards and a minor hotel employee, chosen as scapegoats, were imprisoned.

Corruption creates "phantom factories," whose fictitious output is officially represented as part of the gross national product. As an illustration, Simis cites the example of a major new plant, in the town of Siversky, designed to repair tractor engines. An Inspection Commission report on December 28, 1978, certified that the plant was ready. The Minister of Agricultural Machinery, on February 16, 1979, ordered it to commence operations and assigned a production quota. An existing plant, which the new one was to replace, closed.

Actually, of the 51 workshops and other facilities that were to compose the Siversky plant, only 14 were even approximately ready. The whole place looked like a junkyard, and nothing could be accomplished there. The Inspection Commission had never seen the site. The Ministry of Agricultural Machinery simply had commission members sign the fraudulent certification. Those who refused were replaced or had their signatures forged.

The Central Statistical Office for more than a year listed the work of the nonexistent plant in its official totals of Soviet production. Meanwhile, mounting numbers of broken-down tractors stood idle because the old plant that could have repaired them had closed.

The falsification of the volume of materials delivered and goods produced in industry is so chronic and widespread that Russians have a popular term for the practice—*pripiska*. Even though *pripiska* is well known, even though an extensive inspection system exists to oversee accuracy of reports, the nationwide fraud continues unabated. In the words of Simis, it continues because of "the eternal, ineradicable bribe." And because so many production reports are inflated, the Central Statistical Office does not have reliable data, and its annual compilations of overall Soviet economic output are necessarily misleading—even to the Politburo.

Beyond compounding the inherent illogic and inefficiency of the Soviet economy, corruption on such a grandiose scale inflicts injustice and corrodes the spirit. The man who sees his wife or child die because he cannot afford a black-market appendectomy, the parents who cannot buy the way of their son into a university while others can, the couple that has waited eight years for an apartment only to have it given to others because of bribery, the parents whose child is raped with the tacit sanction of the state, the wife who cannot buy adequate groceries for her family without paying illicit tribute—all feel cheated and debased; they feel that there are no values, that nothing matters save their own survival.

Pipes, who concurs that "the cancer of corruption, previously localized, has spread to the entire Soviet system," points to other effects. "It causes the population to look upon those in authority as a pack of parasites whose exclusive concern is with the gratification of their private needs and wants," he says. "This state of affairs disgraces the government in the eyes of even the most apolitical citizens and robs it of any moral right to demand from them civic responsibility and personal sacrifice. The consequences are particularly disastrous among the young, whose indifference to public affairs and cynicism gives the authorities cause for most serious concern."

A few months after beginning work at the U.N. Secretariat in New York, a young Soviet technician, Aleksandr Sakharov, in 1981 asked for political asylum. The KGB had carefully screened Sakharov; he was not a political ideologue; he had an enjoyable tour ahead in the United States and a secure future back in Moscow. Why then did he and his wife desert their society? His explanation: The Soviet Mission assigns each new family an apartment. But Sakharov was told by the assigning officer that if he wanted a decent apartment, it would cost him $500 under the table. "I am sick and tired of being cheated," he said.

The Soviet oligarchy has tried through the press to signal the population that it intends to do something about corruption. A long *Pravda* story, on April 27, 1982, announced the execution of a Deputy Minister of Fisheries named Ritov. The minister had masterminded a ring that smuggled caviar in cans labeled "herring" to Western Europe. Reportedly, all unraveled after a militiaman accepted a can of herring as a bribe but, upon finding caviar, disclosed his discovery.

The daily newspaper *Sotsialisticheskaya Industriya*, in

January 1983, reported the trial of one Stanislav Ivanov and 14 conspirators, who allegedly embezzled millions of rubles by registering a nonexistent factory and collecting wages for 515 phantom employees over three years. They accomplished the swindle by paying kickbacks to collective farms and bribes to other officials. The newspaper hinted that Ivanov might also be executed.

The oligarchy also recognizes the other fundamental problems. More farmers may be allowed private plots. Russian women are being debarred from certain jobs entailing onerous manual labor and given incentives to bear more children. No resources will be spared in stealing technology from the industrialized democracies, and industrial managers are being exhorted to adapt new technology.

However, the statements of Andropov and others reflect no willingness to confront the underlying causes of Soviet deficiencies. "Yes, we do indeed have difficulties and unresolved problems," Andropov said in 1980. "But they are connected not with the nature of our economic system but above all with the fact that we have not learned to make full use of the tremendous advantages provided by the socialist methods of production."

Hence, the oligarchy resorts to palliatives that will never solve basic Soviet problems. They cannot be solved until farmers, workers, managers and scientists are granted sufficient liberty to work and create as they know best. But the oligarchy dares not grant liberty because of doubts that it could survive in an environment wherein the people are free to exercise some choice about how they are governed. The legions of KGB troops who guard Soviet borders, not so much to keep out foreign invaders as to prevent citizens from escaping the Soviet Union, attest to the oligarchy's fear of what people would do if free.

Insecure and fearful of its own people, the oligarchy preserves itself through tyranny, and in doing so follows precepts enunciated by Aristotle more than 2000 years ago. Aristotle wrote that the successful tyrant must spiritually isolate each citizen one from another; he must persuade each that no one else cares about him, that he is hopelessly and helplessly alone against the overpowering and omnipresent might of the tyrant. A primary means of spiritually atomizing the population, Aristotle said, is to infest society with spies. Fear that the punitive state may always be watching and listening through unseen spies inhibits intellectual communion, and thereby coalescence of opposition.

Since the days of the Cheka, the secret political police have utilized spies and terror to politically paralyze most of the people, by making them feel hopelessly and helplessly alone against the power of the Party. Because of this paralysis, brave generals, heroes of the Party, loyal scientists, artists, industrial managers and dedicated intelligence officers did not resist their own slaughter during the mad purges of Stalin. Fathers, sons, mothers, daughters, sisters, brothers, friends, and comrades feared to raise their voices or offer supplications in behalf of relatives or colleagues. Everyone was cowed; everyone was alone.

Today, stringent censorship, which regulates and constricts the circulation of information and ideas; controls over travel and assembly; the expenditure of excessive time and energy to acquire the routine necessities of life—all help isolate Soviet citizens spiritually and intellectually. But the greatest isolator is still the fear inspired by the secret political police, the KGB.

Comparatively small numbers of Soviet citizens in recent years have dared to speak out, and the KGB has reacted with a ferocity that would seem to outsiders needlessly disproportionate to the threat these citizens present. But the masters of the KGB more keenly comprehend the threat. When a Soviet citizen openly protests perceived injustice or tyranny, he in effect is declaring to the oligarchy: *Do with me what you will. Impoverish my family. Lock me in a concentration camp. Put me in a mental institution and drug me into a zombie. But I no longer will play by your rules. I no longer will be afraid.* The protestor thus strikes at the Soviet system's very foundation, which is fear; and the oligarchy understands that fearlessness, if unchecked, would jeopardize the system.

So the oligarchy must still rely on secret political police to perpetuate fear, and to identify, isolate and suppress any outbreak of fearlessness. To this end the KGB maintains immense networks of informants that reach into every crevice and all levels of Soviet society, into all branches of the armed forces, science, industry, education, agriculture, the arts, the press, the Party itself. Dissidents who do not quickly convert to orthodoxy after a warning visit from the KGB are trundled off to forced labor camps or mental hospitals, where they are tortured and, in many cases, permanently deformed by drugs.

In dealing with the rest of the world, the Soviet oligarchy must struggle from a position of relative weakness, as did the oligarchy under Lenin. Certainly the Soviets have amassed awesome military might, although at crippling costs. By suppressing East German uprisings in 1953, the Hungarian revolt in 1956 and incipient Czechoslovakian liberty in 1968, and by threatening Poland with intervention in 1982, the Soviets have demonstrated that they will employ armed force to preserve their empire. By invading Afghanistan they have shown that they will undertake armed conquest of other nations should they judge there will not be effective resistance. And if the Soviets ever conclude that the West is unable or unwilling to resist their armed forces, they will surely be tempted to set those forces loose. But so long as the Soviets perceive that the West retains equivalent or superior military power, and the will to use it in self-defense, they cannot attempt any expansion that might entail direct military confrontation.

Yet the Soviet oligarchy still vows that all the world eventually must live under communism. Former U.S. Secretary of State Dean Rusk once remarked, "Democracies have paid a fearful price for refusing to believe that dictators mean what they say." Listening to the considered words of the Soviet dictatorship can be instructive. But to understand them, one first must comprehend Soviet language and formulations.

To most Americans, *détente* means just what any standard

English-language dictionary says, "a relaxation of strained relations or tensions" among nations. To the Soviets, *détente* means a diminution of visible conflict, but an increase in *sub rosa* conflict. "Détente in no way signifies a possibility of weakening the ideological struggle," Brezhnev said at the advent of "détente" in 1972. "On the contrary, we should be prepared for an intensification of this struggle."

The president of the World Peace Council, Romesh Chandra, an Indian Communist and Soviet agent who unerringly articulates the official Politburo position, elaborated in 1976: "Détente means essentially a change in the balance of forces in the world in favor of peace and against imperialism. . . . There is the wrong idea that détente means lessening of the struggle against imperialism; détente means the intensification of the struggle but in new forms with greater possibilities, with greater optimism and confidence."

Endlessly, Soviet spokesmen aver that they crave peace, and in so asserting, they indubitably are sincere. But what does "peace" mean? By Soviet definition, "peace" at the current stage of history does not mean an absence of conflict and war. That kind of "peace" can never be realized until communism prevails throughout the world. Once all mankind lives under communism, all will be tranquil. But, in Lenin's words, "As long as capitalism and Socialism remain, we cannot live in peace." Wars of national "liberation" and other forms of conflict are not only inevitable, but commendable. Until the "complete and final victory of communism on a world scale," as *Pravda* puts it, the Soviets are committed to waging war for "peace."

While the Politburo itself makes all the strategic and many of the tactical decisions in this clandestine war without end, the daily combat is directed from KGB headquarters in Lubyanka on Dzherzhinsky Square, a few blocks from the Kremlin. The headquarters, consisting of a six-story Gothic building, owned by an insurance company before the Revolution, and a ten-story Stalinesque addition, built by German prisoners and slave labor after World War II, outwardly looks the same as it has for 35 years. But inside there have been changes.

In the old Lubyanka prison the screams of the tortured and the pleas of the doomed are heard no more. Drunken executioners no longer ram pistols into backs of heads and blow out the faces of "enemies of the people." No longer must cleaning crews come every few hours to wash blood away from the stone walls, swab gore off the oak floors, and cart away the remains of miscreant comrades.

Today these essential functions of the Soviet state are performed more sedately at Lefortovo prison in central Moscow, in pastoral camps outside the city, and in special wards of mental institutions. Lubyanka prison, the shrine and symbol of terror, whose very name still kindles fear in Soviet citizens, has undergone a reincarnation. Unbeknown to the general public, its cells, torture chambers and execution cellars have been remodeled and made part of the Center, as the KGB calls headquarters. In the same spaces where heroes of the Party, the military and the secret political police apparatus itself saw fit to confess to monstrous, unbelievable crimes before being exterminated, KGB officers now work harmoniously alongside famous ghosts of Soviet history.

Conversion of prison cells to KGB offices essentially reflects the need for more space generated by the steady growth of the headquarters staff in the 1970s.* Rooms in the original

---

*The author has been unable to obtain any original, verifiable data revealing the number of personnel in the KGB. Former KGB officers interviewed said that they could not make meaningful estimates because the KGB is compartmentalized into so many different directorates, services and departments, some of whose members are deployed throughout the Soviet Union or the world.

In 1973 two Western intelligence services estimated to the author that the KGB then had about 90,000 staff officers and additionally employed some 400,000 personnel as technicians, secretaries, clerks, security and border guards, and special troops.

The number of personnel assigned to KGB headquarters certainly has increased in the past ten years, and that increase probably reflects growth in the overall complement.

The number of people the KGB employs as informants inside the Soviet Union and as agents outside is unknown. That number, however, doubtless runs into the hundreds of thousands.

building and the postwar addition have been subdivided and partitioned into cramped offices. Most are congested with three or four officers and a discordant hodgepodge of furnishings, some of which were in the old insurance building when the Cheka appropriated it in 1917. When the workday begins or ends, the dingy green corridors, lined with frayed red carpet and patrolled by armed sentries, are packed like a subway station at rush hour.

The Center also has undergone significant organizational as well as physical changes. The Seventh or Surveillance Directorate, for example, formerly functioned as an appendage of the Second Chief Directorate, which bears general responsibility for internal repression and counterintelligence.* Now the Seventh Directorate is empowered to initiate surveillances on its own, and maintain its own analytical division to assess movement of foreign and suspect citizens. The Fifth Directorate—established to crush dissidence, stamp out *samizdat,* or underground publishing, intensify repression of religion, and hound Jews—is still regarded as the dirtiest division of the KGB. Its officers still beat people on the street in broad daylight, as a lesson to others. However, it is now authorized, at its discretion, to try to reform the wayward through persuasion and warnings before hauling them off to camps or mental institutions.

In the First Chief Directorate, which conducts foreign operations, an important new unit, known as Department Twelve, has been formed. Previously, the Second Chief Directorate was solely responsible for suborning foreigners stationed or visiting in Moscow. Over the years, it achieved many notable successes, often through entrapment and blackmail, recruiting at least two Western ambassadors as well as numerous journalists, businessmen and academicians. While the Second Chief Directorate still resorts to these hoary methods, changing mores and new awareness in the West have made them less effective and often counterproductive. Moreover, most

---

*Appendix B delineates in some detail the organization of the KGB.

Second Chief Directorate officers lack the knowledge of foreign cultures and customs that can be acquired only by living abroad. Even if they develop a personal rapport with a recruitment target, its value dissipates when the foreigner goes home.

The new Twelfth Department in the First Chief Directorate has none of these handicaps. It is staffed with senior KGB officers who have distinguished themselves in prolonged clandestine operations abroad. They understand the national mentalities and ways of foreigners, and are accustomed to moving easily among them. From cover positions in the Soviet Academy of Sciences, Chamber of Commerce, and universities, they can naturally and openly meet visitors in Moscow. Such cover also enables them to travel abroad and lure quarry into the Soviet Union, where others can work on them. The ability to travel also permits these officers to maintain any friendships they form.

One archetypical Department Twelve officer is Colonel Radomir Georgevich Bogdanov, who currently masks himself behind scholarly cover—deputy director of the Institute for U.S.A and Canada, in Moscow. A protégé of General Boris Solomatin, who was KGB Resident in Washington and then New York during the 1970s, Bogdanov first reported for duty in India in 1957. He devoted almost ten years there to recruitment of English-speaking Indians, helped develop Romesh Chandra into an important agent, and eventually became Resident in New Delhi. Posing as a serious student of North America, Bogdanov attends international conferences around the world, looking for American prey. He has traveled to the United States, hobnobbed with Congressmen on Capitol Hill, and unsuccessfully sought permission "to do research" at Stanford University.

Department Twelve is one of the few elements of the First Chief Directorate remaining at Lubyanka, most of them having moved to a building of their own, outside Moscow. About ten miles southwest of the city, near the village of Tëplyystan, a narrow road leads from the circumferential highway into a dense forest. A large billboard at this intersection warns: "Halt! No Trespassing! Water Conservation District." Some 200 yards down the access road is what appears to be a militia post; it is actually manned day and night by KGB troops dressed as militiamen. The road ends about a third of a mile beyond, in a traffic circle adjoined by parking lots for more senior or affluent officers who drive to work. Most officers arrive in chartered buses, which depart each morning from assembly points near principal Moscow subways.

Past the circle, a high chain-link fence, topped with barbed wire, protects the premises. Personnel enter through turnstiles in a guardhouse, which bears a bronze plaque inscribed with golden letters saying "Scientific Research Center." Armed sentries from the KGB Guards Division, wearing khaki service dress uniforms, with blue flashes on the lapels and blue stripes on the trousers, inspect the special pass each officer must show. It is a buff-colored plastic card with the bearer's photograph and a perforated code designating areas he is authorized to enter.

Beyond the guardhouse, a driveway runs some 400 yards through lawns and flower beds to the First Chief Directorate building, which was designed by Finnish architects and constructed in part with materials and equipment from Finland. Shaped like a three-pointed star, the seven-story structure is built largely of aluminum and glass; its many windows are edged with blue stone. Stepping through double glass doors, an officer enters an expansive marble foyer and again shows his pass to sentries. A bust of Feliks Dzherzhinsky, the first chief of the secret political police, stands in the middle of the foyer, and fresh flowers are placed beneath it daily. A newsstand is on one side of the foyer, and a large cafeteria and canteen are located beyond the main bank of elevators in the center of the building.

For little more than a ruble, an officer can buy a superior meal, including meat, served by friendly, neat young women hired from nearby villages. The cafeteria sells beer, but no other alcoholic beverages. The First Chief Directorate has

largely extirpated the tradition of drinking on duty that long
benighted the Organs of State Security. The tradition originated and was tacitly institutionalized during the purges of the
1930s, when torturers and executioners were issued vodka
and encouraged to drink during breaks; they needed to be
drunk to do what they did day after day to other human beings.
Drunkenness spread, and at Lubyanka many officers, even in
the 1960s, commonly stopped by the canteen around 10 a.m.
for their first belt of the day. Strictures against imbibing in the
office were not taken seriously until the early 1970s, when the
KGB, under the goad of the Party, began to fire offenders in
large numbers. (Officers are still permitted to drink at operational lunches, and on their own time many still drink
excessively.)

Out of this airy forest redoubt, subterranean networks of
agents reach into the farthest recesses of the earth. The Party
proudly calls the KGB officers who build and manage these
networks "troops of the invisible front." Always, KGB officers
try to remain invisible. But in recent years the scope and
intensity of their clandestine activities have so expanded that
more and more officers expose themselves. Collectively,
these exposures manifest and delineate the kind of war the
Center hourly directs against the world.

Egypt, in September 1981, expelled seven Soviet "diplomats," including the ambassador, and two Russian correspondents. It declared that the Soviets had incited strife between
Coptic Christians and Muslim fanatics, which erupted in
bloody fighting that killed 70 people. The expulsion announcement asserted that the Soviets had also been working
in league with leftist extremists and "an Arab nation hostile to
Egypt," doubtless a reference to Libya.

Norway, in February 1982, expelled two Soviet trade officials for illegally trying to buy components of the American F-
16 fighter, being built in the country, and for attempting to
bribe Norwegian firms into purchasing advanced American
technology for the Soviet Union.

Pakistan, during August and September 1980, ousted nearly

100 Soviets for engaging in subversive and illicit propaganda activities.

Spain, in February 1980, expelled two Soviets for maintaining clandestine contacts with outlawed terrorist and revolutionary groups. In April 1982 it ousted two more Soviets for attempting to influence the press and for cultivating contacts with Spaniards involved in the delivery of U.S. weapons to Spain.

Costa Rica, in August 1979, kicked out two Soviets for fomenting a general nationwide strike.

Canada, in February 1978, declared 13 Soviets *persona non grata* for trying to bribe and subvert the Royal Canadian Mounted Police. In April 1982 it expelled another Soviet for trying to smuggle advanced communications equipment out of the country.

Malaysia, in July 1981, expelled three Soviets for recruiting the political secretary of the deputy prime minister and equipping him with eavesdropping gear, cameras and a transmitter.

Bangladesh, in August 1981, ousted two Soviets after they attacked a security guard, who caught them smuggling in electronic eavesdropping equipment.

Liberia, in April 1979, expelled three Soviets for inciting riots.

The United States since 1979 has expelled five Soviets for espionage. In February 1982 it expelled a Soviet diplomat who turned out to be a GRU major general. The night before, the FBI detected him taking classified documents from an agent in the Virginia suburbs, and captured him after a high-speed automobile chase.

Great Britain in April 1983 expelled three Soviets as a result of their subversive acts.

The Socialist government of France in April 1983 became so outraged by the burgeoning dimensions of KGB espionage that it summarily banished 47 Soviets.

Public trials further reflect the nature and intensity of the clandestine war being waged by the KGB and its surrogates. A British court, in November 1982, sentenced Geoffrey Prime, a sex pervert formerly employed at an ultra-secret communications and cryptographic center, to 38 years' imprisonment. He had been a KGB agent since 1962.

During only 15 months—October 1981 to January 1983—the U.S. Customs Service made 1051 seizures of embargoed strategic materials that were being illegally exported from the country. Much of this contraband, including high technology, was destined for the Soviet Bloc.

Wherever the "troops of the invisible front" are deployed, and no matter which nation is their immediate target, the Main Enemy, the *Glavni Vrag*, is the United States. To intensify the global assault upon the United States, from without and within, Andropov in the mid-1970s formed the extraordinary Group *Nord*, composed of chiefs of all the KGB's operational divisions.* These chieftains meet at least once a month to coordinate efforts of all KGB outposts to shatter the Western Alliance, isolate the United States, induce it to weaken itself and paralyze its will to resist the Soviet Union.

The strategy they oversee has increasingly emphasized Active Measures, tasks undertaken in the field that implement the philosophy expressed by Lenin when he declared: "My words were calculated to evoke hatred, aversion and contempt . . . not to convince but to break up the ranks of the opponent, not to correct an opponent's mistake but to destroy him, to wipe his organization off the face of the earth."

That is what the words and deeds of the KGB today are calculated to do.

*Group *Nord* is known to have been in existence by January 1976; the exact date of its formation is unknown.

II

OFFICER
AND
GENTLEMAN

A MILITARY TRIBUNAL finally convened in Moscow in August 1981 to pass judgment on KGB Major Stanislav Aleksandrovich Levchenko. Because the cause of the trial so acutely embarrassed the Politburo, the Party and the KGB leadership, the proceedings were conducted in even stricter secrecy than usual. The prosecution introduced few witnesses, the defense none, and the evidence was almost entirely circumstantial. But it sufficed to enable the court to reach a verdict quickly. The judges found Major Levchenko guilty of "high treason" and accordingly sentenced him to the "highest measure of punishment."

These days, condemned Soviet criminals often are dispatched more humanely than in the past. The prison warden summons the unfortunate and, with grave politeness, informs him that the Supreme Soviet has rejected his appeal for clemency. There remains, however, one last recourse: the prisoner may draft a personal appeal to the president of the Soviet Union. "Sit down and write whatever you want. Take as long as you need, but the briefer, the better."

Accepting the written plea, the warden assures that it will be promptly posted to the president, and the suddenly hopeful criminal is led back toward his cell. This time, though, the guard, without explanation, takes him along a route different from that by which they came. As they pass the medical dispensary, another guard quietly steps from a doorway and, with a large-caliber pistol, shoots the prisoner in the neck. No hysterical scenes, a minimal mess, and the body need not be carted very far for disposal.

Military executions are conducted differently. Bound but not blindfolded, the doomed man is marched into a courtyard or parade ground and made to stand before members of his unit or before former colleagues, who are drawn up rigidly at attention. As an officer intones the death sentence, an executioner stealthily approaches from behind, pistol in hand. Horrified suspense entrances the onlookers. Will he turn in time to see what is about to happen to him? No matter, the executioner shoots off his head, or much of it, just as in olden times at Lubyanka. And with his last breath, the condemned serves the Party by helping provide an unforgettable lesson to his peers.

Major Levchenko doubtless will be liquidated by military execution or worse, should the KGB succeed in capturing him alive; for in the eyes of the KGB, no crime could be more heinous or destructive than his.* The wrath of the KGB may even be more vengeful, because Levchenko appeared to be an

---

*To deter defections, the Center circulates false reports that many past defectors have died in the West, the implication being that the KGB somehow killed them. The death sentence of course means what it says, and the KGB is empowered to carry it out if it can find the condemned man abroad.

However, in the past two decades, the KGB has been unable to liquidate any of its officers who fled to the West. Its failure results primarily from the new identities, support and protection provided to important officers who flee.

ideal officer. Certainly, in light of the record, no one could be faulted for entrusting him with the crucial assignment to Tokyo back in 1975.

By the mid-1970s, the Tokyo Residency ranked as one of the four or five most important foreign outposts of the KGB, rivaled only by those in New York, Geneva, Paris and New Delhi. Japan, the second mightiest industrial power outside the Soviet empire, had become a target of the highest priority, a treasure trove of wealth and technology to be mined illicitly. Additionally, the Russians gathered most of their covert intelligence about China through Japan. And the KGB had found Japan one of the best locales in the world to steal American secrets and advanced technology.

But in Tokyo, as in Washington, London, Paris, Bonn and other major capitals, Soviet aims transcended the theft of secrets. Above all, the KGB sought to develop Agents of Influence—politicians, government officials, authors, journalists, artists, industrialists, academicians—who could mold the policies of Japan to the benefit of the Soviet Union and the detriment of the United States.

Those targeted usually are intelligent and must be approached subtly on their own plane and terms. Hence, the KGB needed in Tokyo officers who thoroughly understood the nuances of Japanese culture, history, customs, language and contemporary life; officers who, by their own erudition, sensitivity and grace, would interest the Japanese—officers like Stanislav Aleksandrovich Levchenko.

Beginning at age nine, Levchenko attended an experimental secondary school, where many courses were taught in English. Some of the professors had lived in Great Britain, and they strived to imbue the students with the style of English gentlemen. After six years at Moscow University's Institute of Oriental Languages, postgraduate research on Japanese politics, a tour at sea interrogating Japanese fishermen, and six visits to Japan, Levchenko spoke Japanese fluently and understood Japan well. Working with the Soviet Peace Committee, then the Afro-Asian Solidarity Committee, he had shown himself to be an astute propagandist, able to charm or manipulate diverse foreigners, ranging from American Army deserters to PLO chieftain Yasser Arafat. He wrote well enough to prepare commentaries for Radio Moscow, articles for *Novoye Vremya (New Times)* magazine, and ceremonial proclamations signed by Brezhnev. Levchenko also had the advantage of looking the part the KGB desired him to play. His high cheekbones, straight nose, auburn hair and dark, searching eyes combined with a slender, athletic physique to make him a handsome young man—one who naturally belonged in diplomatic salons, elegant restaurants or parliamentary offices.

The KGB had recorded no ideological marks against Levchenko, although it formally investigated him three times. He first underwent scrutiny in 1966, when Soviet military intelligence, the GRU, began training him to undertake a suicide mission in England should World War III seem imminent. In 1968 the Second Chief Directorate took Levchenko away from the GRU to utilize him as an agent against Japanese diplomats in Moscow, and this involuntary transfer necessitated another investigation. Some two years later, the KGB again endeavored to explore every eddy of his life, after the First Chief Directorate decided to induct him as a regular staff officer.

These were serious investigations, each spanning several months. His apartment was bugged, his telephone tapped; he was put under surveillance and tested with provocateurs. Both directly and through informants, the KGB questioned colleagues, neighbors, relatives—indeed, everybody they could find who ever knew him.

Inevitably, they scraped up some derogatory gossip, opinion and facts. Undeniably, Levchenko had seduced female comrades at the Afro-Asian Solidarity Committee, in the cellar of that august organization's headquarters. On a nonstop Aeroflot flight from Tokyo, he had persuaded a stewardess to share one of the crew's rest bunks with him; and after the plane landed outside Moscow, they again repaired to the bunk. Some sources may have criticized him for losing his temper or being too outspoken, for at the onset of the last investigation, a friendly KGB officer privately counseled: "Sometimes you are overly frank. I suggest that for the next few months, you keep your mouth and your pants buttoned up."

There may have been other adverse trivia in his file, but, as successive sets of evaluators concluded, it was just trivia, nothing that called into question his loyalty or fitness. Given his overall background and qualifications, it was logical and sensible for the KGB to post him to Japan under the guise of correspondent for *Novoye Vremya.*

On his last night in Moscow, in February 1975, Levchenko took a taxi to the vicinity of the Russian Orthodox cathedral near the railroad station and reconnoitered the area until he detected a static surveillant—a young man posing as a driver in a parked car. Displaying his red KGB card, Levchenko said, "I'm looking for a man about my height wearing a gray coat and a black fur hat. Have you seen anyone like that entering the church?"

"No, Comrade Lieutenant, only some old women in the past two hours."

"Well, he might have slipped in unnoticed. He's that type. I'll just take a quick look inside."

At the altar, Levchenko knelt and offered the same prayer he had repeated ever since joining the KGB: "Our Father Who art in Heaven, I beg Thine understanding and mercy. I pray that Thou will forgive my many sins and bless me with Thine guidance and deliver my soul unto Thee."

This was something the KGB, in all its investigations, had missed. Levchenko hid his true thoughts so thoroughly that no one, not even his wife, knew that he was a Christian believer. Nor did anyone know that for a decade he had been in violent intellectual revolt against the Soviet system, a system he had come to loathe as a benighting curse upon the Russia he loved.

Doubtless Levchenko's father, a research chemist by profession and army officer by necessity, contributed much to the revolt. Levchenko was born July 28, 1941, in Moscow, and his earliest memory is of a scene that occurred in 1944. His father picked him up and told him something he did not quite comprehend. His mother and the baby brother promised him would not be coming home; both had died in the hospital, moments after childbirth.

About four months later, as he left a playground, a Soviet army truck ran over him, crushing his pelvis. Before losing consciousness, he heard someone bending over him say, "He will not live." A gifted female orthopedic surgeon resolved otherwise, and, by force of will and skill, during ten months of hospitalization, she restored him to health. Visiting him often, his father came to know the surgeon, Anastasia, and at the end of World War II they were married.

The army sent his father to Belgrade as a liaison officer, and upon reassignment to Moscow in late 1947, he admonished Levchenko never to mention that they had been abroad. When Stalin renewed the purges the next year, his father repeated the admonition and also cautioned him not to mention the presence of foreign books in their apartment. "Sometimes it is necessary to conceal the truth," he said. "But always you must tell the truth to yourself."

Levchenko recognized that his father not only spoke of honesty; he behaved honestly. They lived cramped into one room, sharing a communal kitchen and bath with seven other families, and once Levchenko overheard Anastasia imploring his father to exploit the influence of well-placed military friends to obtain a decent apartment. "What of those who have no influence?" his father said. "No, that would be dishonest." On the same grounds, his father refused to ask friends to help Levchenko secure a coveted place in the experimental school. Levchenko had to earn entry on his own merits. (His father did hire a tutor to help him with English.)

His father was an apolitical scientist, the author of textbooks and the chairman of the chemistry department at a military research institute. Levchenko never heard him criticize communism, the Party or any Soviet official; he simply never discussed these subjects. However, he cherished Russia and was proud of being Russian, and he kept proscribed books on Russian history by pre-Revolutionary authors. As they browsed in secondhand bookstores or walked in the parks on Sunday afternoons, he inspired Levchenko to study Russian history and culture. From his father and his father's books Levchenko learned of the Russia that, before the Revolution, spawned music, literature, physicists and mathematicians equal to the world's greatest; which perennially produced enough to feed not only itself, but much of central Europe; which created an industrial base surpassed only in the United States, England and Germany; which, in 1861, the year the Americans began their internecine war over slavery, freed its serfs without strife. And in learning, Levchenko inherited his father's pride and patriotism.

In March 1953 the school superintendent, who wore a glass eye, stood before Levchenko's class and announced the death of Stalin. The students laughed because the superintendent looked comical as tears streamed from only one of his eyes.

That fall the Party ordered Levchenko's father, then a colonel, to witness the trial of dethroned State Security Chairman Lavrenti Beria, who had engineered mass murders and grotesque tortures ordered by Stalin. Coming home nightly, dejected as Levchenko had never before seen him, his father refused to tell any details. "It is too horrible to speak of. I did not believe such things could happen in our country." Fleetingly, Levchenko for the first time thought that there might be some distinction between Russia and the Soviet Union.

Cancer struck Levchenko's father in 1954 and wasted him remorselessly. In an unusual tribute, the army appealed to the Council of Ministers to approve his immediate promotion to general. Barely conscious, he became a major general three days before his death, and shortly afterward the army moved his family into a two-room apartment with kitchen and bath.

Unaccountably, Anastasia as a widow grew irrationally jealous of Levchenko's mother; she burned all photos of her, destroyed all memorabilia pertaining to her, and legally adopted Levchenko. The adoption at the time seemed to him meaningless, but it was to have one enduring and beneficial consequence: it effaced the record of his true birth, a record which would have shown future investigators that his real mother was Jewish.

Anastasia, however, did not allow Levchenko to forget. The same assertiveness, decisiveness and intolerance of imperfection that enabled her to command a surgical theater made Anastasia an autocrat at home. Fatigued at the end of the day, lonely, robbed of her husband and unlikely to find another, she sometimes vented her frustrations by raging at Levchenko for untidiness or tardiness or failure to complete assigned chores. Her rage feeding upon itself, she lashed out uncontrollably, viciously slapping Levchenko and sometimes shouting: "You filthy Jew. Your Jewishness is bred into your blood and bones. You never can purge yourself." Levchenko retaliated by running away. If friends did not harbor him, he slept on the open ground or fashioned crude shelters at construction sites. Emotional reconciliations with Anastasia ensued, yet clashes continued. When Levchenko was 17, he stood motionless during one of Anastasia's outbursts, while she beat him until exhausted. Then he said, "Never hit me again. If you do, I am afraid I will strike back." From his father Levchenko had learned to look for and acknowledge truth; from his stepmother he learned to rebel.

Levchenko escaped Anastasia during his first year at Moscow University by marrying an 18-year-old student, Yelena, a fair, musical daughter of a family of intellectuals. The patriarch of the family, Yelena's grandfather, was an aristocrat who became one of the early Bolsheviks. A man of imposing intellect and bearing, he was educated both as a lawyer and agricultural geneticist, and he defended Communists arrested under the Czar. He sensed in Levchenko a quick mind, and took a paternal interest in him, talking to him for hours on winter nights. It was now safe to speak of the evils of the Stalin era, so he spoke candidly, bitterly.

Despite decades of devotion to the Party, he was imprisoned in Lubyanka during the purges of the 1930s for opposing the lunatic theories of the geneticist Lysenko, one of Stalin's favorite charlatans. Almost daily for two years he was interrogated about alleged involvement in imperialist conspiracies to sabotage Soviet science. For reasons that mystified him, he was not physically tortured, but he saw or heard the torture of others around him in the cellars of Lubyanka. The torturers stuck needles under fingernails and into genitalia, seared flesh with white-hot irons, jerked out teeth with pliers or put victims into the "closet," an iron cage whose walls, with the turn of a hydraulic screw, closed to crack bones or compress bodies into extinction.

A Lithuanian in a nearby cell was accused of masterminding a plot to dig a tunnel and blow up the Kremlin. The bewildered man knew nothing of any such farfetched scheme, and defied the interrogators to show him the tunnel he supposedly had helped dig. All his logic and denials were unavailing. After many crippling visits to the "closet," he in his agony "realized" his error and signed a confession that he had tried to blow up the Kremlin. Such confessions lent credence to the boast of a state security torturer, who, during the purges, reportedly declared: "Give me one night with a man and I will have him confessing that he is the King of England."

The story that most appalled and awed Levchenko was the first to introduce him to the concept of Active Measures. In his indefatigable flirtations with the Nazis, Stalin exposed the Soviet Union to widespread penetration by German intelligence. From the reports of numerous agents, German analysts characterized Stalin as a classic paranoid, who feared gifted and popular men, particularly those in the military, as potential rivals. One of the most popular, able, and, hence, feared military leaders of the 1930s was the chief of the Soviet General Staff, Marshal Tukhachevsky.

With the personal approval of Hitler, German intelligence forged letters bearing Tukhachevsky's signature, copied from a secret Soviet-German agreement he had signed in 1923. Other forged letters bore the signatures, copied from bank checks, of German generals. Collectively, the fabricated correspondence portrayed Marshal Tukhachevsky and many of the Red Army's best commanders as Nazi agents engaged in a plot against Stalin. Aware that Czechoslovakian President Eduard Benes was covertly consorting with the Russians, the Germans allowed a Czech agent to obtain copies of the forgeries. As the Germans anticipated, Benes promptly forwarded them to Stalin, who swallowed the bait whole. He ordered the arrests of Marshal Tukhachevsky, virtually the entire General Staff and thousands of other senior military officers.

In the old concrete cells of Lefortovo Prison, the professional torturers of the secret police set upon the Soviet military leadership to extract confessions of treason. They beat the officers with rubber hoses, wracked them with electric shocks. At night they threw the bleeding, unconscious bodies of the loyal generals back into the cells. When the prisoners regained consciousness, they heard from speakers on the walls the excruciating cries of their wives and children undergoing torture. "Oh, Husband, dearest Husband, spare me! Please confess! I can bear no more!" . . . "Oh, Father, confess; please, for me, confess!"

Some of the generals spat in the faces of their tormentors; most, to save their families and hasten their own deaths, confessed to the most monstrous plots and treason. Drunken executioners shot them from point-blank range in the back of the head, and every few hours squads washed down the cells to prepare for new victims. By 1938, in consequence of the Nazi covert action and Stalin's insanity, the elite of the Soviet military leadership had been exterminated. When the Germans attacked in 1940, they routed and massacred the leaderless Red Army and within a few months overran most of European Russia.

"I can't believe it!" Levchenko said.

"You must," the grandfather replied. "Khrushchev himself has confirmed it. I saved the paper. Here, read for yourself."

To the grandfather, the horrors he had seen did not represent the insane deeds of an individual megalomaniac, as the Party now characterized Stalin. Rather, they were the logical, inevitable consequences of a perversion of Marxism effected, not by Stalin, but by Lenin. It was Lenin who created the system of tyranny that foreordained a succession of tyrants; a tyranny that existed only to perpetuate itself and the privileges of the few who ran it; a tyranny that was founded upon and could only survive through terror. The grandfather argued that, like the walls of the "closet" at Lubyanka, the terror would expand and contract; it would assume new and varying forms; but as long as the system Lenin bequeathed, the Soviet system, continued, terror would continue. If terror ever ceased, the system would collapse, for it had no other foundation.

The grandfather retained in his library the original Russian edition of the writings of Marx. Sensing Levchenko's bewilderment at his heresies, the grandfather urged him to read the theories of Marx and compare them with the realities about him. Levchenko did not complete all the works of Marx, but what he did read, together with what he heard and saw in Yelena's house, afflicted him with doubt.

Life in Yelena's house was pleasant as well as intellectually enriching. He and she rarely quarreled; they enjoyed genuine friendship. Yet it was more the friendship of brother and sister, and after two years of marriage, they decided to part.

Little more than a year later, Levchenko married a stunning architectural student named Natalia. She had the face and figure of a fashion model, beguiling brown eyes, a lovely sensuous mouth, and long raven hair. Their attraction to each other was total and passionate, and the very sight of her made him joyous. Her father was a specialist in forestry and a senior staff member of the Academy of Sciences, her mother an intellectual. From them Levchenko heard macabre stories of the Soviet past similar to those told in Yelena's house. Many of their relatives and friends, Party faithful all, had been swept by the purges into the camps or Lubyanka; and for years Natalia's parents gave much of their means to help sustain the families of the imprisoned.

Still, Levchenko in the early 1960s could reason that perhaps Khrushchev and the Party, as they claimed, had vanquished the evil past. But as he tried to keep the faith of his own father and look for the truth, he could not ignore little omens to the contrary.

Toward the end of a lecture one Monday morning, he noticed a girl crying silently, and after class he asked what was troubling her. "My leg, it hurts so," she said. The day before, she attended an amateur art exhibition put together by young people on a vacant lot. KGB men suddenly piled out of cars; while some tore down the paintings, others beat and routed the artists and bystanders. The girl's leg hurt so, Levchenko later learned, because it was broken. And students continued to disappear from the university, especially those who in class recitation proposed this or that economic reform. They simply vanished, and no one knew where.

Even more poisonous to his thoughts was the evidence he saw year after year of systematic, hypocritical perversion of the truth, of what he came to call Cynicism Unlimited. By 1962, his fourth year at the Institute of Oriental Languages, he could converse fairly well in Japanese, and periodically the International Department commandeered him to escort Japanese visitors. Preparatory to the tours, he and other student guides were coached as to how to respond to certain questions forthright foreigners might ask.

"Why do you make women do hard manual labor?" a young Japanese socialist asked. "In our country, we would never allow women to carry bricks or haul garbage."

Levchenko knew that women worked at any job they could get, in the fields or on the streets, because they had to; few families could subsist without two incomes. He knew that the economy was such that every available body had to be impressed into the labor force. He also knew how to answer. "Socialism does not tolerate discrimination against women, and Soviet women insist upon equal rights, including the right to perform the same jobs as men. That is why so many of our physicians, engineers, professors and scientists are women."

"Yes, but on the train we saw old women carrying heavy railroad ties. It looked as if their backs would break. They could barely manage."

Levchenko's expressive face and eyes flashed righteous indignation. "What! You actually saw that! Just a moment. Let me get some paper. Now. Tell me exactly when and where you saw that. I intend to make a report to the district union leader. I assure you that whoever is reponsible will be punished, severely. That is why we have free trade unions: to protect all workers from abuse."

During his last year in the university, Levchenko volunteered to serve three months interrogating Japanese fishermen aboard a Soviet patrol craft in the Sea of Japan. Impressed by his performance, the Ministry of Fisheries compelled him to work for it in Moscow after his graduation in 1964. However, the International Department continued to employ him intermittently as a part-time interpreter, and in late 1965 it offered him a job with the Soviet Peace Committee.

The Committee and the Soviet Afro-Asian Solidarity Committee, to which he later transferred, were initiating a great Active Measures campaign to force the United States to abandon Indochina to the Communists. And this was a cause in which Levchenko at the time believed. In his eyes, America bared its inherent iniquity by attacking poor, defenseless Vietnamese peasants with super weapons. And unreservedly, he subscribed to the Committees' stated objectives of bringing about peace and nuclear disarmament.

Both the Peace Committee and the Afro-Asian Solidarity Committee were substantially financed by donations that the Party forced the Russian Orthodox Church, along with prominent entertainers and athletes, to solicit in the name of peace. Under the moral suasion of the church, many believers gave of their scant resources; some even sent family jewelry, and an elderly woman once brought a chicken to the Peace Committee's offices. But the Afro-Asian Solidarity Committee used a good portion of these gifts for peace to buy arms and other military supplies for guerrillas in Africa and the Middle East.

Levchenko saw that the International Department used the Soviet Red Cross just as it did the church. To cultivate and influence Moscow correspondents representing the newspapers of foreign Communist Parties, the Soviets provided each with a personal aide and a monthly stipend of 300 rubles. The International Department did not want the courted correspondents to think that these benefits came from the Party or state. So it made the Red Cross pay the stipends and the salaries of the aides. Thus, Soviet citizens who contributed to the Red Cross for charity also unknowingly contributed to the subversion of foreign journalists. Levchenko thought: *War in the name of peace; subversion in the guise of humanitarianism.*

The offices of both the Peace and Afro-Asian Solidarity Committees, as well as several other International Department subsidiaries, were located in an ornate old mansion at 10 Kropotkinskaya Ulitsa. Here, Levchenko and comrades toiled up to twelve hours a day, six days a week, conceiving propaganda, plotting demonstrations and drafting orders to Soviet fronts abroad. All their efforts were intended to create the illusion of widespread popular furor, and thereby to convince Americans that much of the world was appalled and disgusted by their presence in Vietnam, that they must bring about peace by forsaking Vietnam.

After a hard day of fighting for peace, Levchenko sometimes joined friends in the mansion's cellar, where the committees' photographer maintained his laboratory. The photographer, a bachelor in his mid-50s, was skilled at catching and barbecuing doves. With a piece of bread attached to a string, he lured the doves, one by one, down the steps into the cellar. There he wrung their necks, pulled out their feathers and cooked them on a charcoal grill. Accompanied by vodka, the doves tasted delicious. After an enjoyable supper, couples customarily paired off for further pleasures. In a few months, however, these repasts began to occur less frequently, and by the end of the year, perforce ceased entirely, because the peace workers had eaten all the doves in the district.

In the spring of 1966, Levchenko received a telephone call which was the prelude to a dramatic proposition. The call itself was prosaic—a routine summons to a military conscription center. Awaiting him there was a man in civilian clothes who introduced himself as a GRU colonel. "We can't talk here," he said. "Let's go outside."

As they walked in a peaceful park amid blossoming flowers, the colonel spoke frankly of preparations for war. Should it appear that war was about to begin, the Soviet Union intended to land agents by parachute and submarine in Western countries, where they would conduct reconnaissance and sabotage. Because of Levchenko's knowledge of English and England acquired in the experimental high school, the GRU wanted to train him for a mission in the vicinity of Liverpool.

"I don't want to mislead you," said the colonel. "You probably would not survive more than a few days. You are entirely free to decline, and no mark will made against you. But if you accept, you will be a true son of our Mother Country." Levchenko volunteered without question.

Called to active military duty for six weeks that summer, he reported daily to a Moscow apartment for training by GRU officers, who taught him to recognize nuclear weapons storage sites, cryptography, use of an agent radio and other tradecraft. The next summer, at a military camp outside Moscow, he made parachute jumps from a tower, practiced foraging for himself in the countryside, fired small arms, and learned more about his mission.

Liverpool interested the Soviets because it is an important port. An officer briefed him in detail about the city and its docks. He was to acquire all the intelligence he could about military and naval movements, aided by knowledge gained from a study of photographs of war materials, nuclear and non-nuclear. Once he landed in England, no one could help him; he would always operate alone.

"How will I get out?" he asked.

The colonel hesitated. "Well, after you're there, you will be told in due time." They both laughed.

He was scheduled to undergo sabotage training the next summer, and thereafter to take brief refresher courses annually. The GRU officers he met impressed him as brave men contemptuous of the KGB, indifferent to the cant of the Party and concerned only with the defense of the Mother Country. He felt honored to be among them; and had he been permitted to remain with the GRU, his ideological deterioration might have been arrested.

But early in 1968, over a drink in a restaurant, a GRU officer apologetically informed him that henceforth he must serve the Second Chief Directorate of the KGB. To his profane protests the officer replied: "We objected also. But we must obey the KGB. So must you."

And so Levchenko reported to a room in the old Hotel Berlin, near Lubyanka. The hotel was a favorite of the Second Chief Directorate, which had bugged every room and each table in the bar and dining room. Through optical fibers implanted in the ceilings, the Directorate's operatives could watch or photograph the actions of foreigners lodged in the hotel by Intourist. The more salacious photographs of intimate behavior were regularly passed around Second Chief Directorate offices for the amusement of the officers.

A Colonel Azizov, a swarthy, sardonic, pipe-smoking Tartar, awaited Levchenko, who at the outset declared that he would never act as an informant against any Soviet citizen. Azizov smiled, whether out of derision or amusement Levchenko could not tell. "My dear comrade, of course not," he said unctuously. "We have hundreds of thousands of assholes for that dirty work. We sweep them up off the streets like trash. We respect you as an intellectual, and we have a real task for you. You will work against our enemies, the Japanese."

KGB technicians had so thoroughly infested the Japanese embassy and the apartments of Japanese diplomats with marvelously sensitive microphones that they could pick up the least sound, even a whisper or drip of water. By listening and following, the KGB drew profiles to determine which Japanese might be vulnerable to a particular ploy. Noting that one young diplomat never was with women, the KGB concluded he must be a homosexual. "We'll round up a few queers," Azizov said.

"How?" Levchenko asked.

"Simple. We know who the queers are, and we can arrest them at will. We give them a choice. They can go to prison, where they'll probably be killed, or they can serve the Mother Country while enjoying their perversion. They always make the right choice." The colonel thought it was very funny. Levchenko thought, *Cynicism Unlimited.*

Second Chief Directorate officers verified rumors he had tried to disbelieve. Dissidents, malcontents and other ideological saboteurs were being "treated" in mental institutions. By definition, anyone incapable of adapting to socialist reality was insane, and consignment of troublemakers to psychiatric wards obviated the necessity of fabricating evidence now required to confine anyone in the camps. Drug torture had also proven much more effective and much less demanding of the torturers than the bone-cracking of old. It was as Yelena's grandfather prophesied: the terror continued in new forms.

Escorting foreign guests of the Afro-Asian Solidarity Committee, Levchenko traveled through much of the Soviet Union, showing them model farms, factories, hospitals, schools and nurseries specially maintained to edify foreigners. Never did these visitors see typical collective farms, with crops rotting and inoperable machinery rusting in the fields; factories shut down for want of parts or supplies; unsanitary first-aid stations; housing without plumbing; glum lines waiting outside shops whose shelves were half empty. But the exertions he and his colleagues had to make to conceal the real conditions in which most Soviet citizens existed intensified his awareness of their reality.

So did his journeys to Japan, which he visited every year or so on Afro-Asian Solidarity Committee business. Each time, he returned with fresh visions of the surging Japanese economy, which inundated the streets with cars and the stores with food, clothes and an ever-widening array of glittering new products—a booming economy in a society unregimented by the threat of a KGB, of mental institutions and concentration camps.

By 1968, more than half a century after the Revolution, more than two decades after World War II, Levchenko regarded the Bolshevik Revolution as a parody of the French Revolution. He thought no revolution had ever visited such disaster upon those it pretended to liberate. It had cursed his people with a system that robbed them materially while impoverishing their spirit with deceit and corruption.

Yet he could imagine no escape from the system. Opposition would lead only to the camps or a mental institution, and there he could serve no cause. He thought of killing himself but could not capitulate to the cowardice of suicide. And he dared not consult anyone except himself.

In rudderless despair and searching for ideological sustenance, for a sun in his universe, he contemplated religion. For centuries, Christianity had been an integral part of Russian culture and history. In his intellectual judgment, Christian ethics and morality constituted a sound guide to healthy human behavior. When he had taken foreigners to cathedrals, he had found the pageantry and chorales beautiful; and he sensed in the faces of the believers fulfillment. The concept of a First Cause fascinated and encouraged him. There had to have been a beginning of life. Maybe it did begin with some galactic explosion millennia past. But what caused the elements that caused the explosion? Who was to say they were not caused by an eternal, universal God? The quest that began intellectually ended metaphysically. At a time and by means he could not define, Levchenko found faith. Never revealing himself, he also found official pretexts to talk to priests.

Trying to be truthful with himself, as his father adjured, he appreciated the contradictions between religious faith and service to a political system that mocked his God. He attempted rationalizations: He had to live; maybe his work would benefit the Russian people; maybe the compulsions of failure eventually would force changes upon the system. None of these arguments sufficed if he dwelt upon them, so he worked long and hard rather than think.

Diligence combined with natural ability earned him commendations from superiors and, eventually, the attention of the First Chief Directorate. On a dismally gray afternoon in January 1971, a KGB lieutenant colonel assigned to the Afro-Asian Solidarity Committee proposed a drink after work. Like the GRU colonel who recruited him three years before, the KGB officer was frank. He and the First Chief Directorate were impressed with Levchenko and his background. The Second Chief Directorate was an execrable outfit whose principal business was repression of the Russian people. But the First Chief Directorate helped the people, by providing the country with foreign technology and secrets essential to the national security. "It's a real man's work," the officer said. "You will know things few people in the world know. You will see the world, and every day will be a day of excitement." Whether as a result of professional excellence, personal prescience or mere happenstance, the officer sounded the right appeals, and they persuaded Levchenko to become a staff officer of the KGB.

The forests outside Moscow were quiet, fresh and verdant in June 1971, when Levchenko disembarked from a chartered bus at the Foreign Intelligence School, a quarter mile from the village of Yurlovo, off Volokolamskoye Highway. Behind a yellow masonry wall, six feet high and topped with barbed wire, stood a four-story brick building with classrooms, faculty offices, separate libraries for classified and unclassified materials, dormitory, cafeteria and dispensary. A large, well-equipped gymnasium, swimming pool, and firing range occupied the basement. KGB warrant officers wearing civilian clothes and armed with Makarov automatics patrolled the grounds, and at night German shepherd watchdogs accompanied them. When offices and classrooms were closed for the day, sensors detected the slight atmospheric change caused by the body heat of anyone intruding into the sealed spaces, and set off a warning.

There were 120 students in Levchenko's class; roughly two-thirds were recent graduates of the Institute for International Relations, Moscow University or comparably prestigious institutions. The remainder were educated young men plucked from civilian agencies or KGB components outside the First

Chief Directorate. Most spoke one or more foreign languages.

The class was divided into seven sections, each supervised by a colonel. Levchenko's colonel was a white-haired man in his late 50s who treated his wards paternally. He explained that they would be continuously evaluated by him, the instructors and others, "others" meaning the *stukachi**, or informants among the students. At the end of the year, the colonel had to write a detailed professional and personal assessment of each student, which would form the first entry in the student's permanent personnel file. "The evaluation will follow you throughout your career," he warned. "It will be the first thing anyone who looks at your record sees. So your goal is to pass through here unmarked, unwounded."

In a general assembly, another colonel outlined the regimen and rules of the school. Work began six days a week at 8 a.m. with an hour of rigorous exercise—cross-country running, calesthenics, swimming, or training in hand-to-hand combat. Classes continued from 9 a.m. to 2 p.m. and, after lunch, from 3 to 6 p.m., and students were expected to study three hours nightly. Married students residing in the Moscow area could spend Saturday nights and Sundays at home; otherwise, students should expend any free time by exercising or reading. No alcoholic beverages were permitted on the premises.

Students were forbidden to reveal their surnames to each other or the faculty; they would address each other and be addressed by superior officers solely by pseudonyms. (Levchenko's was Livenko.) While they were to maintain comradely relations with each other, security considerations precluded serious friendships or the exchange of personal biographical details. They could visit the village briefly in pairs, but they were not to gather outside school for parties or dinners.

With commencement of the tradecraft courses, Levchenko found that he enjoyed advantages over most of his peers. GRU training had already introduced him to surveillance, ciphers, secret writing, drops, recognition signals and agent radio com-

Stukach is Russian slang for "secret informant" or "stool pigeon." Literally, the word means "to knock." *Stukachi* is the plural form.

munications. Because of extensive experience writing reports, articles and broadcasts, while with the Peace and Afro-Asian Solidarity Committees, he had little difficulty learning to draft logically organized intelligence reports. His work and travels throughout the 1960s required him to speak both Japanese and English, so he needed no help from the language instructors. Engrossing himself in the Theory and Practice of Intelligence, he crossed from the periphery into the real world of espionage. Now he began to see purpose, reason and a certain nobility in activities which heretofore seemed silly, meaningless or squalid.

To dramatize the necessity of clandestine warfare, instructors objectively recited case histories and their import. Levchenko marveled as he heard the story of Soviet penetration of the Manhattan Project, which produced the first atomic bomb and inaugurated the nuclear age. Although the project was the most enormous, complex and costly scientific-industrial undertaking ever attempted, the Americans completely concealed it from the Germans and Japanese. Neither gleaned a hint of its existence until Hiroshima lay devastated under a mushroom cloud. All along, however, Soviet agents kept Soviet scientists abreast of the Anglo-American research and development. By the time the Americans detonated the first nuclear device near Alamogordo, and without having conducted any experiments of their own, the Russians possessed a scientific and engineering blueprint to manufacture a nuclear weapon. The stolen data hastened Soviet production of a bomb by several years—years, an instructor emphasized, during which the Russians would have been wholly at the mercy of the Americans.

Levchenko felt gratitude and admiration for those who rescued his country from such peril, and he felt the same toward those responsible for the Philby operation. According to the fairly acccurate account of KGB instructors, Harold A.R. (Kim) Philby was among the students recruited at Cambridge in the 1930s. Proper Soviet tutelage, combined with his charm, intellect and family background, enabled him to rise so in British intelligence that some colleagues believed he eventually would be its director. During World War II, Philby and agents in the Foreign Office deflected overtures from anti-Hitler elements in Germany who sought a secret alliance with the British. After the war, Philby spared the Russians ruinous damage by enabling them to recapture a Soviet intelligence colonel who was endeavoring to defect to the British in Turkey. Assigned to Washington as liaison to the newly formed CIA, Philby singlehandedly saved Albania by alerting the Russians to an Anglo-American scheme to overthrow that Communist government. The instructors hinted that the Soviet debt to Philby and his band of agents was much larger than they could detail.

Of the many case histories recounted, that of Richard Sorge enlightened and affected Levchenko the most. Sorge, born in the Soviet Union of a German father and Russian mother, enlisted in Soviet intelligence at an early age. As a German newspaper correspondent, he made his way to Tokyo in 1934 to direct a network of agents who had sources and influence in the Japanese government. In Tokyo he also became a welcome intimate at the German embassy and a popular confidant of Japanese leaders, who regarded him as an unofficial Nazi emissary. During the summer of 1941, while German armies swept toward Moscow, Sorge consulted with the Japanese as they debated whether to expand the empire by attacking the Russians in Siberia or warring against the Americans and British in the Pacific. Sorge, the Soviet General Staff and even Stalin understood that at issue was the fate of the Soviet Union. To halt the Germans in the West, the Russians desperately needed to draw fresh forces from their armies in the Far East; yet to deplete the Eastern defenses while the Japanese decision pended was to invite Japanese assault.

In August 1941, Sorge's radioman tapped out in Morse code on a primitive agent radio one of the most momentous intelligence reports of all time: The Japanese will strike America. Immediately, the Russians began the pell-mell transfer of their Siberian armies westward, and some 500,000 troops arrived in time, barely in time, to repel the German offensive which crested only miles from Moscow. Hundreds of thousands of men died to save Moscow; in the end, it was saved by one man, a lone agent who was to die in a hangman's noose in a forlorn Japanese prison.

Throughout their clinical reconstruction of past operations, the instructors interwove and emphasized underlying themes which in Levchenko's mind transformed romantic spy stories into serious, practical lessons:

Each cited operation succeeded because Soviet intelligence was willing to make a general investment in hope of reaping unforeseeable dividends many years hence. When Sorge, Philby and nuclear physicist Klaus Fuchs were recruited as young men, nobody could have predicted that they would ascend to the confidence of Japanese leaders or the heights of British intelligence or the Manhattan Project. Each operation succeeded because of contributions made over a protracted period by many intelligence people—couriers and other support personnel, case officers and senior officers who provided guidance from the Center. But none of the operations would have been possible had not the agents been recruited in the first place. The discovery, development and recruitment of agents, stressed the instructors, constituted the single most important duty of a First Chief Directorate officer.

Generally, agents who can influence the policy or national decisions of their countries are more valuable than those who steal secrets. Priceless as the American atomic secrets were, it would have been better had agents been able to influence the Americans not to attempt the Manhattan Project until after the Soviet Union produced its nuclear weapon. The more Agents of Influence you have, the greater the likelihood of successfully manipulating the actions of other nations. You cannot have too many Agents of Influence.

A military officer may labor throughout his career drilling, studying and otherwise preparing for battle, yet never participate in a single engagement. An officer of the First Chief Directorate is at war on "the invisible front" the moment he steps on foreign soil. However tedious, mundane or unproductive his clandestine duties may seem, all are an essential part of an unceasing war. And there is always the chance that the agent the First Chief Directorate officer recruits or supervises may become another Fuchs, Sorge or Philby.

Now Levchenko understood, and he saw in his life new purpose. The evil in the world, evil which spewed primarily out of America, made war in defense of Russia a necessity; and the First Chief Directorate spearheaded the Russian defense. As the lessons taught in the school proved, clandestine tactics were extraordinarily effective and thus morally justifiable, just as killing in combat was justifiable. And recalling the words of the KGB colonel who invited him into the First Chief Directorate, he thought: *It is exciting. It is a real man's work.* Lectures about foreign counterintelligence methods and intelligence services heightened his sense of imminent involvement in an ongoing patriotic war and his admiration of Russians already in combat.

A Second Chief Directorate general came from the Center one morning to lecture with professional detachment about contemporary CIA methods in the Soviet Union. He stated that although the Second Chief Directorate and Surveillance Department repeatedly uncovered and disrupted American operations, the KGB knew that intolerable leaks from sensitive areas of the Soviet government continued. They could be completely stanched only when the CIA was immobilized by Soviet penetrations. "For that," declared the general, "we count upon you comrades of the First Chief Directorate." Again, Levchenko experienced the excitement of challenge and call to battle, and in early winter 1972, he eagerly began training exercises on the streets of Moscow.

His section moved into a large villa on a side street off Zubovskaya Square. The upper floors had been rebuilt to duplicate a typical KGB Residency, and as Residencies are essentially the same in functions and physical layout the world over, the students might as well have been in Washington, London, Paris or Tokyo. And each day they went out into

Moscow to practice the tactics they would use abroad.

They took turns following and trying to escape each other, loading and unloading drops, making brush passes, signaling for emergency meetings, and receiving messages from agents a few blocks away by miniature radios concealed in their clothing. In the final phase of the practical training, each student was scheduled to meet clandestinely five times a KGB officer posing as an agent. Students were informed that on each occasion they might or might not be followed by professionals from the Surveillance Directorate. If they detected surveillance, they were to abort the meeting and, after the exercise, report exactly when, where and how they recognized the surveillants. If they did not detect surveillance and proceeded with a meeting, they failed the test. But they also failed if they skipped a meeting when they were not being watched and merely imagined that they were. Both the surveillants and officers acting the role of agents filed detailed evaluations of the student's overall behavior, emphasizing whether he acted logically and kept his poise.

Levchenko's first rendezvous was supposed to occur at noon in a restaurant. About 9:30 a.m. he left the villa, took a bus to the GUM department store and bought a newspaper at a kiosk while trying mentally to photograph the disembarking passengers. All dispersed except two men who stayed at the stop talking animatedly, seemingly oblivious to him. Levchenko entered the store and paused by a counter until he saw one of the men from the street step inside and stride off to another area of the store. Having stood in line ten minutes or so, Levchenko bought a toy, a birthday present for his three-year-old son. Waiting outside for a bus, he observed a man loitering nearby. Although the same size as the man he had seen coming into the store, this figure looked much different and older; he wore different clothes, had gray hair, a mustache and glasses. Yet Levchenko knew it was the same man.

He boarded a bus traveling in a direction opposite from his meeting site, had lunch alone, attended a movie, bought a loaf of bread and returned to the villa. Questioned by his colonel, he reported that a surveillant followed him into GUM and while there somehow managed to change clothes, don a wig and mustache.

"How then did you recognize him?" the colonel asked.

"His shoes. He did not change his shoes."

Beginning late that afternoon, Levchenko cleared his path for three hours by bus and subway and, glimpsing no indications of surveillance, kept a rendezvous at a hockey match. As one friendly fan to another, he chatted calmly with his agent and returned without incident to the villa, where his colonel told him he had guessed right: there was no surveillance.

Nor did Levchenko discern surveillance the next night, but upon sitting down with his agent in the assigned restaurant, he was frightened because the "agent," Colonel Altynov, was drinking himself into a stupor. Altynov had burned out in Japan and sought solace in alcohol, and he would have been fired had not a patron saved him with an assignment to the school. If Levchenko reported the drunkenness on duty, Altynov doubtless would be dismissed; if he failed to report it, he himself would be guilty of dereliction punishable by dismissal. And he could not be sure what Altynov in sober guilt might say about their meeting, for he knew that sometimes a man will not forgive you for his own failings.

Despite all Levchenko's entreaties, Altynov insisted on staying in the restaurant, drinking another bottle of brandy and babbling appalling secrets. He wanted Levchenko to understand, to appreciate what he had been through. In Tokyo agents of Line X* reported that Japanese researchers were conducting advanced laboratory experiments with deadly bacteria in search of new antidotes to diseases. On orders from the Center, they stole a sample of the bacteria for use in Soviet bacteriological warfare research. Soviet scientists feared the substance was so lethal that, were it to be released in an accident, such as a plane crash, vast death might result. So the Center sent a freighter to Japan, and the Residency command-

*Line X is the field section responsible for scientific, technological and industrial espionage.

ed Altynov to accompany an operational driver to the dock
with the vial. Altynov began to cry as he recalled how they
drove nearly two hours through heavy traffic, terrified each
minute that a wild driver might crash into them. He sobbed,
"We could have killed hundreds of thousands of people."

Levchenko wrapped an arm around his shoulders and
pulled him to his feet. "Comrade Colonel, you are very tired.
It happens to us all. Let me take you home."

As Altynov tried to break away, Levchenko squeezed him
suddenly and brutally and whispered, "You son of a bitch,
they're about to call the militia. We are in danger. Come on!"

Unlocking the door to Altynov's apartment, Levchenko said
that his report would indicate that their meeting had been
entirely normal.

"Fuck you," Altynov replied.

Having submitted his false report, Levchenko waited in
dread until the colonel showed him Altynov's evaluation. It
concluded: "Throughout, Comrade Livenko demonstrated
the logic, poise and insights of an experienced officer able to
inspire the trust and confidence of an agent."

On his fourth outing, Levchenko rather quickly spotted
surveillance in the form of a succession of Volga sedans which
trailed each bus he rode. According to school lore, if you
outwitted the surveillants twice, they would be sure to beat
you the next time. So on the day of his last scheduled agent
meeting, Levchenko departed the villa at 7 a.m. to give himself five hours to clear his path before a luncheon rendezvous.
He resorted to every evasion he had been taught and could
imagine, darting in and out of stores, doorways and subway
stations, reversing his routes and jumping aboard buses just
before the doors closed. Noticing nothing to indicate that he
was being followed, he decided about 11:30 a.m. to keep the
appointment and took a subway toward the restaurant. Sitting
silently next to him was a middle-aged man with a composed,
saintly face. As the train slowed to stop, the stranger without
looking at Levchenko whispered, "Comrade, you are under
surveillance." Abruptly he rose and vanished out the door,

never looking back.

Stunned, Levchenko got off at the next station to think. Was the man a crackpot suffering hallucinations? No, Levchenko reasoned, he was too serious, and he had seen something Levchenko could not see. Why would he commit the crime of interfering with the Organs of State Security in order to help someone he did not know? Perhaps, Levchenko thought, he is a fellow Christian. With that thought, Levchenko decided to take a chance just as had the stranger. He avoided the agent meeting, dined alone and in the afternoon reported that at the last moment on the subway, he felt himself under surveillance. "I can't say exactly why. Suddenly I just intuitively knew it."

Levchenko, or rather, his mysterious benefactor, was right. As Levchenko had "beaten" the surveillants earlier, this time they enveloped him with the kind of invisible, moving cordon usually reserved for known foreign agents. The entire Moscow subway system, he learned, was specially wired so that surveillants could communicate with each other by secure underground line. The system enabled squads on the trains and posted at stations to stay ahead and behind the subject without being seen. It was necessary to have only one surveillant within sight of him, and that one person could drop off, to be replaced by another. The particular surveillant watching him on the subway car was disguised as a peasant woman carrying a bag of cucumbers, as if to the open-air market. He remembered her but, as he acknowledged, never suspected her.

They accepted his explanation and commended his intuition. But because he could not pinpoint a surveillant, he received a grade of "4" on this last test; the rest of his grades were perfect "5s."

Test grades, though, did not count as much as the personal assessments made by the school's section chiefs and senior officers from the Center who interviewed each student before the final State Examinations. Wives also were interviewed, and one weeknight Levchenko's colonel questioned Natalia

alone for nearly three hours, courteously and respectfully but
searchingly. Obviously, it did not hurt to be bright, beautiful
and socially graceful. She inferred, however, that the KGB
primarily was interested in her emotional stability and that of
her marriage.

After the State Examinations, the colonel in charge of Levchenko's section called him to his office. "I am sorry that I
cannot submit a completely truthful assessment of you," he
said. Levchenko froze and braced himself. The colonel continued, "The truth is, I can find no fault with you. But I must.
Otherwise nobody will believe my evaluation. Since I must
make something up, I want you to help me." To the laudatory
evaluation which characterized Levchenko as one of the more
outstanding students the colonel had observed, they append-
ed two adverse comments: Levchenko tended to write a long
report when a shorter would do. Sometimes out of enthusiasm,
he jumped from one subject to another rather than concentrate
upon tasks one at a time.

"Oh, yes," the colonel said in afterthought. "We can add
that you need more instruction in driving." That was certainly
so. Levchenko was a terrible driver. But then, so were most of
the students, having never sat behind the wheel of a car until
they took driver training at the school.

Credited with GRU and Second Chief Directorate service,
Levchenko was commissioned a senior, rather than junior,
lieutenant and assigned to the Japanese Desk at the Center,
preparatory to eventual duty in Japan. His monthly salary and
allowances exceeded 300 rubles, at the time almost twice the
earnings of the average Soviet scientist, physician, engineer,
teacher or journalist. From Natalia's parents he and she inherited an apartment with two rooms, and private kitchen and
bath, located only a block away from the design bureau where
Natalia earned 120 rubles a month as an architect. Because of
the rigorous daily exercise and nutritious diet at intelligence
school, he felt better physically than he had since boyhood.

To Levchenko, the view of the world from the Center was
breathtaking, at least initially. When he arrived in the sixth-

floor office he shared with five other officers, a stack of cables and dispatches delivered overnight from Tokyo was usually waiting for him. It was exciting to read in them what the President or Secretary of State of the United States had said to the Prime Minister or Foreign Minister of Japan; what the Americans confided to the Japanese about their intentions in Vietnam; which Japanese politicians were taking huge bribes from whom; which Japanese parliamentarians, editors or industrialists were being lured ever more deeply into the snares of the KGB. Daily sensations, however, became routine, and as the distraction of excitement faded, he began to perceive and react to realities heretofore ignored.

In joining the KGB, he now feared, he had locked himself into the core of the Soviet system, a kind of pagan cult or religion, from which there was no honorable escape except death. Members of the cult existed only to serve it. As long as they were of use they would be kept in working order, like essential cogs in an essential machine. But they would be discarded and replaced if they became obsolescent or, sometimes, simply when other, unrelated parts of the machine malfunctioned. The KGB could fire, disgrace, impoverish and ostracize you at any time, for any reason or no reason.

The epilogues to some stories Levchenko had heard in intelligence school began to mold and harden his judgment. He learned that Richard Sorge's Japanese widow and relatives of the other executed members of the Sorge network suffered and died in abject poverty, unaided by Soviet intelligence, even though it knew of their straits and possessed the resources to help them covertly. Another hero portrayed at the school was Colonel Rudolf Abel, who lived for years in a New York slum while directing illegal Soviet agents in the United States. Arrested after the defection of his deputy, he resisted all interrogation and told the FBI nothing. The Americans exchanged him in 1962 for U-2 pilot Francis Gary Powers. The KGB gave him a *dacha* outside Moscow, a car and a driver, and enough Lucky Strike cigarettes to sustain his three-pack-a-day habit. But because he had been in an American prison, the

KGB never fully trusted him or allowed him to work in the Center. He used to sit through much of the day at a coffee shop patronized by KGB officers, near Dzherzhinsky Square, hungering and hoping for their fellowship. Those who approached him were respectful, but none dared offer the fellowship he craved. Another celebrated KGB illegal, Lieutenant Colonel Konan Molodoy, supervised the spies who stole the design secrets of Anglo-American nuclear submarines. Upon his repatriation, the KGB treated him suspiciously and denied him meaningful employment. In his loneliness, he became an alcoholic and died alone, of a stroke, at age 47.

After Lieutenant Colonel Yuri Ivanovich Nosenko fled to the United States in 1964, the KGB cashiered nearly 50 officers, a majority of them colonels and lieutenant colonels. One was fired because investigation disclosed he had failed to report that Nosenko sometimes slept with his secretary. The rest were purged merely because they had known Nosenko, although many knew him only casually.

The 1971 defection in London of Captain Oleg Lyalin, a KGB saboteur, visited similar vengeance upon numerous innocent officers in Department V. The most luckless was an officer who earlier had been dispatched to England to investigate allegations that Lyalin was leading a dissolute life with women and alcohol. He reported that the charges were true and branded Lyalin a security risk. The KGB pigeonholed his report and reprimanded him for denigrating a brother officer. After the KGB discovered that Lyalin had been a British agent for some time before his defection, the officer who warned against him was dismissed for having failed to press his findings with sufficient vigor.

Levchenko also recoiled at what he deemed moral corruption. One of his classmates at intelligence school, whom he knew as Shibayev, turned out to be Aleksandr Shishayev, son of the chief of the Florist Trade Administration of the Moscow City Soviet. When young Shishayev joined the Japanese Department, Levchenko understood why he had been admitted to the KGB, despite hopeless ineptitude. Officers died often and at relatively early ages in the First Chief Directorate. They collapsed at their desks, or in the corridors, of heart attacks or strokes, induced by cumulative fatigue, stress, and perhaps emotions they could not vent. The First Chief Directorate thus had a continuing need for flowers, and for years the senior Shishayev supplied them *gratis*, even in winter, when flowers ordinarily were obtainable only on the black market. The KGB repaid him by giving his son a sinecure and protection.

One morning in 1973, the director of the Seventh Department, Colonel Kalyagin, shouted for Levchenko. "Pronnikov has made Ishida give Brezhnev a car. They're uncrating it right now in the courtyard. Get down there and guard it. Otherwise the bastards will steal everything off it before he ever sees it."

Lieutenant Colonel Vladimir Pronnikov, then chief of Line PR* in the Tokyo Residency, had received the Order of the Red Banner for recruiting Hirohide Ishida, former Minister of Labor, still a member of parliament and prominent figure in the governing Liberal Democratic Party. For his own purposes, Pronnikov represented Ishida as the principal Soviet Agent of Influence in Japan, and the Russians did all they could to magnify his prestige. Soviet bosses, including Premier Aleksei Kosygin, personally feted him in Moscow and at the end of his visits ordered release of Japanese fishermen the Russians regularly shanghai off the high seas. For example, the Tokyo newspaper *Asahi Shimbun,* in a dispatch dated September 4, 1973, reported from Moscow: "The Soviet Union today said it would immediately release all 49 Japanese fishermen detained on charges of violating Soviet territorial waters.

"The announcement was made by the Chairman of the Presidium of the Supreme Soviet Union during his meeting with Hirohide Ishida, head of a visiting Japanese Parliamentary delegation." In Japan, Ishida was able to cite the liberation

*Line PR is the field section primarily responsible for collecting political intelligence and conducting Active Measures.

of the hapless fishermen, who soon would be replaced by new captives, as proof that if you are reasonable with the Russians, they will reciprocate, and as evidence of his personal standing with the Kremlin.

The car Ishida shipped to Moscow was a huge maroon Nissan limousine, adorned with leather upholstery and every gadget known to automobile makers. When Levchenko reached the courtyard, officers from the Guards Directorate, which protects Soviet leaders, were swarming over the vehicle, searching for listening devices, and his presence was superfluous. Obeying orders, however, he stood by until they drove it away.

Levchenko knew that the KGB periodically channeled through Ishida millions of yen, ostensibly for the Japanese-Soviet Parliamentary Friendship Association, which he headed. But the KGB required no accounting from agent Ishida. Obviously, at Pronnikov's instructions, he had purchased the car for Brezhnev, who doted on fancy foreign automobiles, and Levchenko suspected that he bought it with KGB money. Brezhnev would be impressed by Pronnikov for hooking a man rich and powerful enough to give him a car. Once more, Levchenko thought, *Cynicism Unlimited*.

Had the customs and practices that repelled Levchenko been the creation of a few corrupt or despotic individuals, they would have affected him far less. But they were not. Levchenko rated most of the KGB officers he had known as good men who tried to be as fair, decent and honest with each other as circumstances and survival permitted. In his eyes, all were prisoners of a cult that institutionalized cruelty, injustice, corruption and treachery. Some were strong enough to survive in this jungle environment without adopting the ways of the jungle; others were not.

At home he brooded and sulked, and Natalia asked why he was so depressed. For her safety, he could not tell her, just as he could not confess to her his religious beliefs.

A new challenge in late 1973 temporarily rescued Levchenko from his thoughts. The personnel director of the First

Chief Directorate, Colonel Pastukhov, announced that the KGB had decided to send him to Tokyo as correspondent for *New Times (Novoye Vremya)* magazine. The Party founded *New Times* in 1943 solely to provide cover for intelligence officers abroad; by Politburo order, 12 of its 14 foreign bureaus were reserved for exclusive KGB occupancy. However, the new editor, Pavel Naumov, insisted that any officer nominated by the KGB must demonstrate to his satisfaction, during a year of apprenticeship, that he actually could write articles fit for publication. Colonel Pastukhov, a bald, barnacled veteran of 35 years in State Security, explained: "As is well known, Naumov is a famous asshole. But we can't control him because Kryuchkov [Vladimir Kryuchkov, head of the First Chief Directorate] gives him whatever he wants. So you must satisfy Naumov; that is your main duty for the next year. If he kicks you out, we'll have to send you with TASS or *Pravda*, and that's not so good."

Levchenko began work at the office of *New Times*, on Pushkin Square, next to Novosti headquarters, in January 1974. On his third afternoon there, a staff writer named Zhmerynski sidled into his office, flashed a *Newsweek* cartoon lampooning Brezhnev and, giggling like a tipsy prostitute, whispered, "It's funny, isn't it?"

Levchenko grimaced. "It's an obscenity."

Swiftly changing expression and tone like a chameleon, Zhmerynski said gravely: "That's what I mean. It's really funny how desperate they are when they have to stoop to this. It just shows what we're up against."

Levchenko simply stared at him.

"Are you free after work?" Zhmerynski asked. "I'll treat you to a beer. Let's get acquainted."

Food particles stained the oilcloth covering the restaurant table, and a dead fly lodged in the dried beer of a glass the waitress had not bothered to take away. Zhmerynski ordered beer and a bottle of vodka. Levchenko was aware that a *stukach* often needs three or four hefty belts before he has courage enough to begin.

"I think I should alert you," Zhmerynski said confidentially. "Probably you already have heard. But I owe it to you to tell you in case you haven't."

"What?"

"Well, we have a very difficult situation at our magazine."

"What's the problem?"

"Doubtless you know that 80 percent of our writers and technical staff are of Jewish origin. They never will be allowed abroad, and they have to work very hard. Many of them are really mad with this situation. They cannot go abroad, and they are not promoted. It's terrible, isn't it?"

"I don't see anything terrible. Maybe you know something I don't. But so far as I can see, Naumov treats everybody equally."

After more beer and vodka, Zhmerynski threw up his hands. "Let's forget about business and have some fun. We deserve it. Let's go screw. I know a girl who's the best lay in Moscow, and she can get a girl for you."

"Sorry. As you know, I am going to Japan, and I have to be careful. So I've locked my cock in the safe, and only my wife has the combination. Besides, you've never seen my wife."

Having deflected the first provocation, Levchenko set out to breach the invisible wall of suspicion, envy and resentment he knew separated him from the staff. Most were Jewish, and they never would be allowed overseas, though many were more talented journalists than the KGB officers they had to help prepare to go abroad. All of them feared and despised the KGB, and all did have to work hard. As Naumov retorted, when criticized for hiring so many "non-Russians": "Jews work like hell—when they're scared."

By working as hard as everyone else, displaying a willingness to do whatever was needed, and never asking questions or broaching topics that might suggest an ulterior motive, Levchenko gradually earned acceptance. Approximately 30 percent of *New Times* articles were written under pseudonyms by the International Department, about 20 percent by the KGB disinformation service and 20 percent or so by the Foreign Ministry. Not even Naumov could change that. He did demand that all articles meet minimum stylistic standards, and Levchenko gained respect from staff members by competently rewriting many that were unpublishable in their original form. He brightened the question-and-answer columns by writing entertaining replies to queries about Asian subjects. He suggested that the *New Times* correspondent then in Tokyo merely forward notes and newspaper clippings, and let him write the articles under a joint byline. The KGB officer was delighted to be relieved of writing; Naumov was pleased with the articles Levchenko produced; and the Japanese and other security services around the world began seeing the name Stanislav Levchenko in the pages of *New Times*. They could only conclude that he might actually be a journalist.

Before his departure for Tokyo, custom obligated Levchenko to pay for a farewell party in the *New Times* cafeteria. The entire editorial staff of about 100 people was invited, but he guessed probably only 20 or so would attend. He gave the cafeteria manager 100 rubles and told him to procure however much food and drink that would buy.

Levchenko arrived promptly at 8 p.m., the hour the party was to begin, and for a moment he had to fight back tears. The tables were laden with caviar, sturgeon, smoked salmon and cheese, with dozens of bottles of the finest Georgian wines and brandy and ordinarily unobtainable Stolichnaya vodka. He knew that it all would have cost 500 rubles or more, had not Naumov exercised his influence. And nearly 80 people were there, standing and clapping as he entered.

All ate and drank freely and merrily through the evening, and, one by one, each came to say goodbye. Finally, when most were rather intoxicated, Naumov, who remained sober, spoke: "Comrade Stanislav Aleksandrovich has worked only a year for us, but already he has proven himself a worthy member of our collective and a fine journalist. We wish him every success in the difficult and hazardous journalistic tasks awaiting him in Japan. He is a good comrade."

A plump but pretty blonde, with whom Levchenko on occasion had shared the combination to his special safe, squealed,

"And a good *man!*" And everybody laughed.

Taking Levchenko aside, Naumov said, "You are one of our best writers, and I consider you my friend. Good luck in our work and your own. Incidentally, you will fly first class, and you can take your dog in the cabin. That's arranged."

Custom also required Levchenko to give a party for his superiors, and two nights before his flight to Tokyo, he took five colonels from the Japanese Desk to the Cinema Club. A preserve of actors, actresses, producers, writers, and Party functionaries who control the arts, the heavily subsidized club offered caviar, excellent shashlik and the best Georgian wines at modest prices. However, Levchenko chose it because its ambience reminded him of the Russia he imagined had formerly existed; and to cope with the present and future, he needed to be reminded of this past.

From the top floor of a Stalinesque building, the club commanded a fine view of a square and a long *prospekt* leading to the Kremlin. Freshly fallen snow, reflecting the lights of Moscow, hid the reality of the city. Tapestries woven long ago, in rich hues of ruby, gold, copper and emerald, and paintings of village scenes decorated the walls. Perfumed, stylishly dressed women danced to American jazz of the 1930s and old Russian music played by a small orchestra.

In the genteel atmosphere, one of the colonels realized that the six of them, heads bent over, huddling together and muttering in low voices, were anomalous. "Let's stop acting like whores in church and enjoy ourselves," he said.

The evening was amiable but uneventful, until the end, when as they started to leave, one colonel asked Levchenko to remain. The invitation surprised Levchenko because in the office the colonel wore a hard, phlegmatic expression, said little and while civil, had never engaged him in personal conversation.

"I will buy you one drink and give you three pieces of advice," he began. "If you ever repeat any of my words, I will deny I spoke them and prove you a liar five different ways. Then I will cut off your balls. Understand?"

Levchenko nodded.

"First, in real operations there always has to be a first time. The rules you have learned are sound guidelines. The best guidelines will be your own common sense and good judgment.

"Second, stay away from the CIA. You will be under great pressure to recruit Americans; by all means try, if you have the opportunity. But if you play with the CIA, you are playing with fire. The CIA officer will be all too glad to have lunch with you as often as you wish. Sooner or later, he will invite you to dinner at his home, to see how a typical American family lives. There will be a small number of attractive Americans who know a lot about our country, and they will talk reasonably and sympathetically. And there will be an unattached girl who looks like a Hollywood actress and speaks Russian as sweetly as a nightingale sings. She will make you think she thinks you are the only man in the world. At best you will be squandering your time. Worse has happened.

"Third, stay away from Pronnikov as much as you can. He is more dangerous than the CIA."

III

THE SNAKE PIT

DISORIENTED AND FATIGUED after flying across seven time zones, Levchenko looked forward to resting with Natalia in a quiet Tokyo hotel offering immaculate rooms with charming appointments and attentive service. Instead, the KGB booked them into a cheap hotel near the embassy, patronized mainly by couples who rented rooms by the hour. During the night they were intermittently assailed by creaks, squeals, moans and giggles scarcely muffled by the thin walls. Having slept only fitfully, Levchenko dressed in the dark about 6 a.m., drank some tea downstairs to mollify his stomach, and walked aimlessly along awakening streets, composing himself for the trial ahead at the Residency.

He felt as though he were about to descend into a snake pit. From all he had read and heard at the Japanese Desk at the Center, he calculated that fully half the adults in the Soviet colony were informants, and many competed keenly to discover something derogatory. Wives assiduously courted the confidence of each other, then curried favor by informing on the other. Sometimes two people would stay up late drinking together and in the morning hurry to the embassy to write reports about each other. Unless you really knew somebody, you had to guard against everybody, speaking carefully and unambiguously or not at all.

Misjudging the distance he had to walk, Levchenko reached the Soviet compound 15 minutes early, and paced back and forth outside until it opened at 9 a.m. The 11-story embassy is a modern, architecturally presentable edifice, constructed of white stone, set in the greenery of well-tended gardens, shrubs and trees. An apartment building nearby, identical in outward dimensions and appearance, houses a majority of the Soviet diplomatic personnel stationed in Tokyo. Within the compound they enjoy a swimming pool, sauna, tennis courts, a commissary and theater. Some residents rarely find cause to venture beyond the gates, except on officially supervised collective outings. Remote-controlled television cameras concealed behind one-way mirrors scan the entire periphery of the grounds.

When Levchenko entered the marble foyer of the embassy, Major Viatcheslav Pirogov waited to meet him. At first sight, Levchenko decided that during the 14 years since they last knew each other at Moscow University, Pirogov had shed none of his past. A *stukach* at the university, then a Second Chief Directorate Chekist until his father-in-law maneuvered him into the First Chief Directorate, Pirogov was an inveterate lumpen. He suffered from awkward posture, protuberant black eyes and badly snaggled teeth, which fixed his face with a kind of devilish leer. He wore the same suit every day, the shabbiest Moscow make of blue serge, and the seat of his trousers shone like a polished mirror. No matter what he talked about, he spoke in the clichés and hoary, stilted phrases of an old Party manual. Yet Levchenko never condemned him for being what he naturally was, any more than he would condemn a dog for barking. He was so obvious as to be harmless, and Levchenko had been among the few who consented to attend his marriage in Moscow to the very plain daughter of a KGB colonel.

Leaving the elevator on the tenth floor, they stepped into the windowless anteroom of the Residency. With special keys, Pirogov unlocked a gray steel door and by pressing a button hidden in the floor, opened a second door a yard behind the first. Roughly midway down a long corridor, he led Levchenko into a spacious office with artificial wood paneling, a large conference table and a comfortable sofa. There he introduced him to the Resident, Dimitri Yerokhin.

A tall, rugged-looking officer, Yerokhin, at age 42, had become the KGB's youngest major general in consequence of spectacular successes in New Delhi. Brusque and preoccupied, he shook hands perfunctorily and dismissed Levchenko with three sentences: "They tell me you're an outstanding specialist in Japan. Therefore, I expect outstanding work from you. Go and get to work."

In the corridor outside, Levchenko saw striding toward them a short, trim man, wearing a tweed jacket, fresh blue shirt, regimental striped tie and gray flannel trousers. His thick brown hair was carefully combed, his complexion ruddy, and he was rather handsome, except for his gray eyes, which, even as he smiled, seemed to Levchenko predatory and merciless. Offering his hand, he said. "You must be Stanislav Aleksandrovich. I'm Vladimir Alekseyevich. Please come in." Pirogov started to follow, but Vladimir Alekseyevich stopped him with a contemptuous stare, and he slunk away like a cuffed cur.

Lieutenant Colonel Vladimir Alekseyevich Pronnikov, as chief of Line PR, was second in command of the Residency. But, as well-informed officers in the First Chief Directorate knew, Pronnikov was far more powerful than either his rank or position suggested.

The son of a peasant, Pronnikov was ashamed of his heritage and of his height—barely five feet six inches—and he had strenuously compensated for these presumed deficiencies. As a youth, he developed and hardened his body through gymnastics and boxing, and he still kept fit by jogging and playing tennis. He shunned tobacco, drank little and so attended to his health that at 45, he looked 35. Pronnikov also worked inordinately hard in school, and his ability to memorize served him well under teachers who appreciated repetition of their own words. By merit, he earned admission to the Institute of International Relations and brilliantly mastered Japanese. Posted to Tokyo as a junior foreign service officer in the 1950s, he copied the dress and manners of Western diplomats, collected ancient masks, studded his conversation with references to obscure occurrences in Japanese history, and discoursed about the relative merits of foreign automobiles and French wines.

The gloss of urbanity he acquired caught the attention of the KGB, which usurped him as a co-opted agent, that is, one who performs intelligence assignments while continuing his regular job. Within the year, Pronnikov recruited a Japanese journalist, a feat rarely accomplished by a novice, and displayed such a genius for intrigue that the KGB enlisted him as a regular officer. During three subsequent tours in Tokyo, he recruited at least six prominent Agents of Influence, and by suborning former cabinet minister Hirohide Ishida, made himself personally known to Brezhnev, Kosygin and Andropov.

The trajectory of Pronnikov's future career seemed fixed and clear for all to see: another interlude at the Center, probably as deputy department chief, and promotion to colonel; then reassignment to Tokyo as Resident. As commander in Japan, he would have every opportunity to distinguish himself further and vault into the leadership of the KGB; indeed, Levchenko had heard conjecture that Pronnikov eventually would head the First Chief Directorate.

Although exceedingly busy this morning, Pronnikov acted as if nothing were as important as welcoming his new comrade; and, in fact, nothing was more important to him. He habitually appraised each new man, to determine whether and how the officer might be drawn into his personal network of agents and informants. And Levchenko, who embodied the qualities of sophistication Pronnikov had labored so long to gain himself, was an especially desirable prospect.

Trying to be friendly, Pronnikov purposely revealed intimate knowledge of Levchenko that would have been difficult to accumulate except through informants. He dropped the name of Levchenko's prize-winning poodle, Beauty, and inquired how the dog had withstood the flight from Moscow. He asked if Levchenko retained his interest in Shakespeare and Chaucer, showing that he knew Levchenko had attended the experimental high school. He knew about Levchenko's tour at sea, his work with the Afro-Asian Committee, his high marks in intelligence school. He knew also about Levchenko's wife.

"I understand your wife—Natalia, is it?—is remarkably beautiful," he said.

"I am fortunate," Levchenko replied.

"Fortunate indeed. You will have your own car, your own apartment, dine in the best restaurants, meet interesting people. How many young men can say the same? I hope you do not forget that you owe it all to the FCD.* I hope too that you will be wise enough to let me help you. I have had considerable experience in Japan and the FCD, and I will be pleased to share it with you. Frankly, the Resident is heavily burdened these days, and it behooves us all not to add to his concerns. So if you have problems, or if you see situations that need correction, bring them to my attention. My door is always open." Noting that his door was closed, Pronnikov managed a mechanical smile and added, "At least to you."

Levchenko thanked him and stood to leave. As he did, Pronnikov called, "By the way, your wife; is she interested in a job? Perhaps I could help arrange something."

The message Pronnikov imparted was clear to Levchenko: Knowledge is power, and I know everything. Serve me and you will be rewarded with the patronage of the powerful. You know that without my intercession Natalia never will get a job in the embassy unless she agrees to be a *stukach*. And I am not asking you to do anything that would violate your duty or

*First Chief Directorate.

conscience; at least not now.

Later in the morning, after a few more introductions, Pirogov escorted Levchenko through the Residency and explained some of its inviolate rituals. The first room to the right of the entrance was a big one, accommodating 25 work booths, where case officers drafted reports, studied operations and translated documents. Smoking and conversation were prohibited, and the officers silently poring over their papers reminded Levchenko of monks in a monastery.

Past the Resident's office on the right of the corridor, a door opened into two offices, one of which was shared by the chief of Line X and the Illegals Support officer. Of all KGB components, Levchenko respected Line X most because it stole scientific and industrial data he thought could help the Soviet people. And the officers in Tokyo were more productive than any in the world, outside those stealing in the United States. He sympathized with the Illegals Support officer, who had to work long and odd hours, skulking around Tokyo, loading and unloading drops used by Soviet nationals unlawfully infiltrating Japanese society as spies.

The other office in the suite belonged to the chief of Line KR and the Security officer. While endeavoring to penetrate Japanese security services, Line KR also maintained the web of informants within the Soviet colony. For this reason its officers were treated as the outcasts of the Residency.

The Security officer helped manage the informants while supervising the physical protection of the embassy, arrangements for safeguarding visiting Soviet dignitaries, efforts to recapture Soviet defectors and the weekly lectures about the imperialistic perils awaiting Soviet innocents outside the embassy.

The chief of the American Group, chief of the Chinese Group and Active Measures officer occupied the last office on the right of the corridor. Pursuant to Group *Nord* directives, the American Group, with the zeal of scavengers, collected every scintilla of information it could scrape up about U.S. citizens residing in Japan—diplomats, journalists, businessmen, professors, students, servicemen and their families. It targeted for recruitment Japanese and other foreigners who knew or could meet Americans, and compiled lists of Japanese working in the United States, on the premise that they would form some enduring friendships with Americans. The Chinese Group did basically the same with regard to citizens of the People's Republic of China.

The Active Measures officer coordinated the extensive covert actions and disinformation campaigns the Residency continuously mounted through the agent network. Some days he received from the Center half a dozen different directives, defining new covert propaganda themes to be sounded, ordering the circulation of a new rumor or placement of a particular fabrication in the Japanese or world press. In consultation with the Resident and chief of Line PR, he had to recommend which agents could best execute given orders.

Turning back toward the Residency entrance, Pirogov pointed out on the right of the corridor the office of the two regular Reports officers, who edited and refined drafts written by case officers. The next office was that of the Secretariat where two female clerks, both wives of KGB officers, logged all incoming and outgoing communications. Posted on the walls were photographs of known members of Japanese surveillance units and a list of license numbers of vehicles believed to belong to the CIA. A notice beneath stated: "If you ever see one of these machines, please record and immediately report the exact time and location of its sighting."

Pronnikov's office adjoined the Secretariat, and beyond it was an office known as the Zenith room. In it a technician monitored the radio frequencies used by Japanese counterintelligence and police surveillants. Whenever a Residency officer was due to engage in a hazardous meeting with an agent, the technician came on duty and listened. If he heard a flurry or any other abnormality in Japanese communications, he transmitted a signal to a tiny beeper in the officer's pocket, and thereby told him to abort the meeting. The operator also manned the television cameras hidden around the embassy compound, mainly focusing them upon the "first line" of Japanese surveillants hovering outside. If he saw units break away to follow an officer departing the embassy, he signaled by radio. Whenever he wished, he could activate a zoom lens and take a close-up photograph of anyone approaching within view of the cameras.

In the washroom by the entrance, Levchenko remarked that a kind of sepulchral quiet seemed to pervade the Residency, and Pirogov proudly told him why. The walls, ceilings and floors of the entire Residency were double, and both music and electronic impulses constantly were beamed through the voids to frustrate any listening devices and ensure absolute soundproofing. The few exterior windows, formed of special opaque plexiglass, were also utterly soundproof and impervious to any known eavesdropping gear.

Climbing the stairway to the 11th floor, they emerged into a corridor like that below. Two female translators in the first office on the left worked on stolen documents. In the cavernous room adjoining the translation office, Levchenko saw a maze of radio and microwave receivers, tape recorders, sensors, teletypes and electronic equipment. With this array, the Electronic Surveillance officer eavesdropped on communications from American space satellites and military installations, taped conversations from tapped telephones and recorded those transmitted by microwave. The Residency long ago had hooked into the teletype circuits of the Japanese Foreign Ministry and routinely copied all messages sent over them. The setup was so well automated that the officer managed it with the help of two officers' wives.

The last room on the left of the corridor looked to Levchenko like a museum of espionage equipment, some of which he had never seen before. Most items had been made by hand at KGB laboratories in Moscow and were issued by the Technical Operations officer to individual officers for special purposes. The Technical Operations officer also ran the photography lab across the hall, next to the restroom. In the photo lab was the Residency's one photocopier, which could be used only with a key obtained from the Secretariat.

Diplomatic pouches were packed and sometimes small pieces of stolen Japanese equipment were crated in a large open area opposite the electronic surveillance room. In the office beyond this work area, the financial clerk kept officers' expense accounts and readily disbursed operational funds. No reasonable expenses were questioned, and receipts were required only for expenditures exceeding $100.

In the microfilm office by the stairway, the officer in charge photographed the standard contact reports an officer had to complete after each meeting with an agent or prospect, and forwarded a copy to the Center. He also listed in a file the location of each encounter between officer and agent. Before scheduling a lunch, dinner or clandestine meeting, each officer had to consult him, to be sure the officer was not meeting in a restaurant or locale another KGB officer had recently visited.

Aside from the records kept in the microfilm office, the logs in the Secretariat, and a Registry of Active Measures, the Residency retained few operational files in Tokyo. Each officer, upon arrival, received his own Top Secret notebook, whose blank pages were successively numbered. In it he could jot down skeletal details of an operation—true and code names, telephone and license numbers, emergency plans and other essentials to aid his memory—but nothing else. Upon leaving the Residency, he had to place the notebook in a plastic pouch, close the pouch with his individual seal, about the size of a quarter, and put it in his slot in a portable steel safe. At the end of the day, a cipher clerk rolled the safe to the eighth-floor Referentura, protected by a six-inch armor-plated door that could be opened only from the inside. Always, day and night, weekends and holidays, a guard or cipher clerk stayed inside, standing watch over the cryptographic machines and secret satellite transmitters.

Pirogov gave Levchenko some code phrases for use in open telephone conversations with the embassy, the names of a few restaurants and admonitions about drinking. Never drink in the Residency, unless invited by the Resident for a toast on a ceremonial occasion. Never get caught drunk in public. Of course, Pirogov noted with a wink, that did not mean one could not drink at home, or now and then take home a bottle from the ample supply of operational liquor. Levchenko listened to this and other elementary advice courteously and smiled appropriately, but he was preoccupied by bad thoughts. Fearful of betraying them, he pleaded the necessity of meeting his *New Times* predecessor, who was to introduce him around Tokyo, and excused himself.

A contrast had struck Levchenko. In a Moscow store you stand in line looking for something to buy; then you stand in line to pay for your purchase; then you stand in another line to exchange a ticket for what you have bought. Presumably, this redundancy reduces petty embezzlement and pilferage, albeit at staggering costs. In the Residency they had no time for such concerns. They passed out money as freely as ammunition is distributed in the trenches, and they didn't care if someone pinched a few dollars any more than the Red Army cares if a soldier wastes a few bullets. All his life Levchenko had seen the stultifying, choking effects of bureaucracy blight every facet of the Soviet economy. In the Residency, if not at the Center, they disdained bureaucracy. The KGB was not in Tokyo to shuffle papers and keep records. It was there to act, to subvert the nation of Japan, to do in the Chinese and Americans and everybody else. The Residency was a fortress built for war, and officers could expect significant advancement only if they excelled in combat. *Why not apply the same common sense to peaceful pursuits back home? Why not free the people to innovate and produce as best they could and reward those who invented and produced the most for all?*

Except for some of the exotic equipment on the 11th floor, nothing Levchenko saw in the Residency surprised him very much. The Tokyo Residency, though much more modern and larger, was similar to the training Residency in Moscow. He understood that Residencies throughout the world are alike in design and functions; and this universal uniformity contributed to his malaise. He realized that in Washington, New York, London, Paris, Bonn, Rome, Madrid, Mexico City, Ottawa, Brasilia, Bangkok, New Delhi, Canberra and most other world capitals, legions of KGB officers at that very moment were out on the streets doing the same thing as the colleagues he joined in Tokyo. They were among the most brilliant men the Soviet Union could assemble. *Why not invest more of this national treasure in productive pursuits back home?*

Levchenko did not want to inquire and reason further. Again, he fled his thoughts by immersing himself in work.

Initially, he concentrated upon establishing himself in the eyes of Japanese and Western intelligence as a bona fide journalist. He dined with Japanese spotted by his predecessor, called at the offices of parliamentarians, journalists and government officials, attended diplomatic receptions, joined press junkets and generally made himself noticeable. Assuming his phone was tapped, he telephoned leaders of all Japanese political factions, soliciting interviews and asking reasonable questions. To the surprise of Japanese politicians, he showed up at 2 a.m. on election night at the headquarters of the Liberal Democratic Party and behaved like any other serious reporter.

He reinforced his credentials by frequently filing dispatches to *New Times,* and initially keeping them free of polemics offensive to the Japanese. A visit to the huge *Isetan* department store inspired one of his first stories. By chance, an alarm sounded, signaling a fire or earthquake drill. Quickly, thousands of people cheerfully evacuated the building without panic or incident. Levchenko depicted this scene as an illustration of the basic discipline and social responsibility of the Japanese people. And by living his cover so well, he became the first Soviet journalist admitted to the prestigious National Press Club of Japan.

Whereas American and West European correspondents lived in fine apartments or even houses, Levchenko inherited from his predecessor a rickety flat, plagued with cockroaches, in a lower-class neighborhood. He advised *New Times* editor Naumov that the place was an embarrassment to the magazine and the Soviet Union. Naumov at once authorized him to rent a luxury apartment and to furnish it tastefully at magazine expense. Levchenko found a three-bedroom unit in a splendid new building in the exclusive Udagawa district near a beautiful park and the hallowed Shinto Meiji Shrine. The doorman doubtless would report his movements to counterintelligence, and that was fine; he could enter through the foyer, let his presence at home be noted, then slip out by the fire escape for operations.

The apartment, the new Japanese car Levchenko bought with *New Times* money, his well-tailored dark suits, the Western clothes that accentuated Natalia's beauty, their familiarity with fashionable restaurants—all were operational necessities. Pleading operational necessity, they could skip the dreary weekly Party meetings, obligatory for everybody else, and generally avoid the cloistered life of the Soviet colony. All this made them different from the families who had to live in the embassy compound under the watch of Line KR* and its flock of informants, families who would never own a car, who would never fritter away money on clothes or restaurants or foreign films. And to be different was to be feared, envied, disliked and to invite special attentions from the *stukachi*.

A *stukach*, Larisa Petrovna, called uninvited on Natalia in March, ostensibly to offer neighborly counsel about shopping in Tokyo. A fading woman in her 40s, Larisa had both drinking and marital problems, and she confided to all that her KGB husband was impotent. She stayed with him only out of altruism and patriotism, knowing that he would be sent home were they to separate, so she said. Shortly before Levchenko arrived, she and an embassy lothario had driven to a teen-agers' trysting site outside the city, made love in the car and got drunk on vodka. Driving away, they crashed into a parked automobile, severely lacerating her face, and she still was pale and partially bandaged. She escaped punishment partly

*Security and counterintelligence section of the Residency.

because she was an informant, partly because her lover had influence in Moscow.

Exuding the good will of an older sister, Larisa emphasized to Natalia that by saving yen and buying Japanese goods to take home, she could earn a respectable fortune on the Moscow black market. Transistor radios, cameras and watches were good buys, but they were comparatively expensive. She could do better by investing in cosmetics, fabrics, blue jeans, ballpoint pens and condoms.*

To assist Natalia in saving, Larisa recommended that she shave the grocery bill by buying fish heads, bones and other scraps which could be cooked into perfectly adequate meals. Natalia blurted: "My husband works 15 hours a day! He needs real meat." Subsequently, this statement was quoted widely in the colony as evidence of profligacy; and among people obsessed with skimping, so as to trade on the black market in Moscow, profligacy was the gravest of abnormalities. And if further proof of the Levchenko profligacy were needed, you had only to consider their poodle. To waste money feeding a dog was scandalous.

While settling in, Levchenko visited the Residency infrequently, because he had so much to do elsewhere. He did drop off a directory listing the names and office addresses of foreign correspondents accredited in Tokyo. It had come in the mail as an unsolicited courtesy from the Japan Newspaper Publishers and Editors Association, which tried to help foreign journalists. Although every correspondent had a copy, the directory excited Pirogov, who ordered Levchenko to cut off the heading and submit it as a secret document. Shortly, the Center cabled an evaluation: "Comrade Koltsov's** report constitutes a valuable contribution which fills a longstanding need."

---

*The factory supplying prophylactics to Moscow frequently broke down; Soviet women complained about the unreliability of its products and men about the thickness.

**Koltsov was Levchenko's KGB work name; a famous Soviet journalist named Koltsov was liquidated by Stalin and posthumously rehabilitated by Khrushchev.

"You see," Pirogov beamed. "Just listen to me."

Passing in the corridor, Pronnikov expressed surprise that Levchenko had not been by to see him. Somewhat sardonically, Levchenko thought, he asked, "How is your beautiful wife? And your doggie? Your fancy doggie?"

When they chanced to meet in April, Pronnikov said, "Tell me, has your beautiful wife landed a job?" Pronnikov, of course, knew that the embassy had returned Natalia's application with the notation: "No job available."

Among the more interesting of the dozen or so contacts turned over to Levchenko was a leader of the Japanese Socialist Party, to whom the KGB assigned the code name King. While studying him, Levchenko recalled a lecture delivered at intelligence school by a colonel who had served in the United States. In discussing why people become agents, the colonel quoted an American acronym, MICE—Money, Ideology, Compromise, Ego. Usually, he said, one or more of these motivations impel a foreigner to succumb to the KGB; ideally, the case officer should play upon all four.

Briefings told Levchenko that King, a respected intellectual, was a former Communist and still an ideological Marxist. But that did not necessarily mean he was sympathetic to the Soviet Union. Most Japanese disliked Soviets, and many were so hostile that in sojourns around Tokyo Levchenko often posed as an American or Swiss. Many Japanese Marxists regarded the Soviet Union as a traitor to true Marxism, and the Japanese Communist Party was virulently anti-Soviet.

King earned a comfortable salary and lived within his means in a pleasant, small apartment with his wife and two children. He appeared to have no vices that would make him vulnerable to compromise, and to the KGB's knowledge there was no indication of abnormal egotism. Nevertheless, in cultivating him, Levchenko kept searching for means to invoke all the motivations of MICE.

He also guided himself by some general precepts formulated from his analysis of Japanese culture and psychology. The Japanese worked hard, their daily schedules usually were jammed, and they disliked wasting time. Therefore, Levchenko tried to make each luncheon or dinner satisfying to King by subtly flattering him and imparting snippets of information that could be useful.

Invoking a ploy that again and again was to prove effective, Levchenko said, "I want to be frank and tell you in confidence something I would prefer that you not repeat. Officially, it is said that *New Times* is a trade union publication. Actually, it is an organ of the International Department, and it publishes a confidential bulletin which is read by men close to the Politburo and other Soviet policy-makers. So I can't afford to make mistakes; they must know the facts, pleasant or not. That is one reason why our conversations are so important. You are a veritable professor of politics."

In other words, Mr. King, you are not talking to an ordinary journalist. Through me you are speaking to and conceivably influencing the leadership of the Soviet Union.

Drawing from reports of KGB agents already emplaced in the Socialist Party hierarchy, Levchenko asked questions displaying impressive knowledge of the party's inner workings and Japanese politics generally. Often, though, he purposely misstated a fact or erroneously interpreted an event, to allow King to correct him.

"Are you sure?" he asked after King pointed out his error. "My information came from a good source."

Sometimes, to demonstrate the authenticity and superiority of his knowledge, King would amplify and thereby provide insights new to the KGB. Earnestly, Levchenko would thank King for enlightening and again saving him (and, by implication, Soviet leaders) from ignorance. In return, Levchenko occasionally informed King of imminent changes in Soviet policy or of internal Soviet problems which he knew *Pravda* itself would soon announce. The disclosures, which cost the Soviets nothing, made King for a few days more knowledgeable than his peers. And twice he shared with King secrets of the governing Liberal Democratic Party that the Socialist Party could use against its rivals.

Levchenko understood that Japanese do not grant friendship casually. Once they do, however, they tend to regard a friendship almost as binding as a family relationship. And Levchenko slowly earned King's friendship by projecting himself as a sympathetic, sensitive human being, the antithesis of the menacing, dogmatic Bolshevik. He chose modest restaurants and ordered Japanese delicacies repellent to many foreigners, including some hard for him to stomach, such as *awabi-no-kimo*, green abalone liver. Never did he criticize anything Japanese, or in any manner suggest that he agreed with criticisms voiced by King.

As their personal rapport grew, Levchenko, out of overconfidence or inexperience, committed a potentially ruinous error. Talking about his forthcoming 1976 campaign for election to parliament, King said that his principal problem would be raising money. "Well, let us help you," Levchenko responded. "My magazine has funds for such purposes."

King physically recoiled, and his face froze. "No! No!" he said with uncharacteristic harshness. "That would be completely improper." Nevertheless, their relationship was sufficiently cemented to withstand the transgression, and King agreed to lunch the next week.

Levchenko reserved a private room in a stately restaurant, decorated with ancient prints and magnificent antiques. Listening to the rain pounding against the stained glass windows while waitresses in bright silk kimonos served hot sake, he felt as though he were in an enchanting museum. The ambience also delighted King, and they talked amicably through nine courses and three hours. King mentioned that for years he had aspired to publish a newsletter of intelligent political commentary that could unify the Socialist Party. "That's an excellent idea. Why not do it?" Levchenko asked.

The difficulty was money. King had put aside some of his own. But he would need at least a million more yen, and he could not impose such a sacrifice on his family.

Signifying his understanding with a nod, Levchenko shifted subjects. His discussions with King were professionally invaluable to him, but he valued them most of all because of their personal friendship. As a friend, he had to consider King's welfare.

"I am a journalist. You are an important political leader," he said. "We have every right to exchange opinions. But counter-intelligence services usually are over zealous. They often follow Soviets and tap their telephones, just because they're Soviets. I'm not blaming them; that's their job. And maybe some of my countrymen have given them reason to be suspicious. It seems everybody spies on everybody else these days. That's none of my business, but I am worried about embarrassing you."

Accordingly, Levchenko proposed that they cease talking by phone. Henceforth, each time they met, they would schedule two subsequent meetings; if either found cause to forgo the first, they would keep the second. King agreed to the plan, and thereby to a clandestine relationship.

Having lured King across the threshold, Levchenko experienced not professional pride, but self-disgust. He was as hypocritically cynical as the system itself. By deceitfully proffering friendship, he was defiling the soul of another human being and transgressing against the will of God. Yet if he was to survive in the KGB, what else could he do? As always, it was best not to think.

About a month later, Levchenko casually inquired about the newsletter. "Have you found funds?"

"No, I'm afraid that is hopeless; the newsletter never will be published."

"My dear friend, I know you never would take money for yourself, and for that I respect you. But please let me find some way to help you with the newsletter. It's important for all people of good will."

Quickly and nervously King said, "Thank you. Not now; maybe later."

At the Residency, Levchenko reviewed the case with Pronnikov, and together they drafted a cable which Resident Yerokhin approved: "Comrade Koltsov convinced that a payment of one million yen will result in effective recruitment of King, and Residency concurs."

The Center responded promptly: "Give King the money."

During a Friday luncheon at another restaurant, Levchenko waited until they had several whiskies before saying, "I almost forgot. Anything new about your newsletter?"

"No, there is no possibility."

"There is. Please accept our fraternal support," Levchenko said, laying a fat yellow envelope containing a million yen on the table. King hesitated, then stuck the envelope into the inside pocket of his jacket.

Levchenko talked enthusiastically about the potential of the newsletter, how it would augment the power of King, how it might grow into a major publication. Innocently he added: "By the way, that money, of course, is not mine. I must produce a financial accounting, and I need some kind of receipt to show I didn't abscond; anything will do." Red-faced, King hastily scribbled a receipt on the back of one of his business cards.

Pocketing it, Levchenko said, "Thank you so much. I do hope that from now on our cooperation will be more active and mutually beneficial.

King mumbled, "Yes, yes. I will try to help you."

Around 6 a.m. on Monday, the telephone and tremulous voice of King awakened Levchenko. "I must see you at once. It is most urgent."

Joining him later in the day for lunch, Levchenko remarked, "You look ill. What's wrong?"

"I am all right physically. But I must have my calling card back. Do you realize what it means?"

"Yes, it is a receipt for money."

"But do you understand? That document could be used to compromise me, to ruin my career, my whole life."

Levchenko appeared to reflect, as if presented with a wholly new thought. "I suppose it could be used that way; certainly, it never will be so used."

"Where is the card now? In the embassy?"

"No, in Moscow. A courier delivered it."

"What if the plane crashed?"

"The plane did not crash. Your card is locked in a vault for permanent safekeeping. Nobody except me and a financial officer has the right to look at your card—or what you wrote on the back of it." King slumped forlornly, and Levchenko offered no assuagement of his despair.

While maintaining a respectful manner, Levchenko conditioned King to respond to orders. At first they were transmitted in the form of questions, such as: "Shouldn't we do something to prevent this devious Chinese agent from being elected to the JSP convention?" Dutifully King interceded to thwart election of a party member the KGB knew to be working for the Chinese. Prodded by Levchenko, King helped organize the Group of March, to promote Marxist domination of the Socialist Party. His revelations about trends, conflicts and personalities in the party pointed the KGB to additional recruitment opportunities. Whenever his information could be tested against that from other agents, King passed the test.

Analysis of radio traffic and the collective experiences of the Residency showed that Japanese surveillance teams usually did not take to the streets between 11 p.m. and 7 a.m. and that their ranks were thin on weekends and holidays. (The KGB divined that this lapse resulted from government reluctance to pay overtime wages.) Early in December, Levchenko drove from his apartment to King's house at 6 a.m., confident that he would not be followed. Attired in a kimono, King nonchalantly welcomed him into the kitchen, where he was brewing tea. "My good friend, I have brought you three million yen for your campaign," Levchenko announced. "Please accept our fraternal support. We shall never stop supporting you." King calmly counted the money and without being asked wrote out a receipt. By accepting the unsolicited visit and money, he tacitly acknowledged his subservience to Soviet control.

That morning the Residency cabled the Center: "King, for all practical purposes, is now working for us, primarily out of ideological motivation, but also for some material considerations. Analysis of his actions and information demonstrates that he is sincere and not a provocateur. Investigations of King conducted through other sources in JSP confirm this evaluation. Therefore, the Residency considers King to be a Trusted Contact and requests the Center to approve his inclusion in the official network of the Residency."

On December 29, 1975, Moscow replied: "Center approves inclusion of King in Residency Network as Trusted Contact. According to the decision of the leadership of our service, Comrade Koltsov is promoted to the rank of captain and senior case officer. We wish Comrade Koltsov every success in his noble tasks."

The KGB calculated that King could look forward to a political career spanning at least 20 more years. During all those years, at critical junctures, he could slyly uphold Soviet interests in the Diet, Japan's parliament, and the highest councils of the Socialist Party, while appearing to represent what he deemed to be the best interests of Japan. He would give the Russians more than just a single vote. His influence would augment and magnify the influence of comparably placed agents, through whom the KGB expected to wrest control of the entire party. Properly positioned and manipulated, a small core of disciplined agents could decisively affect, if not absolutely control, a political party, irrespective of the wishes of the majority of members. King enlarged and strengthened that core. In rewarding Levchenko with a promotion and accolade, the KGB expressed recognition of the vast potential of King throughout his remaining public life.

Pronnikov was the first to congratulate Levchenko. "My words come true," he said. "I have been able to help you. I gave you rein in the case, and here we have the reward. If you work with me, there will be many more rewards."

Others proposed celebration at a bar. "Maybe tomorrow; I have a meeting tonight," Levchenko demurred. "I thought I might clear my path by visiting the Russian Orthodox church." There was some laughter. "I'm serious," he continued.

"The Japanese say it is an architectural masterpiece. And I hear they sing Orthodox hymns in Japanese. Besides, the Japanese are likely to be less suspicious of anyone they see in church."

The lone Russian Orthodox church in Tokyo was founded in 1891 by a charismatic missionary, Ivan Dmitrevich Kasartskin, who created a faithful congregation of several thousand Japanese converts. They built a stately sanctuary of white stone slabs and an arched roof, whose interior was partitioned by magnificent iconostases. The church opened on old Russian holidays as well as Saturdays and Sundays, and on those days Levchenko sometimes ducked in to meditate and pray in the cool quietude of the sanctuary. That night, he offered the standard prayer for forgiveness he often had repeated since joining the KGB. This time, he also prayed for King and begged that they both be delivered from the evil he did not know how to escape.

Not long afterward, the fall of Resident Yerokhin occurred suddenly and, to everyone at the Residency except Pronnikov, unexpectedly. Many factors, most of Pronnikov's making, contributed to his decline; but his feud with Lieutenant Colonel Gennadi Yevstavyev was fatal. From the moment Yerokhin arrived in Tokyo, flush with his triumphs in New Delhi, Pronnikov saw him as a threat. For if the younger Yerokhin duplicated in Japan his success in India, he would likely remain a fixture at the Residency indefinitely, and thereby obstruct Pronnikov's advancement to Resident. So Pronnikov set out to remove him by subtly sabotaging his operational initiatives whenever he safely could.

Yerokhin brought Yevstavyev with him from New Delhi, promising him a promotion to colonel. When he was unable to immediately deliver the promotion, Pronnikov hinted to Yevstavyev that the Resident was conniving to give it to someone else. Then Pronnikov, as a loyal and concerned lieutenant, informed Yerokhin that an embittered Yevstavyev was making slanderous statements about him. Having sown ill will, Pronnikov inflamed it by periodically reporting to Yerokhin and Yevstavyev disparaging remarks each allegedly had made about the other. Ultimately, Pronnikov suggested to Yerokhin that Yevstavyev was crumbling under the pressure of work and losing his mind.

Whether at Pronnikov's instigation or of his own initiative, Yerokhin began demanding that the Center remove Yevstavyev, claiming that he was insane. One officer on home leave was called in and, in all seriousness, asked, "Is it true that Comrade Yevstavyev stands in the corner of his office and urinates on the floor?"

Pronnikov, of course, made sure Yevstavyev knew that Yerokhin was preparing his consignment to a mental institution as a madman. Therefore, when Yevstavyev was recalled to Moscow, he went directly from the airport to the KGB hospital and insisted upon a complete psychiatric examination. At the Center, a panel of officers spoke to him gently, as to a disturbed child: "We know you have been under enormous stress and tension . . . . You have been working much too hard. . . . You deserve a rest; you've earned it. . . ."

Yevstavyev whipped out a psychiatric certificate from the hospital, attesting to his complete sanity, and proceeded to recount Yerokhin's plot against him. A Party Commission interviewed all officers at the Center who had served in Tokyo during the previous two years; all averred they had never noticed any abnormal behavior by Yevstavyev. Pronnikov, who during the investigation became Acting Resident, submitted a long, dispassionate report praising both Yerokhin and Yevstavyev as splendid officers, lamenting their unfortunate personality clash but fully corroborating Yevstavyev.

Standing before the Party Commission, having been formally accused of falsely slandering a brother officer, Yerokhin initially shouted: "Go to hell! Go fuck yourselves!" But he could not explain away the facts with which the Commission taxed him. In the end, he broke down and sobbed helplessly. To avoid scandal that would accompany dismissal of a major general, the KGB exiled him to the Border Guards.*

*Reportedly, Yerokhin had to retire in 1977, at age 45, after suffering a complete breakdown.

Although Levchenko considered Yerokhin aloof and abrasive, he saw his liquidation as a depravity. It enraged him, and he rashly allowed his anger to surface in the presence of others. "Pronnikov is a snake. The sooner he goes home, the better off we all will be."

The next morning as Levchenko passed his office, Pronnikov yelled, "Come in here!" Pronnikov closed the door, seated himself behind his desk and pointedly left Levchenko standing.

"I really had hoped that we could be friends," he began. "I have made every effort to help you, both in the Residency and the FCD. Now I see that you are ungrateful; I see that you are callous and treacherous."

"What do you mean?"

"You fucking well know what I mean. You underestimate me, and you blabber too much, and people inform me. I know everything that happens here because I am commander-in-chief."

"You mean you have secret informants in the Residency?"

"That is none of your business. But I know everything. I know what you said about me yesterday. For that I will never forgive you. From now on, if you want to keep your head, step very carefully."

"May I go?"

"Get out."

The two scarcely spoke during the weeks before Pronnikov returned to the Center to become Deputy Director of the Seventh Department (which is responsible for Japan), and Levchenko refused to attend his farewell party.

While the KGB looked for a successor to Yerokhin, Pronnikov's replacement, Krarmy Konstantinovich Sevastyanov, acted as Resident. He asked officers to address him as Roman, rather than by his comical first name, Krarmy, an acronym formed from the Russian words meaning Red Army. Tall and gangly, his fingers yellow with tobacco stains, Sevastyanov was nondescript in appearance, soft-spoken and rather profane. His appearance belied his expertise as one of the KGB's premier authorities on Japan. He had served three previous tours there and could recall details of operations 20 years before.

Sevastyanov had a gifted, high-spirited wife, who soon adopted Natalia as her best friend in Tokyo. Through their wives, he and Levchenko became friends. In the security of their apartments, Levchenko came to know him as an essentially honest man, resigned to adapting to a Soviet system he despised, but could not change. This was his last tour before retirement; he merely wanted to conclude it without trouble, and thus urged caution upon all.

Sevastyanov entrusted Levchenko with one of the Residency's more challenging cases, that of Thomas, a senior correspondent of the newspaper *Yomiuri* (circulation 8.7 million, the largest in Japan). A successful author of popular books and a respected political commentator, Thomas was the confidant of a cabinet minister, and personally knew former prime ministers. He also knew who in government was corrupt and who was incorruptible.

As Levchenko realized, Thomas' potential as an Agent of Influence was limitless. Not only could he cause stories to be published in *Yomiuri;* he could cause stories to be omitted, and public understanding of world events is often more distorted by what is suppressed than by what is printed. He could advise the Russians of the true moods, apprehensions and ambitions of Japanese leaders, and thereby enable the KGB to play upon their inner thoughts. Perhaps in years to come, he could, at propitious moments, plant deft arguments in the minds of the prime minister, foreign minister and political leaders, and conceivably thereby affect fundamental national decisions—just as Richard Sorge did in 1941.

However, during 18 months of contact with Thomas, the KGB had discovered no justification to believe that he could be converted into a Soviet agent. Highly educated and widely traveled, he, like his newspaper, was conservative. He derided communism as a moldy political philosophy, which, wherever it was practiced, had discredited itself. His personal life appeared exemplary. He was uncommonly devoted to his wife, a fashionable and educated woman, to his children, home and garden. Salary, book royalties and lecture fees earned him a comfortable income. He had consented to dine once or twice a month with Captain Belov who, as International Books representative of the Ministry of Trade, tried to subvert journalists, authors and publishers. But from Belov, Levchenko derived the impression that Thomas met him partially out of a general interest in foreigners and partially just to show that he was unafraid of Russians. So Levchenko concluded that unless some means to motivate Thomas into subversion could be discerned, the only possible relationship must be founded on personal friendship.

At the first luncheon after Belov introduced them, Levchenko impressed Thomas with his knowledge of Japanese history, literature and politics. Thomas volunteered that he enjoyed conversing with a foreigner in his own language, rather than English, which he understood well but spoke with difficulty. To buttress his journalistic credentials, Levchenko gave him copies of his articles published in the English-language edition of *New Times*, and Thomas promised to read them.

Handing the articles back at their next luncheon, Thomas remarked, "You know, I like the way you write, but if you will forgive me, I must say that *what* you write is, well, rather peculiar."

"Sure, it's propaganda. I have no choice. At least I know it's nonsense. A lot of journalists write absurdities without realizing they're being absurd."

"True, true," Thomas laughed.

While always polite, Thomas revealed his contempt for Soviet repression of dissident intellectuals. "I'm afraid there's some truth in those stories," Levchenko said. "But everything must be viewed in historical perspective. Consider how far we've come since Stalin."

Glancing around the restaurant and lowering his voice, he added, "Of course, I do not deny that we still have far to go."

They joked about the new Soviet ambassador, Dimitri Polyansky, who had been ousted from the Politburo and exiled to Japan.* Polyansky looked, dressed and acted like a peasant. He paced about with his head bent forward and his hands alternately clasped behind him or cupped prayerfully in front of him. At diplomatic functions he grinned constantly, causing people to wonder whether he was all wise or mentally retarded; and he amazed the Japanese with long statistical recitations about Soviet agriculture or childish questions about how they grew so much on so little land.

At the end of a particularly felicitous luncheon some three months after they met, Levchenko ordered a French cognac, and Thomas so enjoyed it that they drank a second glass. "Frankly, I always thought Russians were boors," Thomas said. "But you are a civilized man, and I want you to know that I consider you my friend."

"You are Japanese; I am Russian," Levchenko replied. "First of all, though, we are human beings and friends."

While courting Thomas, Levchenko searched for ways to arouse in him one or more of the motivations of MICE—money, ideology, compromise, ego. Thomas was a gourmet who relished chic restaurants. Handsome and faultlessly groomed, he wore expensively tailored suits, fine silk shirts and ties. Some of his references to his wife suggested that her tastes were also expensive. The upkeep of his house, photographed early on by a Residency agent, also cost him substantially. So Levchenko judged that Thomas would welcome added income.

Levchenko further surmised that Thomas perceived of himself as more than an observer of politics. He liked to think that his ideas and opinions shaped events, and he regarded him-

*In the Politburo, Brezhnev proposed to combine the posts of General Secretary of the Central Committee and President of the Soviet Union, thus arrogating both titles to himself. Podgorny, who stood to lose his position as President, voted against the proposal, as did Shelepin, who generally voted against Brezhnev, whatever the issue. Everyone else voted for the proposal except Polyansky, who foolishly abstained, and thereby provoked Brezhnev to banish him.

self as a wordly sophisticate capable of intriguing with or
against the wiliest of men.

Money and ego, Levchenko decided.

"Last night I realized that I've been both blind and dere-
lict," Levchenko began. He explained that *New Times* published a confidential news bulletin, read by probably no more
than 200 men in Moscow. "But in terms of their impact on
what happens in the world, it would be hard to find a more
influential audience." In each major country, even the United
States, *New Times* invited distinguished journalists to write
for the newsletter. Here Levchenko had been profiting from
the expertise and friendship of the foremost political analyst
in Japan, yet the obvious had never occurred to him. Obviously, Thomas should write for the newsletter. Of course, *New
Times* would insist, as it did in every other country, upon
paying prevailing article rates which, Levchenko recalled, in
Japan were 1000 yen per page.

"What do you want me to write about?" Thomas asked.

"You are the editor. You know far more about the Japanese
scene than I do. So you must choose. Basically, I would say,
write whatever you think the leaders of the Soviet Union
ought to know."

Levchenko had not asked Thomas to betray any secrets,
violate any law or do anything inimical to Japan. What he did
ask seemed like a reasonable journalistic proposal, and Thomas accepted.

The first "article" told the KGB that Thomas welcomed
money, as well as an opportunity to edify the Kremlin. He
submitted a tome of almost 50 pages, bloated with verbose
circumlocutions and irrelevant historical references to increase his payment. After Thomas wrote three or four more
"articles," Levchenko informed him that the newsletter was
adopting a new format. "It will be much shorter, more succinct. So from now on, we will need only a three- or four-page
summary of facts. However, to be fair, we have been instructed to continue paying all correspondents the same amount as
before." When Thomas finally provided a nugget of interest-

ing intelligence—speculation that the Prime Minister inspired conservative criticism of himself to preempt liberal criticism that he was delaying conclusion of an agreement with China—Levchenko announced that he had been ordered to pay him a 60,000-yen bonus. "They thought your last report was quite significant and really appreciated it." Thereafter, Thomas more and more relayed real secrets, and he averaged about $500 a month in payments from the KGB—not a great sum, but approximately a 15 percent addition to his income, an addition he did not have to account for to the tax collector or his wife. And the KGB knew that once he became dependent upon its money, he would be loath to forgo it.

Citing the exaggerated suspicions and snooping of Japanese counterintelligence, Levchenko induced Thomas to meet clandestinely, much as he had done with King. Twice he purposely skipped meetings, even though there was no surveillance, to teach caution and conspiracy. After one of the failed meetings, he said, "I'm sorry, but I noticed a curious car following me, and I didn't want to risk embarrassing you." The secretive arrangements, security precautions and cryptic calls scheduling lunches or dinners in various restaurants amused Thomas, and he played the game with alacrity.

"What are your plans after dinner?" Levchenko asked one evening.

"I am going to have drinks with a professor and talk about Polynesia."

"Will you stop in your office before going home?"

"I hadn't planned to. Why?"

"I have some sensitive financial documents whose disclosure would produce a scandal. I got them just before I came here, and I don't have time to take them to the embassy, because I'm already late for an interview. But I can't take the chance of carrying them around with me. I wondered if you possibly could keep this envelope for me over the weekend."

"I will be glad to, if you can wait until Tuesday. I will be away Monday."

"Fine. Let's have dinner Tuesday evening."

The Technical Operations officer was waiting, late Tuesday night, when Levchenko arrived at the Residency with the envelope. Examining it through a special lens, he said, "No, it hasn't been opened. I'm sure."

Soon, Levchenko put Thomas to another test. In a double-agent operation, Japanese counterintelligence arrested GRU Major Aleksandr Machekin as he left a restaurant after taking film from a U.S. Navy warrant officer. Machekin threw away the film, fought with police and fasted in jail. As he was a Novosti correspondent without diplomatic immunity, the Russians feared he might be sentenced to prison. Levchenko asked Thomas if he could publish something to ameliorate the problem.

"That would be most difficult," Thomas said. "All major newspapers, including my own, are taking a hard anti-Soviet line. It would be impossible right now to publish an article favorable to the Soviet Union."

"Of course," Levchenko replied. "In fact, the first half of the article should be anti-Soviet and say that the Soviets are widely engaged in spying against Japan. But further on you could illuminate some dark spots in the case. Did American Naval Intelligence not arrange the whole provocation? Where is the warrant officer? Why was he, the real spy, if there were any truth to this fairy tale, not arrested? Are the rumors that Machekin is being physically tortured true? Is it a sound practice for Japanese police constantly to prostitute themselves to the Americans? Does Japan profit by involving itself in another major conflict with the Soviet Union when relations between the two countries are already so bad?"

After some reflection Thomas said: "I know a young reporter, quite talented. He loves the sensational and loves to gossip. I will call him in for a general discussion and mention that several distinguished journalists are asking just those questions. Maybe he will do the rest."

After articles reflecting KGB questions appeared in the Tokyo press, augmenting the massive diplomatic pressures the Russians already were applying, the Japanese released the

GRU officer and let him go home quietly.

As Thomas responded to Soviet requests, Levchenko suspected that he realized he was dealing with Soviet intelligence. He had been convinced after Thomas called for an emergency meeting and, in a state of high excitement, detailed an impending scandal. The U.S. government, he said, would disclose that the Lockheed Aircraft Corporation had paid huge bribes to Japanese government leaders. "The Americans are so stupid, so naïve," he declared. "They will ruin some of their best friends."

"How did the Japanese learn of this?" Levchenko asked.

"From that damned Jew."

"Which Jew? So far as I know, there are no Japanese Jews."

"No, he's an American Jew; I don't know his name. I know he works for Japanese intelligence and found out in Washington."

"What will you do with this sensation?"

"Nothing. It's too dangerous. A friend of mine was working on a story like this, and he fell to his death from a ten-story window." Thomas paused and looked Levchenko in the eye. "I thought perhaps your special subscribers in Moscow would want to know ahead of time."

Sevastyanov judged Thomas' report too sensational to be credible and, in the absence of any corroboration, refused to transmit it to the Center. "Stanislav, listen. I like you; you are a talented officer. But you also are a James Bond adventurer. You are going to burn yourself and the rest of us along with you. Now forget about this wild James Bond story and get some sleep."

By now, Levchenko was sure that Thomas would not traffic in misinformation, and intuitively he knew the story must be true. It offered an opportunity to reveal first and dramatize to the world the corruption of capitalism, American and Japanese. He asked himself: *Why discard such opportunity? For what are we wasting our lives; for what are we ruining the lives of others?*

Just as Thomas forecast, in little more than a month the Lockheed scandal broke, convulsing the Liberal Democratic

Party. "What do you think of my James Bond story now?"
Levchenko asked Sevastyanov.

"All right. Sometimes we are not sure, and we make mistakes. Let's forget about the past and consider the future."
They discussed the Thomas case at length, and Sevastyanov
remarked that it illustrated why there is hope, so long as you
can keep seeing a prospect, no matter how slight the chances
may seem initially. Ultimately, he authorized Levchenko to
recommend to the new Resident, Colonel Oleg Guryanov, the
formal recruitment of Thomas.

Guryanov had come from outside the Seventh Department,
having served as Resident in the Netherlands and in Havana,
where he helped supervise the Cuban intelligence service,
the DGI. He was a pleasant if tired-looking man, with thinning, sandy hair, clear blue eyes and a slight middle-aged
paunch. He suffered from hypertension, and sometimes
clasped his hand over his chest in pain.

Levchenko liked him from the first day when he gathered
everyone who happened to be in the Residency into his office.
Without any specific reference to the recent tumult in the
Residency, he declared that he would not tolerate "treachery"
by one officer against another. "You will work together in
Tokyo or you will go home," he warned. "I hope I can come to
know each of you and that we all will be friends. But what we
think of each other personally doesn't matter. You will be
judged, and judged fairly, solely on your performance. I don't
want anyone agreeing with me just to be agreeing. If you
disagree, if you think you have a better idea, tell me. I expect
to be in my office from 9 o'clock in the morning until 8 or 9
o'clock in the evening. Otherwise I will be playing tennis,
which I have to do for my health, or I will be in my apartment.
So I'm always available if you have major problems. I expect
you to solve routine problems by yourself; or if you can't
handle them, take them up with your group chief or the chief
of Line PR."

About two weeks after Levchenko recommended formal
inclusion of Thomas in the Residency network, Guryanov

summoned him. "I have bad news," he announced. "Read this calmly and curb your temper."

The Center's 36-page reply which Guryanov handed him was, within the memory of all in the Residency who read it, unprecedented in length, mendacity and personal vitriol. "The bona fides of Thomas have been inadequately established. . . . Reports from Thomas have been contradictory and false. . . . Koltsov has wasted too much time and money wining and dining Thomas and himself. . . . Thomas is not a progressive; his views are conservative. . . . Thomas cannot be trusted. Recruitment denied."

The chief of Line KR, upon reading the dispatch, exclaimed, "Never in my life have I seen so much shit packed into one document."

"Precisely," said Guryanov. "But we will fight back. Our time will come."

It came when Major General Popov, vice chief of the First Chief Directorate, visited Tokyo. A tall, gentlemanly figure, he had met Levchenko a couple of times at the Center, and now sought him out at the Residency. Levchenko showed him the Center's reply, together with an evaluation Guryanov obtained from Service I, which stated that roughly half of the intelligence Thomas supplied had been forwarded directly to the Politburo.

Popov turned ashen. "Now I remember," he said. "Pronnikov shoved this dispatch on my desk late at night. I was so exhausted I initialed it without reading it. Never would I have approved something so wrong and vulgar had I read it. Trust me to make amends."

Less than 48 hours after Popov returned to Moscow, the Center cabled: "The leadership of our service approves the recruitment of Thomas and his inclusion in the Residency network as a Trusted Contact. We congratulate Comrade Koltsov."

Early in the afternoon of September 6, 1976, Senior Lieutenant Viktor Belenko landed an advanced MiG–25 interceptor at a civilian airfield on the Japanese island of Hokkaido, causing consternation in Moscow and pandemonium in the

Residency. The Center flashed a message commanding the Residency to ascertain why the pilot fled, what he had revealed and what the Japanese intended to do with the ultrasecret aircraft. The message ended: "Urgent questions will be clarified if you can obtain information about two Top Secret electronic devices in the aircraft. One is system of IFF [Identification Friend or Foe]. The other is system of electronic countermeasures. Both devices have demolition buttons. Determine whether pilot destroyed these devices."

The Residency cabled the next day: "Top Secret devices remain intact and already are being examined by American specialists."

Referring to this American exploitation of Soviet secrets, Sevastyanov remarked, "They are shitting on us from a high tree."

A special courier flew from Moscow with a letter concocted by the KGB, in the name of pilot Belenko's wife, and photographs of her and their three-year-old son. The fabrication was a tearful plea from a loving wife beseeching Belenko to come home and rescue his devoted family from inconsolable grief. "I don't care how you do it," Sevastyanov told Levchenko, "but surface this letter in 24 hours in the Western press."

At press functions Levchenko had chatted a few times with a young American working as a stringer for the Tokyo bureau of the Associated Press and laboring hungrily to win a position on the regular staff. Early in the evening he telephoned him: "I have a rather sensational story for you."

In a coffee shop near his apartment, Levchenko outlined the letter and displayed the photographs.

"Where did you get the letter?" the American asked.

"We are both journalists. I don't inquire about your sources."

The stringer wrote in his notebook as Levchenko translated the letter from Russian into English. "This is just a bunch of bullshit," he said when Levchenko finished.

"I will not disagree with you," Levchenko replied. "But it's sensational bullshit, and so far as I know, nobody else has this shit. You can have it and the AP will look very good."

The next day, newspapers in Japan and the United States published the Associated Press dispatch from Tokyo, with excerpts from the forged letter.* It quoted Belenko's anguished young wife: "Lapushka darling, I know what happened to you. I am crying all the time, and our son, seeing me cry, cries also. And then he asked me, When will Daddy return from his flying exercises? . . . I cannot believe you will not find enough strength to return home and join us. I cannot believe you will let people consider us the wife and son of a traitor. I beg you, please make every effort to join us. . . . Don't believe any of their words or promises. They will need you only until you tell them what you know. I believe that our authorities will forgive you even in case you made some mistakes. Hugging and kissing you, your son Dyma and Lyuda."

Doubtless, numerous readers sympathized with the plight and pleas of the apparently sorrowful woman so callously abandoned. None could know that Belenko's wife, who hated military life, had declared her irrevocable decision to divorce him and take their child to her parents, thousands of miles away from his base in the Soviet Far East.

By disseminating the fabrication, the KGB hoped to amplify pressures the Russians were exerting upon Japan to turn Belenko back to them. But, after Belenko contemptuously rebuffed the Residency Security officer during a personal confrontation in Tokyo, the Japanese allowed him to proceed to the United States, as he had asked. Now, the Politburo mobilized all resources of the KGB and Soviet Foreign Ministry to keep the MiG–25 out of American custody. A cable labeled URGENT ordered the Residency:

"Implement at once broad and militant Active Measures to show: 1. The Japanese cannot play tricks with a Superpower. The whole relationship between Japan and U.S.S.R. may be revised as a result of this incident, and Japan will be the loser;

*The dispatch did point out that the letter "purportedly" came from Belenko's wife. It also said the letter was shown by "a Soviet source."

2. The United States is using Japan as a prostitute. The Americans are behaving on the territory of Japan as if in their own house. They do not care about Japanese national interests and are bringing disaster down on Japan; 3. Americans are violating all international rules concerning forced landing of aircraft on foreign soil.

"In all Active Measures, emphasis should be placed upon making it appear that these are the attitudes of the Japanese people themselves."

Officers from the Residency fanned out over Tokyo, instructing Agents of Influence and others with access to the press or parliament to plant stories and propagate themes sounded by Moscow. The ranking Agent of Influence, Hirohide Ishida, personally lobbied the prime minister and cabinet ministers as well as fellow parliamentarians, urging that Japan immediately return the MiG-25 without examining it.*

The sophisticated Active Measures of the KGB, however, were partially nullified by the crudities of Ambassador Polyansky, who stalked the halls of the Foreign Ministry bellowing threats in language the Japanese characterized as "unprecedented in diplomacy." Soviet spokesmen in Moscow accused the Japanese of drugging Belenko, of employing physical force and holding him against his will. Angrily and honestly, Japanese authorities denied the charge, and the Soviet bellicosity provoked rising anti-Soviet sentiment among the public, which, in turn, hardened the attitude of the government. Thus provoked, the Japanese permitted Americans to join them in taking the MiG-25 apart and examining it

---

*In return for such interventions in their behalf, the Soviets continued to reward and aggrandize Ishida in various ways. *Asahi Shimbun,* in a dispatch from Moscow dated June 14, 1977, reported:

"The Soviet Union today decided to release all 23 Japanese fishermen now detained in this country for alleged violation of Soviet territorial waters.

"In announcing the decision, Soviet authorities said the release is a special gesture of friendship in response to a request made yesterday by Japanese Labor Minister Hirohide Ishida now visiting this country.

"Ishida made the request in a meeting with Premier Kosygin . . ."

piece by piece.

But the Active Measures still gave the Japanese sufficient pause to refuse the United States opportunity to fly and test the plane in the air. And the KGB succeeded in damping down hostile publicity and apprehensions caused by the ease with which the MiG–25 flew into Japan without being intercepted. Worried that the incident might stimulate Japanese rearmament, the Center instructed: "Use every possible asset to show the Japanese they are mad. By making a great scandal about the MiG–25 they reveal their weakness. If they are afraid of a defensive weapon, they will lose face as a major nation of the Free World."

Several weeks later, the Center decreed that Levchenko must assume control of a case suffused with danger, that of Ares, who in the past had supplied documents from the files of Japanese counterintelligence. Any Soviet caught with such papers could expect, at the minimum, brutal detention followed by expulsion and public exposure likely to confine him to the Soviet Union for the rest of his crippled career. If the captured Soviet did not enjoy diplomatic immunity, and Levchenko did not, he faced imprisonment. Perhaps, in time, the KGB would ransom him; but it never would trust him again, simply because he had been in a foreign jail.

Pronnikov had recruited Ares more than a decade before, when Ares was a rising young executive with the Kyodo news service. Through a friend in intelligence, Ares obtained a flow of counterintelligence secrets so valuable that the KGB came to refer to him as "the golden fountain." The Japanese eventually suspected a leak, and stanched it by transferring some 30 counterintelligence personnel, among them Ares' source. Line KR, which had taken charge of Ares, because of its responsibility for penetration of foreign intelligence services, mishandled and spoiled him. As a result, for the past three years he had provided little of use, though the KGB continued to pay him about $1300 a month.

Endeavoring to restore Ares to his former productivity, Levchenko tried to build personal rapport and friendship, as he had done with other Japanese. But during their first four or five meetings, Ares behaved with inscrutable indifference. Ares was unimpressed by Levchenko's command of Japanese; after all, Pronnikov spoke the language even better. Political or ideological discussions bored him. Although Pronnikov claimed Ares had been recruited on ideological grounds, Levchenko saw him as a hardened, mercenary spy, bereft of any beliefs.

A slender, well-tailored bachelor with an uncommonly handsome face, Ares had frankly told other officers that women were his favorite avocation, and that he maintained liaisons with three or four simultaneously. Only educated women from cultured backgrounds interested him, and he picked them up mostly from the Foreign Office or Ministry of Justice. So, in quest of a common interest, Levchenko talked about women. "These lovely ladies, do they ever tell you anything interesting?"

"While you can lay them very easily, they will give you no secrets. But frankly, I am uncomfortable talking about my private affairs."

In an appeal to his ego, Levchenko told Ares how famous his past exploits had made him in Moscow and expressed hope that he would repeat them in the future. Ares shrugged, "One always tries."

Late at night, in a car parked on a remote side street, Levchenko announced, "I have brought something special for you."

"What?"

"A letter."

"Oh," Ares muttered in disappointment, probably having had a fleeting vision of money.

Giving him the letter and a flashlight, Levchenko asked Ares to read the "letter," a glowing commendation he personally had typed on expensive stationery and signed "Yu. V. Andropov, Chairman, Committee of State Security."

"I'm getting out of here. This is the most compromising document I've ever seen!" Ares exclaimed, and he almost bolted before Levchenko saved the situation with a spontaneous lie.

"Of course, that is why this whole area is ringed with our countersurveillance squads; why I have orders to burn the letter as soon as you read it. We just wanted you to know how much we think of you."

Somewhat calmed, Ares said, "Well, please give Mr. Andropov my regards, but ask him to cease his personal correspondence with me."

Acting on the Center's instructions, Levchenko told Ares that he would be away for two months, and asked him during the interim to prepare a definitive report on the final Japanese government reaction to the MiG–25 affair.

"Did you find out anything interesting about the MiG case?" he asked when they met some 60 days later.

"No, it seems that what the press says is generally correct."

Again on orders from the Center, Levchenko handed Ares an envelope containing his salary for the current month, purposely omitting his salary for the preceding two months.

When they next met on a street corner, thunderous rain beat down upon them, howling winds threatened to whip umbrellas from their hands, and Ares' breath warned that he had been drinking heavily. Levchenko issued a few assignments and said, "I can't keep you out in this storm; see you in two weeks."

"No," Ares shouted above the gale. "There will not be another meeting. This is our last. You have not treated me fairly. When you were absent, I was working very hard, and now I don't get any money for all my work while you were away."

Assuming the role of understanding idiot, Levchenko yelled, "Now I am beginning to realize. You need that money—and probably deserve it. But I'm afraid you have excited yourself over nothing. We have a huge incoming mail from Moscow, and some clerk probably just forgot to put your money in the pouch. I can understand your feelings. We both are under stress and standing in the middle of a typhoon. Let me go back to the embassy and check. I'll see you tomorrow."

Levchenko awakened Guryanov, and they composed a cable stating the Residency was in danger of losing Ares. By morning Tokyo time, the Center answered: "We approve payment of past salary to agent Ares. We appreciate efforts of Comrade Koltsov to revive case and establish psychological control of Ares. At the same time, we inform you that in the past Ares has displayed sensitivity to money and tried to coerce case officers by threats to discontinue cooperation. We trust that Comrade Koltsov, being an experienced officer, will find appropriate solution."

The next night Levchenko told Ares: "You know, you were right. Sure, it was a mistake. I received a routine answer saying they're sorry and will not make such a technical mistake again. So here's your money. Now, you came here safely, you checked your route. . . ."

"Yes, yes."

"I am concerned about your security; it is of the utmost concern to my whole organization. Therefore, you must not try to deal with your tensions by drinking as you did night before last. To clear your path, you must be clearheaded. I insist that you never again take alcohol before our meetings; afterwards, that's okay; before, never."

Ares agreed, and in agreeing unconsciously accepted the role of a subordinate. And Levchenko sighted the first glimmer of a breakthrough.

"Now, I don't want to embarrass you or to pry. It's your business what you've been doing in the past two months. But I hope that, having received full cooperation from my side, you will pay me back."

In about three months Ares did begin to pay Levchenko back, by handing him films of some 30 documents. Translating them one by one, Levchenko discovered nothing particularly interesting in the first dozen or so, nor could he divine any indication of their source. Then he came across an innocuous, unlabeled document whose import stunned him. It recorded the daily movements for the past week of a promising KGB contact in Tokyo, which meant the contact was under heavy surveillance. Immediately, the KGB alerted the contact to cease all incriminating activity and concentrate upon demonstrating to the Japanese that he was clean. This one document saved the Residency network from possible penetration by the Japanese, and it could only have come from inside Japanese intelligence.

Among documents Ares presented two weeks later, Levchenko uncovered another jewel, a statistical report of the nationalities, numbers and locations of foreigners residing in Japan. As the Center indicated in a commendatory dispatch, this document was an enormous aid to Directorate S in determining where future Illegals could best meld into Japanese society.

Another document, received a month later, listed officers of the Residency whom the Japanese had positively identified as members of the KGB and GRU, and Levchenko happily noted that he was not among them. More significantly, he saw another unmistakable indication that Ares had developed a source inside Japanese intelligence.

With that recognition, Levchenko made the meetings with Ares as furtive as they could be. By telephone he signaled in conversational code the time and place of the next rendezvous.

"Have you brought something for me?" Levchenko, seeing Ares, asked.

"Yes. Here."

"All right, keep moving. I will be right back."

As he hurried with the documents toward the car from which Major Zhavoronkov, the operational driver, kept vigil, Levchenko felt his heart pounding. At the car he placed the film in a special cloth-covered plastic box, locked it and turned a dial 180 degrees. Once the dial was so turned, the film instantly would be incinerated if anyone attempted to open the box without resetting the dial to the safety position, which only Levchenko and the Technical Operations officer knew. Rejoining Ares, Levchenko at once gave him an envelope with money; they spoke quickly, for less than two minutes, and parted as if from a chance encounter. Levchenko then dropped Zhavoronkov off near the official embassy car, and the operational driver delivered the box to the Residency while Levchenko headed home.

Throughout, Levchenko carried a small radio receiver in his pocket, the aerial stretched down his trouser leg. An officer on duty in the Residency's Zenith room listened for any unusual traffic on the counterintelligence circuits, which would cause him to transmit a warning to Levchenko.

By these means, during the next several months, Ares slipped to the KGB films of thousands of pages of documents. Constantly studying the flow, in an effort to isolate the source, Levchenko judged that 30 percent, then 50 percent, and ultimately about 70 percent emanated from the same person inside Japanese intelligence. When certain monthly bulletins, whose circulation was quite restricted, began to turn up in the flow, he knew that the source was highly placed. Delving further, he asked Ares if he could possibly procure a copy of the dossier the Japanese maintained on him.

Ares said he could not obtain the file of a particular Russian without offering a persuasive reason as to why he needed it. So Levchenko decided to write a *New Times* article that would enable Ares to portray him as an anti-Japanese zealot who merited journalistic investigation. He chose the subject of the *eta* or *burakumin*, people who according to ancient tenets of Buddhism are considered "unclean" because they butcher cattle or process meat.

With the help of Takumi Ueda, a member of parliament who was an officer of the *Burakumin* Liberation League, Levchenko visited areas inhabited by the *eta* (*eta* means "outcast"), and *New Times* published his article ridiculing the Japanese for allegedly discriminating against the *eta*. Not long afterward, Ares, with a trace of a smile, handed him a roll of film, saying, "This may be of interest." It was an extract from the Japanese dossier on Levchenko.

The Japanese characterized him as a "possible" KGB officer. But the suspicions seemed to derive primarily from their identification of his *New Times* predecessor as a member of

the KGB. The dossier listed many of his Japanese contacts—
not, however, King or Thomas. It also recorded his travels
outside Tokyo and the results of surveillances. He was
amused to note that the records showed he had traveled to
southern Japan a few months before. He had booked a flight
through the National Press Club but missed the plane because
of traffic. Probably someone in the club was collaborating
with counterintelligence.

The Ares case now assumed both new magnitude and peril,
in the judgment of Levchenko, Guryanov and the Center. If
Ares' source could be formally recruited and molded into a
controlled agent, his value in future years would be incalcula-
ble. It seemed reasonable to assume that the source was, like
Ares, about 40, and likely to ascend still higher in the Japanese service. He would be able to supply more information
and do more for the KGB with each advancement. Yet Ares
was dealing with a senior professional, schooled to recognize
and react to even subliminal cues of espionage. Maybe he had
already recognized and reacted; maybe the Japanese had
started a game, conveying incontestably worthwhile and authentic documents to establish the credibility of a source who
in some future world crisis could give the KGB a disastrously
deceptive document. And in dealing on his own with an
uncontrolled intelligence officer, about whom the KGB knew
nothing, Ares himself was in daily jeopardy. Thus, it was
imperative to ascertain who the source was, to ferret out every
detail of his life. But Ares belligerently refused to reveal the
names of his sources.

Requesting and receiving microfilms of the case file from
the Center, Levchenko analyzed the record, concentrating
upon the early years with which he was least familiar. Late
one night, when he was about to forsake the file for bed, he
read an intriguing notation. About a decade before, Ares had
mentioned among his contacts an unnamed intelligence officer with whom he had become friendly when they both were
beginning their careers. The officer subsequently attended an
advanced intelligence academy and, after graduation, worked

as an undercover agent against terrorists and radicals in Tokyo. Having done well, he was transferred to a semi-overt intelligence post in the provinces, an assignment consistent with regular career rotation and progression. The notation indicated that if he progressed, he eventually should return to Tokyo. Maybe that was the source; maybe he had been reassigned to intelligence headquarters, and that was why the "golden fountain" suddenly began flowing again.

During their next two-minute exchange, Levchenko instructed Ares to leave Tokyo before 6:30 a.m. on Sunday and meet him at 1 p.m. in a private room at a picturesque restaurant near the famous resort of Hakone. Levchenko covered his journey by stopping in towns frequented by tourists and conspicuously taking pictures. If challenged, he would say he was preparing a *New Times* travel article. Ares was waiting, enjoying a whisky, which he drank only when the KGB paid.

"Are you clean?" Levchenko asked.

"I saw nothing."

"Neither did I, so let's enjoy ourselves." Ceremoniously, Levchenko announced that in recognition of his splendid services, Moscow had awarded Ares a bonus that would enable him to buy a new car. The documents Ares provided reflected his worth as a daring, brilliant man. However, Levchenko had been analyzing them and had concluded that they were emanating from a single source; and he recalled that, years before, Ares had a young friend beginning a career in intelligence. If the source of the documents was that friend, then the operation had entered a new and dangerous phase, because working against an intelligence officer was inherently dangerous. If Ares could bring himself to reveal the source, then he could enhance his own security by availing himself of the vast expertise of the Residency and the Center. Levchenko was not demanding. It was Ares' choice. But Levchenko did not want him to take all the risks alone.

"I am glad Moscow remembers me, and I thank you for the present. You are right; the documents in the last months came from one source, my old friend. He came back this year. I have not told you his name because I have not been sure he will give me documents indefinitely."

"What is his position?"

"Section chief."

"The fact that he gives you such sensitive documents suggests that you are still close friends."

"We really are."

"Do you see each other socially?"

"Yes, we often meet girls, take them to dinner and then to some romance hotel. My friend is mad about girls, craves them. But he is married and does not have much time to hunt. So I share my harem with him."

"Would you care to share the name of this Casanova with me?"

"I understand what you are doing. I know that you will rush back to the embassy and write a cable saying you tricked the stupid Ares into naming his source. But I trust you, so I will tell you. Please, though, do not use his true name. Give him a code name."

"All right, let's call him Schweik."

"What does that mean?"

"Nothing. It's just the name of a character in a great Czechoslovakian novel [The Good Soldier Schweik], the first name I thought of. Incidentally, what does your friend think you do with these documents?"

"Use them in my work."

"Doesn't he wonder why he never sees anything in print?"

"Oh, no. I have pledged never to cite them. He understands that they add much to my general knowledge."

"Well, I would like to help you deepen your friendship with Mr. Schweik. Suppose we give you extra money to develop him. You could use it to entertain him, or you could pay him. Tell him your organization has a special fund for obtaining information needed to fight the Communists."

"No doubt that would help get more interesting documents."

"Sure it would. Let's discuss the details next Sunday."

Levchenko, for the moment, had led Ares as far as he dared.

He did not want to anger him by pressing for more details about Schweik, nor frighten him by fully apprising him of the hazards inherent in the operation. The more circuitous route would be the quickest.

The Center replied promptly, almost gleefully, to the cable Levchenko and Guryanov sent that Sunday night: "Comrade Koltsov has managed to revive Ares, and made a major breakthrough in the work with him. Revelation of name and position of source is grounds for hope that Residency can recruit officer of Japanese intelligence under False Flag. However, Residency must be very careful. Check and recheck both Ares and Schweik, never forgetting that this could be a game."

Guryanov authorized an additional monthly payment to Ares for Schweik of 60,000 yen, the maximum amount he deemed plausible. "Now we must put some flesh on this phantom whom we are paying," he said.

Delicately questioning Ares, Levchenko gradually etched in a fairly clear portrait of the phantom. He was a professionally well-regarded lieutenant colonel, about 40; he loved his work, and his career prospects appeared bright. Although a loyal Japanese, and thus anti-communist, he seemed otherwise to be completely apolitical, favoring neither the Liberal Democratic nor Socialist Party. He and his wife, a seamstress, maintained a sort of marriage of convenience, and she did not particularly care that he was "jumping from bed to bed." With a low-interest ten-year loan from a government credit union, he had purchased a small apartment, and the monthly payments consumed most of his discretionary income. He needed both extra money and the good offices of Ares to gratify his passion for women. There was no indication that in passing the documents he had acted out of any motivation other than a desire to help Ares, his best friend. In fact, knowledge that he was helping the Russians would have mortified him.

Once Levchenko defined Schweik's position and the nature of data to which he had legitimate access, he urgently asked Ares for specific documents that Schweik could not legitimately obtain. "He just cannot get them," Ares later reported.

"They are from other offices in which he has no business."
That was encouraging, for provision of the specified documents would have meant that the Japanese deliberately were
giving them to the KGB.

At each meeting, Levchenko also evaluated the words and
demeanor of Ares, looking intently for any changes, listening
for any questions suggesting that Ares might have fallen under
Japanese control.

Month after month, Schweik and Ares continued to open
intelligence files to the KGB. If the KGB wished to investigate
some Japanese, it first checked the secret Japanese records. If
the Residency was worried about the security of a given
operation, it confirmed or assuaged its fears by consulting
Japanese intelligence. One document contained the minutes
of a Top Secret conference of intelligence chiefs discussing
the whole sweep of operations against the Soviet Bloc. From
this rich document alone, the Residency submitted ten separate reports.

After slinking around the back alleys of Tokyo for so long
with Ares, Levchenko concluded that it probably would be
prudent for them to meet sometimes in more natural circumstances, at restaurants late in the evening or on Sundays. He
composed a legend by which Ares could explain dining with
him: "He [Levchenko] is a Soviet journalist and a secret
dissident. Like most Soviet journalists, he is rather close-
mouthed and doesn't reveal any great state secrets. Still, he
discloses a lot about general conditions in the Soviet Union.
As a journalist, I have sort of recruited him for my organization. He is cautious and very afraid that other Soviets may see
him with me, and that is why we usually meet late in the
evening and in out-of-the-way places. He is scared. I don't pay
him money, but he is something of a gourmet and enjoys good
food—if I pay."

Schweik, habituated to removing documents from his office,
obedient to the requests of his friend Ares and accustomed to
a supplemental income, was now, in effect, under KGB control without realizing it. The Center repeatedly commended

the conduct of the operation and placed high valuations on the intelligence it yielded. For all practical purposes, a classic False Flag recruitment had been accomplished, and Guryanov recommended that the Center formally ratify the recruitment.

"If you keep going like this, you will outrank me," he remarked to Levchenko.

However, on a Monday morning, Guryanov opened a 20-page dispatch signed by Orlov, the work name of Anatoli Babkin, then chief of the Seventh Department. "Read it," he said to Levchenko. It said:

"The Center again commends Comrade Koltsov for developing an extremely important contact in Japanese intelligence under a False Flag. At the same time, to be sure that we have a complete picture of the contact and to avoid even the slightest possibility of being victimized by an operational game of Japanese CI,* Residency must make every effort to verify the sincerity of Schweik. Ares also must be checked. We ask the Residency to submit a detailed plan for checking both. Additionally, we want the Residency to consider the following proposals of the Center:

"Ask Ares to photograph Schweik; photograph Schweik's apartment building; make countersurveillance of Schweik near his home and office to determine regular working hours; observe visually a meeting between Schweik and Ares, and afterwards follow Schweik to see where he goes; install a listening device in the office where Schweik works; ask Ares to draw a diagram of Schweik's office; ascertain through Ares names of all superiors and friends of Schweik; draft a plan to check Ares and Schweik by giving Ares a disguised tape recorder with concealed radio transmitter."

When Levchenko laid the dispatch down, Guryanov said, "Stanislav, I know you are a cultured man, so I ask you to excuse my language, but you better go right now and wash your hands, because they have just held a great piece of shit."

*Counterintelligence.

The chief of Line KR, Yuri Dvoryanchikov, laughed often as he read the dispatch. "I would say it was written by an imbecile if I did not know better," he told Guryanov and Levchenko. "Half of these proposals violate the most elementary security rules. Whoever is the author wants to destroy the entire operation or burn somebody in the Residency. Can you imagine Russians trying to follow professional Japanese surveillants around Tokyo? Can you imagine Russians hanging around the headquarters of Japanese intelligence? And bug their headquarters? Preposterous! They know that. They want to sabotage the operation."

"It's Pronnikov," Levchenko said.

"Of course," Guryanov said. "His indecency has no bounds. Still, if we want approval, we will have to check Schweik further. We will do it professionally."

"May I draft the reply?" Levchenko asked, and Guryanov nodded. He wrote: "Every competent officer with previous experience in Japan will recognize that proposals regarding Schweik and Ares made in the name of Center are suicidal. Residency cannot risk ruin of one of its most important cases through such irresponsible and amateurish actions. Investigations will be made professionally."

Guryanov and Levchenko argued about this message, but the Resident acquiesced. "We're all going to hell anyway. Send it." That was a mistake, and both knew it.

Several weeks after Levchenko sent the message, the operational driver, Major Zhavoronkov, hailed him in the compound. "I need your help," he said.

Shared danger had forged an unstated bond of trust between Levchenko and Zhavoronkov. The major had grown up professionally with the Surveillance Directorate in Moscow, hazarding his life in high-speed chases in pursuit of dissidents, suspects and spies. In Tokyo his duty was to protect officers and their agents by sacrificing himself if necessary. If he spotted surveillants during an agent meeting, he was to decoy them away. If police halted him and an officer, he was to have custody of any film or documents, and thus expose himself to

arrest. The week before, Zhavoronkov and Levchenko had
stopped for a drink at a bar near the embassy, after meeting an
agent, and they saw an appalling sight—a Soviet cipher clerk
sitting alone, incoherently drunk. Cipher clerks knew more
than anyone except the Resident himself, and fear that one
might fall prey to a foreign intelligence service was so intense
that they were never allowed outside the embassy compound
without an escort. On this evening, as they later learned, the
escort, a foreign service officer, had drunkenly wandered
away. The offense was inexcusable, and were it discovered,
the cipher clerk would suffer ruin along with the irresponsible
diplomat.

Without a word to each other, Levchenko and Zhavoronkov
acted spontaneously. They picked up the cipher clerk, carried
him to the car, laid him on the floor in the back, drove into the
compound and smuggled him to bed. They did so in full
knowledge that they both would be fired if caught.

"What can I do?" Levchenko asked, willing to do anything
for Zhavoronkov.

"The Resident wants me to write a report about an officer
who is a very good officer, but some bastard in the Center
wants to eat him," the operational driver answered. "I am not
very good with words, and I thought you, being a journalist,
could put my thoughts together on paper for me."

"What do you want to say about this fellow?"

"First of all, I want to write that for many years he's been
working day and night. Second, that he has no private life
because of his field work; his own life is secondary. Third,
that I was involved with him in many high-risk operations,
and he behaved as a cool officer with a realistic assessment of
circumstances in meeting important agents. Fourth, this officer will forget everything else, even in high-risk situations, if
he needs to help one of his friends. Fifth, I personally brought
him to many meetings, and he never was under the influence
of alcohol. Sixth, being an honest and capable officer, he
enjoys the love of his colleagues in the Residency."

Levchenko hastily typed the letter in the Residency and

gave it to Zhavoronkov. "You made a good report, and it will
help that officer," the driver said.

Levchenko thought no more about the favor Zhavoronkov
asked, not even that afternoon when Guryanov spoke gravely
to him. "The Center needs more details of your meeting three
months ago with Ares in the Meguro district."

"Why?"

"There is some misunderstanding at the Center, and they
want to clarify it. Will you be so kind as to write down every
detail of the meeting and your activities preceding it, insofar
as you can remember."

"It was three months ago. I can't remember every detail."

"Please. Please try to remember every detail, every little
detail. It is very important."

"All right, I will give it to you next week."

"No, by tonight."

"I have a meeting tonight."

"With Ares?"

"No, Kamenev [a developing contact]."

"Cancel it and write."

Levchenko remembered more about the meeting in question than he ordinarily might, because it occurred on a Soviet
holiday. Normally, the KGB prohibits contact with agents on
national holidays, because it does not want to risk arrests or
other trouble that would necessitate disturbing relaxing Politburo members. Because all meetings with Ares were by then
considered dangerous, Levchenko had to ask some other officer to interrupt his holiday and come along as driver/lookout.
While drinking beer and watching a volleyball game in the
embassy courtyard, he spotted Aleksandr Shishayev. Here
was one officer who would be glad to accompany him, holiday
or no. Shishayev, who got into the KGB solely because his
father gave flowers to the First Chief Directorate for funerals
and weddings, was so inept that the Residency did not trust
him to handle agents, and he never could recruit one on his
own. So he was always obsequiously willing to perform any
little service that might justify his existence. When Lev-

chenko asked him, he eagerly assented, and in the early evening they set out together. The encounter with Ares, near a small café, lasted only a couple of minutes, and Levchenko recalled nothing unusual about the evening.

Having filed this account, Levchenko forgot about it, until Guryanov frankly raised the subject some three weeks later. "I must tell you that you have been under investigation," he said. "The Center received a report that you were meeting Ares in states of high alcoholic intoxication."

Instantly, Levchenko understood. The "report" could only have come from Shishayev, who obviously was Pronnikov's informant. He felt sick.

Guryanov continued, "The whole matter now has been put right. . ." He paused to answer the phone, then asked Levchenko to excuse him for a few minutes. Whether intentionally or inadvertently Levchenko would never know, but as he rose to go, Guryanov stared at some papers spread on his desk.

Left alone in the Resident's office, Levchenko was able to see that the papers were letters from Residency officers attesting to his skill, devotion and honesty. There was one from Sevastyanov, one from the Resident himself; the last one was from Major Zhavoronkov, the exact letter Levchenko had written for him. He recognized that all three men, including Guryanov, the one true believer in communism he knew, had united in simple decency to save him. He also realized that had they not done so, had each not been willing to incur the vengeful enmity of Pronnikov, then Pronnikov and the system would have destroyed him.

Upon returning to the room, Guryanov had to speak twice to rouse Levchenko from his thoughts. "Stanislav Aleksandrovich, I said, let's get on with Schweik. That will be our best retaliation."

So Levchenko drafted a plan to provide the Center with a photograph of Schweik.

Informed by Ares that he would next be meeting with Schweik in the bar in the basement of the Suntory Building Thursday afternoon, Levchenko replied that he would be there, watching.

"Why? Don't you trust me?" Ares asked.

"Sure, we all trust you. It is great that your friend is a senior intelligence officer and that you virtually have recruited him. But he is an intelligence officer, and when you are up against a professional, it is best that several people analyze every phase of the operation. Remember, for us the most important consideration is your safety."

As planned, Levchenko and his wife waited in the bar, where for the first time he saw Schweik, who was rather disheveled, and poorly dressed. His eyes searching the patrons, Schweik gave Ares a package and took an envelope in return. Friends though they may have been, they were at this moment conspirators eager to be done with their business, and after one quick drink they left the bar. Ares led Schweik close by and Levchenko leaned down, pressed a button, and a camera hidden in his briefcase snapped a picture.

Guryanov cabled the Center: "Analysis of prolonged relationship between Ares and Schweik and of the psychological and personal profile of Schweik developed through questions by Comrade Koltsov demonstrates that each agent is sincere. Additionally, Comrade Koltsov and wife personally witnessed a meeting of the two which in every respect confirms analysis. During the last two years, Residency has obtained through Schweik and Ares more than 3000 pages of documents of varying value, but of enough importance to prove that no game is being played. Japanese intelligence could not possibly gain as much as it has lost through these documents. It would never willingly surrender the one secret document about a conference of Japanese intelligence leaders which disclosed main methods of Japanese counterintelligence. As is known to Center, Residency sent ten cables on the basis of this one document, and some were forwarded directly to Chairman Andropov. Therefore, the Residency considers Schweik ripe for formal inclusion in the Residency network and recommends his inclusion."

Guryanov waited several days to advise Levchenko of the

Center's response. Whether he tried to persuade the Center to reverse itself or delayed to consider the best way of informing Levchenko is unclear. Regardless, the decision of the Center stood: Because of the extraordinary importance of the case, the advisability of just a few more checks and the desirability of long-range continuity, the Ares-Schweik case must be transferred to Line KR.

The order originated, of course, with Pronnikov. When the Center approved inclusion of Schweik in the network, as it surely would before the end of the year, the Line KR officer handling Ares would be credited with recruitment of Schweik. Levchenko would be denied any credit and the probable promotion that went with it.

"If they think Line KR is best qualified, why did they assign the case to me in the first place?" Levchenko asked.

"There is a saying," Guryanov replied, " 'It is better to be stolen from than to have to steal.' Nothing can steal from me and your comrades our knowledge of your worth and accomplishments."

Levchenko made no reply.

"Stanislav, I know you are suffering. But please don't hate the system; it's not the system. It is just that sometimes there are bad people in any system. When we realize true communism, there will be none."

"Of course, you are right," Levchenko said. "Thank you for your decency."

IV

A
SECRET
DECISION

H AD LEVCHENKO believed that he was denied just credit and reward solely because of the malevolent machinations of Pronnikov, he probably would have been only briefly troubled. The KGB considers the tour of an officer most successful if he recruits just one substantial agent; Levchenko already had recruited three and been officially credited with the recruitment of two. Another promotion at the time mattered little to him, and circumstances had robbed him before.

In addition to his other cases, Levchenko had to assume responsibility for one of the Residency's most valued Agents of Influence, Takuji Yamane, whose code name was Kant. A narrow-faced, professorial-looking intellectual suborned by Pronnikov in the 1960s, Kant rose to be an assistant managing editor of the conservative national newspaper *Sankei*, and a personal adviser to its publisher. In May 1982, he became editor-in-chief. He masqueraded superbly as an ardent nationalist—anti-Soviet, anti-Chinese—while masking his Marxist beliefs and sympathies for the Soviet Union.

However, Japanese counterintelligence caught Kant meeting with *Komsomolskaya Pravda* correspondent Nikolai Lossinsky, informed him he was consorting with a KGB officer, and solicited his cooperation against the Soviets. Kant feigned dismay and indignation that the Russians would send a spy to interview him, expressed support for counterintelligence, but insisted that as an editor he could not involve himself in intelligence activities.

The KGB suspended contact for some six months, then renewed it through a Novosti correspondent, Major Boris Smirinov, who after the death of Zhou Enlai in 1976 approached Kant with an imperative assignment. Someone in the disinformation service recalled that a critical letter, written by Lenin just before his death, served to delay Stalin's consolidation of power for several years. To sow discord and confusion among Chinese leaders, the KGB forged "The Last Will of Zhou Enlai" and sent the fabrication to Tokyo, with orders to disseminate it through a respectable conservative publication such as *Sankei*. "As I am not friends with any close relatives of Zhou Enlai, how am I to explain possession of his will?" Kant asked.

The Novosti correspondent told him to say that mainland Chinese smuggled the will through Hong Kong to Japan. Contemplating practicalities, Kant rejected this legend. This will could be published in *Sankei* only if he wrote a story under his own name; from anyone else, the publisher would demand to know the source. And for self-protection, Kant insisted upon indicating in the headline by a question mark that he personally was not vouching for the authenticity of the "will." In Moscow, the Center agreed that would be good enough.

Prominently republished in the Soviet Union, Kant's story did cause consternation among Chinese leaders, who frantically tried to trace the origin and assess the authenticity of the will. Only after much confusion did they establish to their satisfaction that the story was sheer fabrication. But as nobody could immediately prove the will a fake, Kant was unscathed.

Nevertheless, in consequence of the warning from counter-intelligence, his complicity in disinformation and his publisher's antipathy to all things Soviet, Kant could not afford to be seen openly and often with Russians. He could justify only casual encounters with a "journalist," and these had to be brief and inconspicuous. So the Residency turned to Levchenko.

In the spring of 1978 Levchenko made of Kant a request the Center had ordered the Residency to put to every agent in Tokyo. The KGB craved all obtainable information about the positions the Japanese would adopt in forthcoming discussions in Washington between President Carter and Prime Minister Fukuda. The American President and Japanese Prime Minister bring to their annual deliberations a distillation of the best thought and intelligence their respective foreign policy establishments can provide. And the KGB realized that by tapping these candid talks, it could procure the highest, most refined intelligence.

Kant doubted he could help and said that, in any case, he could not see Levchenko again until May 9. That was a Soviet national holiday and Levchenko had to secure special dispensation from the Resident to keep the appointment in the café Din-Don near the *Sankei* offices. Kant stepped quickly into the nearly empty café and whispered that he could not stay because he was in the midst of a meeting of the newspaper brain trust. Laying a large manila envelope on the table, he said, "Here is some background material on the Fukuda talks. Don't publish it in your magazine."

Like most Agents of Influence, Kant almost never stole classified documents, and Levchenko guessed that the "background material" consisted of academic analysis or conjecture. Having spent six hours clearing his path to the café, he drove toward the embassy irritated at losing most of his holiday for nothing. At a stoplight, though, he opened the envelope and pulled out a document far enough to see the words TOP SECRET and the title: "Draft of Positions of PM Fukuda in Talks with Carter." Not expecting such a spectacularly incriminating document, he had neglected to bring along any device to incinerate papers in the event of an accident or questioning by police. Suddenly perspiring, he began driving as if the car were packed with volatile explosives, and proceeded so slowly that irked motorists goaded him with their horns.

Spring sunshine and a holiday atmosphere brightened the compound. Some people were drinking beer or vodka and laughing, while others played chess or volleyball with guests from other Soviet Bloc embassies. Melodramatically, Levchenko strode onto the tennis court in mid-point proudly bearing the document that in a few hours would tell the Kremlin what the Japanese were thinking and what they intended to do in the world, as well as which issues worried the Carter Administration. "This time I have something really exciting," he said to Guryanov. With a wave of the hand to the other players, the Resident excused himself and led Levchenko away.

"What is it?" he asked, and Levchenko showed him the Top Secret resume.

"Stanislav, I hate to tell you this," Guryanov said. "You and Kant are both good men, but two days ago we obtained this very same document from Davey [KGB code name of an editor of the Tokyo edition of *Sankei*]. It already is in Moscow. Please don't be upset; you did your job. Take the rest of the day off, relax and have a few drinks."

KGB Chairman Andropov personally awarded Davey's case officer an official commendation, and Davey got a bonus of 300,000 yen. At Levchenko's insistence, Guryanov authorized a payment of 150,000 yen to Kant, the maximum he could disburse on his own discretion. Levchenko neither asked for nor received anything for himself.

The rule by which the KGB disregarded the accomplishments of an officer and agent merely because someone else produced the same intelligence before them was, of course, unjust. To the extent that it encouraged imprudent operational haste, it was even harmful. But Levchenko understood that no organization of human beings is perfect, that any organization may include weak or malicious or dishonorable people, such as Pronnikov and his lackey Shishayev. And as a Christian, Levchenko could almost forgive Pronnikov and Shishayev personally. The trouble was that he had come to look upon both not as individual anomalies, but as natural products and typical personifications of a congenital, pervasive corruption he now felt to be the essence of the KGB. A host of unrelated incidents drove him to this destructive view.

After Brezhnev made a speech, Guryanov often instructed Levchenko to seek out Japanese journalists and prepare a "sophisticated" report of their reactions. "What if the reactions are negative?" Levchenko would ask with mock seriousness.

"Don't be a pain in the ass. Go do what is necessary."

Both knew that the speech delivered in Moscow a few hours before had not circulated in Tokyo and that even if it had, not one in a million Japanese would pay it the least heed. Fairly typically, a Japanese editor responded to Levchenko: "Oh, he's attacking us again, is he? What's the doddering old fart saying now?" No matter what the Japanese said, Levchenko, as required, wrote variations of the same refrain: A well-placed source close to the Foreign Ministry stated in confidence that the decisive and forceful position of Comrade Leonid Ilyich Brezhnev made the strongest impression in Tokyo. Source revealed that the vigor and logic of Comrade Leonid Ilyich's words prove to Japanese ruling circles that he still is very much in control of Soviet policy. The speech at this very moment is undergoing the closest study by Japanese leaders and, according to source, doubtless will affect their views. However, source indicated that the basic line of Japanese foreign policy is unlikely to change in the near term.

The last sentence signaled to analysts that all this was nonsense, yet the Center could rush the report unchanged to the Kremlin as evidence that Brezhnev indeed was a marvel, and that the KGB was on the job. Levchenko preferred to think that this form of lying was relatively innocuous, that regarding any matters of moment the KGB would communicate reality to the Kremlin. But in an institutional environment that demanded lying, more malign lies could flourish.

Colonel Koshkin, chief of the American Group, had just returned from home leave with a vicious example. The American Group long managed a Japanese agent in the Foreign Office, originally recruited in Moscow by the Second Chief Directorate. Upon retirement, the agent lost access to both secrets and Americans, and he and Koshkin amicably agreed it was pointless for him to continue endangering himself as an agent. Pronnikov, as part of his ongoing campaign to sabotage the Tokyo Residency, spread a report at the Center that the agent had been lost due to Koshkin's premature senility, caused by advanced arteriosclerosis. To buttress the report, he induced a Second Chief Directorate officer to write a memorandum venturing the opinion that the agent could still have been of use in retirement.

Informed that he suddenly was being retired, Koshkin found out about the memorandum and confronted its author. The Second Chief Directorate officer apologized, and gave him a statement that he had written the memorandum only at the behest of Pronnikov, who claimed it was needed for operational purposes, without explaining why. Koshkin then took the statement to the Party representative in the First Chief Directorate who interceded to prevent his forced retirement. Nothing, though, happened to Pronnikov for it was much easier to accept lies and corruption than to duel with a dangerous adversary now widely presumed to have patrons in the Politburo.

Even worse corruption went unpunished when retribution would embarrass or jeopardize the careers of the KGB hierarchy. Because the Singapore Residency had been unproductive, the KGB decided to reorganize and reorient it primarily against China. Led by a new Resident, China hands picked by him began meeting the listed agents of the Residency network, issuing orders and proffering the customary payments. The supposed agents reacted with amusement or incredulity or indignation, for they had never really worked for the KGB. They were merely acquaintances of the previous officers, people they met occasionally over a drink or lunch or at other social functions. The Singapore Residency had conjured up on paper an entire agent network and, for nearly two years, filed bogus reports imputed to these nonexistent spies. However, as senior officers at the Center had approved inclusion of the ghosts in the Residency network, and unquestioningly accepted the intelligence attributed to them, they could take no action against those guilty of the fraud without exposing to the Party their own malfeasance. Hence, the scandal was officially suppressed, though word of it eventually leaked widely through the Seventh Department.

Because of the importance of the Tokyo Residency, chiefs of the various First Chief Directorate divisions could easily concoct reasons to visit Japan. They came principally to vacation and shop; but to justify the journey, they stopped at the Residency to confer with the Resident and individual officers. With the permission of Guryanov, Levchenko briefed visiting Vice Admiral Usatov about a disturbing dereliction. Among the vast number of documents the Residency was extracting from Japanese intelligence through Ares and Schweik were magnificently detailed reports on various international terrorist groups and their *modi operandi*. Failing to receive any evaluations of this exceptional intelligence, the Residency learned that the Center, allegedly because of a shortage of translators, was shredding the documents pertaining to terrorism without even reading them. Levchenko quoted a public statement by former CIA Director William E. Colby, who said that while the KGB was peerless in collecting intelligence, it often could not effectively digest all it gathered. "This seems to show that Mr. Colby is right," he remarked.

"Yes, I'm afraid that asshole Colby is correct," replied Usatov. "In any case, this is against the line of our Party. I'll take care of it. We have all the money we want, and it will be easy to hire a couple more female translators."

But nothing happened, and the KGB continued to disregard and discard the Japanese revelations about terrorism.

In Levchenko's judgment, these and many other wrongs he saw originated in an absence of belief in right or wrong, a lack of belief in anything except personal survival or aggrandizement. The Resident and operational driver were exceptions; Guryanov still believed in the perfectability of communism, Zhavoronkov in fighting for his country no matter what. Levchenko had met others, decent men who tried to be as just and honest as the system allowed. But they were a minority. The faithless majority often could advance their own personal interests by advancing those of the KGB. So in large measure they served the KGB dutifully and expertly, often brilliantly and imaginatively. Thus, the great, ponderous machinery of the KGB ground on more or less as its masters desired, and in the process it ground up people. However inefficiently and inhumanely, on balance it worked.

Again Levchenko cried out to himself, *Why and for what?* The recurrent question recalled a speech that a representative of the Administrative Organs Department of the Central Committee made to the Tokyo embassy staff after consummation of the Helsinki Agreements. The naked cynicism of his declarations shocked even hardened cynics of the KGB. Such things, some said afterwards, never should be stated so starkly and crudely. Levchenko did not take notes, but the speech so burned into his memory that he could almost quote it verbatim: By inducing NATO nations, including the Main Enemy, to sign the Helsinki Agreements, the Soviet Union achieved one of the greatest triumphs since World War II. The Soviet strategy was so ingenious that Western leaders thought they had triumphed. The fools even were eager to sign. Poor fools! They did not understand that they were caught like stupid birds in our trap. They dream now of disintegrating our monolithic society by exploiting the principles of the Helsinki Agreements—free exchange of information, freedom of travel, of emigration, human rights and other bourgeois absurdities. Poor fools! It will take years for them to understand. We will sell their books, magazines and newspapers to foreigners in hotels reserved for foreigners, and we will burn the rest. Western countries think that now rotten dissident organizations will grow like mushrooms in our land. Ha, ha, ha! Let them hope. Our glorious Chekists know their business. In the next few years, we will rid ourselves of dissidents once and for all. We will put them all in prisons and labor camps and reform them by force into productive members of society. Meanwhile, we shall exploit the principles of the Helsinki Agreements to undermine capitalism from within. By all overt and covert means, we shall manipulate public opinion in Western countries as we like, and drown out criticism of our military buildup. We have the resources to create dozens of new organizations in the West and to reinforce existing front-line organizations. Our glorious intelligence services will seize all the new opportunities to operate on a much higher and wider scale, taking advantage of the friendlier attitude toward the U.S.S.R. We shall turn public opinion in the West, particularly in Western Europe, against the U.S.A. Everywhere we shall plant seeds of distrust against the Main Enemy. The Helsinki Agreements offer us historic opportunities to weaken our enemies, and we shall grasp all.

Levchenko asked himself, *Why am I working 15 hours a day, twisting lives, spreading lies? So we can better cheat on the Helsinki Agreements?*

His ever-darkening state of intellectual and moral disarray further frayed an already strained marriage. After the *stukach* Larisa, to excuse her own indiscretions, falsely accused Natalia of gossiping about classified matters, Levchenko subtly blackmailed the security officer. Unless Natalia received an embassy job, he would report to a Party inspector due soon from Moscow that the security officer was utilizing dangerous liars instead of "sincere, honest informants." Natalia thus was invited to work in the consular office, and in a few months became supervisor of the female staff. Her duties were exhausting because of the many Japanese travelers to the Soviet

Union,* and in the evening she wanted companionship and relaxation.

Instead, on the comparatively few evenings when Levchenko was home, she found him in a torpor, preoccupied with heretical thoughts he could not share without making her an accomplice in heresy. She construed his silence, his inability to respond to her efforts to cheer him, his curt refusals to join her at dinner or the theater, as rejection of herself. Minor differences erupted into major disputes, and their relationship deteriorated so that it was difficult for them to talk to each other about anything.

By late August 1978, when they departed for home leave in Moscow, Levchenko longed for sleep, solitude, surcease from combat. He yearned even more for evidence that his perceptions and conclusions were erroneous, evidence that the Soviet system was progressing and redeemable. Most of all, he craved discovery of moral reasons that would justify his not doing what he now dreaded he must do.

Under dingy, sodden skies, Levchenko passed inspection by sentries at the guardhouse of First Chief Directorate headquarters outside Moscow, feeling as apprehensive as a defendant awaiting the momentary verdict of a jury. The first visit to the Center on home leave always was like that. The Residency would have permitted you no clue of trouble, lest you flee. But once you walked in, the Center could simply announce that you were through, demoted to some administrative wasteland and forbidden ever to leave the country again, or exiled to the Second Chief Directorate and the provinces, or just fired. It did not necessarily matter that your record was exemplary. Perhaps someone you once knew had defected, or someone newly in power wanted his man in your place. Maybe they had swallowed disinformation about you purveyed by a counterintelligence service. Almost everyone had to worry about these possibilities. Levchenko,

*Sometimes, Japanese beguiled by images of socialist paradise came to the consular office to apply for Soviet citizenship. Consular personnel considered these applicants insane and treated them as such.

moreover, had to worry about Pronnikov and his interminable plots. And Pronnikov, now a full colonel and deputy director of the Seventh Department, was the first man he had to see.

His senses as keen as those of the hunter or the hunted, Levchenko stepped into Pronnikov's office on the sixth floor, alert to what initial intonations and expressions might tell. Pronnikov regarded him with a broad, condescending smile and, remaining seated while leaving Levchenko standing, pretended to busy himself with papers on his desk. After a minute or so he said: "I am late for a meeting and have no time for you today, so I will come at once to the point. I have underestimated you and your capacity for folly. You embarrassed me by going behind my back to General Popov in the Thomas case. For that I ought to take your head. But I like to think your folly is the folly of youth. I am by nature a magnanimous man, and the strength of my position allows me to be magnanimous. Therefore, I will give you one more chance. Go! Relax and enjoy your vacation. But be sure you report to me before you go back."

So he would be going back; they had not gotten him; he had a reprieve, and at the moment little else mattered.

The finance office gave him that portion of his salary which had accumulated in Moscow, roughly 3000 rubles.* Additionally, he and Natalia had saved some 900,000 yen, mostly from her earnings of 60,000 yen a month, and Levchenko impulsively decided to buy a car. A new Volga cost about 10,000

---

*KGB officers, especially those serving abroad, are paid according to complex formulae. Base salary, which is determined by the officer's military rank, increases only ten rubles per month with each advancement in rank. An officer receives a five percent increase in base salary after five years of service and a ten percent increase after ten years of service. Base salary is augmented by an additional 20 percent for officers who speak two European languages or one Oriental language. Irrespective of military rank and longevity, salary is further raised with appointment to supervisory positions. A major serving as an assistant or deputy department chief at the Center might well earn more than full colonels in the department.

Officers abroad receive one-half of the salary normally paid anyone rubles, or at the official exchange rate $14,000, and a Soviet purchaser paying in rubles had to wait, often years, for delivery. However, by paying in yen, hard currency, Levchenko bought a Volga for 860,000 yen, or $3660, and was guaranteed delivery within two weeks.

Through *New Times* Levchenko obtained a voucher entitling him to stay two weeks at a *Pravda* rest home, located in a lovely forest 30 miles east of Moscow, while Natalia remained with her mother and their son in the city. The three-story yellow brick rest home was more substantially built and less decayed than the typical Soviet structure, and Levchenko understood why. Because *Pravda* was the Party newspaper, the home was a Party facility, and the Party had taken precautions to minimize embezzlement or pilferage of building materials during construction. The home also was well designed, with 50 comfortable rooms, an airy cafeteria, a theater and a pleasant bar. However, the starchy food so offended sight, scent and taste that after three or four days, Levchenko limited himself mainly to bread, butter, eggs, jam and tea. Incessant rain kept him inside, and, as the regular vacation season was past, most of the guests were elderly people retired from *Pravda* or its printing plant. Their general mood was as dour

---

fulfilling the cover job they hold plus one-half of their regular KGB salary. Those under journalistic cover receive extra payments in Soviet currency for each article they write—an incentive to more thoroughly perform the cover job. Additionally, the equivalent of roughly 50 percent of their regular KGB salary is deposited monthly for them in an account at the Center.

By 1978, Levchenko received 247,000 yen a month, an adequate Japanese salary. But since *New Times* also paid for the rental, utilities and maintenance of his large apartment plus his car expenses, and the KGB unquestioningly paid entertainment expenses, his living standard far exceeded that of the typical Japanese. And his account at the Center grew at the rate of about 240 rubles a month.

The Soviet Union arbitrarily has set the value of the ruble at $1.40. In 1982 a ruble could be purchased at American currency exchanges for 23 cents and on the black market in Moscow for as little as 16 cents.

The value of the yen versus the dollar has fluctuated. In 1978 it reached a height of 200 yen to the dollar; in 1982 it dropped as low as 250 to the dollar.

as the weather, and they spoke of little except the difficulty of living on their pensions, the unavailability of goods on the open market, and the impossible costs of commodities on the black market.

Levchenko did encounter one congenial companion at the bar, a 50-year-old widower who specialized in beautifying or doctoring *Pravda* photographs of Brezhnev and other Politburo members. "If we didn't touch them up quite a bit, people would think that the Politburo is a sanitarium for the senile," he said matter-of-factly. He also boasted another skill. To illustrate the fraternal solidarity of Soviet leaders, *Pravda* published pictures showing admiring Politburo members gathered at the airport to see Brezhnev off or welcome him back from sundry journeys. However, as Levchenko's drinking partner explained, some Politburo members seldom troubled to go to the airport. So he inserted photographs of them taken at other times and places into a composite picture represented by *Pravda* as having just been taken at the airport. Levchenko solemnly agreed that this little deception was harmless, indeed, constructive considering the great affairs of state which allowed Politburo members scant time for ceremony.

By way of inquiring elliptically about the status of the economy, Levchenko mentioned the complaints of the pensioners at the home. "I can't say that they're wrong," responded the artist. "Each year it seems more difficult to live on your salary, and everything seems in shorter supply."

Streetwise and privy to information shared by *Pravda* staff members, the artist cited additional adversities. Concentrating resources upon building facilities for the 1980 Olympics, authorities had halted housing construction in Moscow, and hence had to break promises of new apartments made to myriad families. Construction of dormitories, hotels and other structures needed for the Olympics had fallen far behind schedule because of wholesale theft of building materials and insufficient labor. The necessity of interrupting work and clearing sites of civilian laborers, so that KGB teams could install listening devices throughout the new buildings, caused further delays. Tens of thousands of criminals had been imported from prisons to augment the labor force, and they precipitated a dangerous upsurge in rape, robbery and murder. "Frankly, it's best to stay away from those sites even in daytime," the *Pravda* man advised.

He also cautioned about the "thrill killings." Packs of teenagers or young men now murdered people on the streets for no purpose other than the excitement of watching someone die. As these killings were irrational, there was no rational way to defend against them except to keep to areas heavily patrolled by the militia and KGB plainclothesmen. You were safest within a mile radius of the Kremlin. Levchenko knew why. Disguised KGB patrols and militiamen saturated the area around the Kremlin and the Center nearby.

The *Pravda* man mentioned another phenomenon, a new cause of anti-Semitism. Russians were resentful because Jews were being allowed to leave the Soviet Union while virtually everybody else was compelled to stay. "When you think about it, there does seem to be an inconsistency," said the artist. "And Jewish girls have an advantage over the rest. Young men want to marry them on the chance that they can get out as Jews."

In the leisure of the rest home, Levchenko sought relaxation and rejuvenation through reading. Customarily, he began the day in Tokyo with an intellectual feast of world news and competing ideas, presented by a dozen major newspapers staffed with legions of professional journalists espousing diverse political attitudes. Through the Japanese press, he could not help but see a society charged with energy, vibrant with optimism, a society inexorably progressing despite a paucity of natural resources.

He searched Soviet journals, longing to discern credible signs of some comparable movement, however slight, in Soviet society. But what he read only depressed him, because long ago he had mastered the art of deciphering the Soviet press. If an article lauding the work of a particular coal mine mentioned toward the end that, unfortunately, neighboring mines had yet to match the performance of the model mine, that meant there was a crisis in coal mining. If an article singled out the heroic efforts of a railroad manager to ensure maintenance of freight schedules, and noted that all other managers must emulate him, that meant that failure of the railroads to deliver coal would soon cause shortages of heat and electricity. An article glorifying the struggle of farm workers in Asian republics to bring in the cotton, and reporting that they had been joined by tens of thousands of student "volunteers," meant that much of the nation's crop would rot because harvesting machinery did not work. An article openly admitting that organized theft of construction materials in a given region had become a problem meant that the problem of theft was nationwide and overwhelming. Levchenko had learned abroad that whatever the deficiencies of American society, a shortage of food was not among them. Thus, a *Pravda* article reporting widespread malnutrition and near-starvation in the United States signified to him that there were severe shortages in the Soviet Union and that the people must gird themselves for worse.*

The exhortations to conserve that Levchenko read, the excoriations of "economic criminals" and bureaucratic miscreants, the appeals for patriotic sacrifices necessitated by the machinations of imperialists—these all mirrored degeneration rather than progression. To him much of the commentary resembled the "Pleasant News" he sometimes manufactured for the comfort of the Politburo or the disinformation he regularly purveyed to deceive foreigners. And in his eyes, the Soviet leadership, by propagating such massive disinformation at home, was treating the Soviet people no differently than it treated the

---

*Agence France–Presse quoted a TASS article disseminated in the Soviet Union November 19, 1981, as follows:

"The American food distribution system shows 'obvious signs' of crisis; certain products are less and less accessible, Tass declared Thursday, basing [its report] on a study published in the United States. The reduction in the volume of agricultural production carries a 'real threat of food shortages,' notably in urban regions, and the situation is particularly worrisome in the Northeast, Tass went on."

Japanese, Americans or Chinese. It was war with all!

Back in Moscow, Levchenko took delivery of the new Volga. A car symbolized distinction and achievement, and he was proud. The numerous mechanical defects in the car did not unduly irritate him; they were to be expected, and he had already contracted for a complete overhaul by two moonlighting mechanics employed in a secret factory producing guidance systems for missiles. The mechanics inspected the Volga on a Thursday night, stole parts for it at the factory the next day, and worked on the car throughout the weekend, with Levchenko supplying them bottle after bottle of vodka.

Although they were unable to make the right door shut securely, they put the engine, transmission and brakes in good order, and Levchenko set out with a sense of adventure to see his native city for the first time entirely on his own. Inadvertently, he turned left from a center lane, and a police lieutenant whistled him to a stop. Levchenko displayed credentials showing him to be the *New Times* correspondent in Tokyo, and the lieutenant indicated that a present from Japan might spare him a traffic charge. "I have these stereo postcards," Levchenko said.

"Shit! I get those all the time. You'll have to do better."

"I don't live too far away. I can be back in 20 minutes with a cigarette lighter."

"All right. You have an honest face; I'll trust you." When Levchenko returned, the lieutenant grabbed the lighter and cheerfully waved him on, saying, "I knew you were honest."

Friends of Levchenko wanted to organize a party for him, but that was difficult because the Party was waging another campaign against drunkenness, and the head of the First Chief Directorate, being first of all a Party bureaucrat, had banned celebrations among officers. Only recently, he had fired four full colonels who made the mistake of drinking together at a hotel table where a Second Chief Directorate microphone recorded their inebriated conversation. However, Levchenko and three friends were able to dine safely at the National Hotel after one arranged through a pal in the Second

Chief Directorate for the microphone at a specified table to be turned off.

During the evening, Levchenko's recitation of his experience with the traffic lieutenant elicited from his companions numerous other tales of recent bribery and corruption. A man arrested near a secondhand shop peddling Japanese cassettes proved to be a KGB colonel. After six or seven officers angrily reported that their watches had been stolen while they were in the sauna at First Chief Directorate headquarters, Directorate K sleuths trapped the thief—a senior lieutenant who confessed that he was stealing to buy a car.

Then there was the story of another traffic lieutenant similar to the one who stopped Levchenko and invited a bribe. The driver, a KGB investigator in plain clothes, asked what he desired, and the lieutenant said he would enjoy a few brandies at a nearby restaurant. After the lieutenant downed four drinks and returned to duty, the plainclothesman paid the bill and immediately telephoned headquarters: "There is a lieutenant drunk on duty." A patrol forthwith arrested the lieutenant, who vociferously protested his innocence and demanded a sobriety test. The tests showed no trace of alcohol whatsoever.

Upbraided for false accusations, the plainclothesman was so adamant in his account that the KGB placed the lieutenant under surveillance. The watchers saw that he took six or seven motorists a day to the restaurant, and drank as many as 25 brandies, yet appeared none the worse for them. Rising to the challenge, the KGB soon solved the mystery. The restaurant waiter charged the drivers the full price of expensive brandy, but served the lieutenant tea, and the two split the profit.

One of Levchenko's companions suggested that bribery and influence peddling probably had always gone on in Russia and that every society had its corruption.

"I'm afraid there has been a change," commented a Line X colonel. "Two or three years ago, had any of us ever heard of an FCD officer stealing watches at headquarters or hawking contraband on the street like an itinerant Armenian rug peddler? Now, everything is for sale. People even will sell themselves. Maybe it hasn't come to that in the FCD, but I can tell you it has in the MFA [Ministry of Foreign Affairs] and Ministry of Trade. The CIA is picking agents there like apples in an orchard. Andropov himself is very worried."

Two days before his flight back to Tokyo, Levchenko reported to FCD headquarters, and Pronnikov amazed him with a dulcet little speech. "We have had our differences, our misunderstandings. Let's forget them and the past and look to the future. Your future can be full of gold if you can learn to heed advice. I am worried about you. They have given you too many cases; nobody can handle that many cases without eventually getting burned. I would like for you to send me personal letters through the pouch telling me about your situation and the Residency so I can advise you." He added: "And better look after your interests here."

"Certainly I will write you," Levchenko lied. "Thank you."

Cynicism Unlimited, he thought. They ought to erect great red neon signs above the Kremlin, above the Center, above the Afro-Asian Solidarity Committee, and have them flash every ten seconds, day and night, the words "CYNICISM UNLIMITED." Everything was a lie and everybody, including himself, a liar. Pronnikov lied to him, and he lied back. They proclaimed unremitting progress where everybody with eyes could see accelerating deterioration. Material progress and well-being were, of course, in and of themselves nothing; they were only the means to spiritual liberty and fulfillment. That is what they promised; instead, the system corrupted everybody. The whole Soviet Union was like a vast land of exiles ruled by wardens who ceaselessly conducted "militant active measures" against their wards. He came home looking for hope; he saw, especially in the tired, forlorn faces of the people, only hopelessness.

As before, on his last night he went to church and prayed. But this time he went openly, defiantly. He would not desecrate his worship by subterfuge; he would leave to his Maker the decision as to whether worship must be punished.

Moral considerations alone incited his rebellion. Materially, he stood at the apex of Soviet society. He earned in rubles twice as much as the average Soviet professional and while abroad could accumulate hard currency that would make him relatively rich at home. Because of his success in Japan, his career prospects could scarcely have been more promising. By making a few compromises with Pronnikov, he could remain in the Seventh Department and enjoy more tours in Japan, a nation he understood and liked. Or he could transfer to the Twelfth Department, which picked up foreigners in Moscow and pursued them back in their own countries. Given his now well-established journalistic credentials and command of English, he probably could look forward to traveling in the United States and United Kingdom as well as Japan. Very few of his countrymen could ever dream of comparable prospects. Nevertheless, as the IL-62 climbed after takeoff for Tokyo, he knew he was looking down on his homeland for the last time.

Back in Tokyo, Levchenko began to contemplate defection, though at the first thoughts of it he recoiled. He loathed the KGB as an institution, as a symbol and foundation of the Soviet state, and he deemed it congenitally, irreparably evil. He despised Pronnikov and his ilk, personally and as personifications of the KGB. Still, he felt loyalty to Russia and his countrymen, to the honest officers who like himself were cogs in an inhuman machine. Yet, other than flight, what choice did he have?

In his turmoil, he suffered frequent and severe attacks of tachycardia, or rapid heartbeat, for which physicians could find no organic cause. An embassy doctor prescribed Valium, and the tranquilizer calmed him; but upon sensing creeping addiction, he quit it. He knew that alcohol offered no real relief, so again he flung himself into work. Whatever his feelings and thoughts, he had to keep working, meeting agents, developing contacts and, if possible, snaring new recruits. If he manifested symptoms of disaffection or instability, he might suddenly be transferred to Moscow and lose all chance of escape. He had seen it happen. The Resident or chief of Line PR privately informed an officer that he was needed at once for temporary duty at the Center, handed him a plane ticket, and had someone drive him straight to the airport. The officer's family followed in a few days. But, in a couple of cases, banished officers had to wait almost a year before the embassy troubled to ship their household belongings. So Levchenko continued to behave as the energetic and enthusiastic officer his colleagues had always known him to be.

Because of his successes and the confidence the Residency placed in him, he became involved in operations other than his own, including some known to few officers. One of the most guarded centered on a Japanese Foreign Ministry code clerk whom the KGB called Nazar.

An officer from the First Chief Directorate's Department 16, which concentrates exclusively on cipher personnel, spotted Nazar in Tokyo and cautiously cultivated him, never asking for a favor. However, after the code clerk was posted to an East European nation, probably Czechoslovakia, the same KGB officer showed up there and recruited him through the lure of money.

Major Valeri Ivanovich Umansky and then Major Valentin Nikolaevich Belov handled Nazar after he returned to Tokyo. The Center regarded the case as so important that it relieved both officers of all other duties outside the Residency to minimize risk of their compromise. Other extreme precautions were taken. The KGB rarely met Nazar to talk. He transmitted documents by brushing up against his case officer, as if by accident, on the street or by leaving them in hidden drops. Whenever a delivery was to be made, the Residency suspended all other operations. It ringed the pass or drop site with officers who stood watch against surveillance and sent out decoys to lead away any surveillants who might approach the area. These assisting officers were told only that the operation was exceedingly important; few knew its nature.

Access to the cable center in the Foreign Office enabled Nazar each week to photograph or photocopy dozens, sometimes hundreds, of messages from Japanese embassies around the world, including those in Washington and Moscow. Unwittingly, the Japanese embassies and their competent staffs thus served as authoritative reporters for the KGB. Confidences exchanged in Washington, London, Paris, Bonn, and other Western capitals soon were known to the Kremlin. And the dispatches often told the KGB what the Japanese in Moscow were doing and thinking. Nazar's greatest worth, however, perhaps derived from the help he gave KGB cryptographers striving to break Japanese codes. By comparing the plain language text of a message with the encrypted, broadcast version, routinely intercepted and recorded, they could learn much about the Japanese theory of cryptology. Though codes often change, theory does not.

The sheer number of the messages Nazar gave the Residency caused problems of translation and when something very sensitive emanated from Nazar, Levchenko often was called to help.

Early in 1979, Guryanov announced, "I am sorry, but you must help in a high-risk operation that concerns none of your agents. I also am sorry that I can't tell you anything about the case except that you must visually inspect a house and tell me whether it's new."

"Why not send Doctor?" Levchenko asked. A poor freelance journalist and fanatic Marxist, expelled from the Japanese Communist Party because of pro-Soviet views, Doctor was a classic support agent. He photographed offices, houses, and future meeting sites, slipped propaganda under the doors of Chinese offices, posted disinformation letters slandering anti-Communist Japanese, and performed sundry other routine yet essential clandestine errands. Check after check over the years had proven him reliable and competent.

"No!" Guryanov abruptly answered. "This is an extremely sensitive False Flag operation, and only one Japanese is to know about it. I've picked you because I think you can deal with an emergency, if one arises. The problem is that the house is in a remote suburb where foreigners never appear. You must get in, take a mental photograph of the house and block and get out without being burned. If you are burned, you could ruin the most delicate operation we have attempted in years."

Guryanov added that Major Aleksandr Biryuokhov, a *Komsomolskaya Pravda* correspondent, would drive. "Unlike you, he's a good driver."

"We'll go Sunday morning when most of the dogs should be sleeping," Levchenko said.

In America or Europe, the assignment would have been as routine as any intelligence assignment can be. In Japan, it entailed serious perils, and Levchenko appreciated them all. The typical Japanese policeman knows and maintains cordial personal relations with everyone in the neighborhood he patrols. The people in turn look upon their policeman as protector and benefactor, and volunteer to him news of the least unusual occurrence. If anyone in the neighborhood Levchenko had to reconnoiter recognized him and his companion as Russians, the police immediately would be apprised. A counterintelligence investigation, swift and sweeping, would ensue, and the whole neighborhood would know about it.

Such an investigation might very well frighten away the KGB quarry. The Residency obviously was undertaking a False Flag operation because the KGB had determined that the particular Japanese it hoped to ensnare would never knowingly collaborate with Soviets. He was being enticed in the belief that the information or services he might provide were for some secret cause beneficial to Japan. Should he suspect any Soviet involvement, he would surely recoil, and possibly report to the authorities on his own. Regardless, as Guryanov warned, the operation would be ruined, and though the Resident did not say so, Levchenko would be blamed. And back at the Center, Pronnikov could possibly magnify the reversal into reason for forcing his recall from Japan.

Levchenko and Biryuokhov rendezvoused in darkness before dawn and cleared their path for almost five hours before heading into the outskirts of Tokyo. Around 11 a.m., Biryuokhov turned into a congested suburban street only about 15 feet wide. He intended to pass the house slowly, then accelerate out of the area as quickly as prudence allowed but a crowd of children playing in the street forced them to stop. Suddenly the children began pounding on the car and shouting, "Foreigners! Foreigners!"

Smiling and waving at them, Levchenko told Biryuokhov, "Pretend we don't understand and slowly push your way through. Don't let them trap us here."

The noisy gaggle parted enough for them to pass, but toward the end of the block more people—teen-agers and adults—blocked the street. "We must explain ourselves," Levchenko whispered. "Stop and let me try to handle it. Whatever you do, speak not one word of Russian."

Levchenko got out and swaggered toward the Japanese, who stared impassively or hostilely. In English, he identified himself as an American correspondent, stated he had lost his way and *demanded* directions to the main highway back to Tokyo. An elderly man stepped forward and, in broken English, gave directions.

In his best cowboy manner, Levchenko airily said, "Thanks, papa-san." The Japanese bowed and Levchenko saluted.

At the Residency that Sunday afternoon, Levchenko recounted the foray and reported that the house he checked was new. "You did well," Guryanov said. "Now, Stanislav, I ask and warn you: never mention this to anyone. Forget about it. Remember only that I thank you."

While Levchenko never learned the outcome or further details of this particular False Flag operation, he knew of other cases in which the KGB bilked or seduced Japanese who were anti-Soviet. The agent with the code name Maslov was a conspicuous example. A great student of Chinese history, Maslov revered ancient Chinese culture and hated the Communists for their systematic efforts to eradicate it. Motivated by this passion, he began slipping the KGB information he believed would help the Soviets damage the Chinese regime.

Maslov rose to be a senior analyst in the Research Bureau of the Cabinet of Ministers, a euphemism for the analytical division of Japanese intelligence. Here, he had access to the

highest intelligence, as well as sensitive policy papers revealing the real Japanese attitude and negotiating stances toward
other nations, including the Soviet Union. Artfully persuaded
by Major Gennadi Druzhinin that the Soviets needed to know
everything in order to combat the odious Chinese Communists, Maslov shared all he knew with the KGB. He also subtly
inserted into analyses prepared for the prime minister and
other cabinet officers Soviet arguments intended to retard
development of relations between Japan and China. Without
fully comprehending what he was doing, Maslov became one
of the Residency's most productive agents, even though he
disliked Soviet communism only slightly less than Chinese
communism.

Early on the morning of February 9, 1979, the telephone
awakened Levchenko, and a voice asked in Japanese for Mr.
Otsugi—a signal for Levchenko to come at once to the Residency. Again Guryanov wanted his help. During the night, the
KGB had obtained through agent Kamus, a correspondent for
Tokyo Shimbun, a document based on information stolen in
South Korea. It disclosed that in mid-February, Chinese armies would attack Vietnam on three specific fronts. It also
detailed the strength of the Chinese forces and their tactical
objectives.

While Levchenko studied the report, Guryanov and Sevastyanov debated whether to transmit the intelligence to the
Center. If authentic, the information was momentous. The
Chinese publicly had warned that they might "administer a
lesson" to Vietnam, and doubtless the Vietnamese were generally aware of preparations for an attack. With exact knowledge of when and where it would occur, they would be far
better able to blunt it at much less cost to themselves. However, the Residency was not sure that the information was valid.
If analysis in Moscow or subsequent events proved the document to be a fake, the Center would accuse the Residency of
incompetence and recklessness in submitting false intelligence about impending war. If the Chinese did intend to
attack in February, possibly some other Residency would

report their plans, and the Tokyo Residency, by keeping silent, would appear inferior.

Guryanov asked Levchenko, "Can you tell anything from the text?"

"No."

"What do you think?" Guryanov asked him.

"I think we have no choice."

Guryanov stood up, buzzed the cipher clerk on the eighth floor and announced, "We shall send it with an annotation that we do not know whether it is authentic."

"We are supposed to know," Sevastyanov said. "Pronnikov will dump on you."

"Fuck him. Send it, and let them decide whether it's true."

It was true, and when the Chinese attacked on February 17, exactly as the intelligence forecast, the Vietnamese were well deployed and ready. Afterwards, in a rare commendation, the Center cabled: "Tokyo Residency was the only Residency in the world to report this invaluable intelligence."

The second week in May 1979, Sevastyanov shouted in the Residency corridor, "Major Levchenko!" He held a cable announcing that on May 9, a Soviet national holiday, Levchenko had been promoted to major. "Come over tonight and we will celebrate," he said.

"Thanks, but I have to work," Levchenko replied. "Besides, I'm dieting."

No matter how many agents the KGB has, it always hunts more; and the Residency continuously tasked its best agents with the duty of recommending prospective recruits. And early in 1979, Sevastyanov received such a recommendation from Ramses, a Socialist Party member. Sevastyanov briefed Levchenko and instructed him to make a personal assessment of the prospect, journalist Akira Yamada, to whom the KGB gave the code name Vassin. Ramses characterized Vassin as an ideologically sound former Communist and an able journalist who edited a private newsletter, titled *The Insider*, about foreign affairs. His potential, as Ramses saw it, derived from his excellent contacts in the Foreign Office, among Chinese and American journalists and Japanese businessmen engaged in trade with China. Additionally, having once been a Communist Party member, he had some experience in conspiracy and concealed his true name from most people, using instead the pen name Akeo Yamakawa.

Levchenko telephoned Vassin, introduced himself as the *New Times* correspondent, said he was quite impressed by the newsletter, and solicited advice regarding some political questions. Vassin joined Levchenko for lunch three days later in a cafeteria of the Japan Press Building. A lean, haggard-looking man in his 50s, he wore a floppy leather jacket two sizes too large, and his right shoulder slumped under the weight of a bag bulging with papers and news clippings. Levchenko noted that as he entered the cafeteria, he paused to survey the room and the diners' faces.

To induce Vassin to talk about himself, Levchenko first spoke freely of himself, recounting his employment with the Afro-Asian Solidarity Committee, his prior experience in Japan, and his work with *New Times*. As usual, he emphasized the close ties between *New Times* and Soviet leaders and the nonexistent special bulletin the magazine allegedly published exclusively for them. Shifting from himself, Levchenko said, "From your newsletter, I see that you really are a professor of foreign affairs. It amazes me that you know so much."

Flattered, Vassin talked about the newsletter, its circulation and clientele, the problems he had with plagiarists, and his financial difficulties. He also was quite forthcoming about himself, and all he stated accorded with what Ramses had said. Promising to try to brief Levchenko about developments in the Liberal Democratic Party and Japanese relations with the United States, Soviet Union and China, he agreed to another luncheon ten days hence.

During their next three meetings, they got along well, and Vassin volunteered information which, although not new to the KGB, confirmed the quality of his sources. Meanwhile, the Residency investigated him through the network and discovered that several agents, including Ares, knew Vassin personally.

One stated that Vassin was highly informed and well regarded in journalistic circles, even though tinged with a somewhat radical reputation. Ares termed Vassin a friend so skilled at cultivating news sources that he had recruited his own informants in the national defense forces, the Defense College and the National Police Agency. Ares and another agent were sure that he had no covert relationship with Japanese counterintelligence.

"We can make a straightforward recruitment without a prolonged prelude," Levchenko told Sevastyanov. "Three of our best agents all recommend him. Everything they say fits with what he says and my own assessments. Vassin is an expert in many fields; he goes everywhere, and we might even use him in Active Measures. I'm sure I can recruit him at our next meeting under *New Times* cover."

"I agree," Sevastyanov said. "But the Center never would understand how you can recruit someone so good in such a short time. It doesn't fit the mold. Go ahead and recruit him if you can, but we won't report it. We'll just show a gradual development during the next few months, then we will propose his official recruitment."

To relax and disarm Vassin, Levchenko at their next luncheon ordered whisky and made jokes about Ambassador Polyansky before saying, "There is one serious business matter I would like to discuss."

"Really? What business?" Vassin asked.

"I need not only for *New Times*, but for the International Department and even higher Soviet officials, regular analyses of many facets of Japanese politics. I know that you are ideally qualified to make them because I already have learned much from you, and I do not consider myself exactly uninformed. So I would like for you to give me on a continuing basis written analyses. Of course, *New Times* has a fund for such services, and we would insist upon paying you."

Vassin thought for a while. "I am not against cooperating

with you on a businesslike basis," he said slowly. "I am afraid, however, I cannot give you the written analyses you need. You see, I am terribly overworked as it is; I just have no time. And I'm sorry to say I have a chronic inflammation of the nerve in my hand, and writing is very painful."

"Do you have a tape recorder?"

"Sure."

"Well, just dictate your reports. Naturally, that won't affect your payments. I myself will make the transcript from the tape."

"Yes, that I can do. You must tell me, though, the subjects that interest you."

"The topics will vary. Generally, I am interested in what you know most about. In any case, it is important that your reports be short, succinct, and name the sources of information."

Vassin hesitated. "My sources . . . I always protect them. It is not that I distrust you; it is just that I have given my word."

Levchenko guessed that most of Vassin's sources were hidden Communists who since the days when the Party was underground had filtered upward into government or industry. He was confident that eventually he could ferret out their identities, and the best way to begin was to ascertain their general positions. "I appreciate that you must keep your word," he said. "On the other hand, I need to convince Soviet leaders that I am not merely forwarding gossip from off the streets. Would it not be fair to indicate the general position of the source of given information?"

"Yes, that is possible."

"Good. Why don't we start with a report about plans to strengthen the Japanese Self-Defense Forces?"

"It happens that I may have some information about that. I probably can give you something in a couple of weeks."

Two weeks later, as they descended a stairway into a restaurant in the Kanda business district, Vassin slipped a microcassette into Levchenko's jacket pocket. After a quick lunch, during which neither referred to the cassette, Levchenko strolled in and out of a few small shops looking for surveillance. There was none.

Sevastyanov had a personal interest in Vassin because his agent, Ramses, first recommended him, and he questioned Levchenko in detail about the meeting. "Excellent!" he exclaimed. "The way he passed you the tape, all his behavior shows that he understands that your relationship must be clandestine. The fact that he has never bothered to ask how much you will pay him shows he is not a mercenary. Excellent!"

"It seems to me he's as good as recruited."

"He is," Sevastyanov agreed. "However, in your report I want you to make it appear we're moving cautiously. Tell them that although we have checked the contact and he looks very promising, we feel he must be further checked and tested. Otherwise, Pronnikov will make a scandal. Can't you hear him—'The Tokyo Residency has become wild, lost all perspective. They're recruiting agents after only four or five meetings. That's unheard of in Japan. And it's reckless, dangerous.'"

Loitering in a curio shop outside a café, Levchenko watched Vassin scan the area, then dart inside. Waiting to be sure no "dogs" were trailing, Levchenko joined him in the quiet little café and underneath the table handed him an envelope containing 60,000 yen. "The music on the cassette was first-rate," he said. "I would like to hear some more of the same type."

Vassin smiled and nodded. "If I may, I also would like to ask a personal favor of you," Levchenko continued. "We very much need a Foreign Office telephone directory."

"That may be hard; I will try."

Though the directory was not highly classified, its circulation was restricted, and only someone in the Foreign Office could make a copy. The Residency already possessed the directory, but Levchenko wanted to verify whether Vassin had a source who could deliver it. A week later, Vassin pulled a photocopy out of his bulky bag and handed it to Levchenko.

Through the spring of 1979, the intelligence from Vassin increased in both quantity and quality. He reported that a section of the Federation of Japanese Economic Organizations had recommended that Japan begin manufacturing and selling munitions and light armaments to Asian countries in the late 1980s. To the KGB, this signified that industry favored rearmament, and probably that production of light armaments would be followed by heavy armaments in the 1990s.

Another Vassin cassette disclosed that the United States had secretly stationed on Okinawa elite assault forces and put battle-ready groups aboard ships in the Indian Ocean.

In late April or early May, Levchenko brought in a cassette whose contents Guryanov ordered flashed to the Center immediately. It stated that the United States, in concert with Great Britain, Japan and possibly France, was attempting to establish a new Cambodian government under the aegis of Prince Norodom Sihanouk. The Americans saw such a government as the only feasible alternative to Khmer Rouge rule under the maniacal and homicidal Pol Pot or a puppet regime of the Vietnamese. Although the Chinese had been patrons of Sihanouk ever since he fled to Peking in 1970, they declined to participate in the venture, because they believed that the Khmer Rouge, despite the odious Pol Pot, still represented the best counter to the Vietnamese, whom they regarded as lackeys of the Russians. Sihanouk, who had lent his name and charisma to the Khmer Rouge before their seizure of power, had now resolved to cast his lot with the Americans, in hope of saving what was left of the Cambodian people after the prolonged Communist genocide.

Within 24 hours, the Center sent the Tokyo Residency an informational copy of imperative cables transmitted almost instantly to the Residencies in Washington, New York, London and Paris ordering them to corroborate or disprove Vassin's report. Later, the Center advised the Tokyo Residency that the report had been verified as essentially accurate.

Levchenko and Vassin continued to meet three or four times a month, usually in little cafés where surveillants could not sit undetected. Vassin obviously looked forward to the luncheons because he was a natural conspirator, he had come to like Levchenko, and he derived a heady gratification from their relationship. Though he was a good journalist, fame and distinction in his profession had eluded him. Now, though, he believed that his reports were being read by the highest leaders of the Soviet Union, and who among his peers could boast of comparable attention? Unlike most Japanese, he disdained conversational pleasantries, preferring to concentrate all their time together on business. "What are you interested in next?" he would ask.

"China, for example," Levchenko said. "Are you in a position to obtain new information on China?"

"Maybe. I have a friend in the Japan-China trade association."

Levchenko strained to conceal the intensity of his interest. Represented in the association were some of the best brains of Japanese industry, and they had numerous contacts in the Chinese government. Senior Japanese intelligence officers were believed to prepare detailed, authoritative studies for the association, which, in turn, shared information with government agencies. "No harm in trying," Levchenko said, then purposely switched to another subject.

Some three weeks later, Vassin delved into his old leather bag, which always seemed to be stuffed with half his office files, and withdrew a thick manila envelope. His ordinarily haggard face brightened, and he announced, "I've brought you a document."

"I'm eager to read it," Levchenko whispered. "Please, though, keep it until we leave."

To Levchenko and other veterans of the Residency, the sensational had long ago become routine, and a single piece of intelligence rarely excited anybody. But, upon examining the document Vassin had supplied, Sevastyanov blurted, "My God!" and immediately summoned a Reports officer, who also was impressed. The 100-page document, classified Secret, minutely detailed the Order of Battle of the entire Chinese army—force strengths, disposition of all major units, weaponry available to each. And an appendix presented a keen, frank Chinese assessment of the performance of their troops and commanders in the fighting against Vietnam.

The Reports officer said, "We've gotten fragments and dribbles over the years but never such a *tour d'horizon*. This confirms everything." He separated the document into five parts and assigned young officers to translate each during the night. The next day, he drafted four cables summarizing sections of the document, and these were followed by lengthy written dispatches. The Center in a monthly evaluation commended the Residency and termed the cables and dispatches intelligence of the highest order.

By the summer of 1979 Vassin had become one of the Residency's most productive agents, even though he was not yet officially a member of the network, and Sevastyanov decided to try to graduate him into Active Measures. For several weeks the Residency had tried to surface a disinformation story fabricated at the Center by Service A, but no agent could sell it because the yarn was so melodramatic, and it was unattributable to any specific sources. In brief, the KGB fabrication stated:

The popularity of President Carter in the United States is plummeting, and the American public increasingly regards him as a weak, vacillating leader. CIA Director Stansfield Turner is a friend and flunky of Carter. The United States is trying to induce the Arabs to allow American military bases in the Middle East. Therefore, Carter and Turner have concocted a plot to refurbish the President's image and persuade the Arabs to sanction the bases.

The CIA will train some of its Arab agents to hijack an oil tanker in Middle Eastern waters. With world attention riveted on this drama at sea, Carter will order special U.S. forces to rescue the tanker. Landing on the ship by helicopter, the special forces will kill all the terrorists—the CIA's own agents—to prevent them from ever disclosing CIA complicity. The rescue effected, Carter will address the American people as a decisive leader resolute in crisis, and the incident will dramatize to the Arabs the desirability of having American forces in their midst to cope with terrorism. Because so many of the oil tankers plying the routes from the Middle East are Japanese, probably the target ship will be Japanese.

Listening to this tale, Vassin eyed Levchenko sympathetically yet skeptically. "Are you sure this is true?" he asked.

"Absolutely. We have it from the best sources."

"Who are they?"

"I'm sorry, my good friend; they are so secret we can never put them in jeopardy. You see what kind of information they can provide, so you can guess where they are. But if you can't do it, that is all right. We have many other possibilities. We just consider you our best and most able friend, so I came to you first."

"Well, certainly I can't publish it in my newsletter. I never publish anything without knowing the source. I value its reputation, you know. Perhaps I can plant it elsewhere."

One of Japan's most popular weekly magazines, *Shukan Gendai,* in its issue of August 23, 1979, published an abbreviated version of the KGB fabrication. It reported that according to rumor in Washington, the CIA was plotting to hijack a tanker. Referring to Akeo Yamakawa (Vassin's pen name) as "an international affairs specialist," it quoted him as saying: "The rumor is highly credible. With less than 26 percent of Americans now supporting Carter, the Carter camp is desperately trying to erase the image of a weak and vacillating President facing election next year." The magazine insinuated that the allegation had been substantiated because a Kuwaiti newspaper had published it.

After Vassin duped *Shukan Gendai,* Sevastyanov declared that, by all criteria, Vassin now qualified for inclusion in the network, and the Center could not possibly refuse his official recruitment. "Still, we will go through the motions of checking him again so they will have no excuse," he said.

Residency agents were interrogated anew and their statements, all attesting to the steadfastness of Vassin, put into reports. Levchenko bought a small briefcase, into which the Technical Operations officer sewed a tiny recorder that would run for an hour, and also placed a cassette coated with invisible powder that would reveal any tampering. Purposely arriving late for lunch with Vassin, and affecting much apprehension, Levchenko apologized, saying he had just come from a serious business meeting and that he was due momentarily at a Western embassy reception. He was worried because there was not time to go to his own embassy, and he would have to check his briefcase at the Western embassy. "Confidentially, it contains some exceedingly sensitive materials, and I can't be sure they won't search it," he whispered. Nervously glancing at his watch, he wondered if Vassin could do him the favor of keeping the briefcase overnight and returning it to him at breakfast tomorrow, en route to work. Vassin graciously agreed, and insisted that Levchenko leave at once, lest he be late for the reception. The next afternoon, the Technical Operations officer, after studying the cassette under ultraviolet light, assured Levchenko it had not been touched.

The Center's response to Guryanov's emphatic recommendation that recruitment of Vassin be formally ratified came on a rainy night, around eight o'clock, in August. Upon reading it, Guryanov cursed, Sevastyanov laughed, and Levchenko said nothing. The cable stated: "We agree that the case of Vassin shows much promise and has been well handled by Comrade Koltsov. Still, we feel that further testing of contact is required."

"And how shall we further test him?" Sevastyanov roared. "Call in a proctologist? Have him mine the Imperial Palace?"

"I think we will see that after October the need for further testing will evaporate," Guryanov said bitterly. "I'm sorry, Stanislav. As I have said, the indecency of Pronnikov has no bounds."

Everybody understood. Levchenko, who had served in Tokyo since February 1975, was due, in accordance with normal rotation, to return sometime in October 1979 for duty at the Center. By stalling the official recruitment until afterwards, Pronnikov could deprive him of credit and reward for it. Indifferently, Levchenko replied, "It doesn't matter."

That was the truth. Levchenko needed no further evidence that both Pronnikov and the KGB were corrupt. By depriving Levchenko of credit for the recruitment of Schweik, Pronnikov already had robbed him of a promotion. What difference did it make if he were cheated out of another? In fact, the higher he advanced in the KGB, the greater his own iniquity seemed to be.

During this same period, in still another internal cabal, rumors were spead at the Center—probably by Pronnikov— that Tokyo Active Measures Officer Valeri Umansky was a habitual drunk who dallied with prostitutes and the wives of other officers.* Guryanov reported that the allegations were utterly baseless, and submitted testimonials from Residency officers affirming Umansky's good character and competence. Nevertheless, the Center recalled him for "consultations" and forbade his return.

Guryanov called in Levchenko, handed him the Registry, in which covert actions were logged, and announced, "As of today, you are Active Measures officer." Noting that Levchenko's tour at the Residency ended in October, Guryanov instructed him to begin turning over all his agents and contacts, to curtail *New Times* activities and concentrate primarily on Active Measures.

Each day brought Levchenko orders from Moscow detailing specific actions to be initiated in furtherance of basic disinformation themes directed against the United States, China and Japan. Analyzing the Active Measures roster of nearly 100 agents and exploitable contacts, to determine who could best discharge each assignment, Levchenko was impressed by the power the KGB had acquired in an essentially unfriendly land, and especially by its grip on the Japanese Socialist Party (JSP). For his own purposes, he reviewed the Residency network, mentally noting agents with special capabilities for Active Measures:

Hoover (true name: Hirohide Ishida)—former Minister of Labor, Liberal Democratic member of parliament; chairman of the Japanese-Soviet Parliamentary Friendship Association, the leadership of which is KGB-controlled; sponsors bulletin subsidized by KGB;

Grace (Shigeru Ito)—member of parliament and influential

---

*Umansky became Active Measures officer after Nazar, the code clerk he was handling, was sent abroad again.

member of the Central Committee of the Socialist Party; can decisively affect Socialist policies;

Tibre—Socialist Party member; exercises influence on party positions;

Gavre (Seiichi Katsumata)—veteran boss of the centrist faction of the Socialist Party, the faction that spawns many JSP leaders; important for ensuring future KGB influence over JSP hierarchy;

Kant (Takuji Yamane)—assistant managing editor of *Sankei*, conservative newspaper with circulation of 2.2 million; intimate and adviser to conservative publisher; can manipulate views of publisher, plant disinformation in paper and governmental circles;

Davey—an editor of Tokyo edition of *Sankei;* can work in tandem with and reinforce Kant;

Atos (Tamotsu Sato)—General Secretary of Society of Marxism, the core of the JSP; another channel of influencing JSP leadership;

Ramses—Socialist Party member; another key to KGB control of JSP;

Fen-Foking—a Liberal Democratic Party member who can exert influence on leadership of one faction; potential for insinuating disinformation in Liberal Democratic Party;

Krasnov—active in high financial and industrial circles; can spread disinformation among Japanese business leaders;

Yamamoto—professor who heads a group of intellectual agents; active in academic circles; published Soviet-dictated literature;

Ulanov (Takumi Ueda)—member of parliament and officer of the *Burakumin* Liberation League (*Buraku Kaiho Domei*); unwitting agent who can be directed by Yamamoto;

Zum—brilliant secretary of Ulanov; another means of guiding Ulanov through Yamamoto;

Vassin (Akira Yamada)—journalist and editor of a newsletter; unlimited potential as Agent of Influence; KGB can take over newsletter;

Kamus—journalist employed by *Tokyo Shimbun*; specialist

on Korean affairs; can place articles;

Mukhin (Kaneji Miura)—executive of popular television channel *Asahi Terebi*; not an agent but a "friendly contact" who can help slant programs and influence other television personalities;

Tsunami—extremely wealthy and powerful businessman; not an agent and not under KGB control but unwittingly serves as channel of Soviet influence into financial and industrial circles;

Sandomir (Koji Sugimori)—secretary general of the Japanese Society for External Cultural Promotion; cooperates with International Department and unwittingly with KGB.

The motivations and awareness of these, as well as all other KGB assets, varied widely. Ishida and Yamane, for example, were conscious, controlled agents who knew exactly what they were doing and did what they were told. When Yamane slipped Levchenko the secret document outlining positions Prime Minister Fukuda would adopt in private discussions with President Carter, he knew he was handing it to the KGB. When he accepted a bonus for this espionage, he knew who was paying it. Others manifestly understood that they were collaborating with the Soviets—and getting paid for their collaboration. Some may not, however, have understood that they were tools of the KGB. Still others, such as the respected business magnate Tsunami, would never have knowingly done anything injurious to their country. They simply were used subtly, without their knowledge. In influence operations, whether someone was witting or unwitting did not matter all that much. To the KGB, all that mattered were the results.

For personal and very practical purposes, Levchenko in reviewing the roster of Residency agents asked himself one critical question: Do we have any penetration whatsoever of American intelligence in Tokyo? He could find none.

In September and October, Levchenko introduced all his agents and contacts to the officers who would administer them in the future. However, in mid-October, when the chief of

Line KR, Yuri Dvoryanchikov, took home leave, the Resident ordered Levchenko temporarily to resume handling Ares.

The normally phlegmatic Ares beamed upon seeing Levchenko, and warmly shook hands. "I hope we are to be a team again," he said.

"I wish that were to be. But I'm just filling in temporarily. I will be going home soon."

"When?"

"I'm expecting my orders any day. Certainly I'll be leaving before the end of the month."

Ares laughed and shook his head. "At first, I did not like you; we misunderstood each other. Then we became friends, real friends who share danger. We did a lot, didn't we? I will miss you."

"The life of an intelligence officer is like that. You like some people, and you become attached to a few, then you have to say farewell, and you are cheated of the friendship normal people can enjoy for a lifetime. It hurts your heart."

"Will I be able to reach you?"

According to doctrine, Levchenko should have said that he could always be reached through his successor, and that he would always follow the exploits of Ares. Instead he said, "I will not lie to you. No. But we do not have to say goodbye now. We should see each other two or three more times."

"Maybe I can give you a farewell present, something you always wanted."

"What?"

"The directory." The Russians long had coveted a classified, 700-page listing (name, address and telephone number) of Japanese security officers. They considered it a data base that would enable them to track for many years the assignments and careers of those who threatened them.

Ares reported at their ensuing meeting that he could obtain the directory for only two hours, from 1 to 3 a.m., on October 24. This would not be time enough for him to photograph it, so the KGB would have to make whatever arrangements it could to copy it. However, he would have to return the directory to his contact by 3 a.m.

Levchenko thought quickly of an operational plan and instructed Ares to walk in front of the Japan-French Culture Center at 1:15 a.m. "I will walk by, and you hand it to me in a brush pass. At 2:45 a.m. I'll return it to you the same way."

"All right. If anything goes wrong ahead of time, I'll signal by phone."

"I'm afraid the next meeting will be our last. There will be no time to talk, so let me say goodbye now. I wish you good luck always."

Unemotionally, Ares replied, "Good luck to you."

The night was moonlit and still, and only their footsteps could be heard on the street as they approached and, like two preoccupied strangers, bumped into each other. "Excuse me," Ares said.

"Sorry, my fault," Levchenko answered, hurrying onward. A block away he handed the packet to the operational driver and retreated to a restaurant to wait. The operational driver, about a mile farther on, passed the packet to another KGB officer, who drove straight to the Residency, where a team on the 11th floor began furiously photographing page after page. At about 2:40 a.m. the operational driver handed the directory back to Levchenko, and a few minutes later he again bumped into Ares in front of the Culture Center. Levchenko had taken only a few steps when he heard Ares, in a dangerous breach of discipline, call. He turned, and Ares shook his hand. "Goodbye, my best Russian friend."

"Dear Ares, goodbye."

Although Levchenko had not yet received his orders back to Moscow, he knew he would never see Ares again. For he had resolved that today he would do it.

He fell into bed around 4 a.m. and awakened at 8:30 a.m. Although the embassy physician urged him to take Valium whenever tensions caused trembling or tachycardia, he resisted the temptation to tranquilize himself. Instead, he forced down some of the breakfast Natalia had set out before leaving for her job at the embassy—tomato juice, milk, cereal, boiled eggs, ham, croissants, jam and tea. Eating was very difficult, but he would need sustenance, and he did not know when he would next have time for food.

Today, until the last moment, his movements had to appear normal. Because he usually stayed in the apartment until mid-morning reading the Japanese press, he could not leave for a couple of hours. So he thought about the uncertainties and risks ahead, and once more reviewed the questions critical to his survival.

Had the KGB penetrated the CIA at a sufficiently high level to recapture him?

Of all the fates he imagined, this he feared most. He feared death less than the animalistic torture and degradation that would precede it, in the chambers of Lefortovo Prison in Moscow. He visualized the photograph of a Russian colonel, drugged and bound like a mummy, being carted aboard a Soviet aircraft in Istanbul, after he tried to defect to the British. The KGB made sure its trainees remembered that a Soviet agent high in British intelligence, Harold A. R. Philby, had warned the Russians. It could happen again, if a KGB agent were emplaced well enough within the CIA in Washington. The agent could contend quite reasonably that the CIA should invest at least a dozen hours to ensure that Levchenko was not a provocateur, or to determine whether he might be persuaded to remain in place. Accordingly, the American embassy in Tokyo would instruct him to return the next day, and when he returned to wherever it designated, the KGB would take him alive.

The study of the Residency network he was able to make after becoming Active Measures officer and his conversation with the Resident convinced him that the KGB had no agents among U.S. intelligence personnel in Japan. About CIA headquarters in Virginia he could not be absolutely sure. The KGB in past years had penetrated British, German and Japanese intelligence and the U.S. National Security Agency. No institution in the world was a target of greater KGB disinformation and penetration efforts than the CIA. The Soviets habitually fostered rumors that the CIA had been infiltrated, and some American journalists, on their own initiative, echoed this Soviet theme. Levchenko had never had access to the ultrasecret KGB data that would definitively prove them right or wrong.

He could only apply professional logic to the data available to him, and his deductions gave him cause for hope. During his last home leave, he heard from a Line X colonel how the CIA had achieved stunning, recent penetrations of the GRU, the Ministry of Foreign Affairs, and the innermost councils of the Party itself. Visiting Tokyo early in 1979, the chief of Directorate K, responsible for infiltrating foreign services, reported that if the CIA could reach into such secret spheres of the Soviet Union, it could not be penetrated significantly— for emplacement of a high-ranking agent at CIA headquarters would have enabled the KGB to thwart the American schemes.

If he succeeded in escaping, what would he do in America, the land of the Main Enemy, the land depicted to him from childhood on as the fount of evil? Levchenko had not completely shed the encrusted prejudices of a lifetime; he did not consider American society ideal, and he guessed that perhaps there was some truth in what they said about America. After all, the best disinformation is spun around a few kernels of truth. However, Levchenko believed that in Japan he had seen the highest essence of America. Americans dictated the Japanese constitution, patterned after their own, and they imposed democracy modeled after their own. Empirical observation proved to him that Japanese democracy worked magnificently. It bestowed upon the people freedom from political repression and material want; freedom to speak, read, dissent, worship, innovate and create; freedom to honeymoon in Hawaii, to travel anywhere, even to quit and repudiate the country, if one chose. He now believed that the United States, whatever its imperfections, offered much the same freedom.

Levchenko had no idea what he would do in America. He

did know that he could no longer flee from himself, his thoughts and beliefs. Work no longer could be an opiate anesthetizing him against his feelings and convictions. The more he toiled for the KGB, the more he sensed the spirit of the KGB, the more he loathed himself for being part of it, for abetting it. He no longer could profess to worship God while doing what he understood the teachings of God to forbid. Orders to return to the Center would arrive any day now. If he complied with them, he would have to either kill himself or so openly rebel that he would be executed or put in a camp or a mental institution. That is why he was ready to give up everything he had for absolutely nothing, except the chance some way to find freedom. He would take no money from the CIA; he would ask only that the Americans let him go on his own and try to be free, honest and Christian.

Finally, Levchenko asked himself, were the Americans in Tokyo astute enough to accept him promptly, competent enough to spirit him out of Japan before the Soviets could intercede, directly and through fierce pressures upon the Japanese, to recapture him? Again he simply did not know; soon he would.

To suggest to anyone who might follow him that he was not embarked upon business of undue importance, Levchenko dressed casually in beige slacks, brown tweed jacket, white shirt and no tie. About 11 a.m. he drove from his apartment building and began clearing his path. He stopped at the press club and looked for a while at the wire service teletypes, then weaved his car through traffic to the parliament, something he often did when shaking surveillance. Emerging from the parliament about 2:30 p.m., he sped along boulevards and inched through narrow side streets. Leaving his car occasionally, he ducked in and out of book shops and department stores, discerning no surveillance.

At 8:04 p.m. Levchenko pulled into a parking lot and raised the hood of his car, pretending to examine the engine, while waiting to see if any cars joined him. None did, and, glancing conspicuously at his watch again, as if worried about being late for an appointment, he strode purposefully into the Hotel Sanno near the U.S. embassy. The hotel was a kind of U.S. officer's club and social center. Foreigners of many nationalities came frequently as guests of the Americans, and there were parties virtually every evening.

"The reception," Levchenko said to the desk clerk, who directed him down a corridor to a large room where a cocktail party was in progress. He surveyed the room and made his choice, a U.S. Navy commander. Long ago, aboard a ship in the Sea of Japan, he had observed that naval officers are trained to react quickly and decisively, and now the clock had begun to run. "Could you please tell the commander there I wish to speak to him?" he said to a sentry in the doorway.

The officer walked over, probably expecting a message from his office. "My name is Stanislav Levchenko. I am Tokyo correspondent of the Soviet magazine *New Times.* I urgently need to talk to a responsible American intelligence officer."

"Why an intelligence officer?" the commander asked.

"I have very sensitive business to discuss."

The commander hesitated momentarily, and Levchenko imagined him silently counting to ten before making his decision. "Please come with me," he said, and led Levchenko to an empty room. "It will take about 30 minutes. Please wait and relax."

Presently two strapping young military policemen appeared, closed the door, and took up positions on either side. One asked if he could bring him food or drink, and Levchenko declined. "Come on, let me buy you a beer," the soldier said.

"All right, bring me the biggest beer you can find," Levchenko replied. Soon the soldier handed him almost a quart of cold Kirin.

In somewhat less than a half hour, a tall gray-haired man, aristocratic in face, bearing and dress, entered and ordered the military policemen to step outside but remain on guard. "My name is Robert. What can I do for you?"

"Quite a bit, I hope. But before I say anything, I must be sure who you are. I apologize. Can you show me some credentials?"

The American opened his wallet and displayed identification. "Thank you," Levchenko said with relief. "I am not only a correspondent of *New Times*, I am a major of the KGB; and I request political asylum in the United States."

Robert appeared stunned. "I am supposed to know every KGB officer in Tokyo. Although I've heard your name, I never knew you were KGB. How can you prove you're a KGB officer?"

"Whether or not you believe me is your choice. I have no documents, and I have no time. I'm in danger, and the danger increases by the minute."

"I understand," Robert said. "Please try to understand my position. This doesn't happen every day. I have to report to my superior and the ambassador, and they will have to report to Washington. We have to be sure. Now, try to help me. Who is the Resident?"

"Guryanov."

"The chief of Line PR?"

"Sevastyanov."

"Who was the previous Resident?"

"Yerokhin."

"And the last chief of Line PR?"

"Pronnikov."

"Tell me, what kind of a man is Pronnikov?"

"The most dangerous, dishonorable son-of-a-bitch in the KGB."

"Perfect," Robert exclaimed, strongly gripping Levchenko's hand. "Now I have to run to the embassy. Don't worry; I'll never desert you." The military policemen came back and stood almost shoulder to shoulder behind the door. The holsters of their .45-caliber pistols were now unsnapped.

In no more than 20 minutes, Robert and a second American hurried into the room. "The United States grants you political asylum. You can leave for the States immediately. How's that for service?"

"I am really grateful," Levchenko replied. "At the same time, I am very worried. We both are professionals; we both understand that in these matters the Japanese can be difficult. Once the KGB discovers I am absent, the pressures on the Japanese to give me back will be incredible, like an avalanche. So let me just disappear. Take me to Atsugi [air base] and fly me out; anywhere out of Japan."

"I agree; that's what I will recommend. The decision is not mine, though. Right now we've got to get out of here. We can talk on the way."

The other American took the keys to Levchenko's car, so he could hide it, and Robert and Levchenko slipped out a back entrance. Driving from the hotel, Robert circled the block, ran a red light, made a U-turn and once parked a couple of minutes to watch. Every dozen blocks or so he abruptly turned right or left, then sometimes reversed directions; he did everything Levchenko so often had done.

"When are they likely to miss you?" Robert asked.

"I can't be sure; probably not until morning. It's normal for me to come home very late, so my wife will not worry until morning. The Residency might call during the night; that happens."

"When your wife awakens and finds you not there, will she call the Residency?"

"Probably not."

"What time do you usually go to the Residency?"

"If I go, it's between 10 and 11 o'clock."

"We should be gone by then."

In a fashionable suburb they parked and walked about four blocks to a large house, set back from the street behind a formal garden. An American woman, introduced only as "our friend," welcomed them with excellent cognac and offered dinner. The American who had hidden Levchenko's car arrived, took his Soviet passport, and assured Robert they had not been followed. Levchenko assumed they had been trailed by a U.S. countersurveillance squad, probably it was now deployed around the house.

He could not have asked for more than had been done thus far. The Americans had accepted him with professional alacrity; their ability to secure from Washington an almost instantaneous guarantee of asylum astonished him. Yet he was still not beyond reach of the KGB, and trying to sleep, he tumbled about in nightmarish semi-consciousness, assailed by apprehensions and gargoyled images. He visualized the Residency galvanized; Pronnikov flying in to lead agents in parliament and the press; the whole Soviet propaganda apparatus mobilized to cow the Japanese into dragging him away from the Americans; Brezhnev communicating directly to Carter that the future of U.S.-Soviet relations hinged upon his return; Dobrynin confiding, in the office of Secretary of State Vance, that the situation was graver even than it appeared; Gromyko telling the American ambassador in Moscow the same; KGB Agents of Influence in Washington counseling reason, arguing against antagonizing the Japanese and further provoking the Russians over one nutty spook, when so many far more vital issues needed resolution; articles and speeches declaring that U.S. intelligence had run amok again, that it must be reined in once and for all, so that never again could it cause a dangerous international scandal by kidnapping a Soviet citizen.

He imagined other dangers. His friend, the Line X colonel, had told him of an invisible powder. Just before you meet the victim, you rub it on your hand. After you shake hands with the doomed person, you have five minutes to apply an antidote. Seven or eight days later, the person touched dies of cardiac arrest. Certainly he wouldn't shake hands; maybe, though, the KGB had something else: vapors or rays or bacteria, perfected by gifted medical researchers. Abandoning attempts to sleep, Levchenko sat on the edge of the bed and promptly vomited.

Robert, too, was up, talking frequently by phone, in code, to someone at the embassy. After a call around 3 a.m., he told Levchenko he had to drive to the embassy, something too sensitive to discuss elliptically by phone had arisen. Reading the question and fear in Levchenko's eyes, he said, "We will never give you back. I and my friends would resign on the spot and take you out ourselves, before we'd obey such an order. But there will be no such order; it's something procedural, I'm sure."

Dawn was breaking when Robert came back and advised that the State Department, or some Washington committee, had overruled the plan to fly from Atsugi by military aircraft; instead, they would have to take a commercial flight. He gave Levchenko his passport, stamped with a U.S. visa, and a first-class ticket aboard a Pan American flight scheduled to depart Narita Airport that day. "I'm going with you," Robert said. "For me, it is an honor."

"There will be trouble at the airport," Levchenko warned.

"You have a bona fide passport, a visa, a reservation and a ticket. They cannot stop us."

"They will try."

At the airport, they checked in for their flight, cleared immigration and customs without incident, and with only half an hour or so left before departure, Levchenko's anxieties seemed groundless. Then, just before they reached Pan Am's first-class lounge, he recognized two Japanese counterintelligence officers, and they recognized him. "They will instantly alert all their forces," he told Robert. "They will also notify the Foreign Office, and you can be sure that once the Foreign Office knows, the KGB will be on its way."

Soon a dozen or so Japanese swarmed into the lounge, quickly followed by five or six more. "Okay. We have problems," Robert said. "Let's keep calm and deal with them."

The senior Japanese addressed Robert in English. "We wish to speak to this gentleman."

"This gentleman is departing for the United States. He has an American visa. The plane leaves in ten minutes," Robert answered.

"We are very sorry, but this is still Japanese territory. We intend to speak with this gentleman, and, excuse me, we do not wish for you to listen or participate in our discussions. So please remove yourself to another area of the lounge and wait." A wall of Japanese forced Robert and another American escort into the farthest corner.

The Japanese officer ordered Levchenko to sit down and began to interrogate him.

"Before I talk to anyone, I want to know who you are," Levchenko interrupted.

"Some of us are from the National Police Agency. Some are from the Chiba Prefectural Police Headquarters. Some are security officers here to protect you."

"I see no reason to talk to police. I am not a criminal. I have stolen nothing. And I can look after my own security."

"If you desire to leave this country, then you will talk to us. Who are you?"

"You know who I am."

"What is your job?"

"As you well know, I am Tokyo correspondent for *New Times* magazine."

"Why are you going to the United States?"

"I have requested and received political asylum from the United States government. I will not discuss the matter further."

"Are you a KGB officer?"

"I told you, I am a magazine correspondent. I am going to the United States with the permission of the United States government. But you are preventing me from leaving. My plane already has gone."

"It is all right. You are sitting comfortably in an elegant lounge, and there are more flights today." For more than an hour the Japanese interrogated Levchenko, asking the same questions and receiving the same answers, without extracting an admission that he belonged to the KGB.

"This is pointless," Levchenko finally said. "We are all merely repeating ourselves. The second flight has left, and you are detaining me against my will. Do you intend to hold me prisoner?"

Intimidation having failed, the Japanese attempted confidential courtesy. "No, no. You have some influential friends here. But we have a consular agreement with the Soviet Union. We must notify them and give them an opportunity to meet you before we may allow you to go."

"I am surprised that a police officer should be concerned about Soviet sensibilities. As I understand, problems of this nature usually are the concern of the Foreign Office."

"Representatives of the Foreign Ministry are on their way."

Levchenko asked to visit the rest room, and four Japanese gathered about to escort him. "I don't need your help," he said. "I can manage to urinate on my own." They followed, nevertheless.

A cordon of Japanese prevented Robert and his companion from listening to the interrogation or approaching Levchenko. However, a Japanese civilian sat near enough to listen, and twice, when Robert left to make telephone calls, the civilian went outside with him and reported what was being said. And in the rest room Robert stood beside Levchenko, in defiance of Japanese orders.

"As you can see, the story is becoming rather long," Levchenko said in a low voice. "The Foreign Office has been notified, so you can expect a gang from the Residency before long."

Robert whispered, "Our minister counselor is calling the foreign minister personally, and we have men en route. Just keep being yourself. You are superb."

Among the four Foreign Ministry representatives who tried to interrogate Levchenko was a Japanese against whom he had worked in Moscow while an agent of the Second Chief Directorate. Without referring to their past acquaintance, the Japanese said in Russian, "We are not against you, but according to our consular agreement, the Russians have every right to see you before you leave. Otherwise, the Japanese government will be in serious trouble."

"I don't think Japan, the second greatest capitalist country in the world, has to bow and tremble before the Soviets or to be frightened by minor problems with them."

"All problems would be solved if you would simply meet the Soviets and tell them the reasons for your decision."

"A meeting would be a scandal for you and a disaster for me. No."

As a calculated insult, Levchenko ordered champagne for himself, aware that the Japanese could not drink on duty, and remarked about how delicious it tasted. But it was all show, for the third flight to America had left. He was afraid, and the gravity of Robert across the lounge compounded his fear.

While the Japanese conferred among themselves, the senior Foreign Office emissary received a telephone call. Levchenko saw his face turn taut, then crimson. Obviously humiliated, he returned, bowed, and announced tersely: "You are free to leave the soil of Japan. We shall immediately escort you to the plane."

As Levchenko, Robert and some 20 Japanese proceeded across the tarmac and up the steps to a Pan Am 747, a tiny police officer from the Chiba Prefecture kept appealing, "Please, please, tell us just one thing, just one thing. Who is the chief KGB officer working against Japan? Against whom should Japan be most on guard?"

Just before stepping into the aircraft, Levchenko paused and, with an air of ostentatious secrecy, said, "Pronnikov." To his consternation, and the amusement of passengers inside the plane, the beaming police officer exuberantly kissed Levchenko on the cheek.

As Levchenko entered the cabin, the little policeman shouted, "Pronnikov, right?"

"Right. Pronnikov. Vladimir Pronnikov."

By now, Russians had piled out of three illegally parked cars and fanned out in the terminal, searching. A group of rather tough-looking American "businessmen," who for more than two hours had lounged around the international departure gate, dispersed and walked away, their business completed. The men from the Residency had come a few minutes too late. Levchenko and Pan American Flight 2 were airborne, bound for Los Angeles.

Levchenko's sole material possessions consisted of the clothes he wore, yen worth about $30, and a $100 bill that one of the Americans had shoved in his hand, for pocket money, just before takeoff in Tokyo. But on his first day in Virginia,

Levchenko declared that he would not accept a penny from the CIA or any U.S. government agency. He understood that in return for asylum and to establish his bona fides, he must truthfully answer questions about his life, career and motivations. He also understood that in answering he would have to reveal certain KGB secrets, and he volunteered to talk freely about Pronnikov. However, he would betray none of the decent officers he had known in the KGB, nor any of his agents in the Tokyo Residency network, because he felt personal and moral obligations to them. He demanded an official CIA pledge that it would never exploit the information he did provide to harm any individual. Finally, he insisted upon being allowed to consult and confess to a Russian Orthodox priest. If the CIA could not accede to these conditions, then he would appeal to the United Nations, explaining his status, and requesting its assistance in relocating him in another non-Communist country.

The CIA officers who talked to Levchenko in his first days in Virginia thought his position naïve and, in light of his professed hatred of the KGB and the Soviet system, full of logical contradictions. But they also believed he was sincere. A CIA psychiatrist and another psychiatrist with Top Secret clearance characterized him as a highly intelligent, deeply moral and profoundly troubled man. Two polygraph examinations showed that he was being utterly honest. And case officers, whom Levchenko knew as Rob and Mr. Binns, saw him as a Christian spiritually scarred and sapped of all reserves by the years of hell from which he had just escaped. They successfully contended that any hint of coercion would provoke in him revolt that would bring about his destruction. He must be given time to restore and think for himself. His cooperation could never be secured unless, on reflection, he offered it of his own free will. So the CIA agreed to his terms, and Mr. Binns told him, "Tell us as much as your conscience allows. We ask no more."

Practical problems quickly arose. Levchenko asked that officers and bodyguards assigned to his Virginia apartment be

withdrawn; they made him feel like a captive. The CIA elected to take a chance and withdrew them. The problem of
persuading him to take some money remained. The CIA could
stock the apartment with food, drink, books, newspapers, records, and daily necessities. But without money, Levchenko
was a veritable prisoner, which was not healthy. Rob told him
that the U.S. government customarily pays independent con-
sultants a daily fee ranging from $50 to $200. As Levchenko
actually was working as a consultant, could he not accept
some fee? Belatedly, Levchenko agreed to accept $50 for each
day he had to talk to the CIA. Upon receipt of his first payment
of $250, he gave Rob $100 and told him to send it to the
American who had handed him the $100 bill in Tokyo.

At first Levchenko rejected Soviet demands for a personal
confrontation in Washington. To hell with them; he never
wanted to see anyone from the KGB again, and the CIA
assured him he was free to refuse. However, Ambassador
Dobrynin reiterated the demand to Secretary of State Vance,
and hinted that unless the State Department produced Levchenko, the Russians would go to President Carter. Simply to
ease the plight of American officials, Levchenko reluctantly
agreed to confront the Soviets.

Instead of a heavy-handed operative from Line KR, the KGB
sent a suave colonel, Aleksandr Bessmertnykh, minister counselor of the Soviet embassy. He eschewed threats and intimidation, and concentrated upon cryptically asking Levchenko
to cryptically signal to him how much, if anything, he had
disclosed for at the time the KGB was genuinely confused.
The CIA was still digesting and cautiously verifying the intelligence Levchenko provided, without taking any action upon
it. The KGB, which had damped down all operations in Tokyo
while waiting to see what happened, saw nothing happen.

In essence, Levchenko told the KGB emissary that he had
fled for personal reasons and his decision was irreversible,
but that he did not intend to engage in any anti-Soviet activities. From the interview the KGB could have concluded that
Levchenko had betrayed relatively little.

By mid-December 1979, Levchenko had told the CIA all he intended to tell, and he prepared to go off on his own in quest of a job. There the professional story of Major Stanislav Aleksandrovich Levchenko might well have ended, had not the KGB fallen back upon its old and natural ways.

Levchenko had finally decided to flee the KGB upon recognizing that if he remained, he would disintegrate. He could be of no more use to his wife and son; his death or imprisonment would not benefit and might even harm them. Throughout, he had striven to protect his wife by withholding his thoughts from her, even when by so doing he seemed to be cruelly withholding his love. He knew that her maternal and familial instincts were so powerful that she would never flee the Soviet Union with him, leaving their son and her relatives behind. If he had shared his thoughts and feelings with her, he would have made her a criminal; it would have been her duty to report them, and this she would not have done. If, during the intensive interrogations that would ensue after his flight, she could honestly state that she never gleaned the least intimation of his intentions, then she would be innocent. Levchenko had no illusions that the first months would be easy for her. The interrogations would be long, withering, psychologically brutal, and numerous. But once the KGB convinced itself that she was ignorant of his intentions and uninvolved in his ideological insurrection, it would leave her alone. After all, the days of Stalin were over. Now, at least on paper, there were laws precluding children from being brought to the dock with their accused fathers, laws prohibiting punishment of innocent relatives for the crimes of their kin.

However, early in 1980, Levchenko managed to telephone Natalia by calling around 2 a.m. Moscow time, when KGB controls were weakest. And now he learned that the spirit of Stalin still lives.

"Hello, Natasha?"

"Yes, yes. Stas, is it you?"

"It is I."

"Oh, greetings. Oh, oh!"

The burst of happiness prompted by his voice gave way to tears, as Natalia, in answer to his questions, revealed the torment into which she had been plunged. Authorities had confiscated their bank account, consisting mainly of savings deposited from her earnings, and their car. She had been denied employment, except for a part-time teaching job, which paid 73 rubles monthly, less than half the average wage and too little to sustain life for very long. Their son had been expelled from school. The target of organized harrassment and ridicule in a new school, he had developed high blood pressure and a stomach disorder that caused frequent vomiting. Everyone, even relatives, shunned her; no one would talk to her, except her aged mother. She had tried to earn money as a part-time typist, but she could not afford to replace her broken eyeglasses, and without them could not see well enough to type. No, she had received none of his letters or packages or money orders.

"I was told that all of us are guilty under the law. . . . We are living in great poverty. . . . Nobody can advise or help us. . . . We have lost everybody. . . . The only person I have left is my mother. . . . I am terrified to talk. . . . My situation is extremely difficult. . . . It's near the end."

Levchenko cried out, pleading with Natalia to denounce him, to say anything about him, to do anything against him that would help her.

"I can't do anything like that; I can't be a hypocrite," she said, weeping. "I would not agree to some sort of compromise."

To the Soviet embassy in Washington, Levchenko mailed a veiled warning, easily understood by the KGB: He held large reserves of Soviet secrets. Unless the persecution of his wife and son ceased, he would begin expending them in a personal war that would last as long as he lived. He listed an accommodation address and invited a reply.

The instincts of a soldier and fighter that years before made Levchenko willing to undertake a suicide mission in England welled up within him. At the same time, his attitudes toward the United States began to change. Consistent with its original conclusion that Levchenko must be allowed to think his way to freedom, the CIA told him he was at liberty to meet whomever he pleased. It adjured him to be cautious for the sake of security, but imposed no restrictions. Through Rob, he met a number of former intelligence personnel who spoke Russian and understood Russian history and culture, and he found their view of the Russian tragedy similar to his own. While they did not try to impress upon him any particular attitudes toward the United States, they did point him toward realities that contradicted the standard myths of Soviet propaganda. He increasingly saw for himself that American democracy, like Japanese democracy, by and large worked. The freedom of religion and tolerance of religion among those who themselves did not subscribe to religion also affected him. While remaining faithful to the Russian Orthodox Church, he found solace in Catholic, Methodist and Baptist services, which he attended with the blessings of his own priest.

Violating orthodoxy, and without consulting superiors, Rob arranged for Levchenko to meet Viktor Belenko, who had landed the MiG–25 in Japan while Levchenko was there. Bright, daring, ebullient, and irrepressible, Belenko had integrated himself perfectly into American society. He had come to comprehend its functioning better than most native Americans. By car, Belenko crisscrossed the continent, showing Levchenko small towns, the great farmlands and neat cities of the Midwest, the ranches of Idaho and Montana, the wineries and orchards of California, and San Francisco. From San Francisco, Levchenko wrote Rob a note in which he referred to "this awesome and magnificent land of freedom."

Having received no Soviet response to his ultimatum, Levchenko again telephoned Natalia in Moscow. Her plight worsened weekly. She was literally starving, having shrunk from 120 to 90 pounds. Their son, afflicted with dangerously high blood pressure, had run away, to escape the persecution at school. No one dared speak to her. She had been told that she would have to appear at his trial, whether only as a witness or as a co-defendant she did not know. "I am without hope. . . . I am lost. . . . I am only a grain of sand." And then his calls to Moscow went unanswered.

Telling Belenko of her last words, Levchenko wept. "How can you be surprised?" Belenko said. "You know them even better than I. You can never make peace with them. You can only fight them."

With a disciplined fury, Levchenko began briefing the CIA, demanding to work twelve hours a day, seven days a week. He unraveled the entire Tokyo network, constructed by the KGB over decades. He identified important KGB agents beyond Japan. He definitively explained and documented the Soviet doctrine and methodology of Active Measures and disinformation. He charted, as had no one before, the precise interrelationship among the Politburo, the International Department and the KGB. He named many people in the KGB who loathed the KGB, and many who are the most effective in the KGB. He volunteered analyses, some adjudged so profound and important that they were submitted to the President.

In the headquarters and field offices of the FBI, in hidden conference rooms of the CIA, at Air Force Bases, at the State Department and the National War College, in Congress, and at the White House, Levchenko spoke about the KGB, about himself and the Russian people, about tyranny and liberty. His eloquence and sincerity sometimes caused professionally emotionless men to spontaneously stand and applaud in tribute. Always, he asked Americans to understand that the Russian people are the enemy of no one, that the KGB is the enemy of everyone.

Few men understand the KGB better than Levchenko; few, if any, have done as much as Stanislav Aleksandrovich Levchenko to wound the KGB. He understands that, as a consequence, he will always be a hunted man. "Maybe someday they will find me. But as long as I breathe, I will fight them. Unless we fight them, they will degrade all human beings into simple grains of sand."

V

THE
MAIN
ENEMY

$\mathbf{A}$LL THAT Stanislav Levchenko did in Japan, all that he saw others in the Residency do, the KGB does daily in the United States—except on a more grandiose scale. Approximately 400 officers of the KGB and its military subsidiary, the GRU, are permanently stationed in New York, Washington and San Francisco, to spy and conduct Active Measures. Their labors are abetted by hundreds more officers of the Cuban, Bulgarian, East German, Polish, Czechoslovakian, and Hungarian intelligence services, which function as KGB auxiliaries. Some 6000 Soviet nationals annually visit the United States, and a substantial number are tasked by the KGB with special assignments. Additionally, Soviet Bloc nations maintain in America more than 20 legally incorporated companies as fronts or bases for espionage and subversion.

In the United States, as in Japan, an overriding objective of both KGB Active Measures and espionage is acquisition of advanced technology urgently needed to sustain Soviet military and industrial power. At the Center, Levchenko was told that the value of data stolen each year by the Scientific and Technical Directorate (Directorate T) is much greater than the annual costs of operating the entire KGB. Levchenko was in no position to evaluate this claim, and he wondered if it were not merely a bureaucratic boast, contrived to justify larger KGB budgets. Voluminous empirical evidence now available shows that the statement, far from being an exaggeration, probably was an understatement. The fact is that the Soviet Union, largely through the KGB, has succeeded in transforming American research, development, inventiveness and productive genius into a major national resource of the Soviet state. In consequence, American taxpayers in the next few years will be required to spend billions of dollars to offset Soviet weapons that would not be in place or in prospect without American technology. Numerous cases, which can be reconstructed from confessions, court records and other juridical proceedings, illustrate the multifarious means by which the KGB has accomplished and continues to accomplish this singular feat.

Until adversity and tragedy befell him in middle age, William Holden Bell had lived a reasonably successful and happy life. Born May 14, 1920, in Seattle, Bell enlisted in the Navy at age 18 and was aboard a minesweeper at Pearl Harbor when the Japanese attacked. He served honorably and well throughout the war, suffering wounds at Iwo Jima. After the war he married, had two sons and a daughter, earned a degree in physics from UCLA and, in 1950, went to work for the Hughes Aircraft Corporation in Los Angeles.

Hughes has long been a principal defense contractor and a leading innovator of new technology, and Bell took advantage of the professional opportunities it offered to become an expert on military radars. From 1962 to 1965, he managed major Hughes projects in Europe, and the company reassigned him there in 1974, with larger responsibilities. In 1974 the value of the dollar vis-à-vis European currencies declined and consequently the cost of living in Europe so skyrocketed that Bell exhausted all his savings. Additionally, his marriage disintegrated, and an acrimonious divorce that took away most of his assets obligated him to pay $200 a week in alimony.

Returning to Los Angeles in March 1976, Bell felt himself shunted aside at Hughes in favor of younger men and judged that his prospects for career advancement were bleak. The Internal Revenue Service disallowed large deductions he had claimed during his overseas assignment, and four separate IRS offices hounded him for overdue taxes. Overwhelmed by debt, he filed for bankruptcy.

On a camping expedition in Mexico, Bell's 18-year-old son Kevin, to whom he was especially devoted, suffered severe burns and died.

Trying to rebuild his life, Bell married a young Belgian airline stewardess and, with her and her small son, moved into the Cross Creek Village apartment complex in Playa del Rey, Calif. On a fall weekend in 1977, Bell chanced to meet a neighbor, Marian Zacharski, who introduced himself as West Coast manager of Polamco, a Chicago company that, he said, imported and exported industrial machinery. Although Bell assumed that Polamco was an American company, the firm was owned by the Polish government, and Zacharski was a Polish intelligence officer.

Handsome, charming and mannerly, Zacharski was only 26; he could have been Bell's son. And upon learning that Bell specialized in radar fire control systems at Hughes, he began behaving toward him as a son and friend. He insisted on playing tennis daily and downgraded his superior game so that the matches would be enjoyable for Bell. Explaining that he had a generous expense account for public relations, he stopped by with small yet welcome presents. On the tennis court and over drinks or supper afterwards, he gradually came to fill in Bell's life a void created by death.

The two friends naturally discussed their work, and upon request, Bell gladly provided Zacharski with copies of unclassified Hughes publications. When Zacharski inquired about contacts in industry who might be interested in buying machinery through Polamco, Bell gave him a few names. Three or four days later, Zacharski unexpectedly appeared in the evening, thanked Bell for the contacts and, as compensation, handed him $4000 in cash. Bell was sure that his trivial service had resulted in no sales and did not warrant such a large payment. But, as the Pole knew, he needed money, and for it he signed a receipt.

In the fall of 1978, Zacharski proposed that after retirement from Hughes, Bell join Polamco as a consulting engineer. Flattered and excited, Bell saw in the proposal a gratifying new career and an end to financial concerns. He recently had completed a secret study for Hughes entitled "Covert All-Weather Gun System," and to impress Zacharski with his qualifications, he showed it to him on the tennis court. Seeing that the document was labeled SECRET, Zacharski asked to take it to his apartment where he could study it safely. Bell knew that was wrong. But after all, he rationalized, it is not uncommon for engineers being interviewed by prospective employers to divulge trade secrets.

The apartment complex at Playa del Rey was being converted to condominiums, and Zacharski asked Bell if he intended to purchase one. Bell replied that he could not possibly afford a down payment. Perhaps, Zacharski suggested, Polamco could help him since he was likely to become its employee in the future.

Early one evening in January 1979, Bell answered the ring of his doorbell. Smiling, Zacharski silently handed him an envelope filled with 70 hundred-dollar bills. Bell looked at the cash and murmured, "Thank you." A week or so later, Zacharski came again and, without a word, presented an envelope containing about $5000.

The unexpected largesse freed Bell from tormenting financial pressures, enabling him to pay his back taxes and make a down payment on a condominium. In April Zacharski gave him another unsolicited present, a Canon camera that had a zoom lens and could photograph documents frame by frame.

Then Zacharski asked a favor. His company would like to have some documents from Hughes. Could Bell photograph them? Grateful to his friend and benefactor, and lured by visions of more money, Bell agreed, consoling himself with the fiction that he merely was embarking upon industrial espionage. During the next months, he photographed hundreds upon hundreds of pages from documents that he took home with him at night and replaced at Hughes in the morning.

In September 1979 Zacharski announced that Bell must travel to Europe for "negotiations." As directed, Bell flew to Switzerland, drove to Innsbruck and registered at the Grauer Bar Hotel. As he stepped from the hotel lobby in the morning, a man approached, introduced himself as Paul and, in nearly faultless English, asked, "Are you a friend of Marian's?"(Paul was Anatoliusz Inowolski, a Polish intelligence officer posing as a trade representative in New York, who had left the United States weeks earlier.)

Driving away from the hotel with Paul and a younger Polish officer, Bell handed over three cartridges of film, which included plans for an advanced all-weather radar system. At a shopping center, the younger officer left the film with an agent in one of the stores, and they drove to an isolated area in the foothills outside Innsbruck. With his subordinate, Paul led Bell along an empty path and questioned him about his work and access at Hughes.

Abruptly, Paul stopped and showed Bell pictures of his young Belgian wife and her small son, taken near their apartment in California. "You have a lovely family," he said in a tone that chilled Bell. "Only a very few people know about the operation we're engaged in. We depend on each other for our security." Waving the pictures, he warned: "If anybody gets out of line, I personally will take care of them." The clearly implied threat against his family frightened Bell and stripped away all illusions about what he was doing. When they met again that afternoon near the Olympic ski lift, Paul asked him what he thought his future services would be worth. "Fifty thousand a year and two or three thousand a month," Bell answered.

Noncommittally, Paul gave him $5000 in $100 bills and $2000 to compensate for travel costs, together with instructions for their next meeting in Innsbruck May 7, 1980. Additionally, the Poles gave him a list of specific data to be procured at Hughes—details of an air defense missile system, the operational manual for a U.S. Army helicopter, an air defense reference handbook, and plans for a high-energy laser, radar acquisition and tracking system. Bell was amazed that the Poles knew the exact company identification numbers of the documents they listed.

Back at Hughes, Bell dutifully began fulfilling the orders, and he turned over film to Zacharski, who early in 1980 gave him two payments of $5000 each. Carrying film revealing the design of numerous advanced radar and missile systems, Bell returned to Innsbruck and on the morning of May 7, 1980, drove to the ticket office of a cable car company where Paul's younger partner greeted him. Over the mountains in the cable car, Bell passed him the film.

As they alighted from the car, Paul stepped forward to shake hands and led Bell away for a walk, leaving his lieutenant to guard against surveillance. The Poles, or rather, the KGB, had concluded that what Bell was stealing was worth even more than Bell had asked. "A decision has been made to pay you $60,000 and $3000 a month," Paul informed him. "At least at the outset, the payments will be made in gold coins."

Paul insisted that Bell obtain employment at the Defense Advanced Research Projects Agency, which sponsors research to achieve major technological breakthroughs in weaponry. And again he threatened reprisals against Bell and his family if there were any security breach.

While on a business trip to the East Coast in the summer of 1980, Bell did call to see a friend at the Defense Advanced Research Projects Agency. He hoped to gather enough courage to confess to his friend and ask his help in extricating himself from espionage. But the friend was absent. Fearing that he or his family would be liquidated, Bell continued to serve his new masters.

Each month Zacharski delivered a $5000 payment, usually in gold coins, though once he dropped cash into Bell's tennis bag near the court. In midsummer he spoke gravely. He was sure either the FBI or CIA was following him, and Bell also might be under surveillance. They should say nothing incriminating either on the telephone or in their apartments. Playing tennis on the morning of August 30, Zacharski stopped and nodded toward the nearby parking lot. "Look! There they are."

Only two cars were on the lot, each occupied by a lone driver. Bell confronted them, demanding, "Who are you, and what are you doing here?" They stared at him indifferently and said nothing, so he went to his apartment and from the window photographed the cars. He left his camera on the ledge when he returned to the court. When he came home from tennis, the camera was gone. It was a bad portent. But Bell did not know what to do except go on.

Preparing for his next meeting in Europe, Bell photographed secret and vital documents. They betrayed designs of the video correlator of the cruise missile; improvements in the TOW anti-tank missile; two light-weight tactical avionics systems; and the covert all-weather gun system.

On a stormy, forbidding morning in October 1980, Bell kept his appointment with Paul's partner in Linz, Austria, about an hour's drive from the Czechoslovakian border. They drank coffee in a workers' café, whose only other patron was a menacing-looking man dressed as a manual laborer. The Pole took the film, disappeared into the kitchen and upon returning motioned to Bell to accompany him outside. In the gloom, they strode up a narrow path to confer securely in the woods. Above a hedge, the grinning face of the man who had been in the café appeared, and Bell thought he was about to be killed. Laughing at his fright, the Pole explained that their watcher was guarding him because he was carrying so much cash, including $7000 for Bell. The officer instructed him about more documents to be copied and showed him a map of their next meeting site in Geneva.

Early in 1981 Zacharski moved to Chicago to become president of Polamco, and Bell worked on his own. As scheduled, on the morning of April 22, Bell exchanged recognition signals with a contact at the Ariana Museum, across the street from the Soviet Mission in Geneva. With him he had brought on film the most sensitive data yet stolen from Hughes—specifications of a spectacular new "quiet" radar, whose emissions cannot be detected by hostile sensors. This is the radar to be installed on the B–1 bomber and the even more revolutionary Stealth bomber. Bell also brought specifications of the F–15 fighter's "look-down, shoot-down" radar, which enables the plane to spot and destroy very low-flying aircraft or missiles from above.

Bell followed his contact into the nearby offices of the United Nations and on an elevator passed the film from his briefcase. The two men then walked to the edge of Lake Geneva where the contact gave Bell $7000 and instructions for the next meeting, which was to take place at the Museum of Anthropology in Mexico City.

The contact fairly gloated over the loot. But Bell left the rendezvous full of forebodings, fearful that he had been watched everywhere in Geneva. He was more correct than he could imagine. Alerted by Zacharski as to what Bell was delivering, the KGB had sent senior officers from Moscow to monitor the rendezvous and take immediate possession of the film. So the KGB was watching Bell wherever he went in Geneva. In turn, the CIA was now watching both Bell and the KGB officers trailing him.

By means that have not been divulged, the FBI learned that secret documents were disappearing from the Hughes Aircraft Company. Investigation conducted with the cooperation of Hughes focused upon a number of suspects, and Bell eventually became one of them. Although still lacking evidence adequate for prosecution, by the spring of 1981 the FBI was sufficiently suspicious to put him under surveillance and ask the CIA to track his movements in Europe.

When Bell reported to work at Hughes on June 23, 1981, a supervisor summoned him to a conference room. "Bill, these gentlemen are from the FBI." he said. "They would like to speak to you."

Bell slumped into a chair, buried his head in his hands and, for a while, said nothing. Then over the next six hours he confessed and ultimately agreed to help gather additional evidence against Zacharski. On June 28, wearing a body microphone, he recorded a clandestine conversation with his friend that further and conclusively proved their guilt.

On December 14, 1981, William Holden Bell stood in a federal court in Los Angeles. Because of his cooperation with the government, he was given only an eight-year sentence. But for a man of 61, eight years can be a long time.

Zacharski, then 30, was sentenced to life imprisonment, and all his appeals have been denied. The Soviet Union did all in its power to extricate him—suggesting various prisoner exchanges—for its debt to him was great. In a damage assessment submitted to the Senate Permanent Subcommittee on Investigations, the CIA revealed some of the data the KGB acquired through Zacharski and Bell. The CIA study states:

"Among the classified reports, those of prime importance to the West included: the F–15 look-down, shoot-down radar system, the quiet radar system for the B–1 and Stealth bombers, an all-weather radar system for tanks, an experimental radar system for the U.S. Navy, the Phoenix air-to-air missile, a shipborne surveillance radar, the Patriot surface-to-air missile, a towed array submarine sonar system, a new air-to-air missile, the improved HAWK surface-to-air missile and a NATO air defense system. The information in these documents put in jeopardy existing weapons and advanced future weapon systems of the United States and its allies. The acquisition of this information will save the Polish and Soviet governments hundreds of millions of dollars in R & D efforts by permitting them to implement proven designs developed by the United States and by fielding operational counterpart

systems in a much shorter time period. Specifications will
enable them to develop defensive countermeasures systems."

The arrest of William H. Bell shocked the people of Playa
del Rey, many of whom also worked in the aerospace industry.
They knew him as a model husband and father, a good and
friendly neighbor, who looked after their children as well as
his own stepson. Some of them could not bring themselves to
believe the espionage charges against him until he confessed
in open court.

If acquaintances of Bell in Playa del Rey thought him an
improbable spy, then some 50 miles to the east in Corona,
Calif., anybody who knew Walter Spawr would have been
outraged by the suggestion that he might sell out to the
Soviets. In a superbly researched article published by *New
West* magazine, author Ehud Yonay characterized him as "a
Reagan Republican, father of three, pillar of his church, and
former president of the Corona Little League." Disdainful of
bureaucracy and regimentation, Spawr indeed personified
American ingenuity, self-reliance, initiative and entrepre-
neurship. And entirely by himself in his garage workshop,
Spawr, by age 30, had learned to make something the United
States very much needed and something nobody in the Soviet
Union could make—some of the world's finest laser mirrors.

A laser projects energy through a narrow light beam that can
be used to perform delicate surgery, to control industrial
robots, and for many other purposes beneficial to mankind.
Laser beams also can guide bombs with exceeding accuracy,
and in the future they may be able to disintegrate missiles in
flight. Of all technologies, few, if any, are more important to
national security than technology pertaining to lasers.

Because high-power laser devices are big and cumbersome,
the beam must be reflected off a mirror that can be aimed
easily and precisely. Unless the mirror is perfectly smooth,
though, the beam and its energy will scatter. The metal mirror
thus is a major determinant of the force and effectiveness of a
laser weapons system.

Beginning with a few thousand dollars in savings and the

administrative help of his wife, Spawr produced mirrors so excellent that the Los Alamos National Laboratory, the Redstone Arsenal and the Naval Weapons Laboratory eagerly bought them. He also made sales to industrial customers, and through Wolfgang Weber, a free-booting West German broker of scientific wares, he sold a few mirrors to medical and industrial research centers in Europe.

In 1975, Spawr received a letter inviting him to exhibit his mirrors at a Moscow trade show sponsored by the Soviet Chamber of Commerce, and Weber emphasized the riches to be had by tapping the vast Russian market. Spawr in the fall shipped mirrors of varying sizes to Weber, who took them to the Moscow exhibition.

The Soviet Chamber of Commerce is, purely and simply, a front of the KGB and International Department, the Soviets having no internal need for a "Chamber of Commerce." The senior vice president of the Soviet Chamber of Commerce at the time was KGB General Yevgenni Petrovich Pitovranov, who during a more rigorous stage of his career in the 1950s masterminded kidnappings and assassinations in Western Europe. Scientific, technical and industrial exhibitions in the Soviet Union actually are planned and overseen by the State Scientific and Technical Committee (GNTK), which is closely intertwined with the KGB. The exhibitions allow the Soviets to assess which equipment or processes they wish to buy or steal in the future. And sometimes the Soviets are so tempted that they steal wares right on the spot in Moscow.

A former Soviet engineer, who appeared before a Senate committee under the name Joseph Arkov, testified: "I know a man in Russia who had been assigned as a security guard at a trade fair in Moscow. This assignment was the turning point of his career. In league with the KGB, the man used his position as security guard to steal several pieces of high-technology equipment. He was rewarded handsomely for his thievery. Not an expecially intelligent man, he could never have earned on his own the Ph.D. degree he subsequently was awarded. He was then made director of a department in a research institute, a position for which his training, experience and ability left him totally unqualified."

The following dialogue between Senator Sam Nunn and Arkov ensued.

Nunn: "You are saying this individual stole equipment . . . and he was rewarded for that with a Ph.D. degree?"

Arkov: "Yes."

Nunn: "Was it an honorary degree, or do they have such a thing in the Soviet Union?"

Arkov: "It is an honorary degree, and it is awarded not only academically but materially."

Nunn: "It is an honorary degree for thievery?"

Arkov: "Yes."

Rather than steal, the Soviets elected to buy Spawr's mirrors from Weber and attempt to duplicate them in their own laboratories. But because their scientists could not decipher the process by which Spawr polished them so magnificently, they could not "reverse engineer" them on their own. All they could discern was that the mirrors were far finer than any they had ever seen and would vastly increase their laser capability.

In January 1976, the Soviets, through Weber, placed an order for mirrors, and Spawr quickly put his men to work filling "the Russian order," as they called it. The mirrors were on the list of proscribed strategic items that cannot be shipped out of the United States without express Commerce Department approval. But because the order identified Weber's West German company, not the Soviet Union, as the ultimate recipient, Spawr rationalized that he did not need an export license, and he applied for none.

Meanwhile, the Soviets became so excited by what they expected to do with the mirrors that in April 1976 they ordered 29 more. All were to be water-cooled; about half were to be unusually large—up to 15.74 inches in diameter. If Spawr had any delusions about the purposes to which the Soviets intended to put his products, the nature of this order surely dispelled them. A laser beam powerful enough to disintegrate targets generates intense heat that will distend a metal mirror unless the mirror is continuously cooled by water pumped through conduits at its base. These were the kind needed for weapons and weapons research.

Now Spawr equivocated about whether to seek an export license. Finally, in May he applied for permission to sell 14 smaller mirrors to the Soviet Union. His application omitted any mention of the first Soviet order or of the 15 larger mirrors in the second. When mirrors to fulfill the first order were ready in the summer, Spawr and his wife, Frances, shipped them to Weber in Germany with fake invoices showing their value to be less than $500. Weber promptly forwarded them to Moscow.

In October, the Commerce Department for "national security reasons" categorically rejected the application Spawr had submitted in May. It wrote that "these laser mirrors . . . have important applications in the military arena." Disdainful of government interference in private business, Spawr conspired with Weber to ship the 29 additional mirrors to the Soviets through a freight forwarder in Switzerland. Again, they faked invoices and valued the mirrors at $500 or less.

Actually, the price was about $40,000—a trivial sum compared to the value the Russians received. As the Soviets indicated to Weber, they loved Spawr's mirrors. But to develop large numbers of laser weapons and conduct advanced research on a broad scale, they needed thousands of them, not just the comparative trickle obtainable through the clandestine channel running from southern California to Germany to Moscow. So, according to author Yonay, they offered to pay $1.5 million if Spawr would sell them the secrets of his production process and the necessary polishing equipment, which he would have to teach them how to use.

However, through one of Spawr's former employees, the FBI learned of his illicit exports. On March 9, 1978, Customs and Commerce Department investigators informed the Spawrs that they were under investigation and subpoenaed their records. Subsequently, a federal grand jury indicted them for conspiracy, submission of false statements to the government, and illegal exportation of laser mirrors to the Soviet Union.

Standing on his reputation for patriotism and rectitude, Spawr was a resourceful and attractive defendant. He represented himself as a hard-working, self-made small business-man victimized by mindless, bullying bureaucracy, which could not understand what it was talking about. The mirrors were innocent items of no military value and, in any case, he did not know they were destined for Russia.

Given the technical complexities of the case, the Spawrs might well have escaped, had it not been for Assistant U.S. Attorney Theodore Wai Wu of Los Angeles, probably the one man in the United States most qualified to handle the case. With his mother and sister, Wu came to the United States at age 9 from China after the Japanese confiscated his family's home. The three brought with them no possessions or money, only hope. But Wu made his way to the U.S. Naval Academy, served six years as a naval officer and then put himself through law school. A few years after graduation, he eschewed more lucrative private practice in favor of government service. A grateful patriot, he once explained: "We came here in poverty. This country gave me freedom and opportunity. I owe so much to America."

From his naval background Wu keenly comprehended all that was at stake, and he communicated forcefully to a non-technical jury. To each of Spawr's contentions, he retorted with a disprov-ing witness or document. And in a masterstroke, he introduced as a government witness Wolfgang Weber, whom he had con-verted in exchange for immunity from prosecution.

On December 12, 1980, a federal jury convicted Walter Spawr of five charges and Frances Spawr of eleven. The judge suspended all but six months of Spawr's ten-year sentence and put Mrs. Spawr on five years' probation. He ordered both to perform 500 hours of community service and fined their company $100,000. The Spawrs are appealing their convictions.

While Wu was marshaling evidence in the Spawr case, he was assigned to unravel another KGB operation of enormous magnitude and import. It was born in the mid-1970s out of acute Soviet need. The Russians continue to experience extreme difficulties in building and operating factories to manufacture integrated circuits and microcomputers. Using semi-conductors and other technology bought or stolen in America, they have managed, after a fashion, to copy the IBM 360 and 370 computers. But to establish a sound base for the production of future weapons dependent upon micro-electronics, they need to produce, reliably and efficiently, their own semi-conductors. So the Soviets charged the KGB with a formidable mission: steal all the latest American equipment and technology necessary to build a modern American integrated circuit/micro-computer plant in the Soviet Union.

On June 20, 1977, the United States received the first warning of this operation in the form of an anonymous letter written in German and mailed to the American consulate in Düsseldorf, Germany. It stated that a syndicate of companies, headed by the California Technology Corporation, was falsifying export documents and illegally shipping embargoed equipment from the United States to forbidden countries. Already they had smuggled out an underwater sonar system and accessories. But, the letter stressed, their prime objective was to assemble illicitly a "complete system for the manufacture of semi-conductors, ICs [integrated circuits] . . . which will be purchased in the U.S.A." for delivery to the Soviet Bloc. The anonymous author understood that the chief of the CTC group was a West German living in an American community called "Marinabay."

Another anonymous letter to the consulate on February 11, 1978, named six U.S. and European companies in the CTC syndicate. It reported that they were smuggling large quantities of embargoed and strategically vital equipment to the East along an underground route running through Germany and Switzerland. Specifically, the letter said that the conspirators in recent months had transferred high-technology components manufactured by IBM, RCA, Hewlett-Packard, Tektronic and Varian Palo Alto. And the author offered other specifics that could be checked relatively easily.

Translated into English, the letters were forwarded to the Compliance Division of the Office of Export Administration in the Commerce Department. This was the division of government charged by a 30-year-old statute with enforcing U.S. export laws and investigating allegations of their violation. The FBI, Defense Department, Customs Service and other government agencies might help when asked. But the Commerce Department's Compliance Division bore the legal responsibility for overseeing the laws and initiating investigations; if it did not act, ordinarily nothing was done. Even though the threat to national security posed by technology transfer had never been as great in American history, in 1978 the Compliance Division had fewer than 10 inspectors and only about 25 personnel. Few had any meaningful background in criminal investigation or in science, technology, intelligence, or Soviet affairs. The division had no formal training program, not even a manual telling personnel what they were supposed to do. And as late as spring 1979, the Commerce Department was far more interested in promoting "trade" and détente with the Soviet Union than in stanching the hemorrhage of secret technology to the Soviets and thereby risking troublesome Cold War incidents.

Someone familiar with the KGB operation had sent warnings so explicitly detailed that their validity could be proven or disproven quickly. But the Compliance Division failed to act and ignored the letters; and it let nobody else know about them.

A competent, elementary investigation at the time would have shown: The California Technology Corporation and other companies named in the anonymous letters had been incorporated by Werner Jergen Bruchhausen, a West German not in "Marinabay" but in Marina del Rey, Calif. All of the companies existed only on paper; none had any visible assets; none did what it purported to do. In Los Angeles, the chief officer of CTC, which was to reincarnate itself under 18 different corporate titles, was Anatoli Maluta (alias Tony Metz), born January 25, 1920, Kharkov, Russia. His only employee was Sabina Dorn Tittel, a young German woman who was listed as an officer of many of the companies.

A serious professional investigation would have disclosed more: Bruchhausen was the head or founder of 16 different companies in America and Europe, and he dealt often with the Soviets. Maluta and Tittel were the beneficiaries of a steady flow of cash emanating from mysterious origins. For example, in 1979 Maluta spent $190,358.66 in cash to make 17 purchases of gold and silver coins from Jonathon's Coin, Inc. in Inglewood, Calif. In 1978 and 1979 Tittel made a $198,400 down payment on a $295,000 house in Rancho Palos Verdes; a $49,345 down payment on a $126,000 condominium in Palm Desert; a $19,400 down payment on a $92,000 house in Torrance; and a $15,700 down payment on a $33,000 house in New Cuyama. She also bought a new Mercedes-Benz 450 SLC, paying $41,595 in cash and a cashier's check.

Awareness of these facts would surely have caused the Compliance Division to conclude that perhaps something was odd about the CTC syndicate, Bruchhausen, Maluta and Tittel. And such awareness doubtless would have caused the Compliance Division to take much more seriously yet another warning received in April 1979.

The administrative officer of the Perkin-Elmer Company in Wilton, Conn., Robert Markin, was advised that CTC had ordered sophisticated semi-conductor manufacturing equipment costing more than $150,000. Export of the equipment, marketed under the name Micralign, to the Soviet Bloc was illegal, and it could not be exported anywhere without express Commerce Department approval. Markin told the Commerce Department he had learned that the Soviets so desperately wanted Micralign that they were offering millions for it. Consequently, Perkin-Elmer had looked into the California Technology Corporation and decided it was simply a front for a group that intended to transship the sensitive semi-conductor equipment to the Soviet Bloc.

Eight days later, a Compliance Division representative in-

terviewed Maluta, who had now changed the name of the
CTC syndicate to Consolidated Protection Development Corporation. Feigning ignorance of complicated laws, Maluta
said that his company was quite small and did not itself export
items. Rather, it served as a broker, locating suppliers for
foreign customers. Somebody in Düsseldorf wanted the Micralign system for sale to a West German customer. No, he did
not have any documentation of the order; he took it by phone.
But as the government was so concerned, he too was worried.
Anatoli Maluta did not wish to involve himself in anything
questionable. Therefore, he would cancel the Micralign order. In May the Compliance Division ascertained from Perkin-Elmer that the order had been cancelled, and decided that
no further action was required.

But in January 1980 the Fairchild Test Systems Group in
San Jose wrote the Commerce Department raising questions
about Maluta and asking for guidance as to whether it should
deliver $740,000 worth of sensitive semi-conductor equip-
ment to him. The next month, Phillip Gohr, security manager
for the Watkins-Johnson Company in Palo Alto, conveyed his
anxieties about the CTC syndicate: "Since they have changed
names frequently, we are concerned that there may be a
reason. Could you please check on their current name and
past identities and advise me by telephone." Gohr also cited a
Dun & Bradstreet report of January 1980 that described Maluta's outfit as a manufacturer of surveillance equipment for the
Air Force, Army and Atomic Energy Commission.

Finally the Compliance Division put its most experienced
investigator, Robert Rice, on the case. In Palo Alto, Gohr
informed him that Watkins-Johnson had pending orders total-
ing $983,663 from Maluta. The largest was for a $700,000
microwave receiving and antenna system designed to intercept communications. Maluta also ordered a $258,000 micro-
wave system; he claimed it was to be used for intrusion
detection at the Fort Huachuca Army base in Arizona, but
Gohr doubted such a complex, advanced system was needed
there. Gohr was worried also about the CTC syndicate fre-

quent name changes, its under-capitalization, abnormal credit arrangements and, most of all, the ultra-sophisticated nature of equipment it was always trying to buy.

From Gohr's office in Palo Alto, Rice drove to nearby Sunnyvale and there discovered further grounds for alarm. He talked to Robert Chamberlain of Applied Materials, Inc., the sales representative of Gasonics, Inc., one of the few companies in the world that manufactures high-pressure oxidation systems. Such systems, trademarked Hipox, control the atmosphere and temperature during conversion of silicon into a wafer or chip, onto which integrated circuits are impressed. Without Hipox, chips simply cannot be produced, and the rest of an integrated circuit factory is useless. Chamberlain reported that Maluta had ordered two Hipox systems and, when challenged about their ultimate use, pledged that they would be utilized only by his company in California. Nevertheless, Chamberlain was dubious.

Late that same afternoon, Rice spoke to the president of Gasonics, Monte Toole, who stated that Maluta had refused to supply any information about the intended use of the systems except to say they were destined for a top secret installation at Fort Huachuca, Arizona.

Queried by Rice, a senior intelligence officer at Fort Huachuca reviewed the records of both the Army and a nearby Immigration and Naturalization Service installation. Neither had ever ordered anything from Maluta nor done any business with him whatsoever.

Rice now flew to Los Angeles and briefed Assistant U.S. Attorney Wu about his findings. Both men felt the Commerce Department was incapable of sustaining the kind of massive investigation that must be started at once. Cutting through bureaucratic red tape, Wu consulted Kenneth Ingleby, special agent in charge of the Customs Investigations Office at Terminal Island, California. Ingleby agreed to make available 15 Customs investigators, and later the Internal Revenue Service volunteered to lend Wu four of its best men. These Customs and IRS agents were trained, armed investigators empowered to make arrests and use firearms which, as it turned out, would be needed.

To gather evidence, Wu chose to allow Maluta to continue illegal shipments and to trace them with assistance from West German authorities. On March 25, 1980, Gasonics advised that it had sent the two Hipox systems to Maluta, who said that because fire had damaged his (nonexistent) plant in the San Fernando Valley, he would store them temporarily at the Kamino International Transport warehouse in Inglewood. Kamino willingly cooperated in the investigation.

At Maluta's instructions, Kamino on May 5 delivered crates containing the Hipox systems to Los Angeles International Airport. The accompanying Shipper's Export Declarations stated that the crates contained "furnaces" worth $3445 and that their destination was a company in Bad Reichenhall, West Germany.

As Maluta falsified and undervalued the shipment by $259,129, Wu had legal grounds to act, and he informed the Compliance Division at the Commerce Department that he planned to remove the Hipox systems and substitute sand. When the Compliance Division objected and refused to pay the cost of flying sand to Germany, the Customs Service underwrote the freight charges.

A Lufthansa plane carried the phony Hipox shipment to Munich; from there it was trucked to a Vienna freight forwarder representing Dietmar Ulrichshofer. At his behest, the forwarder arranged to fly the equipment aboard KLM flight 940 to Amsterdam June 6. There, it was to be transferred to Aeroflot flight 702, departing for Moscow June 7, for final delivery to Mashpriborintorg, a Soviet purchasing agency. However, on the night of June 3, Ulrichshofer went to the Vienna storage area and opened one of the crates to insert a manual Maluta had delivered. He found only sand. At 1:10 a.m. June 4, he cancelled the scheduled shipment to Amsterdam.

Meanwhile, U.S. and West German Customs agents seized the records of Bruchhausen-Maluta companies in California and Europe. Scores of documents and telex messages proved that everything Maluta illegally exported from the United States went to the Soviet Bloc. The records, together with numerous interrogations conducted by the investigative team in Europe and California, ultimately established that Maluta had made at least 300 shipments of embargoed semi-conductor and electronic equipment worth more than $10.5 million.

Kept under surveillance, Maluta and Tittel were arrested as they sat in a parked car in Palm Desert, Calif., August 19, 1981. There were three pistols in the car. Prosecuted by Wu, Maluta was convicted of 13 counts of conspiracy, falsification of Customs declarations and unlawful exportation. The judge sentenced him to five years' imprisonment and fined him $60,000. He was released on bond pending appeal. Tittel, who pleaded guilty to export and income-tax violations, received a two-year sentence and a $25,000 fine. Bruchhausen and his confederate in Austria, Ulrichshofer, also were indicted, but they remain fugitives beyond the reach of American law.

The KGB operation had ended, but not before it achieved a coup without known precedent. Dr. Lara Baker of the Los Alamos National Laboratory concluded that the Soviets acquired everything they needed to build an entire semi-conductor factory.

"Because of CTC, the United States gave up technology, much of which the Soviets could not have obtained elsewhere," Dr. Baker said. "The Soviets purchased everything they needed for their plant. . . . They showed no interest in purchasing production equipment that was not state of the art.* The sequence in which they purchased things and the quantities indicate the production plant would be of medium size and capable of delivering a high-quality product . . . High-quality integrated circuits are the basis of modern military

---

*American equipment smuggled to the Soviet Union included: saws for cutting silicon crystals, gear for making masks for integrated circuit production, plotters to draw the circuits, basic computer-aided design system, scribers for separating integrated circuits on wafers, testers, bonders for connecting leads to integrated circuits, and even equipment for finally packaging the circuits.

electronics. The production tooling and equipment obtained by the Soviets will significantly improve their capability to produce such circuits."

Dr. Baker noted that in their meticulously planned operation, the Soviets were careful to procure four of each item they needed. Thus, for some time they will have spare parts for their new semi-conductor plant—made in America, delivered by the KGB and assembled in the U.S.S.R.

Striking as the Bruchhausen-Maluta operation might seem, it is merely one example of how the Soviets systematically have looted the American semi-conductor industry to feed their armament industry, which would be faltering technologically without U.S. sustenance. In the looting, the KGB has sometimes employed the same False Flag techniques Stanislav Levchenko used in Japan.

An Israeli national, Jacob Kelmer, served as the principal agent in an especially successful False Flag operation spanning several years.* Having obtained a master's degree in electrical engineering from Rensselaer Polytechnic Institute, Kelmer returned to Haifa and founded DEK Electronics, ostensibly to represent American firms in Israel. The Commerce Department in 1971 allowed him to buy high-frequency American oscilloscopes, which can be used to test nuclear weapons, lasers and other military equipment; the department believed his claim that they were for Israeli customers. However, Kelmer had them shipped to Vienna, where they disappeared, doubtless into the Soviet Bloc. Because he refused to explain their disposition, the Commerce Department in 1972 debarred him and his company from doing further business in the United States.

A few months later, Peter Virag, a Hungarian Jew who had emigrated to Canada and become a lawyer in Montreal, received a visit from an American acquaintance. The American said he had a cousin in the Israeli army who needed to

*For many details of this case, the author is indebted to R. Jeffrey Smith, who wrote an excellent account published by *Science* magazine, January 23, 1981.

purchase electronic equipment secretly; he asked if Virag would be willing to help. Virag agreed to meet the "cousin," who turned out to be Kelmer. "Are you ready to help the state of Israel?" he asked. Virag said that he was.

As a lawyer, Virag easily incorporated a new company, DeVimy Test Lab, Inc., whose purported business was the testing and manufacture of integrated circuits. He told one and all that the company was being established with funds from European investors and a New York bank and that he had leased a plant site near Montreal. With this legend, Virag commenced purchasing American equipment specified by Kelmer, and because U.S. firms may ship even strategic items to Canadian customers without an export license or government review, he obtained whatever he sought without difficulty. And the Soviets supplied him bountiful, untraceable funds from two Swiss bank accounts.

Virag first purchased from a California concern a reaction chamber for production of arsenide, which is used in microwave communications devices. He promptly shipped it to Amsterdam; from there it was transferred to East Berlin. When a representative of the California company arrived to assist in installation of the chamber in Montreal, Virag told him that for tax reasons he had decided to build his plant in the Netherlands.

Guided by Kelmer, Virag proceeded to buy the production components the Soviets needed for a semi-conductor plant. From the GCA Corporation in Bedford, Mass., he bought, for several hundred thousand dollars, one of the world's best photorepeaters, which etch circuits on semi-conductor chips. Customarily, GCA dispatches engineers to help purchasers install a photorepeater but Virag explained that the equipment would be stored in a warehouse pending completion of his plant. The day after the photorepeater arrived by truck in Montreal, Virag and "Major" Kelmer, as he represented himself to his Canadian agent, transshipped it to Prague via Amsterdam.

For $40,000 he bought an autoprober, which tests contact

points on semi-conductor chips, and transferred it to Warsaw
by way of Amsterdam. A California company verging on bankruptcy gladly sold him two computer simulators, and they
were consigned to a Vienna freight forwarding firm.

Whether Virag ever realized that all his purchases were
being diverted from their European destinations to the Soviet
Bloc rather than to Israel is unclear. Regardless, between 1973
and 1977 he and Kelmer supplied the Soviets with the basic
components of a semi-conductor plant, the best the United
States could make. They might still be doing so had the
Soviets not become greedy.

The GCA photorepeater so pleased the Soviets that they
demanded another. Virag placed the order but the company
began asking questions. What happened to the first photorepeater? Why had Virag not called for the standard technical
assistance in installing it? He explained that labor problems
and political unrest had prevented the opening of his plant.
Then why did he need another photorepeater? Dissatisfied
with the answers, GCA in early 1977 told the Commerce
Department about its suspicions. An ensuing investigation
soon exposed both DeVimy Test Lab and Kelmer.

But closure of this one subterranean channel into the U.S.
semi-conductor industry troubled the Soviets only slightly. As
the record demonstrates, they simply opened another through
Bruchhausen and Maluta. Doubtless there have been many
others. The fact is that for more than a decade the Soviets have
looted the U.S. semi-conductor industry of virtually whatever
they wanted and could not make. The enormous dimensions
of the U.S. losses are indicated in the CIA analysis submitted
to the Senate Permanent Subcommittee on Investigations in
May 1982.

"Western equipment and technology have played a very
important, if not crucial, role in the advancement of Soviet
microelectronic production capabilities," the analysis states.
"This advancement comes as a result of over ten years of
successful acquisitions—through illegal, including clandestine, means—of hundreds of pieces of Western microelectron-

ic equipment worth hundreds of millions of dollars to equip their military-related manufacturing facilities. These acquisitions have permitted the Soviets systematically to build a modern microelectronic industry which will be the critical basis for enhancing the sophistication of future Soviet military systems for decades. The acquired equipment and know-how, if combined, could meet 100 percent of the Soviet's high-quality microelectronic needs for military purposes, or 50 percent of all their microelectronic needs."

The United States enjoys a wide lead over the rest of the world in computer software, the art of programming computers to meet user requirements. The Soviet Union lags well behind the U.S. in software, and in the judgment of some experts, even Japan is behind several years. And future computer development depends in large part upon software. Hence, repair of Soviet deficiencies in software has become another high-priorty duty of the KGB.

Software AG in Reston, Virginia, has developed a Data Base Management System called ADABAS, which contains 200,000 detailed instructions for computer programmers. According to the company's president, John Maguire, ADABAS increases the productivity of computerized information systems up to 1000 percent, and thus many customers are willing to pay the standard price of $160,000 for it.

Although customers can understand and profitably use ADABAS, they cannot deduce the source code or logic upon which it is based. Thus, like most other software, it cannot be reverse-engineered. Maguire draws an analogy to a bottle of Coca-Cola. From the beverage itself, no one can figure out the formula of its essence and thereby produce it; but anyone possessing the formula could produce Coca-Cola.

The Soviets knew that if only they could learn the ADABAS source code, in one fell swoop they could advance their computer industry by several years. So in 1979 a Belgian industrial spy, Marc DeGeyter, approached James Addis, the only Software AG executive other than Maguire with access to the source code, and offered him a $150,000 bribe for it. Apprised of the proffered bribe and the significance of what the Soviets were after, the FBI asked Maguire personally to play along with DeGeyter for a while.

As the two negotiated during the next six months, DeGeyter became foolishly frank. The Soviets, he said, had given him a "shopping list" of high-technology items to be acquired by any means in the United States, and much of the time he prowled California's "Silicon Valley" trying to pick them up. The ADABAS source code had been on the list for three years, but suddenly the Soviets wanted it more than anything else.

DeGeyter doggedly tried to persuade Maguire to come to Brussels to transfer the source code and take the payoff; Maguire insisted on consummating the deal in the United States, so that the FBI could arrest DeGeyter. As he stalled, DeGeyter raised his offer to $200,000 plus some California real estate and eventually to $450,000. Negotiations broke down because Maguire refused to go to Europe.

Soon, though, DeGeyter contacted Charles Matheny, the owner of a computer firm in the building housing Software AG offices, and asked him for help in securing the ADABAS source code. Again the FBI interceded, and its disguised operatives entered into negotiations with DeGeyter. The Soviets and DeGeyter became so desperate for the source code that DeGeyter agreed to take delivery in the United States. At Kennedy Airport in New York, an FBI operative handed him a dummy code, and he gave the agent $500,000 in cash. The FBI handcuffed him and hauled him away to jail in Virginia, where he later pleaded guilty to violating the Export Administration Act and the Virginia Commercial Bribery Statute.

Still the Soviets did not give up.

At two trade exhibitions in the Washington area during the summer of 1981, KGB officer Georgi Veremey sidled up to the Software AG booth and interrogated company personnel about ADABAS, its internal logic and source code. Then on September 25, 1981, Veremey showed up uninvited at the offices of Software AG in Reston and introduced himself as a member of the Soviet embassy staff in Washington. Bluntly he told executive Sunday Lewis that he wanted a complete list of all Software AG products and any documents that pertained to them. Asked the purpose of his request, Veremey said he was "just interested." Asked what he did at the embassy, he was vague and evasive. He left after Lewis gave him a published list of products, available to anyone, and an order form.

A week later, Veremey appeared again at Software AG and, while waiting for Lewis to return from lunch, wandered in, out and around the offices, despite a receptionist's request that he sit down and wait for Lewis. When Lewis came back, Veremey gave her an order for all Software AG documents—which would fill a dozen boxes. "This type of technical documentation tells one how to use various systems produced by our company," Maguire explains. "One would have no use for this unless you have the system or are planning on acquiring it; or you are attempting to develop the system via knowledge of user techniques."

Maguire had instructed Lewis and other executives that Software AG would do no business of any kind with the Soviets and would give them nothing whatsoever. So Lewis brushed Veremey off by saying he would have to present a valid U.S. government export license before he could buy any documents.

Maguire estimates that over the years U.S. companies collectively have spent at least $1 billion developing the data base management technology that made possible creation of ADABAS. So for the KGB $500,000 would have been a "bargain-basement" price.

As much as hardware or software, the Soviets need the general know-how that can be absorbed only inside American research and industrial centers. Thus, the large majority of Soviet Bloc exchange students coming to the United States study the sciences at universities that are abreast of the latest technological developments and methods. And increasingly, the KGB sends agents, disguised as emigrés, on technological espionage missions.

The credentials Gennadi Popov* presented when he applied for employment at the main plant of a leading American electronics corporation in February 1980 were impressive, and his manner appealing. Born in 1952 in Russia, Popov appeared to be something of a mathematical prodigy. He had earned master's and doctoral degrees in math, worked as an analyst at the Institute of Applied Mathematics, and engaged in advanced research in computer-aided design at the Soviet Academy of Sciences. By age 27 he had published some 30 scientific papers and been nominated for a state award in the Soviet Union. Moreover, Popov specialized in the art of designing with computers, a field in which the American corporation is a world leader. And though the Soviet Union lags badly in the practice of computer-aided design, young Popov exhibited theoretical knowledge equal to that of the U.S. scientists who interviewed him. His command of English and American scientific jargon was nearly faultless, and he evinced enthusiasm well calculated to please prospective American employers.

Although the company wanted to hire Popov, there were questions that cried out for answers. The Soviets are usually not all that obliging in facilitating the emigration of citizens possessing the talents and education of Popov, yet without any difficulty he received a visa just 90 days after requesting it. His mother, father, brother and grandfather still lived in the Soviet Union, as did relatives of his wife. What would he do if the KGB tried to blackmail him through pressures upon his family? "They wouldn't do that," he answered.

To resolve doubts, Popov volunteered to undergo a polygraph examination, during which he was asked: "Regarding your background, do you intend to answer truthfully each question? Do you intend to lie to any question about your background? Are you applying for a job here for any reason other than employment? Are you directly or indirectly employed by the U.S.S.R? Were you deliberately sent to seek

---

*Because this case still has not been resolved, a pseudonym is used for the Russian involved. The author and researchers have seen documentary evidence verifying the details reported.

employment in a high-technology company in the U.S.?"

None of Popov's answers to these questions were satisfactory.

Informed that the company could not hire him because his close relatives remained in the Soviet Union, Popov moved on undismayed and found a job at another major U.S. corporation with many defense contracts. He has since failed to pass another polygraph examination. But he has as yet committed no crime, and as the KGB well understands, until the FBI gathers proof that he has, it can do nothing about him.

Only the Soviets know how many scientific secrets they have stolen. But the inventory of high technology that the U.S. knows the Soviet Union has acquired from the West in the past decade is staggering. Consider the table of acquisitions, all with important military applications, that the CIA submitted to the Senate:

Type of Technology	Soviet Acquisitions
Computers	Complete systems designs, concepts, hardware and software, including a wide variety of computers and mini-computers for military purposes
Lasers	Optical, pulsed power source and other components, including special optical mirrors and mirror technology for future laser weapons
Manufacturing	Automated and precision manufacturing equipment for electronics, materials and optical and future laser weapons technology; technology related to weapons, ammunition, and aircraft parts, including turbine blades, computers, and electronic components; machine tools for cutting large gears for propulsion systems

Communications	Low-power, low-noise, high-sensitivity receivers
Guidance and Navigation	Marine and other navigation receivers, advanced inertial-guidance components, including miniature and laser gyros; missile-guidance subsystems; precision machinery for ball-bearing production for missiles and other applications; missile test-range instrumentation systems; precision cinetheodolites for collecting data critical to post-flight ballistic missile analysis
Structural Materials	Titanium alloys, welding equipment, and furnaces for producing large titanium plates for submarine construction
Propulsion	Missile technology; ground propulsion technology (diesels, turbines and rotaries), advanced jet engine fabrication technology and jet engine design information
Acoustical Sensors	Underwater navigation and direction finding equipment
Electro-Optical Sensors	Information on satellite technology, laser range-finders and underwater low-light-level television cameras and systems for remote operation
Radars	Air defense radars and antenna designs for missile systems

The KGB stole the design plans and drawings for the huge C–5A cargo plane even before Lockheed began producing it. The silos of the SS–13, the Soviets' first solid-propellent missile, are strikingly similar to the U.S. Minuteman silos. The Soviet SAM–7 missile, which shot down so many American fighters over Vietnam, is largely a duplicate of the U.S. Redeye missile. Through theft of U.S. equipment and technology, the Soviets have gained the capability to catapult aircraft from ships, which they previously could not do.

In addition to these illegal acquisitions, the Soviets have acquired via legal commercial transactions immense quantities of equipment and technology for military purposes. Beginning in the early 1970s, they orchestrated Active Measures to convince Western companies that the Soviet Union constituted a veritable El Dorado that could be lucratively mined through trade and credits. In the heady spirit of détente, the Nixon Administration opened heretofore secret laboratories and forbidden factories to inspection by Soviet scientists, engineers and technicians.

Soviet delegations methodically toured the great Boeing plant in Seattle and the Lockheed plant near Burbank, conjuring up for their American hosts the alluring prospect of billions of dollars' worth of aircraft sales to the Soviet Union. Naturally, to decide which aircraft to buy, the Soviets needed all sorts of technical data about how the planes are built. And they got it.

Late one night, a Soviet engineer came furtively to the hotel room of the U.S. officer escorting the prospective buyers. Intoxicated, he told the American, who spoke fluent Russian: "Don't be fooled. We will never buy your planes. We don't have the money. And besides, how could we force the East Europeans to use our aircraft if we bought yours? No! We are here only to learn your secrets."

Of course, the Soviets never did attempt to buy any American aircraft. But ten years later, they finally are beginning to produce their first wide-bodied jet, the IL–86, which looks remarkably like the Boeing 747. Their new IL–76 transport closely resembles the Lockheed C–141.

Encouraged by the U.S. government, U.S. companies sold the Soviets technology and production equipment, including that for the $1.5 billion Kama River truck factory, which produced the military vehicles that carried Soviet invaders into Afghanistan. The basic Soviet Bloc computer, the Ryad, is a copy of the IBM 360 and 370 series. Additionally, the Russians and East Europeans have legally bought more than 3000 minicomputers and are using them for military purposes.

From the West, the Russians in 1978 bought one of the world's largest floating dry docks, which their existing shipyards could not build. Though they assured one and all that the dry dock would service only merchant vessels, the first ships to be overhauled in it were destroyers. The dry dock can accommodate several warships, including carriers, simultaneously, and it has been made part of the Soviet Pacific fleet. By obviating the necessity of long passages back to shipyards for repairs, it enables the Soviets to keep more ships on station for longer periods.

In allowing purchases and wholesale theft of advanced technology, the industrialized democracies are subsidizing the Soviet war machine and economy by sparing the Soviets the risks, cost and time entailed in original research and development. They are ameliorating the consequences of the congenitally inefficient and backward Soviet economy, and thereby helping the Soviet oligarchy preserve a totalitarian system. They are endangering themselves by enabling the Soviets to develop weapons they could not perfect if dependent solely upon their own resources. And they are adding grievously to the burdens of their own taxpayers.

In stealing American technology, the KGB operates from three major sanctuaries within the United States. They are the Soviet Mission to the United Nations at 136 East 67th Street in New York; the Soviet embassy at 1125 Sixteenth Street, N.W., five blocks from the White House, in Washington; and the Soviet consulate at 2790 Green Street, overlooking San Francisco Bay. The KGB Residencies at these three diplomatic installations are redoubts similar to the Residency in Tokyo. And, as in Tokyo, the top floor of each Residency is packed with electronic gear linked to forests of antennae on the roofs.

With this equipment, the KGB daily intercepts and records hundreds of thousands of private American telephone conversations transmitted by microwave. Today more than half of all telephone calls made over any distance go by microwave, and nobody ever knows just when a call may be automatically switched from land-line to microwave. Tapes of conversations, intercepted at random, are fed to computers programmed to select out calls made to designated numbers. By keying the computers to calls made to known telephone numbers of defense contractors, research laboratories and military facilities, the KGB gathers masses of technological data, which are digested and analyzed at leisure by the Center in Moscow. And if the KGB is interested in an individual American official or citizen, it frequently can peer into his or her personal life by keying the computer to his or her telephone.

The problem is particularly acute in California because the Soviet consulate, purposely perched on one of the highest slopes in San Francisco, can focus interceptors southward into "Silicon Valley," where many of the world's most advanced research centers are congregated. The problem will worsen in Washington when the Soviets complete their new embassy, which the State Department doltishly agreed to let them build on Mount Alto, the highest point in the capital. From here the KGB will be able to intercept microwave communications among many of the government's most vital installations in the Washington area.

Senator Daniel Patrick Moynihan, vice chairman of the Senate Select Committee on Intelligence, has said of this widespread Soviet invasion of American privacy: "I cannot stress too strongly that modern technology has given to foreign espionage a new dimension which needs to be understood in this country. The targets of Soviet interception of telephone communications now include our businesses, our banks, our brokerage houses, as frequently as our government agencies. Soviet espionage seeks to penetrate into other aspects of American life—commercial, intellectual, political—as much as it seeks illegal entry into the councils of governments. This is precisely why the problem is now one of interest to all Americans in their daily lives—not an abstract problem for intelligence operatives in trench coats."

In intercepting telephone conversations and in all else it does within the United States, the KGB seeks to penetrate and debilitate American intelligence services, particularly the CIA and FBI. They constitute the first line of defense against the KGB, and their immobilization is a Soviet objective equaling acquisition of technology in importance.

So far as is known, there have been few, if any, ideological defectors from American intelligence to the KGB. Two employees of the National Security Agency, Bernon Mitchell and William Martin, fled to the Soviet Union together in 1960. However, they had suffered from financial and homosexual problems, at a time when homosexuals were still widely scorned in the United States. Some FBI officials in the early 1960s believed that the KGB had recruited an agent in its New York field office but were never able to so prove. The agent denied the allegation and resigned, and the case was never fully clarified. Army Sergeant Roy Rhodes, while on a tour of duty at the National Security Agency in 1966, dealt with the KGB. Upon learning that he was being investigated, Rhodes committed suicide before he could be questioned. The FBI discovered that the Soviets had paid him approximately $30,000 in cash. The CIA in 1968 forced Philip Agee to resign for a variety of reasons, including his irresponsible drinking, continuous and vulgar propositioning of embassy wives, and inability to manage his finances. Gradually he became embittered and began to consort with the Cuban intelligence service, the DGI, and later the KGB. He eventually proclaimed himself a Communist and emerged as a fierce ideological enemy of the United States and open ally of the KGB. But it appears that his conversion did not occur or even begin until some time after he left the CIA.

The most serious known breaches of the CIA have resulted not from KGB actions but from the initiatives of former employees motivated by egotistical or monetary considerations. One of these was William Kampiles.

An only child, Kampiles grew up in Indiana under the care of his mother, his father having died when he was a young child. The mother worked in a cafeteria to sustain them and subordinated all else to his welfare. A handsome young man, Kampiles earned good grades at the University of Indiana, where acquaintances considered him smart or "smart-assed." During the first semester of his senior year, he presented himself for an interview by a visiting CIA recruiter, and suddenly his future was clear: he would be a spy.

The processing of his application and a security investigation took more than a year, and Kampiles had to wait until March 1977 to begin work at the CIA. He had hoped to join the Clandestine Service (Operations Directorate), which engages in worldwide collection of intelligence, and combat against the KGB. Instead, after brief orientation, he was assigned to the Watch Center at headquarters in Langley, Virginia.

Manned twenty-four hours a day, seven days a week, the Watch Center receives continuous reports from CIA posts throughout the world. The duty staff examines the reports and routes them to whoever needs to see them. It also maintains the CIA link to the circuit over which the U.S. intelligence community, White House, State Department and Pentagon communicate in an emergency.

To some the Watch Center is an exciting place. But Kampiles found the Watch Center tedious and boring. He wanted to be a James Bond 007, not a GS-7, and he did not want to wait and work his way up. Although he fancied himself a Casanova, female colleagues rejected his overtures, and supervisors criticized him, warning that his work was barely adequate. And in light of his performance, his requests for transfer to the Clandestine Service were rejected. So in early 1978, after less than a year, Kampiles gave up and quit.

Available to all in the Watch Center is a small operational library of manuals, some Top Secret, left there on the premise that to understand reports from the field, watch personnel might need to refer to them. Some months before he resigned, Kampiles slipped inside his jacket a loose leaf manual, just as James Bond might do, and took it to his apartment. It was classified Top Secret; probably it should have borne a higher classification; certainly it should not have been left 24 hours a day on an open shelf where anybody could pick it up, even though access to the Watch Center requires Top Secret clearance.

Unemployed and a failure in his first foray into espionage, Kampiles in late February 1978 departed upon an expedition to prove that he could be a real spy. In Athens, Greece, he walked into the Soviet embassy and proposed business. He was an accomplished man, worldly beyond his years, who had procured a Top Secret American document that he was prepared to sell. The Russian who spoke with Kampiles was cautious. (The KGB has become leery of "walk-ins," as they are called in the trade, because so many turn out to be agents of foreign counterintelligence services.) He asked for time to study the document and advised Kampiles to rendezvous with him in a park two days later.

Perhaps Line X officers in the Athens Residency lacked the specialized background necessary to evaluate the pages Kampiles delivered. Possibly the description of them the Residency doubtless cabled to the Center was unclear. Maybe the Soviets doubted their authenticity. Whatever the reason, the Soviets apparently did not immediately comprehend the value and import of what Kampiles had. For the Russian who met Kampiles in the park paid him only $3000 and concentrated upon persuading him to try to rejoin the CIA.

However, at the Center, analysts quickly gleaned from the document two of America's most precious secrets, which had long been kept from the Soviet Union. Kampiles had given away a manual that revealed the precise workings of the KH–11 reconnaissance satellite. Heretofore, the Soviets had assumed that American satellites, like their own, periodically dropped packages of photographs, which had to be caught in mid-air by aircraft or recovered on earth and flown to a laboratory for development and analysis. Now, to their amazement, they realized that the KH–11 continuously flashed photographs from overhead to the United States. Whatever its cameras saw, analysts back in Washington instantly saw.

The KH–11 manual disclosed something else even more stunning. For years the United States had doctored all satellite photographs made public so as to conceal and mislead the Soviets about their incredibly fine resolution. The Soviets had disguised intercontinental missiles as smokestacks in chemical and other industrial plants. To fool American reconnaissance, artists had painted the nose cones so that from above they looked like openings of smokestacks. The manual told the KGB that the cameras in the KH–11 were so powerful that they could see through this ruse by detecting even small chips of paint on the nose cones.

A month or so later, U.S. analysts began to see a new and disturbing pattern of activity in the Soviet Union. Whenever the KH–11 approached, the Russians started covering things up, trundling aircraft inside hangars and otherwise trying to hide weapons—this even though the SALT I agreement stipulates that neither party will interfere with the other's "national means of verification"—that is, overhead reconnaissance—by resorting to camouflage. Then the United States obtained intelligence indicating that the KGB had the KH–11 manual. Urgently FBI agents throughout the country were galvanized into an investigation to find out how the KGB procured it.

Back in Indiana, Kampiles deposited the $3000 the Soviets paid him in his mother's bank account instead of his own. Smart spy that he was, he was not about to be duped. If the money proved to be counterfeit, then his mother would be blamed, not him.

Kampiles also was smart enough to realize that if the CIA accepted his application for re-employment, he would have to undergo a polygraph test and that he could not evade a standard question about contact with Soviets. To cover himself, he told CIA officer George Joannides that he had contacted a Soviet in Athens to purvey disinformation and received $3000 from him. Now, he explained, he was positioned to participate in an operation to deceive the Soviets.

One outgrowth of the Congressional assault upon the CIA in the 1970s was an executive order forbidding the agency from investigating any American citizen in the United States other than its own employees. The CIA interpreted the order as precluding it from questioning Kampiles, who was no longer an employee. So to acquire evidence which could be forwarded to the FBI, it ordered Joannides to tell Kampiles to write a letter explaining his actions. The letter arrived just as Joannides was entering the hospital, and it lay unopened until he returned to work weeks later.

Upon finally hearing of Kampiles' tale, the FBI assigned one of its best counterintelligence agents to question him, and eventually Kampiles confessed. Though he later repudiated his confession, a federal court jury convicted him of espionage, and he is now serving a 40-year prison term.

While egotism motivated Kampiles, greed and desperation drove David Henry Barnett to the KGB. His business foundering, Barnett was so far in debt that he could see only one escape. On a Sunday afternoon in October 1976, he called at the home of a Soviet cultural attaché in Djakarta and passed him a typewritten note stating he would tell the KGB all he knew about the CIA in return for $70,000.

Barnett had quite a bit to tell. He worked as a contract employee for the CIA in the Far East from 1958 until 1963, when he became a regular staff officer. After serving covertly in Korea for two years and spending two years at headquarters in Langley, he was assigned to Surabao, Indonesia. As the CIA ran no operations against the friendly government of Indonesia, there was little to do except assess and try to cultivate Soviets there. The work was not overly demanding, and the social life was pleasant. But, as the post offered scant prospects for career advancement and he wanted to earn more money, Barnett resigned in 1970 to enter business for himself. The seafood processing company, P.T. Trifoods, and other ventures he started all floundered, and he had to borrow more and more.

Though the Soviet cultural attaché was not a KGB officer, Barnett knew him to be an intelligent man who would transmit his message discreetly, and he obliged by inviting Barnett to return in a week. The next Sunday, a KGB officer calling himself Dmitri drove Barnett from the attaché's home, and in the car they talked business. Dmitri listened attentively as Barnett outlined his financial straits and CIA operations he could divulge, and the two agreed to meet again two weeks hence at the Soviet compound. There, on another Sunday afternoon, Barnett began to recite names of CIA agents and officers about whom he knew, and Dmitri gave him $25,000 cash.

Having received instructions and $3000 more for travel from Dmitri, Barnett flew to Europe on February 25, 1977, and in Vienna rendezvoused with a KGB officer, who escorted him to a safe house in the suburbs. Three officers from the Center—Pavel, Mike and Aleksei—waited in a large, dim living room behind shuttered windows. On a table in the center of the room was placed what looked like a big, square metal box. Seated on opposite sides of the table, Barnett and Pavel put on earphones and face masks and talked to each other through the box, their conversation secure from eavesdropping even by the other two KGB officers.

During the next ten hours, Barnett reconstructed CIA operations and, in so doing, explained to the KGB why Soviet SAM-2 missiles so rarely had been able to hit U.S. B-52 bombers over Vietnam. Up until the Indonesian military crushed an attempted Communist coup in 1966, the Soviet Union deluged Indonesia with military hardware in hopes of drawing the strategically located archipelago into its orbit. One night CIA operatives sneaked into a warehouse where SAM-2s were stored, removed the guidance system from one and hauled it in a shopping cart to a van outside. On an isolated beach the guidance system was transferred to a small boat, which at once put to sea. A few miles offshore, a larger vessel waited to transport the guidance system to the United States. Its possession enabled Air Force scientists to equip the B-52s with countermeasures that largely nullified the effectiveness of the SAM-2 and thereby saved the lives of countless American air crewmen in combat.

This same CIA network, code-named HABRINK, learned the designs and workings of numerous other Soviet weapons, including the surface-to-surface Styx naval missile, the W-Class submarine, the Komar guided-missile patrol boats, the Riga class destroyer and the Kennel missile.

During three days of interrogation through the machine in Vienna, Barnett supplied the KGB with identities of approximately 100 agents and officers with whom he had worked in the Far East and Washington. He also identified some KGB officers whom the CIA had marked as possibly being susceptible to recruitment.

This was all quality intelligence, and the KGB gladly paid him another $15,000 toward the $70,000 he asked. However, Barnett had not had access to any CIA secrets for seven years, so much of his information was rather dated. And neither in South Korea nor the tightly compartmentalized CIA headquarters had he been privy to any really extraordinary data. To the KGB his value lay not in the past but in the future, not in Indonesia but in Washington. So the KGB urged him to seek employment with the CIA, the State Department's Bureau of Intelligence and Research, the Defense Intelligence Agency, the White House Intelligence Oversight Board, or the Senate or House Intelligence Committee.

Assuring the three officers that he could worm himself back into U.S. intelligence, Barnett flew home to Djakarta, and in March Dmitri gave him $30,000, bringing the total the KGB had paid to $70,000. Twice in the summer of 1977 he flew to Washington to look for a job, receiving $3000 for each trip. Among government officials he called upon were David Kenny of the State Department, Joseph Dennin of the White

House Intelligence Oversight Board, and William Miller, staff director of the Senate Select Committee on Intelligence.

Back in Djakarta, Dmitri again told Barnett to reapply for a CIA staff job and gave him $3600 to prepare for his move to Washington. In November KGB officer Vladimir Popov of the Washington Residency flew to Djakarta via Moscow to brief Barnett about clandestine communications in the United States. At 3 p.m. on the last Saturday of each month, Barnett was to stand in one of two phone booths near an Exxon station on Little River Turnpike in Annandale, Va., and wait for a call from Popov, whose work name was Igor. If the phone did not ring, he was to wait for Popov the next afternoon in an Annadale bowling alley. If he had film or documents to convey, he could leave them by a described rock near Lock 11 of the C & O Canal in Maryland and make a mark with red tape on a telephone booth not far away, to signal that the drop was loaded. Popov, a congenial, seemingly competent officer, and Barnett, who had been a calm, calculating officer, talked easily with each other. Both were professionals; both understood.

On April 21, 1978, his businesses in Indonesia liquidated, Barnett, his wife and 12-year-old son settled in Bethesda, Md., and he renewed his search for an avenue back into American intelligence. He spoke to many people, including Richard D. Anderson, Jr., of the House Permanent Select Committee on Intelligence. In discharging oversight functions, the House and Senate Intelligence Committees necessarily share many of the nation's highest secrets, and the law requires that they be informed of any covert actions attempted by the CIA. From a position on the staff of either committee, a skilled KGB agent could do much to sabotage the CIA.

The legend Barnett presented made him appear eminently qualified for such a position. Since leaving the government, he said, he had become a man of independent means, and salary was not a consideration. Only the opportunity to utilize his special experience in intelligence serving his country mattered. From his CIA background he could discern any CIA activities that might be questionable. But he did not want to pretend. Basically he was sympathetic to the CIA and believed in its mission.

Considering his legend and talents, Barnett probably found it remarkable that he was not able to find work until January 1979, when the CIA hired him as a contract employee to teach agents going overseas how to resist interrogations. His pupils came, two or three at a time, to hear the counsel of a veteran who concluded his lecture with the advice: "If all else fails, tell everything."

Barnett communicated according to schedule with Popov from public telephone booths and periodically flew to Djakarta to confer personally with the KGB, which kept urging him to regain the status of staff officer in the CIA. Given his lengthy residence and business involvement in Indonesia, the trips were not surprising.

When Barnett came to the CIA safe house the morning of March 18, 1980, none of his pupils was there. Instead, two FBI agents awaited him. "We would like to discuss your relationship with the KGB," one announced. Once they started talking about Popov, Barnett realized that all had failed. During the next days he told everything.

In sentencing Barnett to 18 years' imprisonment, the judge took into consideration his confession and cooperation, as well as the fact that he would be 65 at the end of his sentence. And the Justice Department allowed him a week of liberty to arrange personal affairs in the interest of his family before entering prison.

Barnett cared about little except his teen-age son, whom he adored. By chance, FBI agents called for Barnett and handcuffed him just as his son was leaving the house, school books in hand. As they drove away, an agent saw the boy standing and crying as he watched his father disappear.

In the aftermath of the case, critics ridiculed the CIA for being so stupid and incompetent as to hire a KGB agent to teach its agents. Finally, Senator Daniel Inouye, a member of the Senate Intelligence Committee throughout the period the case unfolded, spoke out. He revealed that the FBI had known about Barnett in consequence of detecting his communications with the KGB.

Had not Barnett been detected early on, the KGB almost certainly would now and for years to come have a professional inside U.S. intelligence.

While Line KR tries to infiltrate U.S. intelligence, and Line X plots the theft of American technology, Line PR officers from the Washington and New York Residencies execute Active Measures, resorting to the same ploys Levchenko used so effectively in Tokyo. Just as Levchenko did, they often tell Congressmen, Administration officials, and journalists that they enjoy direct access to the Kremlin. The implication is that whatever the American says will be considered by the highest Soviet leadership, and whatever the KGB officer says reflects the private opinions of the highest Soviet leadership.

KGB officer Sergei Chetverikov, who during the early 1980s cultivated legislators and staff members at the best Washington restaurants, claimed that he was the "direct channel" between the U.S. Congress and the Politburo. Diplomatic and debonair, Chetverikov in this pose sought to influence Congressional attitudes toward arms limitation agreements by "confiding" which conditions were acceptable and unacceptable to the Kremlin. He also earnestly assured American contacts that he personally would report their views to Soviet leaders when home leave next took him to Moscow.

Similarly, KGB officer Boris Davidov, masquerading as a secret emissary of the Kremlin, tried to persuade Congressmen, their assistants, and journalists that the United States ought to shut up about Afghanistan. To one contact on a Congressional committee, he confidentially explained that by focusing world attention on the invasion, the United States was making it more difficult for the Soviet Union to withdraw from Afghanistan. To others he "confided" that no matter what the United States did, the Soviets would persevere in Afghanistan, hence U.S. boycotts embargoes and other countermeasures were futile and ought to be abandoned.

One of the hoariest themes of the Soviet disinformation

which KGB officers propagate orally in the United States, as well as in Europe, runs as follows: The Soviet leadership is rent into two factions, the "hawks" and the "doves." To help the moderates gain ascendancy, the United States must make concessions which will enable them to demonstrate that "moderation" is best. Otherwise the hard-liners will prevail, and détente will be jeopardized. Despite the bellicosity of his words and actions, Brezhnev was secretly a "moderate," just as Andropov is a "closet liberal."

Line PR officers sometimes attempt to form *ad hoc* lobbies to agitate for Soviet interests. After President Carter ordered a U.S. boycott of the 1980 Moscow Olympics, KGB officer Viktor Tyutin approached a prominent American who he believed opposed Carter. Tyutin offered to pay him to organize politicians and athletes into a committee, which would mail 60,000 letters urging Congress to override the boycott. He further proposed that the committee issue a press release declaring its disregard of the boycott and asserting that its members would travel to Moscow in defiance of it. While the Soviets would pay the costs of the campaign, their involvement, of course, would not be known. The scheme failed when the FBI learned of the proposal.

Officers from the Washington Residency laze around Congressional corridors and hearing rooms and regularly attend committee sessions of intelligence interest. Whenever FBI representatives testify in open hearings, the KGB is likely to be there. In testifying before the Senate Subcommittee on Security and Terrorism on February 4, 1982, FBI Director William H. Webster informed the committee members that an official of the Soviet embassy had been present that morning to monitor the hearings.

Productive as the Washington Residency is, the presence of the United Nations enables the KGB to maintain an even larger and more important base in New York. In January 1983 there were 330 Soviet nationals employed in the United Nations Secretariat, 310 members of the Soviet diplomatic delegation to the U.N., and more Soviets working in New York under journalistic or commercial cover. Approximately 30 to 40 percent of them were KGB or GRU officers. Additionally, there were hundreds of East European and Cuban nationals employed by the U.N. in New York or assigned to it as diplomats. A goodly number also were professional intelligence officers available to execute clandestine tasks dictated by the Soviets.

KGB officers hired by the U.N. enjoy unique operational liberties in the United States. Whereas Soviet diplomats may not travel beyond a 25-mile radius of New York without U.S. permission, U.N. employees are free to travel about the country as they please. The U.N. grants such liberal sick leave that a KGB officer may take as much time off from work for operations as he wishes, simply by presenting a statement from a Soviet Mission physician certifying illness. U.N. work rules are so lax that KGB officers freely abandon their jobs during work hours to deliver reports and receive instructions at the Residency on East 67th Street. Since many KGB officers are unqualified for the U.N. work they are supposed to be performing, their absence matters little; in any case, supervisors are reluctant to discipline them because whenever a Russian employee is rebuked, the Soviet Mission belligerently protests. And, to the continuing amusement of the Soviets, American taxpayers directly subsidize KGB operations mounted out of the New York Residency.

The United States pays one-fourth of the assessed budget of the U.N. and voluntarily donates more to the many special U.N. agencies. The over all U.S. contribution in 1981 totaled $1,098,502,013. (The Soviet Union pays 12 percent of the basic U.N. budget, contributes little or nothing to many of the special volunteer programs, often ignores assessments, and currently is nearly $200 million in arrears in payments it is obligated to make.) Thus, at least one-fourth of the salaries of Communist spies on the U.N. payroll comes from the U.S. Treasury. In defiance of the U.N. Charter, the Soviets require their nationals to rebate part of their salaries to the government. Some of the American dollars given to the U.N. doubtless find their way into the New York Residency's operational fund.

The Residency itself is a snake pit of internecine intrigue, just like the one in Tokyo. The present Resident, Vladimir Mikhailovich Kazakov, is an American affairs specialist now on his third tour in the United States. Kazakov is an able but tormented man. Apprehensive about how the Center is evaluating him, he sees in innocent acts or circumstances malevolence which causes him to lash out irrationally at subordinates. These outbursts tend to estrange and divide his lieutenants into suspicious factions. Because the United Nations constitutes such a rare sanctuary for subversion, the KGB loads the Residency with experienced officers, some of whom enjoy higher military or diplomatic rank than the Resident. And the competition among them to aggrandize their careers by excelling in New York, even at the expense of each other, is keen and occasionally vicious.

Tensions in the Residency notwithstanding, the KGB has thoroughly infested the United Nations bureaucracy, infiltrating many officers into positions of authority and influence. The current special assistant to the Secretary General of the U.N. is Gennadi Yevstavyev, the same KGB officer whom Resident Yerokhin tried to railroad out of the Tokyo Residency into a mental institution back in 1976. His predecessors were the prominent KGB officer Viktor Lessiovski, an intimate of Secretary General U Thant, now deceased, and KGB General Mikhail Krepkogorsky.

After Arkadi Shevchenko quit the lofty position of Under-Secretary General of the U.N. and gained asylum in the United States in 1978, the Soviet Union demanded that another Russian replace him. His successor was KGB General Mikhail Sytenko.

As supervisor of international civil servants at U.N. headquarters, KGB officer Geli Dneprovsky posted people where the Soviets wanted them and favored employees willing to obey the Russians. Several defectors have exposed him, and Russians themselves regard him as an overbearing, self-serving bureaucrat. Nevertheless, the U.N. in 1978 appointed "Colonel Dneprovsky," as he is widely known, personnel director in Geneva, and he helps honeycomb its offices there with KGB officers.

Yuri Pavlovich Chestnoy, having served at the KGB Residencies in Havana and Buenos Aires, is now an efficient propagandist and fixer inside the U.N.'s Economic Commission for Europe, based in Geneva. Affable on the surface, Chestnoy is feared by other Russians because be provokes them with anti-Soviet jokes and reports those who laugh.

KGB officer Aleksandr Sergeevich Bryntsev exploits his position as counselor inspector to generate studies and reports whose adoption by the U.N. would give the Soviets what they desire. Because of the extravagance of his wife, Eugenia, his U.N. expense accounts are quite creative works.

Valeri Pavlovich Yevstigneyev arrived in Geneva as an interpreter, but the KGB maneuvered him into a job on the Joint Inspection Unit where he assists Bryntsev in operations. Senior translator Vladimir Ivanovich Lemesh specialized in Active Measures as a member of Line PR in the Geneva Residency. Igor Guriev, First Secretary of the Soviet Mission, concentrates upon theft of technology. Though relatively unpolished and a heavy drinker, Guriev is a tough and effective officer with lengthy experience in scientific and technical espionage.

In New York, KGB officer Vladimir Nikolaevich Orlov has been director of the U.N. library since 1979. As such, he orders at U.N. expense microfiches of governmental publications and archival records from all over the world, then also at U.N. expense copies them for the KGB.

The Soviet Union contributes only 0.7 percent of the budget of the U.N. Development Program, which bestows money and technical assistance upon Third World nations. The Soviet Union, however, does contribute the services of KGB officer Nikolai Bogati in New York. As regional project coordinator of the Development Program, he tries to make sure that the millions the United States gives to benefit the Third World ultimately benefit the Soviet Union.

Among numerous other KGB officers who have burrowed within the United Nations administrative heirarchy are Nikolai Fochine, Special Political Affairs Department of the Secretariat; Ivan Alekhnovich, Department of International Economic and Social Affairs; Grigori Myagkov, International Labor Organization; Leonid Guryanov, Department of Administration, Finance and Management; Vladimir Kartashkin, special legal assistant to the Under-Secretary General; Aleksandr Nikolaevich Kashirin, section chief for Coordination of Political Information; Viktor Kryzhanovsky, Department of International Economic and Social Affairs.

Continuously, these and other KGB officers strive to pervert the United Nations into an instrument of Soviet policy, to project through the U.N. images the Soviets desire the world to accept. Sometimes their success is conspicuous. For example, on October 14, 1982, the Joint United Nations Information Committee leaked a 12-page "report" denouncing the Western press for tarnishing the U.N. by depicting it as "an irrelevant, inefficient and swollen bureaucracy." The pronouncement declared that in contrast to "grossly inaccurate" dispatches by Western journalists, reporting by correspondents from the Soviet Union and other socialist countries helps inspire "continuing support in these countries for the United Nations." While neglecting to cite a single specific example of inaccurate reportage by even one Western journalist, the Information Committee's statement did propose a solution to the problem perceived: allot more money and hire more publicists to burnish the image of the U.N.

New York Residency officers at every opportunity cultivate influential Americans and try gently to guide them in the right directions. Sergei Paramanov, a handsome, charming First Secretary of the Soviet Mission, typifies their operations.

Paramanov is interested in peace, and in furtherance of international understanding, he gladly helps arrange for selected Americans to visit the Soviet Union. Carol Pendell, a bright and energetic Californian, is also interested in peace and amity among nations. As President of both the Women's International League for Peace and Freedom and the U.S.A.-U.S.S.R. Committee for Citizens Dialogue, she visits the United Nations and Soviet Union to further peace. So it is natural that Paramanov and Pendell should be drawn together by common interests, that they should consult and confer with each other.

Pendell, of course, is unaware that Paramanov is a KGB officer assigned to manipulate nongovernmental organizations such as those she heads. She rejects any suggestion that her organizations unwittingly abet Soviet interests to the detriment of the U.S. Yet the positions of WILPF and the Soviet Union often do coincide.

WILPF, for example, has advocated abandonment of military bases abroad, termination of military alliances, cessation of nuclear-weapons production, and destruction of existing stockpiles. It also has advocated "public ownership of the sources of wealth." WILPF's U.S. section has developed, in its own words, "a strong and friendly" relationship with the Soviet Women's Committee, another front for propaganda and covert action. And the U.S. State Department in 1982 classified the Women's International League for Peace and Freedom as one of the "nominally independent organizations that are controlled by the Soviets."

But as an American citizen who violates no laws, takes no money and gives away no secrets, Pendell has every right to advocate what she believes and talk to whomever she pleases. "Paramanov does not influence us one way or another," she states. "He is a contact person for when I need to get in touch with a person in the Soviet Union. He puts us in touch with what's going on." Pendell explains that Paramanov also helps expedite issuance of a visa when she desires to travel to the Soviet Union.

No doubt he does, although as first secretary of the Soviet Mission to the United Nations KGB officer Paramanov ordinarily would not concern himself with visa matters.

From the United Nations, KGB officers additionally maintain clandestine contact with the U.S. Communist Party, delivering money and instructions in behalf of the International Department. The U.S. Party exists almost entirely on secret Soviet subsidies, which now average about $2 million annually. KGB officers pass the cash in furtive meetings with Party officials, usually in the New York area. The KGB communicates with Party leaders through open personal meetings and secret means.

Though numerically small and taken seriously by few people, the U.S. Communist Party provides a corps of disciplined activists dedicated to serving the Soviet Union however they can. The origin and growth of the protest movement against U.S. policies toward El Salvador illustrate how useful they can be and why the KGB concerns itself with them.

In 1980, pursuant to the objective of installing Marxist regimes in Central America, the Soviets, assisted by the Cubans, initiated Active Measures to arouse foreign support for leftist insurgents in El Salvador. In February Farid Handel, brother of the chief of the El Salvador Communist Party, visited the United States to solicit support for the revolutionaries. Subsequently, his detailed report of the trip was found among papers confiscated at a guerrilla safe house in El Salvador. The House Permanent Select Committee on Intelligence published the following excerpts from his report in December 1982:

"Route: San Jose-Mexico-New York-Chicago-San Francisco-Los Angeles-New York-Washington-New York-Mexico-San Jose. . . .

"New York: 1. Interview with members of the Cuban Mission to the United Nations. This took place in the house of Alfredo Garcia Almeida [an officer of Cuban Intelligence, which when required functions as an appendage of the KGB] . . . .

"With regard to my stay in the U.S.A. and the work which I would accomplish there, they recommended that I should carry out work of an informational nature about the situation in El Salvador with progressive Congressmen for the purpose of making the rest of my work appear more natural. And in that way protect my visa.

"They offered to facilitate contacts in Washington. And they did that.

"2. Interview with members of the Directorate of the CPUSA. At their invitation, in spite of the fact that I insisted that I did not represent the CPS (Communist Party Salvador), they insisted that they needed to meet with me because they wanted information.

"Attended: Secretary of Education of the CC (Central Committee) of the CPUSA . . . Person Responsible for the U.S. Peace Council; Sandy Polak [Pollack], member of the CC of the CPUSA. . . .

"Meeting with Sandy Polak [Pollack], Solidarity Coordinator for the U.S. Peace Council.

"Sandy proposed a national conference under the auspices of the U.S. Peace Council, the National Council of Churches, Amnesty International, WOLA (Washington Office on Latin American) and unions, the most important ones in the U.S. The objective of the conference is to establish a support mechanism for the solidarity committees and to help create solidarity committees in those states where they do not exist yet."

The "support mechanism" the Communists proposed to the guerrilla leader materialized after conferences in Washington and Los Angeles during October 1980. Its title was and is the Committee in Solidarity with the People of El Salvador (CISPES). The steering committee of CISPES includes activists from the U.S. Peace Council (Sandy Pollack), the Ecumenical Program for Inter-American Communication and Action, the Interreligious Task Force, the North American Congress on Latin America, and the Religious Task Force on El Salvador.

The U.S. Peace Council is headed by American Communists and affiliated with the World Peace Council. It is a transparent tool of the Soviet Union.

The Ecumenical Program for Inter-American Communication and Action (EPICA) has acknowledged receipt of funds from a division of the National Council of Churches. One of its prominent leaders, the Reverend Philip Wheaton, served as a "contributing editor" of *Counterspy,* which has published Soviet disinformation and names of American intelligence officers.

The Interreligious Task Force, composed of religious leaders from different faiths, is based at National Council of Churches headquarters in New York. It has praised the Marxist guerrillas in El Salvador as the "chosen" leaders of the people and claimed they are "committed to the establishment of a democratic, pluralist government."

The North American Congress on Latin America is a radical organization, which long has disseminated pro-Cuban, anti-American propaganda, while supporting Marxist guerrilla movements. Philip Agee has credited NACLA activists with assisting him in efforts to undermine the CIA.

The Religious Task Force on El Salvador is an *ad hoc* group which opposes the existing government of El Salvador and defends the guerrillas.

In one of its early actions, CISPES circulated a sophisticated forgery labeled "Dissent Paper on El Salvador and Central America." It looked exactly like an official document distributed through the regular Dissent Channel and available to State Department officers who disagree with prevailing policies. The anonymous authors claimed to represent views widely held in the State and Defense Departments and in the American intelligence community. In sum, they warned that continued U.S. support of the El Salvador government and opposition to the guerrillas would end in disaster requiring military intervention in Central America.

The fabrication appeared so authentic that the New York *Times* on March 6, 1981, published a story based upon it. Three days later, however, reporter Flora Lewis, stating that she had been misled by a fabrication, repudiated her story.

Other propaganda issued by CISPES, often through its publication *El Salvador Alert,* has been no less mendacious than the forgery. CISPES has claimed that the Catholic hierarchy in El Salvador unequivocally supports the guerrillas. Actually, the church unequivocally and clearly has decried both the guerrillas and right-wing radicals. CISPES asserts that labor unions speaking for 90 percent of the organized workers in El Salvador are part of the insurgency. In fact, the major unions, representing both urban and agrarian workers, outspokenly oppose the guerrillas. CISPES tracts state that the insurgents are pledged to creating a nonaligned democracy affording equal political rights to all. Demonstrably, the guerrillas are allied with the Soviets and Cubans, whence comes most of their support, and they have made clear that only their adherents would share political power.

In demonstrations and literature, CISPES has cried out against the land reform the El Salvador government is trying to implement with the help of the American AFL-CIO and its own unions. CISPES has lobbied against any form of U.S. aid to El Salvador—economic, humanitarian or otherwise. While depicting the Marxist insurgents as native democrats (much as the Viet Cong and Khmer Rouge were pictured), CISPES has suggested incessantly that U.S. assistance to El Salvador will lead to "another Vietnam." And it somberly warns: "There is always the chance that a frustrated U.S. leadership could resort to 'tactical' nuclear weapons to show its resolve not to 'lose' Central America."

In March 1982, just before the El Salvador elections, CISPES sponsored a demonstration in Washington that attracted some 23,000 protesters, who chanted, "No draft, no war: U.S. out of El Salvador." (At the time, there were 54 U.S. military instructors in the country.) Almost simultaneously, small demonstrations against U.S. policy in El Salvador occurred in Europe.

By all accounts of impartial observers, the national elections in El Salvador on March 28, 1982, were fair and honest. The guerrillas did try to disrupt them. They attacked numerous polling places and assaulted the central voting center in San Salvador three times. They stole identity cards to prevent people from balloting and threatened candidates and voters alike with death. Yet while shots rang out about them, many voters stood in line eight to ten hours waiting to cast ballots, and in the end, 80 percent of the eligible electorate succeeded in voting.

The election's results astonished even the U.S. State Department. More than 95 percent of the voters repudiated the guerrillas by voting for candidates dedicated to their elimination.

Still, CISPES, the "support mechanism," chants on about "another Vietnam," about U.S. imperialism thwarting the natural revolutionary will of the downtrodden people of El Salvador. In Europe alarm about "another Vietnam" in Central America persists. And from the United Nations in New York, the KGB "troops of the invisible front" fight on, paid in part by the American society they would destroy.

VI

REALITY UPSIDE DOWN

THE SOVIET UNION stands before the world swathed in the banners of peace. Millions upon millions of words issuing from Soviet broadcasts and publications aimed at the rest of the world depict the Soviet Union as the archenemy of war and hideous nuclear weapons, which menace mankind with extinction.

Having exhorted citizens to mail protests against Western nuclear arms to NATO headquarters, Soviet authorities reported in the spring of 1982 that 273,000 messages, bearing 8.6 million signatures, had been sent. As the movements in the West to prevent the United States from modernizing missiles in Europe progressed, Soviet spokesmen urged them on and could barely contain their glee. On March 26, 1982, ideologue Boris Ponomarev declared: "The present upsurge of the anti-war movement is without precedent. The anti-war movement in Western Europe encompasses millions and millions of people. We are witnessing the biggest explosion of truly popular indignation in the continent's history."

Two days later, a Deputy Director of the Institute for U.S.A. and Canada, Vitali Zhurkin, hailed the nuclear freeze movement in the United States "as a completely new phenomenon." Central Committee member Leonid Zamiatin on September 29 boasted that "the anti-war and anti-nuclear forces are now perhaps more widespread and influential than ever. In the United States itself, public protest is growing against the buildup of armaments and the White House's aggressive course." And in his last address, just days before his death, Brezhnev called for reinvigorated Soviet support of peace movements in the West, asserting: "The masses of people on all continents angrily protest against Washington's aggressive policy, which is threatening to push the world into the flames of nuclear war."

However, as it turns out, "peace" is more for export than for internal Soviet consumption.

In July, a European peace group called Greenpeace sailed into Leningrad harbor in a small craft, the *Serius*, and released 2000 balloons saying "U.S.S.R. Stop Nuclear Testing Now." The Soviets evicted them forthwith, towing them far out to sea. Greenpeace, they said, was polluting the harbor.

Eleven young Soviets led by Sergei Batovrin, the 25-year-old son of a former Soviet diplomat to the U.N., in the summer formed the "Group to Establish Trust Between the U.S.A. and the U.S.S.R." They advocated "four-sided dialogue" among the Soviet and American people as well as their governments, and they asked permission to demonstrate in favor of disarmament. The KGB arrested members of the embryonic peace organization August 6 on charges of "hooliganism" and incarcerated young Batovrin in a mental institution. And other lone Soviet citizens with the temerity to speak out in favor of peace and disarmament were beaten, fired from their jobs or locked in psychiatric wards throughout the latter part of 1982.

While lauding Western peace movements as "the indomitable will of the people," *Pravda* in another issue warned the

Soviet people against the perils of pacifism. "Our propaganda must display firmness and principle in upholding the Soviet Union's positions and in popularizing the ideas of Marxism-Leninism and must resolutely get rid of the touches of pacifism that sometimes emerge in certain information and propaganda materials."

In July 1981 Marshal Nikolai Ogarkov, chief of the Soviet General Staff, lamented that younger Soviet generations have grown up without the "personal experience of what war is. . . Questions of the struggle for peace are sometimes interpreted not from class positions, but somewhat simplistically: any kind of peace is good, any kind of war is bad. This could lead to unconcern, smugness and complacency. . . ."

Possessed by "imperialists," nuclear arms are "fearsome weapons of war," asserts Major General A. S. Milovidov, but in the hands of Communists, they are a "protective shield of peace." As Milovidov puts it in *Questions of Philosophy* (which could not have been published it if did not represent Politburo policy): "While speaking against the use of nuclear weapons, the Soviet Union does not exclude the possibility of using them in extreme circumstances. . . .Marxist-Leninists decisively reject the assertion of certain bourgeois theorists who consider nuclear missiles unjust from any point of view."

The legitimization of double standards; the readiness of so many people to judge the Soviet Union by one set of criteria and America by another; the turning of things upside down—all exemplify the success of what the KGB terms Active Measures. By Soviet definition, Active Measures consist of a diversity of tactics including overt and covert propaganda, mass demonstrations, controlled international assemblies, disinformation, forgeries, use of Agents of Influence and occasionally acts of sabotage, terrorism and even murder, committed for psychological effect. Any of these tactics may be invoked individually for a limited purpose, such as defamation of a foreign leader or a powerful anti-Soviet figure like Aleksandr Solzhenitsyn. In strategic or global campaigns, all or most forms of Active Measures are employed in concert to propagate a general theme that plays upon natural human fears and yearnings.

All Active Measures, however couched and conducted, aim at perverting perceptions of reality. To the extent they succeed, they cause popular attitudes and public policies to be formulated on the basis of specious or unrealistic premises. Grounded in illusions rather than reality, the thought and behavior induced can secure benefits for the Soviet Union unobtainable through rational debate, reasonable negotiations or even force. As will be shown, Active Measures have persuaded millions upon millions of honorable, patriotic and sensible people who detest Communist tyranny nevertheless to make common cause with the Soviet Union.

Soviet Active Measures frequently succeed for several reasons. With the possible exception of Japan, the industrialized democracies recognize the threat posed by KGB theft of technological, military and state secrets, and have erected defenses against Soviet espionage. Though the defenses are often breached, Western nations at least restrict their losses by combating Soviet spies.

But because the concept of Active Measures is not popularly understood in the West and Third World, few societies have prepared any institutional defenses against them. Although many Western security specialists understand Active Measures, their services generally are neither organized nor authorized to do much about them. This remains so even though Active Measures, by weakening and dividing free societies, can inflict more damage than espionage ordinarily does. Additionally, Active Measures strike at the inherent vulnerabilities of free societies, whose functioning depends upon unrestricted flow of information, rigorous competition of ideas, and unfettered criticism of public officials and policies. Through Active Measures the Soviet Union strives to debilitate and misguide other societies by debasing the coinage of this essential democratic debate with counterfeit data. Finally, Active Measures succeed because to prosecute them, the Soviet Union has developed an immense apparatus unique in modern history.

"The initiative in introducing propaganda as a regular instrument of international relations must be credited to the Soviet government," observes historian E. H. Carr. "Soviet Russia was the first modern state to establish, in the form of the Communist International, a large-scale, permanent international propaganda organization. Since the end of the Middle Ages, no political organization had claimed to be the repository of universal truth or the missionary of a universal gospel. . . . So revolutionary did this innovation appear that the Communist International purported at the outset to be wholly unconnected with the power of the Soviet government."

The Communist International, or Comintern, from its inception in 1919 was, of course, totally controlled by the Soviets. Initially it tried to foment revolution abroad through the embryonic foreign Communist Parties, which the Soviets regarded, quite simply, as instruments for expansion of their own power. After worldwide revolution failed to materialize, Lenin in 1921 damped down the calls for open rebellion and, while seeking trade and credits from the West, introduced more refined tactics.

While the Comintern directed the foreign parties and proliferating front organizations with secret ties to these parties, the Organs of State Security maintained a "disinformation desk" to supplement overt and covert propaganda with clandestine deceptions. They also developed in the West hidden agents, who could affect opinion and governmental policy, and they helped dupe foreigners by stage-managing visits to the Soviet Union. Viewed in retrospect, the results they achieved surely must be classified as brilliant.

At a time when the secret political police were murdering hundreds of thousands of Soviet citizens, and when countless others were being herded into concentration camps where ghastly conditions ensured the deaths of most, famous Western authors, scholars, journalists and lawyers acclaimed Soviet feats of "human regeneration" and "social correction." Even as millions perished from deliberately caused famines, playwright George Bernard Shaw praised Stalin for blessing the Soviet people with plenty. Equally luminous Westerners averred that Stalin was not a dictator but rather a great humanitarian actually entrusted with less power than that vested in President Franklin Roosevelt. While the secret political police cracked the bones of revolutionary leaders and threatened to do the same to their children unless these leaders confessed to the most preposterous imaginary crimes, the Dean of Canterbury proclaimed the Soviet Union the most moral nation he had known. When the tortured did, like zombies, mouth their incredible confessions at Moscow show trials, American journalist Walter Duranty wrote that surely they must be guilty, otherwise the good Stalin would not have put them in the dock. And French author André Malraux opined that, in any case, the show trials no more sullied the purity of communism than the inquisitions tarnished the essence of Christianity.

Many Westerners were emotionally disposed to be duped because the Soviets so effectively portrayed themselves as the principal bulwark against Nazism. Announcement of a formal alliance between the Soviet Union and Germany in 1939 awakened some Western intellectuals, but many remained blindly faithful. European and American Communist Parties, which had been among the shrillest in warning against Nazism, suddenly reversed themselves and began opposing the Allied war effort against Nazism. (Only when Germany attacked the Soviet Union in 1941 did the foreign parties rediscover the evils of Nazism.)

The contemporary Soviet Active Measures apparatus is essentially a continuation of that constructed before World War II, and its methodology is fundamentally the same. The International Department of the Communist Party, U.S.S.R., has assumed the role of the defunct Comintern in exploiting the foreign Communist Parties and directing international front organizations. The KGB has taken over and expanded upon the missions traditionally performed by State Security.

There are, however, some differences. The oligarchy has elected to allot seemingly limitless resources—human, monetary, material—for Active Measures. Whatever the apparatus thinks it needs, it gets, and the magnitude of current efforts dwarfs those of the past. The present practitioners of Active Measures are more learned, astute and sophisticated than their predecessors. Many of the KGB's most gifted and imaginative officers are congregated in its Service A, which conceives and oversees clandestine Active Measures, and the Service has upgraded the quality of personnel even while doubling in size during the last decade.

Perhaps the most significant difference between past and present is that anyone who wishes to peer inside the Active Measures apparatus now can do so. For within recent years, important members of that apparatus have fled to the West, bringing with them encyclopedic knowledge. In consequence of these KGB losses, it is possible to delineate the interrelationship among the Politburo, KGB and International Department to see just how the Soviets today go about turning reality upside down.

The KGB participates in virtually all forms of Active Measures, and it is principally responsible for those with which the Soviets fear to be publicly associated, such as terrorism. Bombings, arson and killings by terrorists can buttress Active Measures campaigns by generating social unrest and the impression that a society may be degenerating into chaos. During the last years of the Vietnam War, Weather Underground terrorists in the United States perpetrated at least 40 bombings, targeting public buildings, police stations, corporate offices, banks and the U.S. Capitol itself. Their primary intent was not to cause physical damage, though in some cases damage was substantial. Rather, they sought to persuade the public that American involvement in the war was so evil that idealistic young people were impelled by their moral outrage to violence.

At the trial of former FBI executives W. Mark Felt and Edward S. Miller in November 1980, heretofore secret evidence concerning the true nature of the Weather Underground was made public in federal court. The extensive data, derived from hundreds of U.S. intelligence reports, conclusively demonstrated that the KGB, directly and through Cuban surrogates, supported the American terrorists in their efforts to undermine the war effort. The support included training, financial aid and instruction in maintaining clandestine communications. According to an FBI report cited at the trial, after three terrorists blew themselves up on March 6, 1970, while experimenting with explosives in a New York townhouse, another Weatherman "was in Canada being instructed by a Russian adviser on how to make bombs."

The KGB regularly produces forgeries which the Soviet press and agents then cite as "proof" that the United States is guilty of whichever perfidy it is being accused of at the moment. The KGB, sometimes with help from its East European proxies, has concocted and disseminated more than 150 forgeries of official U.S. documents and correspondence.

Service A of the First Chief Directorate specializes in using stolen documents to make forgeries. Even so, the difficulties of replicating every detail of format, classification, terminology, and frequently changing procedures are such that the KGB has yet to manufacture a document that cannot be proven to be false. But by the time the necessary evidence is prepared, the damage sometimes cannot be fully undone.

During the last years of Egyptian President Anwar Sadat's life, the KGB plagued him with defamatory forgeries. Some sought to besmirch and isolate him in the Arab world; others to show that the United States secretly held him in contempt and was plotting his overthrow or assassination. The first purported to be the transcript of a speech delivered by Treasury Undersecretary Edwin Yeo to the Detroit Economic Club. Remarks imputed to Yeo insulted Egyptians generally, depicted Cairo as a hellhole and the Egyptian economy an unsalvageable mess, portrayed Sadat as a hopeless incompetent and suggested that Yeo favored U.S. intervention to replace him. Publication of the bogus speech in December 1976 by an Egyptian magazine, which received a copy anonymously mailed under a U.S. Information Service label, caused such concern that the Egyptian government officially asked the

United States for an explanation.

A forged letter, ostensibly from U.S. Ambassador to Egypt Hermann F. Eilts to the Saudi Arabian ambassador in Cairo, indicated that Sadat, with American assistance, intended to subvert the government of Sudan. The forgery, delivered anonymously to the Sudanese embassy in Beirut, caused dismay both in the Sudan and Egypt. Another forgery, purporting to be a photocopy of excerpts from a confidential report on the Mideast submitted by Secretary of State Cyrus Vance to President Carter, warned that Sadat was not to be trusted. "His concepts of what the U.S. should do in relation to Egypt are unrealistic, even absurd," declared the forgery. Summarizing an alleged conversation with Saudi Prince Fahd, it continued: "He warned us not to exaggerate our trust in Sadat. He does not think Sadat's fall will lead to complications. (The Saudis may be doing something in this respect without telling us.)" After delivery of this forgery to the Egyptian embassy in Rome, the Egyptians again were sufficiently perturbed to ask for an official U.S. explanation. In June 1977 ten newspapers and magazines in Egypt received photostatic copies of yet another forgery, this one a TOP SECRET OPERATIONS MEMORANDUM drafted on a genuine State Department form bearing a good facsimile of Ambassador Eilts's signature. The bogus memorandum concluded: "[Sadat's] leadership style leaves much to be desired, and this could be an obstacle to our plan for a settlement in the Middle East. Close associates of the President are shocked to see that recently he has displayed reluctance to read reports, analyses and proposals prepared on the country's affairs or to devote proper attention to the country's problems."

A forged dispatch from the U.S. embassy in Tehran, mailed the same month to the Egyptian embassy in Belgrade, showed that Iran and Saudi Arabia were conniving with tacit U.S. assent to oust or kill Sadat. In July 1978 copies of a fabricated press release from the U.S. embassy in Paris quoted Vice President Walter Mondale as saying in an interview that both Sadat and Israeli Prime Minister Menachem Begin were worthless because the former could not govern and the latter was dying. Yet another forgery over the signature of Eilts, this one ostensibly a letter from the ambassador to CIA Director Stansfield Turner, stated that the United States should be ready to "get rid of" Sadat "without hesitation" and should clandestinely overturn the leadership of the PLO.

A forgery published in 1979 by the Moslem Brotherhood's magazine *Al-Dawa* in Cairo may have contributed to the murder of Sadat. It purported to be a report from an American professor to the CIA outlining foul means by which members of the Brotherhood and other Islamic organizations opposing the peace settlement Sadat advocated could be bribed or duped and their religious beliefs corrupted. The wording was calculated to affront and enrage Muslims generally and particularly the fanatic Moslem Brotherhood, whose followers in 1981 finally killed Sadat.

Another of the more significant KGB forgeries in recent years was the "Top Secret" *U.S. Army Field Manual FM30-31B*. Field Manuals *FM30-31* and *FM30-31A* did exist, but *FM30-31B* was entirely a KGB creation. Typed over the forged signature of General William Westmoreland, the manual detailed the operational procedures to be followed by U.S. military security personnel in foreign countries. In these instructions, two sinister themes were apparent. Wherever U.S. military forces or advisers are stationed, they are to interfere in the internal political affairs of the host country to ensure vigilant anti-Communist and anti-leftist policies suitable to the United States. In extreme cases, they are to manipulate and incite ultra-leftist groups to violence so as to provoke the host government into militant anti-Communist actions.

A minor Turkish newpaper referred to *FM30-31B* in 1975, but few paid any heed. The KGB next attempted to surface the forgery by leaving a facsimile at the embassy of the Philippines in Bangkok. U.S. specialists immediately pointed out defects which proved the document a forgery. Unable to fool the Filipinos, the Center ordered the Tokyo Residency to mail copies of the manual to two conservative Japanese newspapers with an anonymous note saying, "Westmoreland manual is a threat to Japan." Here again, the forgery was ignored, and the KGB put aside the document until later, when it was used with stunning effect.

On March 16, 1978, terrorists from the radical leftist Red Brigades shot down five bodyguards protecting Aldo Moro, President of the Italian Christian Democratic Party. They dragged away Moro and later killed him. A popular pro-Western moderate, Moro had done much to maintain political stability in Italy by achieving practical understandings between his governing party and the Communist Party. His murder constituted a serious loss to the United States and the West.

Nevertheless, on the very day of Moro's abduction, the Soviet Union began a campaign to persuade the world that the United States was responsible. Radio Moscow declared that the kidnapping was one of several "attempts by a right-wing force to aggravate the situation in Italy." In a broadcast beamed to Italy March 18, Moscow charged that the crime was "prepared by internal and international reactionary forces." The same day, it quoted the French Communist newspaper *L'Humanité* as reporting that "secret services whose activity is connected with the NATO military base in Naples" participated in the kidnapping. The next day Radio Moscow implicated "a far-flung organization with connections far beyond Italy's borders." Four days later, it elaborated: "It is no secret that the Central Intelligence Agency is actively operating in the Apennines Peninsula." Subsequent broadcasts, reinforced by a KGB whispering campaign in Italy, escalated hints that the CIA abducted Moro. Finally, on April 2, on the Moscow Radio International Service, commentator Anatoli Ovsyannikov said: "Well, to call a spade a spade, that service [which kidnapped Moro] is called the Central Intelligence Agency, and the foreign power that it belongs to is the United States of America." Thereafter, the Russians openly repeated this charge, and KGB officers as well as Soviet diplomats in Western Europe confidentially assured anyone who would listen that it was true.

But the allegations had minimal impact because they were unsupported by any evidence or plausible explanation of why the United States would desire the death of such a valuable ally as Moro. How could evidence and a motive be concocted? During the summer of 1978, someone in the KGB obviously thought of the forgery, *U.S. Army Field Manual FM30-31B*. Someone also thought of ordering the KGB's satellite service, the Cuban DGI, to help.

According to Congressional testimony, Cuban intelligence officer Luis Gonzalez Verdecia offered a Spanish newspaper the forged manual, along with an analysis by Fernando Gonzalez, a Spanish Communist who dealt with the KGB. In his article, Gonzalez cited the manual to support claims that the United States was involved with various terrorist groups, including the Red Brigades.

The leftist Spanish magazine *El Triunfo* published both Gonzalez' article and parts of the forgery on September 23, 1978. Immediately, Italian and other European newspapers replayed the Spanish stories. Soviet propagandists now set up a new hue and cry, pointing to all the articles in the non-Communist European press as "evidence" that the CIA really killed Moro and that the United States was the actual sponsor of left-wing terrorists all around the world.

Soon the press in 20 different nations published these allegations, along with the forged manual or excerpts from it. In the minds of millions, the KGB again had succeeded in inverting reality.

As the use of forgeries and the fanciful allegations about the fate of Moro indicate, Soviet propagandists and the KGB are not inhibited by or concerned with truth, in the Western sense, in their conduct of Active Measures. By Leninist definition, the "truth" is whatever at the moment seems most likely to advance Soviet interests. Hence, to the Soviets there is nothing immoral about propagation of "disinformation," which usually is an amalgam of fact, distortion and fiction, but sometimes is pure fabrication.

The KGB purveys disinformation through Soviet journalists, academicians and scientists, both within the Soviet Union and abroad, and by planting articles in the foreign press. A majority of the 500 or so Soviet journalists working abroad are regular intelligence officers, and among the minority who are not, few can easily refuse *ad hoc* assignments from the KGB. Irrespective of which publication or news organizaton they claim to represent, Soviet journalists, without exception, are full-time employees of the Soviet state—paid by it, controlled by it, allowed abroad only at its suffrage. However, they pretend to be journalists as independent as are representatives of the Associated Press, Reuters, Agence France-Presse or any other reputable private news organization. Like Stanislav Levchenko, they enjoy membership in press clubs, access to their foreign colleagues and wide entrée to politicians and policymakers, and they exploit these privileges subtly to transmit disinformation orally. They and KGB officers under other covers also bribe or recruit foreign journalists to publish or cause to be published disinformation in the foreign press.

In the most subtle and artful form of Active Measures, the KGB employs Agents of Influence to spread disinformation as well as to mold opinion and policies by other means. A typical Agent of Influence, exposed in 1979, was Pierre-Charles Pathé, a French journalist of aristocratic heritage. A KGB officer on the staff of UNESCO in Paris recruited Pathé in 1960 as an intelligence source, but the KGB gradually converted him into an agent whose primary mission was to influence public attitudes and governmental actions rather than supply information. The Russians saw such potential in Pathé that they allowed his recruiting officer to remain in Paris handling him until 1967, when another officer from the Paris Residency assumed control.

Over the years, the KGB regularly supplied him with data which, under Soviet guidance, he transformed into articles or passed along to other journalists as if they were the product of his own research and thinking. Between 1960 and 1979, Pathé caused to be published, under his own name or that of others, more than 100 articles about Latin America, China, NATO, the

CIA, and other topics important to the Soviet Union. With financial support from the KGB, he wrote a newsletter read by leaders in government, politics and industry. Additionally, he enjoyed personal ties with several major French publications as well as numerous journalists. In print and conversation, Pathé adroitly circulated the beliefs the KGB wished to implant, sometimes making them more persuasive by accompanying them with mild criticism of the Soviet Union.

The French arrested and convicted Pathé in 1979, sentencing him to five years in prison. (He was pardoned in 1981, reportedly because of his age.)

The KGB additionally participates in Active Measures by assisting the International Department of the Party in maintaining an interlocking web of front organizations or "Innocents' Clubs," as German Communist Willi Münzenberg called them in the 1930s. Although all these fronts are controlled or manipulated from Moscow, they are not popularly perceived as the subversive instrumentalities they are. Yet they constitute in the 1980s what Andropov's mentor, Otto Kuusinen, proposed more than half a century ago—"a whole solar system of organizations and smaller committees around the Communist Party." Among the more important fronts are the World Peace Council, the Afro-Asian People's Solidarity Committee, and the Institute for U.S.A. and Canada.

The World Peace Council emerged in Paris in 1950* to foment "Ban the Bomb" propaganda at a time when the Soviets had not succeeded in arming themselves with nuclear weapons. Expelled from France for subversion in 1951, the WPC took refuge in Prague until 1954, when it moved its ostensible headquarters to Vienna. The Austrians evicted the WPC because of subversive activities in 1957, but it retained a European outpost by leaving behind in Vienna a branch titled the International

---

*The origins of the World Peace Council are as follows: In 1948, the Soviets sponsored the "World Congress of Intellectuals for Peace" in Poland. Out of this gathering grew the "First World Peace Congress," which in 1949 established the "World Committee of Partisans of Peace" in Paris. That organization renamed itself the World Peace Council in 1950.

Institute for Peace. In 1968 the WPC established headquarters in Helsinki to orchestrate the global propaganda campaign to compel withdrawal of American forces from Vietnam.

The president of the World Peace Council is Indian Communist Romesh Chandra, who has long been a controlled and witting Soviet agent. Intelligent, vain and arrogant, Chandra is almost embarrassing in his slavish adherence to Soviet dictates and his paeans to all things Soviet. "The Soviet Union invariably supports the peace movement," Chandra said a few years ago. "The World Peace Council in its turn positively reacts to all Soviet initiatives in international affairs."

Nevertheless, the Russians supervise Chandra closely by assigning both International Department and KGB representatives to the permanent Secretariat of the WPC in Helsinki. The KGB further ensures Soviet dominance by recruiting Agents of Influence within the WPC organizational hierarchy and among its affiliates. KGB officers placed on the Soviet Peace Committee in Moscow also recruit agents from among the many foreigners journeying to the Soviet Union under auspices of the WPC. Together, the International Department and KGB guarantee that positions of power in the WPC and associated "peace committees" in foreign countries are occupied by pro-Soviet personnel or people amenable to Soviet manipulation.

The public record alone amply demonstrates the totality and effectiveness of Soviet control of the World Peace Council. In its 32 years of existence, the WPC has not deviated from the Soviet line of the moment. It did not raise its voice against Soviet suppression of East German workers in 1953, Soviet slaughter of Hungarians in 1956, Soviet abrogation of the nuclear test moratorium in 1961, the clandestine installation of nuclear missiles in Cuba in 1962, the invasion of Czechoslovakia in 1968, the projection of Soviet military power into Angola, Ethiopia and Yemen. Never has the WPC criticized a single Soviet armament program; only those of the West. And it endorsed the Soviet invasion of Afghanistan.

WPC finances further reflect Soviet control. Huge sums are necessary to maintain offices and staff in Helsinki, Vienna, and, since 1977, Geneva; to pay for continuous far-flung travel by WPC officials; to publish and distribute around the world monthly periodicals in English, French, German and Spanish; to finance international assemblies, for which hundreds or thousands of delegates are provided with free transportation, food and lodging. Yet the World Peace Council has no visible means of support. Virtually all its income comes clandestinely from the Soviet Bloc.

Even so, many people, including politicians, scientists and journalists, do not see the World Peace Council for what it is, or if they do see, they do not care. The United Nations officially recognizes the WPC as a "non-governmental organization" and joins it in "discussions" of issues such as disarmament and "colonialism." The national peace committees with which the WPC maintains both open and secret ties in more than 130 nations are rarely stigmatized in the press as puppets of the Politburo.

Given the façade of an earnest institution uniting sincere men and women from all parts of the world in the quest for peace, given the expertise of KGB and International Department specialists in Active Measures and propaganda, given virtually limitless funds, the World Peace Council frequently rallies millions of non-Communists to Communist causes.

The Afro-Asian People's Solidarity Organization, founded jointly by the Soviets and Chinese in 1957, set up headquarters in Cairo with permission of Gamal Abdel Nasser. Shrewdly, the KGB enlisted a respected non-Communist journalist, Yusuf As-Sebai, to be titular head, and prevailed upon prominent personalities from other nations to lend their names to the organization. However, ever since the Sino-Soviet split, the Soviets alone have dominated the AAPSO. KGB officers assigned to the Cairo offices make sure that the staff and leadership hew to the Soviet line, and they also develop agents among AAPSO affiliates in Third World countries. Plans and policies governing the whole organization are conceived and issued in Moscow by the Soviet Afro-Asian Solidarity Committee, which long shared offices with the Soviet Peace Committee in an ornate old Moscow mansion at 10 Kropotkinskaya Ulitsa. About a fourth of its staff members are active or retired KGB officers.

The AAPSO and affiliates in 50 nations form a conduit for funneling propaganda into the Third World to further regional Soviet aims and generally defame the United States. They also provide convenient cover for Soviet dealings with terrorist and guerrilla movements. The Soviet Afro-Asian Solidarity Committee long represented the Soviet Union in relations with the Palestinian Liberation Organization, arranging delivery of arms and training of personnel in Soviet camps. The committee considered the insurgents that brought Marxism to Angola, albeit with the help of Cuban troops, its own creation, and today it maintains ties with revolutionary groups throughout Africa and Latin America.

The Institute for U.S.A. and Canada affords disguised Soviet operatives entry into much higher levels of American society than does the WPC. Ostensibly a scholarly branch of the Soviet Academy of Sciences, the Institute actually is a front for the International Department and the KGB. Its quick-witted director, Georgi Arbatov, a long-time intimate of Andropov, is a pudgy man with a melancholy face and the sad eyes of a hound dog. Arbatov in recent years has been a regular commuter to the United States, where he hobnobs with prominent politicians and airs Soviet views on national television.

Fully a third of the Institute's staff members are now KGB officers, and its deputy director, KGB Colonel Radomir Bogdanov, privately is referred to among clerical personnel as "the scholar in epaulets." After an underling wrote a doctoral dissertation for him, Colonel Bogdanov became Dr. Bogdanov, and to enhance his academic standing further, the Institute allowed him to appear as co-author of two books written by others. Galina Orionova, who fled from the Institute to England in 1979, recalls Col./Dr. Bogdanov in this way: "He was a drunk, a womanizer and a bully," she says. "It was after his arrival that the staff came under renewed pressure to inform against foreign visitors."

However he appears to subordinates, Bogdanov is an effective professional who ventures often into the West, peddling the Soviet line and hunting Americans who can be seduced into following it. And once he has memorized what the KGB wants him to say, he can say it smoothly and earnestly.

The KGB also assists the International Department in sustaining foreign Communist Parties. Many of the parties survive only through secret Soviet subsidies, often delivered by the KGB. As noted earlier, the Soviets regularly smuggle about two million dollars annually to the U.S. Communist Party. Similarly, local security services have detected and, in some instances, photographed KGB officers handing over cash to Communist Party functionaries in Ecuador, Venezuela, Mexico and Brazil. For some time, the KGB funneled money to the West German Communist Party through clandestine meetings in Copenhagen. During the 1970s, KGB officers frequently met Filipino Communists in deluxe Japanese hotels and gave them large sums of cash hidden in false bottoms of suitcases.

The Soviet Union spends millions on the foreign parties because, even if bedraggled and numerically small, they still contribute significantly to Active Measures. Their members can be counted upon to circulate pamphlets and daub the walls of cities with political graffiti promulgating Soviet themes, which then creep into respectable discourse. Members elected to democratic parliaments can insert these same themes into the reportage of the non-Communist press by echoing them in official debates. The parties constitute a ready reservoir of obedient demonstrators who can take to the streets simultaneously in different cities and nations to foster an illusion of widespread popular concern spontaneously expressed. And they provide the indefatigable cadre of planners, organizers and agitators who help stage mass demonstrations that attract non-Communists.

The vast Soviet Active Measures apparatus—the overt propaganda organs, foreign Communist Parties, international fronts, the KGB Residencies around the world, the factories of forgeries and disinformation at the Center, the Agents of Influence—is so well coordinated and disciplined that it can respond to commands rapidly and flexibly. When the KGB or

International Department senses opportunity, a detailed operational plan is submitted to the Politburo. Once the Politburo approves, everybody from Andropov on down pitches in. The basic themes and sub-themes of the campaign are then propagated through tendentious arguments and simplistic slogans repeated massively and thunderously, as some primitive chant, to drown out reasoned debate or dissent.

Currently, the Soviets are waging one of their greatest campaigns of all time. Its name is "nuclear freeze." This campaign actually began in 1977 in reaction to the Enhanced Radiation Warhead (ERW), which soon was mislabeled the "neutron bomb." The ERW was born of the most realistic considerations. By 1976, the Soviet Union and its satellites had deployed some 20,000 main battle tanks against West Germany. The tanks were augmented by many more thousands of armored personnel carriers, sealed to survive chemical and bacteriological contamination as well as normal nuclear radiation.

NATO, with only some 7000 tanks and numerically inferior ground forces, could be sure of repelling an onslaught by Soviet armor only through use of tactical nuclear weapons. However, the smallest of the nuclear weapons then stored in Europe had a destructive force roughly equivalent to the bomb dropped on Hiroshima. The blast and heat from such a weapon would wipe out not only Soviet invaders but everybody and everything within a four-mile radius of the detonation point; radiation would kill men, women and children within a wider area.

Through their hydra-headed propaganda apparatus, the Russians were able to say and in effect continue to say to the West Germans: If there is war, that is, if we attack you, the Americans will lay waste to your country and people. Since defense is impossible without annihilation, you should quit NATO, cease being pawns of the Americans and come to peaceful and profitable terms with us. The most imminent objective of the Russians in arraying armor on West German borders in such profligate numbers was to reinforce this argument—not to attack but to intimidate and fragment by threat.

The United States developed the ERW solely to neutralize this threat. Fired with extreme accuracy from a howitzer or short-range missile, the Enhanced Radiation Warhead obliterates everything within a radius of about 120 yards, inflicting no physical damage beyond. But it releases neutrons, which flash through the thickest of armor with the ease of light passing through a window. The neutrons instantly kill tank crews, soldiers and anybody else within a radius of 500 yards, and cause death in hours or days to all within a radius of a mile. The radiation effects dissipate, though, and the area affected soon may be safely entered.

After technological breakthroughs in the mid-1970s made production of an ERW feasible, military strategists advanced the following arguments: The ERW in one fell swoop would render the masses of Soviet tanks menacing NATO by and large useless, *politically* and militarily. The ERW could wipe out the crews of entire Communist armored armadas, while causing minimal civilian casualties and physical devastation. In other words, with the ERW, NATO could defend West Europe without blowing up much of West Europe and its population. Because the ERW was a low-yield, tactical weapon valuable only in defending against massed, attacking armor, the Russians could not legitimately construe it as an offensive threat to them.

Accordingly, in April 1976 President Gerald R. Ford approved the Enhanced Radiation Warhead, and the last budget prepared by his administration included funds for its production. But in June 1977, President Jimmy Carter announced that he had not yet personally approved production of the ERW and would delay his final decision until November.

That announcement gave the Russians time and opportunity to initiate a worldwide campaign to force President Carter to do as they wished. In little more than a month, the Politburo, the International Department of the Central Committee, the KGB, their worldwide web of agents and front groups and the Soviet press all were ready. They began July 9, 1977, with a cry from TASS aimed at Carter himself: "How can one pose as a champion of human rights and at the same time brandish the

neutron bomb, which threatens the lives of millions of people?"
Pravda the next day accused the United States of embarking
on an "old, bankrupt policy of American imperialism." The
Kremlin warned the world that the neutron bomb "can only
bring the world closer to nuclear holocaust."

Throughout July the Soviet press and radio, in an ever-
rising chorus, sounded variations of this refrain: The ghastly
new American weapon, the neutron bomb, threatens mankind
with nuclear war and extinction. To be for the neutron bomb is
to be for war. To oppose the neutron bomb is to be for peace.
Faithfully, the state-controlled media of Eastern Europe and
the newspapers of Communist Parties in Western Europe
echoed the bombast emanating from Moscow.

Initially, the Active Measures against the ERW were mostly
overt and the propaganda traceable to Communist sources,
but in August the campaign advanced into semi-covert and
clandestine phases. The World Peace Council proclaimed
August 6-13 a Week of Action, and its front groups, abetted by
the KGB and local Communist Parties, promoted public demonstrations whose Soviet sponsorship was less perceptible.
That week, crowds pleading the name of humanity against the
"killer neutron bomb" demonstrated before U.S. consulates
or embassies in Bonn, Stuttgart, Frankfurt and Istanbul. A
motley group of Ghanaians even turned up at the embassy in
Accra. Though subtly directed by Soviet agents, the demonstrators, in Germany at least, were mostly non-Communists
attracted by intensive advertising and motivated by impulses
ranging through anti-Americanism, pacifism, abhorrence of all
nuclear weapons, and sincere longing for peace.

Elsewhere, in lands where the ERW never would be used,
KGB Residencies did their job by planting disinformation in
the local press. One prestigious Latin American newspaper
published an anti-neutron-bomb article attributed to the "International Institute for Peace" in Vienna, but the Institute
was not identified as the Soviet front it is. A little Communist
claque in Lima dispatched a formal protest to the United
Nations. A spate of Soviet-inspired articles appeared in India,

Pakistan, Mauritius, Ghana, Ethiopia and Libya.

Concurrently, the Soviet Union, within its own empire, beat the propaganda drums to a new crescendo. From East Berlin, Reuters on August 8 reported: "Twenty-eight European and North American Communist Parties today joined an unusual display of public unity to call on the United States to ban production of the neutron bomb." In Soviet cities, where demonstrations never occur unless prompted by the Party and overseen by the KGB, there were "popular" demonstrations against the "neutron bomb," casting it as an issue of war and peace. A sturdy worker in Moscow recalled the suffering of World War II; by coincidence, another man, 1500 miles away in Uzbekistan, spoke almost exactly the same words.

In October Secretary of Defense Harold Brown announced that President Carter would approve production of the ERW only if the NATO allies agreed in advance to its deployment on their territories. Western European leaders recognized the ERW as a much safer, more credible deterrent than the nuclear warheads already on their soil and privately wanted it added to NATO defenses. But by temporizing and publicly shifting the burden of decision to them, Carter exposed Allied leaders as well as himself to intensified pressures.

Accurately assessing Carter as a devout Baptist, the Soviets played upon his deep religious faith. In a dispatch quoted by the American press, TASS reported: "Soviet Baptist leaders today condemned production of the neutron bomb as 'contrary to the teachings of Christ' and urged fellow Baptists in the United States to raise their voices in defense of peace." As President and Mrs. Carter worshiped at the First Baptist Church in Washington on Sunday, October 16, 1977, six outsiders disrupted the service with shouts against the neutron bomb. And on two more occasions, protesters harassed the Carters at church.

In January 1978, Brezhnev sent letters to heads of all Western Governments asserting that the "neutron bomb" would "pose a grave threat to détente." Western parliamentarians received similar letters from members of the Supreme Soviet and Soviet "trade union" leaders. The letters did not explain why preparations by NATO to defend itself would jeopardize détente.

Emboldened by the initial furor the Active Measures campaign had incited, the KGB and International Department moved on the U.S. Congress itself. American Communists joined by non-Communists formed a "National Committee" to welcome Romesh Chandra and the World Peace Council Presidential Bureau to a "Dialogue on Disarmament and Détente" in Washington, January 25-28, 1978. U.S. Rep. John Conyers, Jr., heartily welcomed the group. "You have joined us to give us courage and inspiration in our fight for disarmament and against the neutron bomb," he declared.

Agent Chandra was delighted. "The wide interest in the work of the Bureau and the Dialogue was indicated by participation in the sessions and also in special meetings of Bureau members inside the U.S. Congress itself with several Congressmen, among which [sic] were Congressmen John Burton, Ted Weiss, Ronald Dellums, John Conyers, Jr., Don Edwards, Charles Rangel and others," Chandra asserted. "The movement to ban the neutron bomb has assumed the widest dimensions in the U.S.A., with a large number of Congressmen opposing this dastardly weapon."

The KGB provided the star of this show at the Capitol. Reporting the proceedings, which included a luncheon in the House of Representatives, the Communist *Daily World* said: "Every now and then, one of the speakers would strike an emotional chord that was both personal and political, a human plea that sank deeply into the listeners. One such speaker was Radomir Bogdanov of the Soviet Academy of Sciences." The *Daily World* neglected to inform readers that Radomir Gregorovich Bogdanov is actually a senior KGB colonel from the Twelfth Department, First Chief Directorate.

Having given "courage and inspiration" to U.S. Congressmen, agent Chandra and Colonel Bogdanov proceeded to New York, where the WPC group had "long and fruitful discussions" with United Nations Secretary General Kurt Waldheim.

In late February 1978, 126 representatives of "peace groups" from 50 nations gathered in Geneva to denounce the "neutron bomb." They also attracted attention from an uncritical press, which did not ask who was paying for this extravaganza, allegedly sponsored by a heretofore unknown outfit calling itself the "Special Nongovernmental Organizations Committee on Disarmament." The actual organizers and sponsors were the World Peace Council, its Swiss allies, and East European "diplomats" accredited to the United Nations in Geneva. The presiding officer was the ubiquitous agent Chandra. Chandra also helped turn a symposium in Vienna on "Nuclear Energy and the Arms Race," sponsored by the World Peace Council and the U.N. International Atomic Energy Agency, into another anti-"neutron bomb" forum.

On March 19 in a rally organized primarily by the Dutch Communist Party, some 40,000 demonstrators, drawn from throughout Europe at considerable expense to organizers, marched through Amsterdam inveighing against the horrors of the "neutron bomb" and the nuclear holocaust it would surely precipitate. The protest, part of the "International Forum Against the Neutron Bomb," doubtless constituted to many evidence that the "neutron bomb" must be very bad indeed.

Despite the illusion of a worldwide tide of sentiment welling up against the ERW, President Carter's three principal foreign policy advisers—Secretary of State Cyrus Vance, Defense Secretary Harold Brown and National Security Adviser Zbigniew Brzezinski—all urged production. So did the Washington *Post* and the New York *Times*, scarcely redoubts of Dr. Strangeloves. Declared the *Times*: "Ever since the Carter Administration asked Congress last summer for funds to produce enhanced-radiation nuclear warheads, critics ranging from Soviet propagandists to Western cartoonists have had a field day attacking the so-called 'neutron bomb.' The archetypical capitalist weapon, Moscow has called it, destroyer of people but not property. Grim forecasts of lingering radiation deaths have filled newspaper columns worldwide. Rarely have the relevant questions been asked: Is the neutron weapon really more terrible than other nuclear weapons? And more important, would its deployment make nuclear war more likely?

Hirohide Ishida

Takuji Yamane (Kant)
Photo: Kyodo News Service

Stanislav Levchenko

Vladimir Pronnikov

The Soviet Embassy compound in Tokyo.

Apartment house where Levchenko lived.

Ketel German Restaurant, where Levchenko had some clandestine meetings.

Typical street in downtown Tokyo, with small restaurants and cafés in almost every building.

KGB PERSONNEL WORKING IN GENEVA, SWITZERLAND

Valeri Yevstigneyev

Eugenia Bryntseva
(Bryntsev's wife)

Aleksandr Bryntsev

Igor Guriev

Vladimir Lemesh

Yuri Chestnoy

Geli Dneprovsky

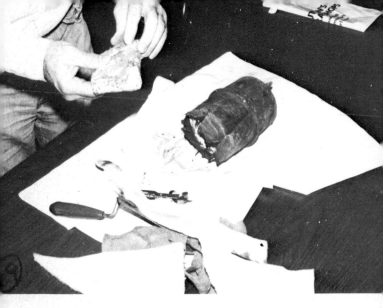

In May, 1979, at a drop site in Rockland County. N.Y. $5,000 in cash was picked up by Rudi Herrmann. These photographs show how part of an automobile exhaust was used to conceal and protect the money at the drop, and the money that was concealed.

Vasili V. Averyanov, a Soviet employed by the United Nations Secretariat in New York City, clears a drop in Westchester County, N.Y. in September, 1977. The drop had been loaded by Herrmann.

Yuri S. Serpokrylov, First Secretary at the Soviet Mission to the United Nations in New York City, clears a drop in northern New Jersey in May, 1975.

Hugh G. Hambleton
(Photo©Popperfoto)

Yuri Andropov
(Photo: Sygma)

"The answer to both these questions is almost certainly 'No.'. . . Neutron weapons in Western hands would significantly complicate Soviet tactical planning: If its tanks were to attack in mass, they would be highly vulnerable. If they were to disperse, they would be easier targets for conventional precision-guided anti-tank weapons."

Such logic was unavailing. On April 7, after America's two leading liberal newspapers adjured him to order production of the ERW, President Carter announced its cancellation. The Communists chortled. "The political campaign against the neutron bomb was one of the most significant and successful since World War II," boasted Janos Berecz, chief of the Hungarian Communist Party's International Department. And Brezhnev himself decorated the Soviet Ambassador to the Netherlands, Aleksandr Yosipovich Romanov, for his services in inciting Dutch demonstrations.

In unilaterally abandoning plans to produce the Enhanced Radiation Warhead, the United States secured no reciprocal or compensatory concessions from the Soviet Union. It gained no good will from those people endemically hostile to it or those convinced that it had pushed the world to the precipice of nuclear war by developing a ghastly, misanthropic weapon. Far from being appeased, the Russians pressed on with the campaign to exacerbate the fear and loathing of the United States they had incited through the "neutron bomb" scare. The KGB forged and, in June, surfaced a letter, over the signature of NATO General Secretary Luns, advising the U.S. Ambassador to NATO that a list of journalists opposed to the "neutron bomb" had been compiled. The wording insinuated that they would be subject to unspecified but harsh retribution.

By arming NATO with the Enhanced Radiation Warhead, the United States had intended to demonstrate to friends that it possessed the will and capacity to participate effectively in their defense. By vacillating, then capitulating before the pressures of Soviet Active Measures, the United States showed itself to be irresolute and, in the eyes of many friends, witless. The retreat especially frightened Europeans because they were now threatened by the Soviets' newest weapon of mass destruction, the SS-20 missile. The SS-20 is an accurate, mobile weapon, which can be hidden from space satellites and reconnaissance aircraft. By 1977 the Russians had begun deploying the first of 333 missiles, each with three nuclear warheads that can be directed at separate targets. Thus, the Soviet Union now boasted an intimidating new force, which within 15 minutes from launch could obliterate 999 European targets—including every sizable city from Oslo to Lisbon, from Glasgow to Istanbul.

At the insistence of the Europeans, particularly West German Chancellor Helmut Schmidt, the Carter Administration finally agreed to emplace, under joint U.S.-NATO control, 572 Pershing II and cruise missiles as a counterpoise to the SS-20s. Unlike the old missiles they would replace, the intermediate-range Pershing II and cruise missile could reach Moscow and other cities in the western Soviet Union. Both are mobile and can be concealed and thus could probably survive a surprise attack. Unlike the SS-20, the new American missiles would be armed with only a single warhead. NATO strategists reasoned that the 572 warheads would suffice to void the threat of the SS-20 by convincing the Russians that attack upon Western Europe automatically would precipitate catastrophic counterattack. The balance of nuclear terror that has kept peace in Europe for more than three decades would be restored; neither side could credibly threaten the other with nuclear assault. NATO ministers in December 1979 overwhelmingly approved deployment of the modern missiles, and the United States promised to put them in place by late 1983.

Throughout the 1980 Presidential campaign, candidate Ronald Reagan declared that if elected, he would restore American military power to the degree necessary to deter Soviet intimidation or attack. A few days after Reagan won, the Soviet Union instigated the great new Active Measures campaign to prevent NATO from countering the SS-20s and to reverse the American election results by nullifying the rearmament program implicitly mandated by the voters. After the success of the anti-"neutron bomb" drive, their expectations were high.

The sub-themes of the new campaign were: The missiles the United States plans to emplace in Europe bespeak American intentions to fight a nuclear war on European territory and invite destruction of Europe. The world is teetering madly, uncontrollably, toward the abyss of nuclear extinction. It can be saved only if good men and women, irrespective of nationality, ideology, age or station, unite for peace. All must raise their voices in unison to curb the profiteering American military-industrial complex and the aging cowboy, the movie actor Reagan. All must join in demanding a pause so the superpowers can reason and negotiate together. We must demand a moratorium on development of all new nuclear weapons systems; we must have a "nuclear freeze."

After President Reagan routinely confirmed that the Enhanced Radiation Warhead was being produced, just as he vowed it would be, Chandra cabled the White House in the name of the World Peace Council. Claiming credit for having forced President Carter to cancel the weapon, Chandra demanded that Reagan do the same. "The World Peace Council with national committees in 137 countries embracing hundreds of millions of people is deeply shocked," Chandra averred. "The overwhelming majority of humanity has already expressed itself as one voice in condemning these illegal, inhuman weapons."

With the World Peace Council, its foreign affiliates, and local Communist Parties again the principal organizers, a new series of mass demonstrations occurred in Europe. An estimated 250,000 people marched in Bonn, protesting against any new missiles or nuclear weapons. Some carried placards saying, "*Ich habe angst*," or "I am afraid," which is just what the Soviet Union wanted everybody in Europe to be. Only a miniscule portion of the Bonn demonstrators were Soviet sympathizers, but many of the "marshals," who kept everybody in line, were Communists.

Soviet fronts helped assemble throngs estimated at 350,000 in Amsterdam, 400,000 in Madrid and 200,000 in Athens. In West Germany the furor in the streets was accompanied by terrorist attacks on U.S. military personnel and installations and by virulently anti-American articles in the press and programs on television. French television correspondent Michel Meyer, having monitored German television for seven weeks, stated "I didn't see a single program that was either friendly or clearly positive about the United States."

The KGB all along played its traditional part. Dutch authorities, in April 1981, expelled KGB officer Vadim Leonov, who in the guise of a TASS correspondent associated intimately with leaders of the Dutch "peace" movement. Leonov made a number of professional mistakes, including a drunken boast: "If Moscow decides that 50,000 demonstrators must take to the streets in the Netherlands, then they take to the streets. Do you know how you can get 50,000 demonstrators at a certain place within a week? A message through my channels is sufficient," Leonov bragged.

In January 1982 Portugal ousted two KGB officers, Yuri Babayants and Mikhail Morozov, for attempting to incite riots against NATO.

The same month the Portuguese Socialist Party boycotted a Lisbon march, deriding it as a "reflection of the diplomatic and military logic of the Soviet Bloc." However, the march of about 50,000 people proceeded with U.S. Congressman Gus Savage as one of its leaders. In a newsletter to constituents, Savage boasted of his participation in activities of the World Peace Council, which he described as "the largest non-governmental peace organization in the world."

All the while, the KGB was surfacing forged documents to buttress the theme that American, rather than Soviet, nuclear weapons imperil Western Europe. It succeeded in circulating in Great Britain, the Netherlands, Norway, Belgium, Malta, Greece and France a pamphlet entitled *Top Secret Documents. . . U.S. Forces Headquarters in Europe. . .Holocaust Again for Europe*. The contents consisted of alterations and fabrications based upon authentic Top Secret military contingency plans stolen by a KGB agent, Sergeant Robert Lee Johnson, from the Armed Forces Courier Center vault at Orly Field in 1962. The fabrications purported to show that the United States planned to blow up much of Europe with nuclear weapons to save itself.

Reproducing a standard, unclassified U.S. government map of Austria, the KGB labeled it "Top Secret" and marked "targets" on it. Both the Austrian Communist newspaper *Volksstimme* and *Komsomolskaya Pravda* in Moscow then published stories alleging that the map proved the United States planned to destroy Austrian cities and installations with nuclear bombs.

Soviet Agents of Influence also were active. Danish writer Arne Herløv Petersen, a KGB agent since 1970, helped organize a propaganda drive advocating a "Nordic Nuclear Weapon Free Zone," i.e., stripping the northern flank of NATO of all nuclear defenses. As part of this effort, he composed an advertisement, signed by 150 Danish artists and intellectuals, and bought newspaper space with KGB money. In the summer of 1981, Petersen sponsored a "peace march" from Oslo to Paris, and he also published under his own name propaganda tracts written by the KGB.

Danish counterintelligence monitored 23 clandestine meetings between Petersen and Major Vladimir Dmitrevich Merkulov, the Active Measures officer at the KGB Residency in Copenhagen. Finally, in October 1981, they arrested Petersen as a Soviet agent. Merkulov, who had been active in the Danish "Cooperation Committee for Peace and Security," a Communist-dominated subsidiary of the World Peace Council, was expelled.

While the Soviet-inspired demonstrations against NATO and the Euromissiles raged across Europe, protests in America were initially scant and inconsequential. After all, each of the new American weapons systems had been long and carefully considered. A consensus between both political parties had been reached, and in the Presidential election just concluded, the people had spoken. Seemingly there was nothing more to argue about. All that soon changed.

Brezhnev, addressing the 26th Party Congress on February 23, 1981, called for a halt in production of all nuclear weapons and a ban on the "neutron bomb." He also issued the first official Soviet appeal for a nuclear "freeze" or an immediate cessation of development and deployment of the new missiles the U.S. planned for Europe. As the Chairman of the Soviet Peace Committee, Yuri Zhukov, states, the Soviets then "proposed that the 'freeze' be extended to strategic—intercontinental—nuclear armaments." The KGB, the International Department and the immense Active Measures apparatus quickly heeded his call.

At first glance, the nuclear freeze seemed to some both reasonable and alluring, as it was meant to seem. A pause in the "arms race" at least might be a beginning. Mankind could step back from the brink and reflect calmly upon how to avoid plunging into extinction.

However, the Brezhnev proposals would instantly achieve the fundamental Soviet objective of aborting American production of the Enhanced Radiation Warhead, the MX, Pershing II and cruise missiles, and a new manned bomber. It would leave Western Europe vulnerable to relentlessly expanding Communist forces—now including an astonishing 42,500 tanks and the 333 deadly SS-20 missiles. It would leave the United States with a fleet of old, obsolete strategic bombers, unlikely to penetrate Soviet air defenses, and with an aging force of fixed land-based missiles, vulnerable to a first strike by great new Soviet missiles.

On March 20, 1981, less than one month after Brezhnev called for a nuclear freeze, the first national strategy conference of the American "Nuclear Freeze Campaign" convened in the Reiss Science Center at Georgetown University in Washington. The idea of a nuclear freeze was not new in the United States. It had been advanced two years earlier at the convention of the Mobilization for Survival, which is composed of three dozen or so organizations, including the U.S. Communist Party, the U.S. Peace Council, and Women Strike for Peace. One energetic leader of the Mobilization for Survival is Terry Provance, a longtime World Peace Council activist who in 1979 helped found its American branch, the

U.S. Peace Council.* Provance earlier led the campaign against the B-1 bomber and then became coordinator of the disarmament program of the American Friends Service Committee.

MFS leaders endorsed the nuclear freeze when it was first suggested back in 1979. But whether by happenstance or otherwise, the idea floundered until Brezhnev embraced it, and the admirably organized Nuclear Freeze Campaign began at Georgetown. The topics of the "Skill Sharing Workshops" suggest just how farsighted and well considered the planning was. Working sessions were conducted to teach future agitators about: "Congressional District/Petitions Approach; Referendum/State Legislator Approach; Organizing Around Nuclear Weapon Facilities; How to Approach Middle America—Small Group and One-to-One Techniques; Media; Reaching and Activating National Organizations (Including Your Own); Working with the Religious Community; Working with the Medical and Scientific Community; Working with Groups with a Human Needs Agenda."

From March 20 to 22, 1981, virtually the entire blueprint for the nuclear freeze campaign that followed was drawn in clear and comprehensive detail. Speakers stressed that the beauty of the nuclear freeze derives from its simplicity. It would enable all people sincerely concerned about the danger of nuclear war to answer for themselves the question, "What can I do?"

According to the Mobilization for Survival publication *Mobilizer,* the organizers at Georgetown comprised "between

*After a *Reader's Digest* condensation referred to Provance as a World Peace Council activist, Provance wrote the magazine, stating th it he never had been a member of that organization. The *Digest* replied, "Despite your statement that you are 'not and never have been a member of the World Peace Council,' your name appears on page 142 of the publication entitled *World Peace Council List of Members, 1980–83*, published by the Information Centre of the World Peace Council in Helsinki, Finland." Provance also is listed in the *World Peace Council List of Members, 1977–1980*.

The agenda of the "U.S. Peace Council Founding Conference" lists Terry Provance as óne of the "Workshop Leaders." The two people listed as co-leaders of his workshop were James Jackson, member of Presidential Committee, World Peace Council, and William Hogan, Chicago Clergy & Laity Concerned, Chicago Peace Council.

Provance did not respond to the *Digest* letter.

275-300 predominantly white middle-class people from 33 states, Great Britain and the Soviet Union." Records available today identify two of the invited Soviet guests. One was Oleg Bogdanov, an International Department Specialist in Active Measures, who flew in from Moscow. The other was Yuri S. Kapralov, who represents himself as a counselor at the Soviet embassy in Washington. Kapralov was not merely an observer. He mingled with disarmament proponents, urging them on in their efforts to abort new American weapons. He was an official member of the discussion panel, and as one listener put it, his statements were "very impressive."

Yuri Kapralov did not speak just for himself. Kapralov is a KGB officer who has dedicated himself to penetrating the peace movement. Thus, little more than two miles from the White House, the KGB helped organize and inaugurate the American nuclear freeze campaign. While many civic and church groups of unassailable repute were to join in advocating the "freeze," in terms of the strategy and organization of the drive, this little-noted conference at Georgetown was a seminal meeting.

Kapralov had long been at work in the United States. Expelled from Egypt in 1974, he arrived in Washington in June 1978 and told everyone that his last post was on the American desk in the Soviet Foreign Ministry. By December 1978 he had ingratiated himself so well that the Riverside Church in New York invited him to a disarmament rally. There, Kapralov argued that it would be foolish for the United States to arm itself further against the Soviet Union because the Soviet Union threatened nobody. "We are not going to attack anybody," he assured the friendly audience at the church. Even after the Soviets conspicuously attacked Afghanistan, Kapralov continued to assure American audiences that because the Soviet Union only desires peace, it menaces no one. However, as a professional intelligence officer, Kapralov was interested in more than merely articulating Soviet views. Wherever he melded into American gatherings, it was his duty to identify for the KGB Americans who, by whatever means, might be persuaded to propound Soviet views as their own.

After participating in the first nuclear freeze strategy session at Georgetown, Kapralov showed up at other forums advocating peace and disarmament. According to press accounts, he received "some of the loudest applause" given speakers by about 800 Harvard students and faculty members, and the Boston *Globe* termed him "one of the most effective speakers." Blaming the arms race on the United States, Kapralov said, "It's funny that when our leaders talk about their desire for peace, some of your people just discredit it as transparent propaganda. We would prefer that your leaders would talk as clearly and as forcefully for peace and arms control as ours." More applause.

When Brezhnev called for a "freeze," he adjured scientists to join in warning the public of the horrors of nuclear war. On March 20, the same day the Nuclear Freeze Campaign strategy conference began at Georgetown University, a new outfit, titled International Physicians for the Prevention of Nuclear War, held its first annual conference. The Soviet delegation to the meeting in Virginia included Brezhnev's personal physician, Evgenny Chazov. But the head of the delegation was not a physician at all. He was none other than Georgi Arbatov, the International Department operative, one of the masterminds of the whole Active Measures campaign. And Arbatov did much of the talking.

The Cold War, he contended, was entirely the fault of the United States. America started it by dropping an atomic bomb on Hiroshima. The Russians always have believed, declared Arbatov, that the first atomic bomb was aimed as much at them as at the Japanese. New weapons will not enhance the security of anyone, he argued. America should spend its money on the needy, the underfed, the starving, not on arms. According to the Toronto *Star*, the assembled rewarded Arbatov with "thunderous applause."*

---

*The International Physicians for the Prevention of Nuclear War held their second conference in Cambridge, England, in April 1982. Delegations from Bulgaria, Czechoslovakia, Hungary, Poland and the Soviet Union took part along with those from 23 non-Communist countries. The Soviet delegation included one M. A. Milstein, who was identified as a "Senior Researcher" from the Institute for U.S.A. and Canada. Milstein also is a general from the GRU, Soviet military intelligence.

Following the Georgetown and Virginia conferences, the U.S. Peace Council arranged for a World Peace Council delegation, led by agent Chandra, to tour American cities. Their most beneficial appearance was on Capitol Hill, where in May Representatives John Conyers, Jr., Don Edwards, Mervyn Dymally, George Crockett, Jr., Ted Weiss and Mickey Leland invited colleagues to meet and listen to the WPC delegates. Whether or not the delegation's lobbying in behalf of Soviet interests affected any of the Congressmen, the cordial welcome Chandra and associates received at the U.S. Capitol lent them a useful measure of respectability as bona fide seekers of peace.

Continuing organizational efforts resulted in a series of conferences, at which assorted "peace" and allied special interest groups planned specific actions. The strategy envisioned a rising furor of demonstrations, agitation and propaganda against the Euromissiles and new U.S. weapons and for the nuclear freeze proposed by Brezhnev. Various leaders repeatedly emphasized the necessity of rounding up "newly aroused individuals and constituencies" so, as one put it, the demonstrations would not appear to be "a primarily 'peace movement' event."

The Mobilization for Survival sponsored a strategy conference, attended by representatives of some 46 "peace" and disarmament factions, in Nyack, N.Y., October 23-25. Terry Provance, who had spoken at a peace rally in West Germany earlier in the year, announced that Europeans active in the disarmament movement would come to the United States in ensuing months to adrenalize the American movement. Participants in the Nyack conference were told that the months ahead would be "a key time to organize local public meetings and/or demonstrations," demanding a "suspension of all U.S. plans to deploy Pershing II and cruise missiles." The action agenda adopted at Nyack called for support of the nuclear "freeze," solidarity with the European peace movement, "creative dramatic action" against large corporations, propaganda against both nuclear arms and nuclear power, and attempts to attract more followers by blaming social ills on the "military budget."

Two weeks later, agent Chandra flew to New York to confer with American Communist leaders and attend a conference of the U.S. Peace Council, which attracted representatives from a mélange of "peace," religious and radical organizations. Chandra and Achim Maske, of the West German peace movement, implored the Americans to redouble agitation to block the Pershing II and cruise missiles. As a pattern for their lobbying, Chandra commended recent pronouncements of Brezhnev.

U.S. Representative Gus Savage spoke about how to induct blacks and other minorities into the disarmament drive. Representative John Conyers, Jr., exhorted the activists to rally behind efforts to transfer funds from the defense budget to welfare programs. The Executive Director of the U.S. Peace Council, Michael Myerson, a longtime Communist functionary, asserted that the USPC and World Peace Council had a unique responsibility to fuse the cause of disarmament with that of the Palestine Liberation Organization and guerrillas in El Salvador, Chile and South Africa.

On November 15, 1981, the day the U.S. Peace Council gathering ended, the Riverside Church in New York opened a conference on "The Arms Race and Us." Serving as host and hostess were the Reverend William Sloane Coffin and Cora Weiss, whom he engaged as the Riverside Church disarmament-program director.

During the Vietnam war, Weiss was a leader of Women Strike for Peace, characterized by a Congressional study as "a pro-Hanoi organization," which from its inception "has enjoyed the complete support of the Communist Party." Even while the fighting continued, Weiss traveled to both Hanoi and Paris to consult with the North Vietnamese. Subsequently, she became a director of Friendshipment, established to funnel American aid to Vietnam after the Communist victory. In 1976 she joined a coalition formed to stage anti-government demonstrations during the bicentennial celebrations. Weiss has also helped sponsor the Center for Cuban Studies, a group to which Fidel Castro personally expressed his appreciation on its tenth anniversary.

About 500 disarmament proponents from around the nation

attended the conference Weiss organized. A prominent new performer on the disarmament scene, Australian-born pediatrician Helen Caldicott, did her best to instill fear and loathing. "We are on the brink of extinction," she warned. While Caldicott had no criticism of Soviet weapons, she likened the U.S. Trident submarine to "Auschwitz," to "a gas oven full of Jews burning up."

Caldicott, who now devotes herself fully to running another peace lobby, Physicians for Social Responsibility, did sound one positive note. She had just toured Europe, whipping up support for the freeze. "It was a wonderful feeling to be over there," she said, because "the fear was palpable but realistic." By contrast, she lamented, "the Americans seem to have no panic. Why?" Caldicott concluded by quoting an ecclesiastical appeal for unilateral American disarmament.

The Mobilization for Survival convened its climactic strategy session in early December 1981, on the campus of the University of Wisconsin in Milwaukee. Some of the MFS leaders were frank in their statements of tactics, strategy and goals. A staff organizer from Boston, Leslie Cagan, said that current expediency necessitates a coalition which "makes it easier to call out more people to demonstrate." Construction of a coalition with "diversity of composition," she explained, requires "a common enemy as well as a common vision." As useful enemies, Cagan cited President Reagan, "our military-industrial complex, racism and sexism."

Mel King, a Massachusetts state legislator active in both the World Peace Council and U.S. Peace Council, demanded a more militant spirit. "We've been too damn nice," he declared. "It's time we stopped just getting mad and started getting even." In workshops, allies of the revolutionary Weather Underground lobbied for terrorism in general and "direct action" against installations involved in production of nuclear power and weapons. Lauded as "genuine people's leaders" were Puerto Rican Rafael Cancel Miranda, one of the terrorists who shot up the House of Representatives, wounding five Congressmen, and American Indian Movement leader Leonard Peltier, who killed two FBI agents from ambush.

The business of the conference included the practical planning of 1982 demonstrations at air bases, missile sites and defense plants, and the formation of task forces to write letters to newspapers and importune elected officials in behalf of the "nuclear freeze" and against major American weapons systems, such as the MX missile. The Reverend Robert Moore, an MFS national staff member and a leader in the Nuclear Freeze Campaign, together with MFS staff organizer Paul Mayer, stressed the advantages of bringing the campaign to a climax during the U.N. Special Session on Disarmament beginning in June.

The World Peace Council in the December 1981 issue of *Peace Courier* happily reported that its U.S. Peace Council was progressing well in collecting signatures on petitions advocating the nuclear freeze, promoting a California referendum on the freeze, and advertising the "Jobs for Peace Campaign," another ploy to divert money from defense to welfare.

The World Peace Council, its parent the International Department, the KGB and the Politburo—all had ample grounds to be pleased. From East Coast to West, here and there town councils and county boards of supervisors paused in their deliberations about zoning, sewerage systems and school budgets to pass resolutions favoring the "nuclear freeze." Prominent religious leaders, educators, scientists, artists, entertainers and other public figures endorsed the "nuclear freeze." And Helen Caldicott's Physicians for Social Responsibility toiled tirelessly.

Then on March 10, 1982, Senators Edward Kennedy and Mark Hatfield, with 19 co-sponsors, introduced a resolution demanding an immediate nuclear "freeze," and in the House of Representatives, a parallel resolution was introduced.

Meanwhile, on orders from the Center at Lubyanka, the KGB Residency in New York concentrated much of its manpower upon the freeze campaign. U.S. counterintelligence identified more than 20 Soviet agents endeavoring to influence elements of the peace movement, particularly leaders in religion, labor and science.

Typical of them were KGB officers Sergei Paramonov, Vladimir Shustov and Sergei Divilkovsky, all of whom masquerade as diplomats at the U.N. Paramonov participated in the inaugural meeting of the Riverside Church Disarmament Program. Shustov and Divilkovsky have made numerous visits to Riverside Church and have shown up at other churches and meetings of prestigious organizations concerned with peace.

The Soviets supplemented the labors of their New York and Washington Residencies by sending people from the Center into the United States on temporary assignments. Even before the freeze movement materialized, a Soviet delegation, including KGB officer Andrei Afanaseevich Kokoshin, toured the United States, visiting many who were to be prominent in the campaign. Another delegation led by Nikolai Mostovets, who heads the North American section of the International Department, plotted strategy with the U.S. Peace Council.

Of the Soviets who applied for visas to attend a disarmament conference sponsored by the National Academy of Sciences in Washington in January 1982, roughly half were known intelligence officers. The State Department refused entry to most of them. Nevertheless, of those who came, almost half were co-opted KGB agents or International Department operatives. One of the Soviet "scientists" was Vitali Zhurkin, who, back in the 1960s when agent Chandra was being groomed in New Delhi, used to give money and orders to the Indian Communist Party.

In anticipation of a massive nuclear freeze rally on June 12, 1982, emissaries from 13 Soviet international fronts flooded into New York City. They joined more than 500,000 Americans who paraded and spoke out for peace.

The following week the Soviet Union staged a terrifying rehearsal of a surprise nuclear attack on the United States and Western Europe. For several hours, they fired land- and sea-based missiles designed to kill American satellites, destroy U.S. retaliatory power, obliterate American cities and wipe out Europe. The firings, over Soviet territory and waters, exactly duplicated wartime distances and trajectories, and shocked those monitoring them in Washington. Never before had there been such a realistic and comprehensive practice for starting a nuclear war.

There has been no great outcry against these ominous Soviet preparations. Nor has there been any outcry against the relentless Soviet buildup of offensive nuclear weapons.

In Europe demonstrators did not protest against the 333 Soviet SS-20s and 999 nuclear warheads, weapons already emplaced and aimed at them, weapons that in 20 minutes could incinerate European cities. Instead, they protested against the 572 weapons that NATO *plans* for defense of Western Europe. In America the demonstrators did not protest against the 1400 intercontinental missiles aimed at America, many of which are designed to annihilate U.S. missiles in a first strike. Instead, they demonstrated against *projected* American missiles, bombers and submarines, whose deployment would more than anything else ensure that Soviets will never dare launch the kind of surprise attack for which they practiced in June 1982.

While the demonstrations proceeded in Europe and the United States, seven young European tourists—a Belgian, two Spaniards, two Frenchmen and two Italians—attempted a tiny demonstration in Moscow. On April 19, 1982, in Red Square, they unfurled a banner saying in Russian, "Bread, Life and Disarmament." Instantly, the KGB seized them and carted them to jail before they could pass out a single leaflet in behalf of peace. On August 8, 1982, the Associated Press reported from Moscow: "A co-founder of Moscow's only independent disarmament group is being administered depressant drugs against his will in the psychiatric hospital where he is being held, his wife said today." And at Harvard students and faculty reserved some of their loudest applause for a spokesman from the KGB, a man from the Lubyanka Center.

Once again the KGB had succeeded in inverting reality.

The House Permanent Select Committee on Intelligence, in secret session during July 1982, heard testimony from the assistant directors of the FBI and CIA regarding Soviet Active Measures and Soviet involvement in the peace movement. In the declassified portions of the testimony, released December 9,

1982, Edward O'Malley, FBI Assistant Director for Intelligence, stated:

"A primary focus of the KGB has been arms control and disarmament matters and the American peace movement. KGB officers have recently instructed their contacts to devote serious attention to the anti-war movement in the United States, especially with respect to coalitions forming among the various factions within the movement. . . .In addition, KGB officers have recently asked their contacts in the peace movement to report on meetings, participate in the planning of demonstrations and distribute leaflets and other publications. Some KGB officers are also directly involved in efforts to influence the U.S. peace movement. A Soviet diplomat involved in Active Measures operations assigned to the Soviet embassy in Washington has been actively attempting to influence the American peace movement."

Pointing out that the U.S. Communist Party (CPUSA) is wholly subservient to the Soviet Union, that KGB officers are in regular contact with its leaders, and that the KGB secretly supplies the party with money, O'Malley testified:

"In the last few years, the Communist Party Soviet Union instructed the CPUSA to place high priority on issues of arms control and disarmament and the peace movement. The Soviets have used the Communist Party U.S.A. to mount campaigns against the neutron bomb, NATO theater nuclear force modernization and administration defense policies. Furthermore, the Soviets have requested the CPUSA to reinforce and mobilize the peace movement in this country. . . .

"In April 1982 the CPUSA held an extraordinary conference and Central Committee meeting in Milwaukee, Wisconsin. . . . The purpose of the meeting was to move the entire party to bolder, more militant positions on various issues, including the peace movement. . . .According to some CPUSA officials, the Party takes credit for the current popularity of the peace movement, estimating that one-third of the anti-nuclear movements across the United States were a direct result of CPUSA action and suggesting that the CPUSA had input into many others."

O'Malley cited further Soviet involvement. "The World Peace Council is, of course, the largest and most active Soviet front organization, with affiliates in approximately 135 countries. The WPC is one of the major Soviet instruments for political action and propaganda in the peace movement. The World Peace Council has placed the highest priority on the peace movement, and a program of action for 1982 calls for a worldwide campaign against the danger of nuclear war and is clearly directed at U.S. defense and arms control policies.

"The World Peace Council has taken a direct hand in organizing and mobilizing the American peace movement. . . . With the establishment of the U.S. Peace Council, World Peace Council-related activities in the United States have increased noticeably."

Asked by a committee member about Soviet involvement in the June 12 demonstration in New York, O'Malley replied: "The U.S. Peace Council and the World Peace Council, as well as CPUSA members, were actively involved in the planning and implementation of the June 12 demonstration . . . . There were some 500,000 people who participated in that demonstration. I would not attribute the large turnout at this demonstration to efforts of the U.S. Peace Council, the World Peace Council or the CPUSA. However, there was significant involvement by all these people concerned."

O'Malley additionally disclosed that KGB officers "are in regular contact" with members of the National Council of American-Soviet Friendship and have urged them to concentrate on the peace movement. "The NCASF has responded by sponsoring letter-writing campaigns, rallies and demonstration to support Soviet interests in this matter. Affiliate chapters of the NCASF were urged at an NCASF executive meeting in April 1981 to join peace coalitions in their areas to ensure that such matters as a freeze on nuclear weapons are promoted and Soviet attitudes towards peaceful coexistence are brought to the attention of the American public."

CIA Deputy Director John McMahon cited numerous examples of direct KGB and Soviet involvement in the West European peace movement, including dissemination of forgeries, use of Agents of Influence and clandestine funding.

"This committee," he told the Congressmen, "is well familiar with the Active Measures that the Soviets undertook against the INF, the intermediate-range nuclear forces, in Europe some years ago. That campaign, which began in 1979, continues unabated, and there is evidence that the Soviet Union is manipulating and financing activities by some elements of the so-called peace movement in Western Europe. . . .

"We all well know that not all opposition to NATO nuclear forces modernization is Soviet-inspired. Many people are sincerely concerned about the potential danger of nuclear weapons. We do have good evidence, however, that the Soviets have sought to exploit and manipulate the movement, and we believe that the Soviet covert support has enabled it to grow beyond its own capabilities. . .," McMahon testified.

"We have information that some recruited Soviet agents in the peace movement were given instructions by the Soviets on actions to take. But we're well aware that the peace movement in Europe did have a very native and genuine spawning. Yet the Soviets were able to capitalize on that and drive it much further than what the Europeans expected. We also have reporting. . .which shows that the Soviets tried to do the same thing in New York when they knew there was going to be a very large 'peace' demonstration up there. The Soviets came in and tried to acquire all of the information they could about who was who in the peace movement, what coalitions were getting together, who were the key players, in order that they could begin to pressure them in the direction the Soviets wanted to go."

McMahon also outlined extensive involvement of the World Peace Council in the European peace movement. "The hand of the World Peace Council, the major Soviet-controlled international front organization with headquarters in Helsinki, is often apparent in the planning and coordination of anti-nuclear 'peace campaigns' in West Europe and elsewhere. . . .Providing funds for peace movement activities is one important means of WPC involvement, but the WPC seeks to conceal this aspect of its support."

Representative Edward P. Boland (D., Mass.) presided over the House committee hearings. On December 9, the day the FBI and CIA testimony was released, Boland said of it: "The bottom line is that the hearings provide no evidence that the Soviets direct, manage or manipulate the nuclear freeze movement."

His statement received the widest national publicity. It was accepted and represented as factual and definitive by many reporters, commentators and editorialists, who obviously did not trouble to read the testimony of the hearings.* As a result, most Americans remain ignorant of what the FBI and CIA actually reported to Congress.

However, even those who do read the entire record of the hearing still will be denied certain facts because the House committee under Chairman Boland withheld them.

The World Peace Council regarded the feat of its representatives in gaining admission to the U.S. Capitol in January 1978 as an "outstanding landmark in WPC history." Agent Chandra, Colonel Radomir Bogdanov of the KGB and Oleg Kharkhardin of the International Department delighted in inducing members of Congress to join in discussions of "peace" and disarmament. To herald the triumph, the WPC "Information Centre" in Helsinki published a 48-page brochure about the proceedings.

The House Intelligence Committee judged the brochure sufficiently significant to merit inclusion in the exhibits it published as examples of Soviet Active Measures. But, in reproducing the brochure as Exhibit XI, the committee omitted pages 3, 4, 12, 13, 14, 18, 19, 21, 22, 23, 45, 46, 47 and 48 of

---

*One exception was *The Wall Street Journal,* whose editors did take time to read the actual testimony and, having done so, challenged Boland's conclusion. The newspaper declared in an editorial: "There is reason to suspect, in short, that Communist efforts within the freeze movement have been successful in shifting attention away from the Soviet Union's massive military buildup and toward the Reagan administration's defense programs. Perhaps this does not meet Rep. Boland's definition of 'manipulating' the freeze movement, but it certainly meets ours."

the original WPC document. The table of contents lists Exhibit XI as "Materials from World Peace Council Presidential Committee Meeting, Washington, D.C., June 25-28, 1978." (As the WPC brochure states, the actual month was January.) But the exhibit itself as reproduced provides no indication that portions of the WPC document have been deleted. And, unlike the original document, the Committee reproduction bears no page numbers. Thus, readers cannot see that there are omissions.

Omitted pages 3 and 4 contain the following statement:

"The National Committee set up in the United States to host the WPC session included prominent trade union leaders such as William Winpisinger, President of the 900,000 member International Associaton of Machinists, and three leaders of the Amalgamated Meat Cutters and Butcher Workmen of North America: Patrick Gorman, Chairman, Abe Feinglass, Vice-president, and Charles Hayes, Secretary-treasurer. (Hayes is also a leader of the Coalition of Black Trade Unionists).

"Other labour leaders who endorsed the meeting included James R. Herman, President of the International Longshoremen's and Warehousemen's Union, Leon Sverdlov, General President, International Jewelry Workers Union, and David Chaney, Vice-president, Central States Joint Board, Amalgamated Clothing and Textile Workers Union, AFL-CIO.

"Congressman Ron Dellums and a number of Democratic Party state legislators also joined the committee together with other outstanding U.S. personalities . . .

"The wide interest in the work of the Bureau and the Dialogue was indicated by the participation in the sessions, and also in special meetings inside the U.S. Congress itself of Bureau members with several Congressmen among which were Congressmen John Burton, Ted Weiss, Ronald Dellums, John Conyers, Jr., Don Edwards, Charles Rangel and others."

Page 12 shows photographs with the caption: "Participants in the dialogue listen to Congressman John Conyers, Jr., tell them: 'You have joined us to give us courage and inspiration in our fight for disarmament and against the neutron bomb.' "

Page 18 shows a photograph with caption: "Congressman Ron

Dellums talking to WPC President Romesh Chandra during a lunch for the WPC Bureau members at the US Congress."

Page 19 shows photographs with the caption: "Congressman Charles Rangel (left) and Congressman Don Edwards addressing participants in the WPC events."

Page 21 shows a photograph with the caption: "Deputy Mayor of Boston, Sandra Graham addressing a session of the Dialogue."

Page 22 shows a photograph with the caption: "Members of the WPC Bureau on the steps of the US Congress after discussion with US Congressmen."

Page 23 shows a photograph with the caption: "Representative of the Palestine Liberation Organization, Zuhdi Tarazi, presenting a review of developments in the Middle East to participants in a session of the Dialogue in New York City."

Page 45 shows a photograph with the caption: "Congressman John Conyers, Jr. addressing a luncheon for participants in the Dialogue on Disarmament and Détente. The luncheon was given at the restaurant of the U.S. House of Representatives."

Some may argue in good faith that any association with Soviet agents in furthering the disarmament cause is irrelevant, that all that matters are the merits of the cause. Of the millions upon millions of patriotic citizens who favor a nuclear freeze, many doubtless would adhere to their advocacy even if fully informed about the extent of clandestine Soviet involvement in the cause. They honestly believe that a moratorium on new nuclear weapons systems would benefit the United States and the world, irrespective of what the KGB is doing. Others, though, might take pause at awareness that, pure though their motives are, they nevertheless are aligning themselves on the same side as the KGB—which serves neither the cause of American security nor human liberty.

In any case, all citizens are entitled to all verifiable facts, whose import they may assess for themselves, according to their own values.

VII

DEVOTED AGENT

T HE SOVIETS cannot believe that other nations will forever allow crowds of spies to be openly stationed in their midst, that they will indefinitely permit professional subversives to prey upon them with relative impunity from the sanctuary of embassies. Always, they fear the mass expulsions or severance of diplomatic relations that would deprive them of these sanctuaries of subversion.

For the Soviets, this apprehension is primordial. Many nations denied the Soviet Union diplomatic recognition during the early years of its existence, thus Soviet intelligence officers and agents could enter and live in these nations only illegally. Of necessity, Soviet intelligence perfected the art of training men and women to assume fictitious foreign identities and to function as normal citizens in alien societies. Such officers and agents were and are known today, in the parlance of espionage, as "Illegals."

The Illegal may act as a saboteur or assassin, but the highest calling of an Illegal is the administration of agent networks, ordinarily directed by the legal Residency out of an embassy or other diplomatic installation. And in all major nations, the KGB keeps an Illegal Resident, whose primary duty is to be ever ready to take control of the networks and maintain clandestine communication between them and the Center, should the legal Residency be closed.

To embed one of its own officers in American society so deeply that he can penetrate the most secret spheres of government, the KGB is willing to wait decades and expend untold resources. No clandestine undertaking is more difficult or more susceptible to failure. Yet the KGB keeps trying, for a single success will far offset myriad failures; there are times when a lone agent or one scrap of intelligence can doom or save an entire nation.

Of the many critical stages in such a prolonged operation, the most critical is the first—the selection of the agent who is to infiltrate himself into a position from which he can strike at the vital organs of the United States. Only an extraordinary man will do, because the extraordinary will be continuously demanded of him. He must enter and live in the United States under a fictitious identity, always dissembling and deceiving, always hiding his true self and thoughts, always soliciting friendships with intent to manipulate, exploit and, if expedient, to betray his friends. By his own devices, he must secure a normal job and work at it as hard as would any ambitious American. At the same time, he must work just as arduously at his secret job, surreptitiously discharging assignments that are usually tedious, frequently exhausting and sometimes dangerous. Cut off from his own culture, language and relatives, he must adapt to the American way of life, yet never succumb to the appeal it exerts upon so many other immigrants; rather, he must remain implacably committed to its destruction. He may labor for years without accomplishing anything noteworthy, except his own survival. No matter how well he does, he can never be sure that a security breach elsewhere in the KGB will not bring a fatal knock on the door and the dreaded words, "We are from the FBI." Simultaneously inhabiting open and subterranean worlds, subjected to unremitting stress and anxiety, he nevertheless in all moments and situations must retain emotional and mental stability, and to do so he can depend only upon himself. The further he advances, the more he succeeds, the more and the longer the Center will require that he endure.

The requisite personal traits for such an agent—high intelligence, physical stamina, an ability to deal with people from all social strata, courage, tenacity, initiative and imagination— are not enough. They must be accompanied by an invincible loyalty to the Soviet cause, a willingness to die anonymously or to give up most of life for the cause. In 1955, the KGB found a young man who had these traits in large measure. And it found him in an improbable locale, outside the Soviet Union.

As the armies of Germany, France and England mobilized for war in the fall of 1938, British Prime Minister Neville Chamberlain cried out for peace. "How horrible, fantastic, incredible it is that we should be digging trenches and trying on gas masks here because of a quarrel in a faraway country between people of whom we know nothing," he declared. On September 29, Chamberlain flew to Munich to bow before Chancellor Adolf Hitler and to beg the Führer for peace.

Among the unknown people in the "faraway country" to which Chamberlain referred were the 1602 peasant souls who comprised the Czechoslovakian village of Zdounky. In all the world there scarcely could have been found a less likely breeding ground of future peril to the United States. This ancient village stood, isolated and obscure, in the Moravian lowlands. Thick stone cottages sheltered the villagers comfortably; their gardens, orchards, poultry, pigs and cows yielded abundant food; and they made their own wine and potent plum brandy according to formulas passed down through the centuries. Like their forebears, most were conservative Catholics who exalted family, work, frugality and self-reliance.

Until the creation of an independent Czechoslovakia at the end of World War I, the Moravians had always been ruled by aliens. Now they were fiercely proud of their nationhood, passionately patriotic. And so on the night of September 29, neighbors crowded into the house of Josef Zemenek—who owned the one radio capable of receiving short-wave broadcasts—to await news from Munich.

Zemenek stood barely four feet eight inches tall and looked even shorter because he was slightly hobbled and bent by chronic rheumatism, which he contracted in dank trenches after his conscription into the Austrian army during the First World War. When Hungarian Communists tried to recapture territories from newly formed Czechoslovakia in 1919, Zemenek joined the armed Czech volunteers who repelled the invasion. Returning from combat a second time, he became a photographer. He and his wooden tripod were a familiar accompaniment at weddings, christenings, confirmations, wakes and reunions. He refused few jobs, no matter how small or how many miles he had to trek on his perpetually swollen feet. He never failed an appointment; his prints were excellent, his fees fair. In fact, he had been known to shave them for poorer clients, and if someone lagged in payment, he never pressed his claim. Zemenek managed handily until the great worldwide depression reached Moravia in 1930. With fewer and fewer people able to afford photographs, and recognizing that the loss of his house was imminent, Zemenek responded typically. As circumstances had halved his income, he reasoned that he would have to double his business. Although his wife Heidi had only recently, on December 22, 1929, given birth to their first son, Ludek, Zemenek subjected her to a crash course in business. He then made her responsible for photography in the Zdounky area, while he solicited business in another village.

It never occurred to Zemenek to consider, much less ask, whether his wife wished to learn photography; whether she could run the business, raise a family, and keep house at the same time. And it never occurred to her to ask any such questions either. Similarly, as the child Ludek grew, he never thought of questioning his father's orders to deliver photographs, haul coal, stoke the furnace, indeed, to work at something almost constantly. Within the family, Zemenek's instructions were natural law, to be obeyed promptly and without reservation.

Probably, Zemenek perceived of himself not as a patriarchal tyrant, but rather as a devoted and loving husband and father, and in ways he was. In his view, rather than exploiting Ludek by levying so many tasks, he was teaching him. Ludek reacted with adoration. From his mother, he learned to read and study, and he attained high marks in school. But in life, it was his father whom he wished to emulate.

The Munich Conference formally convened at noon September 29 and continued through the night, and the events of this night spawned the spy who was to become known as Rudolf Herrmann.

While villagers kept vigil by the radio in the Zemenek house awaiting word from Munich, Ludek, now almost ten, listened with them and watched his father. The radio reported that *Il Duce* Benito Mussolini of Italy, Herr Hitler's spiritual comrade, and Premier Pierre Daladier of France, Mr. Chamberlain's equal in courage, had joined the deliberations. Czechoslovakian delegates had arrived in Munich to be informed of whatever the Great Powers decided. To be informed—not to participate, not to be consulted, not in the least to be asked about decisions that would determine whether Czechoslovakia lived or died as a nation.

As hour after hour passed without any news, Ludek sensed the villagers' mood growing more and more foreboding. "They are selling us," Zemenek said calmly. "There is no hope." Then shortly after 2 a.m. there was a news flash. The conference had concluded with a communiqué signed by Germany, France, Great Britain and Italy. The essence was as simple as it was brutal. In the interests of peace, Czechoslovakia would be forced to cede the entire Sudetenland to Germany.

In the house, women screamed, and some men wept. Others

cursed the rotten, degenerate, corrupt, lying Western democracies who had given birth to Czechoslovakia, and then only 20 years later, out of treacherous cowardice, condemned it to death. With some difficulty, Zemenek stood on a chair and, his voice rising above the bedlam, commenced singing the Czechoslovakian national anthem.

"The Nazis soon will be upon us," he told Ludek. "We will find ways of fighting and surviving. But never forget how we were betrayed."

On March 15, 1939, the Wehrmacht sprang from newly consolidated positions in the Sudetenland and marched into Prague unopposed. Germany absorbed Moravia and Bohemia as vassal provinces, awarded a sliver of Slovakia to Hungary, and converted the remnants of Czechoslovakia into a puppet state. To Ludek, the timid protests voiced in the West were outrageous in their impotence.

Under tutelage of his father, who reported and interpreted the news nightly, Ludek became a sedulous student of contemporary history. Throughout World War II, the progression of events fortified his trust in his father's judgments, each episode hardening the contempt for the weakness and worthlessness of the perfidious democracies.

Although Zemenek disdained communism, from the onset of the war he sympathized with the Russians. At night, he sat in the kitchen, ear close to the speaker, listening through the static to German and Russian broadcasts. Everywhere, the Russians were falling back, and even if you discounted claims of German broadcasts by half, they must be suffering terrible casualties. But, as he kept emphasizing to Ludek, who was always at his side, at least the Russians were fighting, by God! They had not thrown up their hands in craven surrender like everybody else. After the Russians held at Leningrad, halted the Wehrmacht outside Moscow, destroyed the German army at Stalingrad, and slowly began to push the Nazis back westward, Zemenek's admiration of the Russians grew even greater.

Zemenek knew no more about the theory of Marxism-

Leninism or the Soviet practice of communism than he knew
of ancient hieroglyphics. But when Soviet forces liberated
Czechoslovakia, he announced first to his family, then to the
village: "I am a communist."

Ludek accepted communism as a natural bequest, but unlike his father he was eager to learn the philosophical tenets of
his new faith. With the passion of a convert, he studied the
writings of Marx, Engels, Lenin and Stalin. And unlike most
who venture into this intellectual thicket, he could actually
see; he could understand their most abstruse, convoluted and
tedious thoughts, for, as a sophisticated examination many
years later was to show, nature had endowed Ludek with the
mental capacity of a genius.

By his 16th birthday in 1945, Ludek had found in communism
a great cause in which he could wholly lose himself. Marx,
Lenin, Stalin were his gods; communism his religion; the
Party his church. His life had acquired meaning, purpose,
direction, and nothing the Party asked was too demeaning or
too challenging.

At the *gymnasium* (secondary school), he founded and led
the first league of Communist students. Like an itinerant
evangelist, he traveled the countryside as a Party organizer
proselytizing among youths. Throughout the summer of 1946,
he passed out leaflets, ran errands and made speeches in
behalf of Communist candidates who won 38 percent of the
national vote. And while he was still 17, the Party granted him
full membership, despite the requirement that a member be
18 or older.

After Stalinist Communists took control of the government
in 1948, the purges began, and, as in the Soviet Union itself, a
kind of madness stalked the land. But Ludek was unafraid.
Lenin had taught him that revolution required sacrifice, suffering, even individual injustices, as in the case of his own
father.

By his espousal of communism, which largely was loathed
in Zdounky, Zemenek forfeited many of his friends. Once the
Communists started to nationalize small enterprises, he gave

his business to the state voluntarily even though, strictly speaking, it was not really a business. He continued to work in photography as he had for a quarter of a century but now he relinquished all his earnings to the state. In return, he was given a subsistence wage of 1200 crowns a month, far less than he earned for the state. As an entrepreneur and landlord—he rented two small apartments on the upper floor of his house—Zemenek had, by definition, been an exploiter of the proletariat. Although the sincerity of his conversion and loyalty to the Party were unquestioned, he still must make restitution. Zemenek accepted the Party decision in good grace, and Ludek admired him all the more.

In 1949, Ludek joined the elite admitted to the study of international relations at historic Charles University. The opportunity to prepare himself better to serve the Party, and the prospect of eventually serving in the engrossing field of foreign affairs suffused him with enthusiasm. And he arrived in Prague resolved to excel academically, because the Party had decreed students must subordinate all activities and interests to their studies.

The students were given a monthly stipend of 2000 crowns, but when Ludek received his first payment, he counted only 600 crowns, and he asked the university administrator about the deficiency.

"You are not from the working class. Your father even now collects rent. You are fortunate even to be allowed in the university and to be given anything."

Ludek did not try to explain that his father in fact was providing subsidized housing to families who otherwise would have none; that unless the meaning of the word was grotesquely distorted, his father was a *worker* who each month made thousands of crowns for the state in exchange for a miserable wage. A sense of duty rather than fear kept Ludek silent. The Party required sacrifices of him, the Party had spoken and he was morally bound to obey.

To survive, Ludek worked as a proofreader for the Party newspaper, *Rudé Právo*, squinting at type nightly from 8 p.m.

to 2 a.m. On weekends, he scraped up a few more crowns by unloading freight trains at the railway terminal and sweeping dance-hall floors. Sometimes while studying, he was so tired that to stay awake he propped his eyes open with thumbs and forefingers. Even so, he gave freely of his time to tutor others who asked his help, and they asked often because on examinations he regularly ranked among the top three or four in the class. Ludek also participated energetically and spoke out at Party meetings. In his judgment, it would have been unthinkable heresy to challenge any principles of the Party and indecently selfish to dispute any Party decision that solely affected him. But duty impelled him to speak when he felt principles were being wrongly applied. Hence, he accused the administration of dereliction in not providing a separate room for a student suffering from tuberculosis, and he protested to the student leadership the appointment of a classmate who flaunted his homosexuality.

Such outspokenness—at a time when people still were disappearing—coupled with conspicuous honesty and brilliance made Ludek popular among students and faculty alike. At the first opportunity, his classmates selected him as a candidate for the chairmanship of their Party organization. Immediately, Party officials voided the nomination and ordered another. Ludek preferred to believe he was being punished for his candor, but succeeding events proved otherwise.

During the next three years, he was chosen as the student most qualified to study in the Soviet Union; the student most qualified to study in China; to be a guide at the exhibition celebrating the Communist Party's 30th anniversary; to serve as a Czech representative on the international truce team in Korea. In each case, unseen Party functionaries vetoed his appointment, because he was "not from the working class."

Ludek was graduated in the summer of 1953, one of only four students to receive the highest of honors, a Red Diploma. The majority of his classmates, after basic military training and reserve officer commissions, had choice government jobs awaiting them. But, again because his father was not a worker,

Ludek was assigned as a private to a border guards brigade in a rural region on the German frontier. In off hours he began to write a history of the area, getting on so well with villagers he interviewed that the brigade commander appointed him as a kind of liaison. Ludek could not resist attempting to teach communism to his fellow soldiers, who were five or six years his junior and had little schooling. He volunteered to write a political speech for an officer, and it was such a success that thereafter he became the brigade speech-writer. To the Soviet advisers assigned to the brigade, the commander cited Ludek as the personification of the efficient, politically conscious Czech soldier. Probably, one of the Russians took note and made a recommendation.

An order, which mystified even the brigade commander, summoned Ludek to Prague in March 1955. At the Ministry of Interior, he was ushered into a large, high-ceilinged conference room, where eight well-dressed civilians interrogated him for two hours. Though none identified himself, Ludek surmised that a majority were Russians. To him, their presence was neither unusual nor significant; in those days, Russians were everywhere in Czechoslovakia, teachers and "brothers" from whom it was a privilege to learn.

The initial questions explored Ludek's political knowledge and attitudes, and here he stood on the securest of ground; he probably knew more about communist theory than anyone in the room. He responded quickly, elaborating sometimes with quotations from Marx, Lenin or Stalin, and his directness and erudition evoked approving nods.

The men politely questioned him about his personal attitudes, and after a few queries, he realized they knew his entire life. "I believe that in the university you experienced certain disappointments," remarked one Russian. "That is, you were recommended for several positions of honor, but the Party or individuals in the Party denied you the fruits of your achievements."

Ludek fell back, as he so often had, upon Lenin's dictum about the necessity of sacrifice in time of revolution, concluding: "Lenin cautioned that we may not expect the revolution to be completed overnight. The Party did allow me to complete my studies, and I am grateful."

"Your posting after graduation hardly was commensurate with your record at the university. Do you not harbor some resentment?"

"At first, I considered the Party guilty of waste by not placing me where I could exploit the education it gave me. Then I realized that each member must serve as the Party decides best."

"And today you would be willing to serve wherever and however the Party thinks best?"

"Absolutely, comrade."

Recalled again to Prague early in May, Ludek was told: "The Party has selected you to work in secret intelligence. It is a position of the highest trust and importance. You would have to live abroad many years and, we must warn you, your life might be in danger. The choice is yours, and it must be entirely voluntary. If you decline the assignment, that will not prejudice your future. I am sure we can locate you in good and productive work here. Take a few days and think by yourself about your decision."

"There is no need," Ludek said. "I accept."

Ludek told his fellow soldiers that he was being transferred to Prague and told his parents that he was going to China indefinitely for political work. When he returned to Prague, a Czech officer, who called himself Jenda, led him to an apartment with tall windows in a handsome old building, gave him the keys and some money and his first assignment. It consisted simply of accustoming himself to living alone and moving about a city under an alias. After a few weeks, Jenda revealed, Ludek would go to East Germany to master German, then eventually to West Germany to combat neo-Nazis.

"For how long?" Ludek asked.

"Three, five, ten years. Who knows?"

On a starlit night a few weeks later, Jenda drove him across the East German border to the ancient university city of Halle.

There, inside the Soviet compound, KGB Major Aleksandr Afanosovich greeted them with coffee, then a luxury in Eastern Europe. The Russian was a broad-shouldered officer with thick coal-black hair, equally dark eyes, and an uncreased olive complexion. The son of a Ukrainian farmer, he had joined Soviet intelligence in his early 20s and served mostly abroad for nearly a quarter of a century, surviving the purges of the 1930s and the convulsions within the KGB that followed upon the death of Stalin and execution of Beria. He spoke with easy confidence, and Ludek liked him.

"Your head must be teeming with questions," he said, "so let me try to answer as many as I can."

To facilitate Ludek's study of the German language and customs, the KGB had arranged for him to monitor classes at Halle University, use the library and hire a tutor. Not being formally enrolled, he could absent himself as necessary for individualized instruction in clandestine tradecraft from KGB officers at the Soviet Kommandatura in Karlshorst, outside Berlin. According to his KGB legend, he was a junior Soviet trade official born in an area of Czechoslovakia absorbed by the Soviet Union in 1945—which explained his Czech accent, imperfect command of Russian and need to learn German.

"Before we put you to work, though, we have a surprise for you: a trip to Moscow," Aleksandr Afanosovich concluded. "Many friends are eager to meet you."

Flying from East Berlin in a Soviet military transport, Ludek approached Moscow in the spirit of a pilgrim approaching Mecca. Two courteous KGB officers drove him to the Hotel Peking, handed him a packet containing rubles, ballet tickets and an emergency telephone number, and encouraged him to explore the city in between meetings at a nearby apartment. Except for the superb subway system, museums and a few theaters, the sights of Moscow were a shock. Long lines of drably dressed customers waiting hours before near-empty shops, buildings with cracked or crumbling façades, and patients emerging from clinics wearing bandages seeping blood reminded him of a medieval city. But these scenes did not dent his faith. The squalor was simply the consequence of noble wartime sacrifices by the Soviet people, an emblem of heroism rather than evidence of Communist failure.

Different officers, a dozen or so in all, visited Ludek at the apartment to which he daily reported. Two asked a series of both personal and abstract questions, which suggested to him that they were psychiatrists. Others steered him into discussions of Marxist-Leninist theory, academic subjects and world affairs. None mentioned intelligence work. The Russians became progressively friendlier, and on the last night they honored him with a lavish dinner, replete with flattering toasts to his future. As in Prague, he had fulfilled and exceeded the expectations of the evaluators. By so doing, he unknowingly cast his future for decades to come.

Back in Halle, the Czech officer Jenda informed him that he would now be working for Aleksandr Afanosovich, that he was solely the property of the KGB. "We have given you a code name," said Aleksandr Afanosovich. "All messages to you will be addressed to Douglas; you must sign all your reports Douglas; and I will call you Douglas. Since you and I will be partners for a long time, call me Aleks."

If I am to work permanently in Germany, they should give me a German name, Ludek thought. *Douglas is an English name—or American.*

One evening a girl appeared in the university library: she was slender and buxom, with flaxen hair, impish blue eyes, a slightly upturned nose and a wide, tempting smile. Springing from his chair, Ludek introduced himself and invited her for a glass of wine. The chance to talk to a "Russian" delighted her, as she was an advanced student of Russian literature and Slavic languages. And the more they talked, the more they found in common.

Inga Juergen was born in the Sudetenland of German parents who out of opposition to Hitler became devoted Communists. After the war, the Sudetenland reverted to Czechoslovakia, and most inhabitants of German descent were expelled, irrespective of their political beliefs. Driven from their home like hundreds of thousands of others, Inga's family settled as refugees in East Germany. Yet, like Ludek's father, her parents kept faith with communism. Like Ludek, she inherited the faith, joined the Party as soon as she could and consecrated herself to its service. Once Inga agreed to tutor him, Ludek could not find enough time for German lessons, and Aleks complimented him on the sudden spurt in his fluency. In February 1956, Aleks instructed Ludek to report in his one suit the next evening for a special dinner at the Soviet Kommandatura in Karlshorst. There Ludek was introduced to a lovely 20-year-old Argentine woman, Rosemarie.

"What did you think of the girl?" Aleks asked the next morning. "How would you like to live with her?"

Inwardly, Ludek froze; outwardly, his face manifested amazement.

"Think of the advantages," a KGB colonel pressed. "You would have a trusted comrade at your side day and night, and she would take care of you—in every way. You would not have to waste your time chasing after girls and risking falling into bed with the wrong one. You would not have to explain your absences and unusual hours. No, your partner would be a trained agent who could help with communications, photography, drops—with everything. You would not be alone behind the lines. There would be someone to talk to. I assure you, we have had much experience, and this is the best way."

"Of course, this question cannot be finally answered today," Aleks interceded, in an effort to control the discussion and relax the pressure on Ludek, who sat motionless with tension. "But Comrade Colonel is absolutely correct. And there are additional advantages to be considered. Marriage would greatly facilitate your safe passage into the West, and it could cut years from our preparations. By marrying an Argentine citizen, you acquire Argentine citizenship. It is well known that many Germans have emigrated to Argentina, and by joining them you could gain a right-wing reputation. An Argentine passport is accepted throughout the West, and after building your legend, you could move on, as many other

German émigrés have done."

In the next days, Ludek agonized alone and, for the first time, wavered. If compelled to choose between Party duty and Inga, he was unsure what his choice would be.

Aleks did not broach the subject of marriage again for three weeks. "That Argentinian girl turned out to be a very silly child," he announced. "In Paris she prattled about Communist Party headquarters, boasting that she had been approached by the KGB. Obviously, we will have to forget about her."

"That's good," Ludek exclaimed, "because I have a real girl."

"Who is she?"

"My tutor, Inga. As I told you, she is a Party member; absolutely reliable."

"And you wish to marry her?"

"Yes."

"Do you think she would be willing to work with you; that is, do our work?"

"I have no doubts."

"She sounds worth investigating."

That night, Ludek broke the rules by confiding to Inga who he was and reporting his conversation with Aleks. She was proud and thrilled.

Soon, an East German official—or a Russian who spoke German very well—visited the university to interview Inga, explaining that she was under consideration for a government teaching position after her graduation in the summer of 1956. He questioned her in inordinate detail about her personal life, family background, and friends. Other visitors followed to assay her ideological attitudes, her intellect and personality. Her parents were investigated, friends questioned. Inga proved to be as politically sound and committed as Ludek. When asked if she would be willing to perform a secret and hazardous Party assignment in West Germany, she unhesitatingly replied, "For sure."

Meanwhile, his continuing training in the basics of espio-

nage conditioned Ludek more and more to think and act as a
spy. Each Saturday he submitted to Aleks a written summary
of his activities and characterizations of persons he had met
during the preceding week. He learned to write terse, factual
intelligence reports and to discern traits of character or outlook that might make an individual of interest to the KGB.
When walking about Halle, he practiced looking for prospective drop sites, applying the criteria drilled into him by one of
the Karlshorst instructors. Was the hiding place plausibly
accessible, that is, could an agent explain his presence there if
challenged? Was the drop or hiding place so situated that the
agent could "load" or "unload" it unobserved? Was it secure
from disturbance by curious children, small animals, future
construction? Would it be safe for repeated use or only one
delivery? He also studied his boardinghouse room searching
for nooks and crannies where he could conceal a cipher pad
and microfilmed radio schedule, as he would have to do in
foreign houses in future years. On the streets he made a game
of watching for and eluding surveillance, even though in
Halle there was none.

To test Inga, the KGB sent her into West Germany on
practice missions. Once she filled a drop outside Bonn with a
pencil supposedly containing microfilm. She executed such
assignments without incident, and in late August, Aleks announced to Ludek: "Inga has proven herself. You have chosen
well, and I am confident your marriage will be approved.
However, first they would like to see Inga in Moscow."

There, she was subjected to ideological and psychological
scrutiny by some of the same officers who had questioned
Ludek the year before. They were satisfied, and in a farewell
toast, a KGB colonel said, "We wish our dear young comrades
health, happiness and success in their life together and in
their noble work in behalf of the Party."

Back in Germany, Inga and Ludek were sequestered in the
Karlshorst compound while they learned the legends that
would transfigure each into a new being. "From this day
forward, you are Rudolf Herrmann," Aleks said. "Not Ludek;

Rudi. Think of yourself: Herrmann, Herrmann, Herrmann!"
From Soviet archives, the KGB had found the ghost of a real
Rudolf Herrmann, a worker in a German auxiliary labor battal-
ion, who perished in the Soviet Union in 1943. Guided by a
few papers taken from his body and retained all these years for
possible clandestine purposes, the KGB had ascertained the
outline of his actual life and determined that he had no close
living relatives. He was an ideal candidate for resurrection.

Ludek studied and rehearsed daily until he was able to
stand before KGB interrogators and confidently recite his life
history:

"My name is Rudolf Herrmann, though most people call me
Rudi. I was born April 22, 1925, in the Sudetenland. My
parents were German. My father worked as a glass-cutter, but
because of his contagious tuberculosis, I went to live with my
grandmother and attended Czech schools, where I had to
speak Czech. Later I was denied admission to the *gymnasium*
because I could not speak German very well, so I attended
vocational school." (The KGB had forged a report card from
the vocational school containing a notation that although pupil Herrmann did not appear to be stupid, he was not linguisti-
cally apt, and his knowledge of German was poor.)

"After the war started, I worked as a handyman for a construction company which repaired military vehicles. At 17, I
volunteered for Organization Todt and was transferred to
Prague as a driver. I drove mainly from Prague to Breslau and
Vienna hauling supplies.

"On February 13, 1945—a day I will never forget—I was
instructed by an engineer to deliver some construction plans
to Berlin. I left Dresden just before the great bombing, and
my truck was hit on the Autobahn about 45 miles south of
Berlin. I was wounded by shrapnel"—scars on his left leg,
incurred when he tried to climb a barbed wire fence as a boy,
attested to the wound—"and put in a Luftwaffe hospital.
When the Russians approached to within a few miles, the
hospital was disbanded, and I hitchhiked, trying to make my
way back to Bohemia. I got as far as Dresden, where I was

hospitalized again because I was losing so much blood.

"My mother and grandmother both died during the war. After the war ended, I tried to find an aunt and uncle, the only other relatives I had, but I could never find them. So I stayed in Dresden and got a job with a canning factory, buying produce from the Slavic-speaking minorities in East Germany.

"But I always loved to read, so when I learned about a vacancy in the state bookstore in Magdeburg, I applied. I worked there as a salesman from late November or early December 1951 until late 1957. I quit to be close to my girlfriend, who had obtained a very good job as a secretary in Frankfurt an der Oder, east of Berlin."

Here the legend for the moment was necessarily blank. The KGB planned that Rudi, as everyone now called him, would in January 1957 on his own find a job around Frankfurt. The blanks would be filled by what he did.

The legend, drafted by specialists of the Illegals Service at the Center, was technically excellent. If vital statistics recording births in the Sudetenland during the 1920s still existed anywhere in Germany, they would confirm Rudolf Herrmann's birthdate. Very likely, records of Organization Todt had been lost or destroyed in the chaos of collapse and occupation. But if they were intact anywhere, they would show that young Herrmann volunteered in 1942. Personnel files at the cannery in Dresden and the state bookstore in Magdeburg had been duly altered to reflect his employment—and inquiries at either establishment instantly would alert the KGB. While accounting for his lack of a profession or particular vocation, the fictitious history also accounted for the erudition that might seep into his conversation: he loved books and had worked in a bookstore.

Over all, the strength of the legend derived from its very dullness. It projected the profile of a quite common man with a plebian past unlikely to arouse interest, much less suspicion; a past that blended him facelessly into the millions of refugees and migrants from the East.

Rudi inspected the canning factory and the bookstore and spent several days studying Dresden and Magdeburg. He bought etchings depicting scenes of each locale in his legend, intending to take them with him to the West as tangible evidence of his past. From somewhere the KGB brought forth an old German truck and a mechanic to lecture Rudi about its peculiarities. He looked for hours at photographs of certain co-workers alongside whom he would have worked, and he memorized details of their lives and deaths.

On a Saturday night in November, when Rudi arrived at a café for his weekly meeting, Aleks was standing outside rather than waiting inside as usual. "I have sad news," he said, putting his arm around Rudi's shoulder. "Your father died this morning. We have a car with a Czech driver who will take you to Zdounky. Here are your old papers and some crowns; better let me keep your Soviet passport."

At the wake after burial, Rudi's mother announced to assembled relatives and friends: "Beginning tomorrow, I will work for the Party. That is what he would have wished of me." She was then 60.

Inga had become Ingalore Moerke, born February 10, 1931, in Stettin, assuming the identity of a young woman who perished along with her family during a 1944 bombardment. An authentic birth certificate was still on file at the city hall in West Berlin. Courtesy of the KGB, she had a job as a secretary in a state design bureau in Frankfurt an der Oder. Aleks, however, insisted that Rudi find work on his own, because the KGB wanted his last listed employment in the East to be legitimate and preferably to be in one of the relatively few remaining private enterprises whose personnel were not chosen by the state.

Rudi began the job hunt in January, going from shop to shop in the town of Fürstenwalde, about 25 miles from Frankfurt an der Oder. Wet with sleet and still uncomfortable speaking German, he was turned away again and again. But on the fourth morning he confronted a stern-visaged, 70-year-old, white-maned patriarch who ruled a small auto-parts store staffed by his elderly wife; spinster daughter and a retarded clerk. Because the old man was almost deaf, he habitually shouted. "What? What? Why do you want a job here?"

"Because I don't want to work for the goddamned Communists," Rudi yelled back.

"You're hired!"

The KGB could not have conceived a more ideal situation than the one Rudi wandered into at the shop. He had landed in a nest of unregenerate, unapologetic Nazis, in whose eyes Hitler's only mistake was neglecting to win the war. The son of the family even had tried to blow up a Soviet headquarters and now was in prison. The old man, however, was far from a crackpot. He simply was a super-Nazi, just as Rudi in Czechoslovakia was known as a super-Communist. He had been a senior tax auditor under Hitler, and he retained his professional acuity, along with his personal and ideological acerbity. He taught Rudi bookkeeping, how to administer a small business and how to cheat safely on income taxes. Rudi also absorbed Nazi lore, the words and melodies of Nazi songs, and virtually every argument ever invented to prove that barbaric, godless communism was the scourge of mankind.

On January 16, 1957, Rudi rode his bicycle to the city hall to marry Inga at 9 a.m. A female magistrate, however, refused to proceed with the ceremony because he had failed to bring flowers. He explained that florist shops were not yet open and that they both had to be back at work in an hour. The magistrate placed a potted plant on her desk and performed the ceremony. Rudy and Inga spent their wedding night in the unheated garret of a widow's house. When he opened the bottle of wine bought for celebration, he found that it was frozen.

The KGB delayed Rudi's departure for West Germany until after his first child, christened Peter, was born in October 1957. On November 26 he left West Berlin by train to search for employment in the vicinity of Stuttgart.

Locked in his small room in an inexpensive hotel, he removed a specially coated sheet of paper from an ordinary tablet and, placing it on a normal piece of paper, wrote a brief message reporting his arrival. Then, writing directly on the regular paper, which now bore his invisible message, he drafted a routine letter, which he mailed to an accommodation address in West Berlin. About 7 p.m. his first Saturday, he opened a hairbrush hollowed out to hide a cipher pad and schedule of radio broadcasts. Tuning a common commercial radio to the frequency the schedule specified, he took down the dots and dashes which designated numerals in groups of five. Deciphered, the broadcast message read: "Congratulations on your safe arrival. Continue explorations and reporting. Wife and child well."

While reconnoitering the picturesque old town of Freiburg, Rudi was stopped by an elegantly dressed man in his mid-60s, who introduced himself as Otto Seefelder. He wondered if Rudi could recommend a restaurant. Both his family and peasant heritage had taught Rudi always to behave respectfully and generously toward others, especially elders. So he took Seefelder to the only place he knew, a student cafeteria. After a plain but satisfying meal, Seefelder inquired about a hotel. Rudi mentioned that his *Pension* was clean and quiet, and Seefelder took a room there.

On a sightseeing walk through the town the next day, Seefelder told Rudi of his life. He had made a fortune from cattle and textiles in Argentina during the 1930s. When Hitler called upon German expatriates to return to the Fatherland with their money, Seefelder came and built a textile factory in Ichenhausen, Bavaria. He had more money than he could ever use. But to his great regret, he and his wife had no children.

About six o'clock in the morning, Seefelder pounded on Rudi's door. "Herr Herrmann! Wake up and come with me to the railroad station. I have something important to tell you."

Seefelder wanted Rudi to go to work for him and eventually be manager of his factory. He and his family could live on the third floor of Seefelder's large villa. Rudi noted that he knew nothing about textiles or manufacturing. "Young man, you have a quick mind and good manners. That is enough."

Just before Christmas, Rudi slipped into East Germany, and the KGB instructed him forthwith to accept Seefelder's offer. In the manner of a professor proud of his pupil, Aleks informed him that by order of the Council of Ministers of the Soviet Union, he had been awarded the rank of senior lieutenant. "You have been my best pupil. I expect brilliant accomplishments from you."

The Seefelders in effect adopted Rudi and Inga as their children and doted on Peter as a grandchild. Seefelder insisted on buying Rudi a fine dark suit, on grounds that it was a business necessity. Shedding the imitation leather jacket, worn sweater and frayed shirt of a refugee and putting on his new garb, Rudi suddenly looked like a banker or diplomat.

Seefelder presented him to clients and other businessmen as his "future manager." In his capacious cellar stocked with magnificent vintages, he taught him about wines. Knowledge of wines, he declared, was a business as well as a social necessity. Accompanying Seefelder everywhere, Rudi absorbed the mores, manners and methods of the financially and socially elite. He acquired status, poise, and ability to maneuver in the upper echelons of Western society—attributes the KGB could not have expected him to develop in less than several years.

One evening in the drawing room, Seefelder announced that he had decided to bequeath his factory to Rudi. The thought of breaking with the KGB to accept the factory and a secure life of independence never occurred to Rudi. Instead, he worried. Were he to become manager, he would be totally confined to Ichenhausen and could not move about for the KGB. And when the KGB eventually required him to relocate, his departure would leave the Seefelders heartbroken.

Some days later, Rudi spoke somberly to Seefelder: He was unfit to be manager. The future of the factory depended upon employment of someone with expertise he could not soon acquire. Manly and gracious, Seefelder said he understood. He would find other work for Rudi.

With Seefelder's guidance and 5000 marks, delivered by a

pretty KGB courier at a Frankfurt café, Rudi bought a small mail-order house that sold supplies to public schools. In a used Volkswagen, also purchased with KGB funds, he began calling on customers, gaining experience as both salesman and manager.

On a Friday in July 1958, an official letter from the Office for the Protection of the Constitution, the West German security service, chilled Rudi and Inga. It announced that at 10 a.m. the next Friday, a representative of the agency would call to interview Herr Herrmann concerning official matters. Rudi suffered nightmarish visions of catastrophic arrest.

The security officer, a Herr Hoffman, was a tall, imposing man, whose quiet, gentlemanly manner reminded Rudi of a distinguished professor. He apologized for taking Rudi away from work and assured that his visit was no cause for concern. The law required that all refugees from the East be interviewed about their background, and he had come simply to fulfill that legal requirement. At his behest, Rudi and Inga easily recited their legends.

"If I may ask, Herr Herrmann, why did you decide to flee to the Federal Republic?"

Rudi stood up, paced the room, and with ever more ringing conviction, enumerated the evils of communism. Workers and peasants were oppressed and exploited; Party bureaucrats fattened themselves on the people. The Communists were the real imperialists, murderers who would kill anybody according to the whims of their mad dictators. At least the Nazis killed only selected people.

"I can understand your passion, Herr Herrmann. As I am much older, I know a bit more about Nazism than you. Neither the German nor Soviet people are bad. Both peoples—and all peoples—have suffered terribly because each was afflicted by bad systems. We are creating a good system, a sound democracy in the Federal Republic, and I am glad you can contribute to it. Thank you for your courtesy in answering my questions."

Though they rarely drank except out of social expediency, Rudi and Inga celebrated with a bottle of champagne.

Herr Hoffman unexpectedly reappeared four nights later to proffer Rudi "a position of the highest trust and honor." Rudi's personal characteristics and convictions had so impressed Herr Hoffman and his superiors that they desired to train and send him to Czechoslovakia as a West German agent. The work would be difficult, yes, even dangerous, and it would entail prolonged separation from his lovely wife and child. But it would be a noble work, for by his anonymous toil, he would help extirpate the very evil that he himself so loathed from the body of mankind.

"I realize my proposal necessitates a great decision, and we want you to think about it carefully. I will stop by week after next. Meanwhile, you must say nothing to anybody, not even to your wife. Her well-being could depend upon your silence."

"My God!" wailed Inga. "What shall we do?"

Instinctively, Rudi ruled out consulting the KGB; he feared that unseen and unknown men at the Center would disbelieve any explanation of how he became an intimate of West German intelligence. But how could he reject such an earnest and patriotic offer without stigmatizing himself as a poseur, a coward and maybe a suspect, without inviting further pressures and perhaps investigation?

A week later, still brooding and deliberating, Rudi passed a notorious brothel in Ulm, frequented mainly by American enlisted men, and there he suddenly saw deliverance. Straggling out of the brothel was none other than the distinguished, if somewhat besotted, figure of Herr Hoffman. Draped on either arm were two garishly rouged and outlandishly dressed prostitutes, drunkenly giggling and pawing him.

Rudi dashed up, grabbed and vigorously pumped the mortified officer's hand. "Herr Hoffman! Herrmann from Ichenhausen. What a surprise and pleasure to see you here! My wife and I are looking forward to your next visit—and to meeting your colleagues." The disgrace on Hoffman's face guaranteed Rudi that he would never see or hear from him or his colleagues, at least not about the matter they had discussed.

With Rudi seemingly secure in his own business, he and the Center exchanged messages only about once a month. Sometimes the Center did request political analyses, such as: "Provide assessment of prospects of progressive candidates in future elections. Provide assessment of attitudes of refugees toward socialism." To each, Rudi replied with the bluntest honesty: "There is no chance whatsoever of any progressive candidate or any candidate perceived as progressive winning any election anywhere in the foreseeable future. Refugees side with the imperialists and will form a core of revanchism for years to come." The Center responded: "Your report received."

Browsing in a photo shop, Rudi picked up a new Japanese camera. In those days, many Germans still looked down on Japanese products, considering them cheap and inferior copies of their own. But Rudi knew enough about photography to recognize that the camera was excellent, despite its relatively low price. So he obtained a franchise to sell Japanese optics, liquidated his mail-order business and opened a store in Heilbronn, north of Stuttgart. Soon, business boomed.

The Center commended him. He had entrenched himself as a good German citizen and businessman with impeccable references. His real past in West Germany more and more overshadowed his fictitious past in the East, and as the events of his legend faded with time, they became less checkable, less significant. On December 31, 1960, the Center congratulated him upon his promotion to captain.

In late February, he received a message prefixed URGENT: "As soon as practicable, visit Canada and United States as tourist. Determine whether you can live and work effectively in these countries."

Rudi sailed from Bremerhaven for Montreal in April aboard the tourist ship *Seven Seas*. He tarried several days in Montreal, then visited Ottawa, Toronto, Windsor and Detroit. After a few days in Michigan, he traveled by train to New York and stayed a week before flying to Frankfurt.

He liked what he had seen of America, most of all the casual and relaxed friendliness of the people and their spontaneous willingness to be helpful. Back in Heilbronn in early June, he concluded the report of his trip, "I would be comfortable in either country and am confident of my ability to work there."

The Center soon commanded: "Apply immediately for immigration visa to Canada. Commence intensive study of English. Prepare to dispose of business. Desire to confer with Gerda (Inga's code name) at Center in August. Instructions for her travel will follow."

Inga crossed into East Berlin just before the Wall arose, left Peter with her parents (who thought that she had married a Russian diplomat stationed in Asia) and, with a KGB escort, flew to Moscow. She returned in September with new cipher pads, a complicated radio schedule, a little brown cube oscillator to be fitted into a Hamerlund HQ180 radio to improve short-wave reception in Canada, 5000 U.S. dollars and a set of instructions. Upon receipt of their visas, they were to leave for Canada; settle in Toronto; open a small business, preferably a camera shop; and become good, loyal Canadians, just as they had become good, loyal West Germans.

Inga also brought from Moscow a new attitude. Heretofore reluctant to resettle so far away from her relatives in the East, now she was almost fanatical in her zeal to get to Canada, in her exhortations about Party duty, about how hard Rudi must strive in their new homeland.

"I do not need lectures from you or Moscow, or from Khrushchev himself, about work and duty," Rudi said with a warning edge in his voice. "You listen to me, not them. Remember that."

"It is just that they are counting so on us," she persisted.

"And just what do they expect?"

"I don't know exactly. They will tell us later, after we are safely there."

After purchasing their tickets, settling all accounts, and shipping belongings (including a BMW sedan), Rudi had $8300 of his own, plus the Center's $5000. They flew from Germany on February 16, 1962, and landed in Montreal on the

coldest day Rudi had ever known. Within two weeks, they had
bought a pleasant three-bedroom suburban home outside Toronto, making a down payment of $7500.

Rudi's real estate agent advised that Toronto was surfeited
with camera shops and recommended that Rudi take over a
delicatessen that was for sale. It was in disrepair, but the
location was superb, and with rehabilitation and proper management, the little establishment could become profitable.
With the assistance of a local bank, Rudi paid $5600 for
Harold's Famous Delicatessen on Yonge Street—having ascertained that it was near the headquarters of the Canadian
Broadcasting Corporation.

Upon first entering Harold's Famous Delicatessen, Inga
cried; everything there insulted, indeed outraged, her Ger-
manic sense of order and cleanliness, and she felt as if she had
sunk inextricably into a quagmire of filth. But they set to work
clearing the place out and washing away decades of grime,
expending countless gallons of disinfectant and insecticide.
Rudi repainted and papered the walls and installed new
equipment, a new counter and little butcher-block tables. As
word spread of Inga's homemade German potato salad and
fresh-baked bread and the attentive service from her affable
husband, the delicatessen attracted more and more customers,
among them cameramen, technicians and other employees of
the CBC. Some also were German immigrants, and occasionally they stayed after closing to drink wine and listen to Rudi's
recordings of Nazi war songs. The music and his right-wing
views caused him to be known as "Rudi the Nazi." But he was
popular, and ingratiated himself with the CBC employees,
letting cameramen borrow an impressive new Arriflex motion
picture camera he had brought with him from Germany. They
were so enamored of the camera that the CBC started renting
it for $25 a day.

Besides posting monthly reports in invisible writing to an
accommodation address in Berlin, Rudi's only clandestine
duty consisted of recording and deciphering transmissions
from the Center. Often the messages, which took as long as 18

hours to unravel, turned out to be congratulations on May Day, the anniversary of the liberation of Czechoslovakia, or the advent of socialism in the German Democratic Republic, or birthday greetings to him, Inga or Peter. Finally, he pleaded with the Center to cease all non-operational messages except in case of an emergency involving relatives in the East.

Periodically reassessing his circumstances, as a prudent officer should, he began to worry about keeping the Hamerlund receiver in his house. It was too unusual, too powerful, and within it was the incriminating Soviet oscillator. Reacting to his apprehensions, the Center directed him to dig up a new receiver buried in a forest 80 miles north of Ottawa. In a locale minutely described by the Center, Rudi retrieved the package exactly five feet west of a birch tree, exactly four feet underground. He wondered who put it there and how long ago; no matter, it was meant to stay there for years if necessary.

Taking off an outer wrapping of rubber and an inner wrapping of plastic, Rudi opened a waterproof metal box and, upon removing yet another rubber wrapping, saw the radio—steel gray, ten by five by three inches in size, with earphones and an antenna that could be raised six feet. He had never seen such a radio, and neither had anybody else except spies. The device fairly shrieked "espionage" and "made in Moscow."

"My God!" blurted Inga when she saw it. "Does it come with a hammer and a sickle also?" After six months of feeling as though he was putting his head in the noose every time he used it, Rudi dismembered the radio with a hacksaw, discarded the pieces in different areas, and bought a Braun receiver, which served well.

The birth of their second child, Michael, in December 1963, forced Inga to withdraw from the delicatessen. Aware that he could not maintain the quality of food and service without her, Rudi decided to sell while business still thrived, and he found a purchaser willing to pay $10,000.

Commanded to spend two weeks in Moscow in April, Rudi flew to Paris and took a train to Vienna. At 6:05 p.m. on the corner of Hellwag Strasse and Dresdner Strasse, he was approached by a man carrying a yellow book in his left hand. "Excuse me, do you know where Brown's Curiosity Shop is?" the man asked in German with a Russian accent.

"No, I'm sorry, I am a stranger here. I just came from Gault."

"Welcome, comrade. I hope you have had a good journey."

Rudi slipped the KGB officer an envelope containing his Canadian passport, driver's license, social security card and other papers identifying him as Rudolf Herrmann. The officer handed him an envelope containing a West German passport, driver's license, workbook and a ticket for a flight the next day to Moscow via Sofia.

Beginning with the greeting at the airport and an excellent dinner in a comfortable apartment, the KGB officers who dealt with him were friendly, respectful, professional and, he thought, sensible. Nearly nine years had passed since his induction into intelligence, and in his mind he could credit himself with not a single clandestine accomplishment of substance. But the earnestness with which his hosts praised his achievements in legitimizing himself as a German émigré in Canada caused him to think that perhaps he did not entirely understand, that perhaps they knew much more than he— which, of course, was the case.

Max, the officer who seemed to be most responsible for him, brought a handful of pens and a stack of paper in the morning. "Please write a complete history of everything that has happened to you since you were last here. Put down everything you can remember; it's impossible to include too much detail. Sometimes, what seems meaningless in the field is of significance here. Don't worry about the words; just write whatever comes to your head."

A procession of specialists conferred with him in between his writing. Security officers reviewed the physical layout of his house, discussed hiding places for his cipher pad, radio schedule, and the chemically treated paper needed to write invisibly. A communications expert detailed new emergency signals and pinpointed on a map drop sites around Ottawa where he could deposit urgent messages. A technician instructed him about improved paper for secret writing, and an accountant calculated how much the Center, which allotted him $800 a month for living expenses, owed him. A professional political analyst questioned him about Canadian politics, the strength of separatist sentiment in Quebec, Canadian-U.S. differences, and prospects of Canadian relations with the Chinese.

At the conclusion of his written history, Rudi outlined his future plans. He intended to enter photography and gradually establish a business producing advertising and commercial films. Acquaintances at the CBC would help him. With his own business, he could control his time, as he was unable to do at the delicatessen and could not do if he took a regular job. As a filmmaker, he could justify travel anywhere, and he would be likely to meet a diversity of interesting people.

"Excellent," Max said. "However, always you must think first of all about your real work. From now on, your main mission is to prepare yourself to take charge of the agent networks in Canada as Resident in the event of war or a break in diplomatic relations. Continue to solidify your position economically and socially.

"Secondly, we want you to search for progressives everywhere, particularly among politicians and journalists, and we want you to report about anyone interesting you meet, progressive or not."

Max outlined the format of the "personality reports" Rudi must submit: name, position and approximate age of subject; importance or potential of subject; date and circumstances of encounter; assessment of political and social views; reasons for inferring subject sympathetic to Soviet Union or hostile to United States; assessment of character and personality, with emphasis upon any pronounced vices or eccentricities; possible means of approaching (does subject collect stamps or coins; study a particular period of history or area of the world; play golf or tennis avidly; have any unusual interests; evince any signs of homosexuality; acutely need money?).

Returning via Prague to Vienna under yet another identity, Rudi retrieved his Canadian passport and personal documents from the same KGB officer on the same street corner. Then in Germany he spent his $10,000 in back pay to buy the latest motion picture cameras and microphones. Back in Toronto, through a photographer cultivated at the delicatessen, he obtained a part-time job with CBC as a soundman while studying and practicing filmmaking. An advertising agency hired him to help produce a campaign film for Liberal Party candidates, and his superior work earned him subsequent assignments from other agencies. Within a year, he became known as a skilled and reliable filmmaker who scrupulously kept his commitments, worked overtime without charge, and was never sick or intoxicated. In 1966, he netted nearly $30,000, investing a goodly part of the profit in more advanced equipment, some of which he rented to the CBC. Meanwhile, he duly filed dozens of personality reports on Canadians he judged of possible interest to the KGB.

Increasingly, however, the Center exhorted him to devote less time to his business and more to assessing prospective targets, admonitions which initially perplexed, then angered him. His overriding responsibility, as clearly enunciated in Moscow, was to so entrench himself that he could assume control of the agent networks if necessary. To do that, he needed to succeed as an independent entrepreneur, but the Center's demands interfered. In early 1966, a message from Moscow included the command: ". . .Visit nightclubs and pubs two or three nights a week to meet people and listen to what they are saying."

"Fools!" he exclaimed to Inga. "Important Canadians don't hang around nightclubs gossiping about important business. They don't have time for that nonsense, just as I don't."

In the summer of 1966, the KGB ordered Inga to come to Moscow by way of Vienna to pick up money, a new radio schedule and ciphers, and before she left, Rudi invisibly wrote the Center a long message, polite and reasoned but emphatic. Describing the improbability of making significant contacts or obtaining valid samples of public opinion in bars, he stressed that unless his stated mission had been changed, neglect of his business would be ruinous. He predicted that as his business expanded, he would encounter more and more people of interest. However, he believed that the limitations on his social status imposed both by his legend and the nature of his work would preclude him from circulating socially at the highest levels. If that is what the Center actually desired of him, then perhaps he should consider entering a university to equip himself for a profession that would provide higher social entrée.

Inga returned from Moscow with no direct response to his analysis. Rather, as if she had been metamorphosed into a Party agitator, she chastised him for concerning himself so much with business and not hunting hard enough for "progressives." Rudi was enraged. Inga he could and would straighten out. But the myopia of the Center and its attempt to use his wife as a goad against him provoked contempt.

In February 1967, Rudi, Inga and Peter joined some 70 other émigrés in a solemn Toronto courtroom. Like a congregation in church, all sat in silent reverence awaiting the naturalization ceremony that would transform them into Canadian citizens. Rudi looked up, inwardly recoiled, and thought, *It's all over.* Standing over him were two huge Royal Canadian Mounted Policemen wearing red coats. "Are you Herrmann?" one asked in a tone Rudi construed as challenging and ominous.

"Yes."

"Then come with us."

Feeling like a man being led to the gallows, Rudi followed them into a chamber, where an impassive flinty-eyed judge was studying papers on his desk. "Rudolf Herrmann?" the judge asked.

"Yes, I am Herrmann."

"I have been reviewing your record," said the judge. "In light of all you have been through to acquire Canadian citizenship, I have decided that at the end of the proceedings you shall lead everyone in taking the Oath of Allegiance to the Queen."

Ten days after Rudi reported acquisition of citizenship, he labored into the early hours of Sunday morning to decipher a message. The words that emerged astounded him: "Make all necessary preparations to obtain U.S. visa and to move to the United States."

He had assumed that he was permanently stationed and had oriented his whole life on that assumption. Peter was thriving in school, loved Canada and thought of himself as Canadian. Inga enjoyed their home, her Canadian friends and the ethnic diversity of Toronto. He had built a flourishing business that would make $50,000 in 1967. He cared nothing about money per se, but it afforded the independence and security essential to his secret purpose. And he was beginning through filmmaking to converse with important men. Already, he had met and filed reports on Canadian leaders—former Prime Minister John Diefenbaker, Prime Minister Lester Pearson and politicians Joseph Smallwood, René Lévesque and Walter Gordon. To be sure, he reported nothing that could not be read in the press, and he found no indications that any of these leaders were "progressives" or could be suborned by the KGB. But the Center praised his ability to observe them closely and personally in their unguarded moments. And the prospect of forsaking the foundation so laboriously laid in Canada and starting again from nothing exasperated him.

Rudi conjectured that the KGB would not compel him to abandon a strong and safe position in Canada unless it required something much more important from him in the United States, and he suspected that whatever that was could be dangerous. He was correct on both counts. What he did not understand at the time was that the United States always had been his final destination. Doubtless, had need arisen, the Center would have activated him as Illegal Resident in Canada. But Canada was just a way stop, the country from which it was easiest to immigrate normally and legally to the United States.

Dutifully, Rudi began studying U.S. immigration laws and

procedures and concluded he was more likely to obtain a visa if he possessed a needed skill. Further study showed that there was a plethora of photographers in the U.S., but a comparative shortage of electronics specialists. So that he could claim a background in electronics, he joined the Canadian Society of Motion Picture and Television Engineers, and on his visa application stressed his technical expertise.

The depressing necessity of liquidating his business so preoccupied him that he thought little of a seemingly routine and tedious instruction the Center sent in the fall of 1967: "Verify address of Professor Hugh Hambleton of Laval University in Quebec City, Quebec." Too busy to waste a day in Quebec, he dispatched Inga, and she had no trouble ascertaining that Professor Hambleton did indeed live where the KGB said.

Soon afterward, the Center informed Rudi that Professor Hambleton was a "highly trusted agent" who spied under the KGB code name "Roman." He was to track the professor down forthwith in Quebec City and, having introduced himself with the recognition signal "I bring you greetings from friends," relay instructions.

The KGB decision to bring Rudi and Hambleton together represented a singular departure from standard procedures and reflected uncommon trust and confidence in both men. For once they met, each thereafter would be at the mercy of the other. Rudi surmised that the Center judged the professor to be so valuable that it dared not endanger him by contact with an Ottawa Residency officer who might be under Canadian surveillance.

Failing to find Hambleton at home, Rudi wandered about the Laval University campus looking for his office. In the corridor of an administration building he spotted a man who fit the Center's description—tall, trim, wavy gray hair, gray eyes, handsome face, baggy tweed suit.

"Professor Hambleton?"

"Right."

"My name is Douglas. I bring you greetings from friends."

"How good of you," Hambleton replied with a glint of amusement on his face. "I was thinking of a beer. Would you care to join me?"

The ingenuous speech and manner of Hambleton surprised Rudi, who vaguely expected a more conspiratorial manner from a major Soviet spy. The professor seemed as relaxed talking to a representative from the Center in a public café as he would chatting with a colleague at the faculty club. Rudi put him down as an intellectual explorer with a broad array of interests and knowledge, and a worldly man whose wry self-deprecation suggested he did not take himself too seriously. The more Hambleton revealed of himself, the more Rudi liked him, and it occurred to him that here was the one man he had encountered in the West with whom he freely could be his ideological self. Nevertheless, whether because of his training or pure peasant prudence, Rudi chose to try to disguise himself slightly.

"Have you come far?" Hambleton asked.

"Well, yes and no. Originally I am from Finland; now I work in New York," Rudi said. "Our friends wanted me to relay some requests they consider important. Would you like to take notes?"

"I think I can remember."

Rudi instructed him first to submit an analysis of the Canadian economy, then to prepare reports on the prospects of the separatist movement and Canadian-Chinese relations. His permanent assignment was to collect general intelligence about the United States and China. Hambleton agreed to rendezvous two weeks hence at Place Ville Marie in Montreal to deliver the economic report.

Rudi drove from Toronto so there would be no record of the trip. Believing that "two are less suspicious than one," he took Peter along, waking him up at 3 a.m. As if sightseeing, they stood at the monument on Mount Royal, the highest site in Montreal, lashed by bitter December winds in sub-zero weather. Rudi told Peter to wait while he attended to some brief business, and dashed off to meet Hambleton.

The professor had typed a lengthy analysis which Rudi, when he later read it, thought masterful. Rudi gave him an address in East Berlin, to which he was to send future reports, and two new orders from the Center: Develop a personal relationship with McGill University Professor Paul Lin, whom the Center believed had access to Mao Zedong, and try to obtain an appointment to the Canadian Foreign Service. They parted in little more than a minute, and Rudi called, as if repeating directions to a stranger, "That's right. Two blocks, then left."

To justify his presence in the area, if justification were needed, he stopped in a camera shop, spoke amiably with the proprietor for a while and asked for an unusual model of a light meter. The proprietor apologized and suggested he try another shop. There, Rudi again visited with the sales personnel and bought a few items. Pretending to window-shop, he spent a half hour or so checking for surveillance, then took refuge from the cold in a coffee shop. Suddenly he thought, *My God, what have I done?*

Racing his 1966 Thunderbird back to the monument, he saw his ten-year-old son still implanted there, his face blue, his small body trembling. Peter apparently had not moved in more than four hours. He said only, "I'm so cold."

VIII

THE
INHERITOR

P ROMPTLY AFTER Rudi received a U.S. visa early in 1968, the Center advised that New York would be his base and told him to buy a house either on Long Island or in Westchester County. Radio reception, privacy and fear of street crime doubtless were considerations in the KGB decision to locate him outside the city. Rudi guessed there was one other reason. In the event of nuclear war, the KGB needed him to survive at least the first few days, something relatively few in the city could expect to do.

The Center subsequently radioed some specifications the house must meet. It could not be located on a main thoroughfare or near high tension power lines, and there could be no nearby obstructions to the East, whence messages from Moscow originated. Ideally, the house should stand on high ground and not be directly observable from other dwellings.

Flying from Toronto on weekends, Rudi eventually discovered the ideal house—an attractive split-level at 5 Andover Road in Hartsdale, about 15 miles north of the city. It was isolated on a hilltop amid tall trees, open to the east. A house below blocked any view from the road and no other houses were nearby. From Hartsdale he could easily commute into the city or drive to corporate headquarters and offices in the vicinity of White Plains. With a $12,000 down payment, Rudi bought the house for $32,000.

He notified the Center that his family would move in June, at the end of school. Moscow replied by commending his choice of the house, which the New York Residency had evidently inspected; announcing his promotion to major; and inviting him to Paris in May for briefings about his mission in the United States.

On a balmy Sunday morning when all of Paris seemed painted golden by sunshine, Rudi met Pavel Pavlovich Lukyanov at a bench by the Seine on the Left Bank. Lukyanov, then 48, was an able and experienced KGB officer who understood the United States well, having been stationed in both New York and Washington. As they strolled along with throngs of Parisians, he stated that in the United States, as in Canada, Rudi would be the Illegal Resident. Again he must position himself so well in society that he could assume control of all agent networks should the Legal Residencies be lost. He must constantly hunt for "progressives." And he would be tasked with many more subsidiary missions—among them penetration of the Hudson Institute, which the KGB considered one of the most fecund research centers in America.

The directive to penetrate an institute that symbolized practical intellectualism caused Rudi to raise anew the question of whether he should not enroll in a university. Again he defined the structural defect in his legend, which left him bereft of any qualifications for an intellectual profession and any foundation from which to ascend into upper social strata. Unprepared and unauthorized to cope with these issues, Pavel evaded them, saying only that for the time being Rudi would have to establish himself as best he could.

To Rudi that meant duplicating in New York his business in Toronto, and he founded a firm titled Documatic Films, Inc. Canadian friends steered him to a few American clients, and one of them proposed that they form a joint venture to produce a movie biography of Senator Edmund Muskie for his Vice Presidential campaign. Foreseeing a possibility that Rudi could forge a personal relationship with a potential U.S. President and his staff, the Center added: "Do whatever necessary to produce Muskie film. Spend any amount necessary. Will reimburse all expenses." However, Muskie campaign officials rejected their bid because, in Rudi's opinion, his would-be partner asked an exorbitant fee.

Rudi met IBM people and interested them in renting his sophisticated film editing machine, and soon IBM awarded him jobs producing training and sales films. Able to cite as a reference a prestigious corporation renowned for insistence upon technical excellence, he attracted many other clients, more in fact than he could accommodate. For beginning in 1969 the KGB often diverted him from lawful business to execute sensitive assignments which could not be entrusted to officers from the Legal Residencies in Washington or New York.

In March 1969 the Center ordered him to type and to mail from Atlanta to Cape Kennedy an anonymous letter warning that the next manned space flight would be sabotaged before launch. "Do it at once, no later than tomorrow," the message commanded.

Canceling photo assignments, Rudi bought a typewriter at a pawn shop, typed the words dictated by the Center, cut the typewriter into pieces with a hacksaw and discarded the pieces in storm sewers. So as to leave no trace of his travels, he drove nonstop to Charlotte, N.C., parked his car in a 24-hour lot, took a bus to Atlanta and posted the letter, which was signed "Patriotic Citizen"—who claimed to have overheard the sabotage plans on a plane flight. Returning by bus to Charlotte, he drove straight to New York, sometimes steering with one hand and holding an eye open with the other to stay awake, as he had done long ago while studying at Charles

University. But the puerile KGB attempt to interject a costly delay into the space program had no effect; NASA officials tossed the letter into the crackpot file.

A couple of months later, the Center routed him back to Quebec to seek out Hambleton and ascertain why he had not appeared at a rendezvous scheduled in a remote area outside Ottawa. Happy to see Rudi, Hambleton explained with equanimity. "I would have been an idiot to attend that meeting. Do you know where it was to take place? Right in front of a dynamite factory! How could I have explained to the guards what an economics professor was doing lolling around a dynamite factory in the middle of the night?"

Rudi laughed. "Whoever picked that site is an idiot. If I were in charge, I would send him home to work in a dynamite factory. Forget about it. I will straighten them out."

In autumn 1969, the Center directed Rudi to try to track a Soviet defector believed to be residing in a large apartment building in Arlington, Va. The cable instructed him to chart the exile's daily pattern of movements—when he left for work, in which direction he drove, the make of his car, when he came home, where he usually parked. The KGB warned that the reconnaissance involved danger because the CIA used several apartments in the buildings, and American professionals would be suspicious if they spotted him prying.

On three occasions, Rudi drove from New York at 1 a.m. so he could begin his vigil in Arlington before 7 a.m. The apartment building had multiple entrances; no matter where he positioned himself, he could observe only one at a time; and he never saw the hunted man. Nor did he ever learn his name or why the KGB wanted to know his movements. The detailed physical description the Center provided of the man, however, fit that of KGB defector Yuri Ivanovich Nosenko..

Sometimes, Rudi had to journey on short notice to distant sections of the country to perform tasks meaningless to him but classified "urgent" by the Center. He flew to California in January 1970 and drove toward Thousand Oaks until locating and verifying the address of "an Italian-looking woman with two children." Why Moscow was so intent upon obtaining such data he never knew. Later, he flew to Dallas and, exactly as he had been told, dialed a telephone number and to a male who answered said: "The friend you are expecting will not come as planned. You will be advised of new arrangements later." He hung up without awaiting a reply and flew back to New York.

Rudi did appreciate the importance of one type of clandestine assignment, the selection of drop sites in the vicinity of research centers and military bases. Tradecraft training told him that the drops could be needed because there were agents inside those installations who could communicate safely only through drops. He also understood why the Center wanted someone such as himself to pick the sites.

While officers from the legal KGB Residencies might escape FBI surveillance in the environs of Washington and New York, it was much more difficult for them to venture undetected into remote areas of the country. If the FBI in silently following a known KGB officer noted the drops he picked, then it had only to wait and watch until the spy for whom they were chosen showed up at the site. Rudi, seemingly a reputable commercial photographer and filmmaker who could concoct a reasonable excuse for traveling anywhere, presumably was of no interest to the FBI and thus was unwatched. So as he slogged through muddy woods, paced stretches of hot desert, trod lonely roads in the night, perused cemeteries in the rain looking for secure drop sites, Rudi did not object. He realized that the drops could be crucial to the Party, to socialism, to mankind. Through them, unknown comrades might someday pass intelligence that could hasten the advent of universal communism and liberate the world from the curse of capitalism.

The KGB in late 1970 rewarded Rudi with promotion to lieutenant colonel, and he continued to ensconce himself so as to be ready to assume control of the entire Soviet network of agents in the United States, if necessary. Inga unfailingly supported him, often recording and deciphering radio messages, drafting his reports in invisible writing and charming his business associates. To clear space for addition of a formal living room needed to entertain, Rudi and Peter over a period of five months chipped away a rock formation too close to the house to be blasted.

Though they missed Canada and their friends, Rudi and Inga came to enjoy the openness and informality of American society, the ease of doing business, making friends and traveling. But these superficial baubles did not seduce them. They knew that beneath the glitter and pleasantries of the U.S. lay the incurable corruption and degeneracy of capitalism. This certitude armored them with a psychological shell that made them politically impervious to any allure of American society. No matter how benign and hospitable, the United States for them was still enemy territory, a battlefield on which they fought uncorrupted. On those few occasions when they had time to dream, they looked forward upon completion of their tour of duty on the front lines to retirement in Communist Czechoslovakia.

They worried, however, about Peter as they saw him growing into an American, one of the enemy, and they felt an acute dilemma. In the presence of guests at home, Peter heard his father speak as an ardent anti-Communist who looked upon the Soviet Union as a land of benighted, backward butchers. Rudi could not safely contradict privately what he said openly nor inculcate Peter with Marxism as an antidote to the traditions of democracy he was absorbing at school and from his peers. To reorient his maturation, they agreed that Inga would take him abroad for eight to ten weeks each summer to imbue him with European culture and expose him to its forms of socialism.

Operationally, the Center's importunities about the Hudson Institute posed the most vexatious problem. Rudi asked IBM technicians about the institute; he read about it; he talked to gas station attendants about it; he drove around it. Ascertaining that members of the institute frequented the Tarrytown House on Sunnyside Lane, just off Route 9, he dined there several times on the improbable chance that he might overhear snippets of information and contrive artifices to approach noted scientists and thinkers. But he could think of no practical pretext. As Dr. Ludek Zemenek from Charles University or Herr Doktor Professor Rudolf Adolfus Herrmann from Heidelburg, he could have approached them. But what was Rudi Herrmann, the smiling, accommodating, diligent, self-effacing commercial photographer, to say to them? Short of applying for a janitorial job, he could conceive no way to cozen the Hudson Institute.

To his explanation of the difficulties, the Center replied simply: "Renew efforts to penetrate Hudson Institute." He asked the Center to recommend *how*. The reply: "Renew efforts." As the Center chose to ignore his explanations and request for guidance, he resolved to ignore any further adjurations regarding the infernal institute.

Without explanation, the Center in April 1972 summoned Rudi to a meeting in Quito, Ecuador. He decided to take Peter along to deflect suspicion and to show the boy a different part of the world. At 6 p.m., Rudi stood in front of a theater in downtown Quito, and a thin, balding man, six feet tall, joined him in looking at the marquee. In excellent English he said, "Good evening. Have you read any books by Elie Wiesel recently?"

"No, I have been reading Hemingway."

"I am very glad to meet you, Douglas. My name is Yuri. I'm sorry but because of unexpected business, we will have to postpone our visit until the morning. Meet me at ten o'clock at the Equatorial Monument."

"My son is with me. May I bring him along?"

"Peter? Why, certainly. I would like to see him. You and I can speak German."

At the monument, Yuri asked Rudi a host of questions, mostly personal. His phrasing connoted the sympathetic interest of a friend, rather than the suspicion or hostility of an interrogator. "How is your health? . . . Is Gerda (Inga) happy? . . . Do you like New York? . . . Are you willing to stay indefinitely?"

Rudi was tempted to mention the Center's obsession with

the Hudson Institute and the admonitions to spend more time in bars. But Yuri was so gracious that he did not wish to appear petty and carping; besides, there had been a pause in the demands, and he hoped they had been forgotten. So he said only, "I am willing to do whatever the Party requires. We wonder, though, how long we will be in America."

"I need not tell you how important the mission of Illegal Resident is," Yuri said. "The longer you stay in the United States, the more valuable you become; the more you succeed, the more difficult it is to bring you home. And you are succeeding. If I had to guess, I would say that you would remain in the U.S. many more years."

Sensing the end of their conversation, Rudi asked, "Do you have new tasks for me?"

"No. I came only to convey our appreciation of your service and to let you know that always we are interested in your welfare. We know that when far away from home for so long, one sometimes can be quite lonely even while quite busy."

Yuri impressed Rudi as both a sensitive man and an accomplished professional. Having seen in some messages from the Center evidence of insensitivity and incompetence, he was reassured to know that those in command were like Yuri, and he left the monument feeling gratified, honored.

Rudi's feelings were justified. For Yuri was General Yuri Ivanovich Drozdov, who was later to become KGB Resident in New York. He had journeyed all the way to Quito to evaluate, then encourage Rudi, because the KGB considered him essential to operations Drozdov would direct.

Flying back to New York, Rudi reflected pridefully upon Peter, who had proven to be a splendid traveling companion: undemanding, obedient, yet eager to explore, and inquisitive and perceptive about all they saw. Attempting to make the same kind of assessment of him that he would make for the Center, Rudi asked himself: *What are his qualifications for intelligence work? Perfect,* he thought.

The KGB had obligated itself to pay for the university education of both Peter and Michael. Noting the mounting tuition charged by better American universities, Rudi winced at the burden their education would impose upon socialism. His familiarity with IBM convinced him that the corporation's stock represented a profitable investment, and he calculated that were the KGB to invest $10,000 through him, the appreciation would defray a substantial part of the college costs of Michael, if not Peter. Accordingly, he forwarded an analysis to the Center recommending the purchase of IBM stock. He might as well have profaned Lenin.

"Proposed Wall Street investment unthinkable and anti-Marxist. Stop thinking about money and the *dolce vita*. Stop acting like a capitalist," the Center radioed in reprimand.

The rebuke infuriated Rudi, both because of its personal innuendo and because of its idiocy. Like a Moravian peasant, Rudi was compulsively thrifty and obsessed with saving. During his first exploratory visit to the United States, he discovered that Americans give or throw away much of value. He learned to buy for a few dollars expensive suits and ties donated by the wealthy to the Salvation Army. In secondhand shops he found broken yet fine furniture and restored it himself. At a junkyard he bought a hot water heater for $10 and with $3 worth of piping made it as functional as a new one. While on trips he never took a taxi if he possibly could walk or ride a bus; he never treated his family to dinner in a restaurant.

However, Rudi did not stint in entertaining others, and his house became a veritable social center, frequented by dozens of clients and corporate executives living in Westchester County. Inga prepared delectable sauerbraten, schnitzel, dumplings, sausage and other German dishes, and Rudi served choice wines and costly brands of liquor. But all this was for operational purposes, not the goddamned *dolce vita*. "*Dolce vita*, my ass!" he shouted. "I'm paying for this whole fucking operation with my sweat, working 14 hours a day, trying to save them money, and those assholes think just because I have a house and a car, I'm living like a millionaire." Still, faith and duty prevailed over his anger at stupidity.

KGB ability to gather intelligence through Soviet and Cuban assets in Chile declined precipitously after the anti-Communist coup and the suicide of Salvador Allende. So in the spring of 1974 the Center directed Rudi to devise a pretext to travel throughout Chile and assess the prevailing political situation. With Peter along, he landed in Santiago in the guise of a producer hopeful of securing government cooperation in the making of some films. He thereby obtained interviews with several Chilean officials and moved around the country unencumbered by the suspicions that would have attached to any Russian. Peter, who spoke Spanish well, was always at his side, frequently serving as an interpreter. From Chile they flew to Lima, where Rudi would write his report, which he was to deliver to the KGB in Mexico City. And it was in Lima that he reached what was to be the second greatest decision of his life.

Its gestation doubtless had begun long ago in his subconscious; his conscious contemplation started after he and Peter returned from Quito. His contemplation had been objective, analytical, clinical, as befitted the gravity of the subject. He knew, and the KGB in various ways had acknowledged, that he already had fulfilled his principal mission in the United States; he now was ready and able to take control of the agent networks at any time. He could justify travel on the shortest of notice. He had integrated himself so well into American society that had the FBI initiated a background investigation, its agents would have learned from his friends, neighbors and associates, from patriotic executives at IBM and elsewhere in business, that he was a man of estimable character and an ideal citizen, albeit with rather right-wing views. Rudi had accomplished every reasonable clandestine task assigned. If he could not penetrate the Hudson Institute, he could handle an agent emplaced there—or anywhere else, even the White House. Given his legend and age, he could never expect to place himself into any of the most secret areas of America. Yet he knew someone who in time probably could—Peter.

Peter's high-school grades were outstanding; on the Scholastic Aptitude Test he ranked phenomenally high. Already he spoke Spanish and was learning Japanese and French; and he possessed the linguistic gift to master any language rapidly. He disdained alcohol, loathed narcotics. In conversation with adults, he manifested poise and maturity far beyond his years.

Were the KGB to commence now to indoctrinate and train Peter, by the time he completed undergraduate work, he would be a professional intelligence officer. After finishing graduate school at, say, Harvard, Yale, Stanford or the Massachusetts Institute of Technology, he could step, by virtue of his own abilities, into literally any area of U.S. government the KGB preferred. The vistas of what he could accomplish in the service of the Soviet Union were limitless.

Rudi had given his life and wife to the Party. In Lima he decided to give the dearest and most meaningful gift left to him to bestow—his son.

Sitting on a bench in Lima's central square, Rudi said: "Peter, I must tell you something very serious. It may shock you at first. In the end, I hope you will understand and be proud.

"My name is not Rudi Herrmann. I am not German; I am Czech. And I am a Soviet intelligence officer, a lieutenant colonel in what is called the KGB. I have been working with the KGB ever since before you were born. It is because of intelligence work that we moved to Germany, Canada, then the United States. I have been on an intelligence assignment in Chile. Everything I do is part of my duty as an intelligence officer.

"Sometimes you have heard me talk like I am a Nazi, and each time I have had to speak that way in front of you, I have been ashamed. I am the antithesis of a Nazi. I am a Marxist and always have been. I hope you will come to see, as I do, that the principles of Marx and Lenin are the scientific solution to the injustice and misery that afflict the world."

Peter remained composed and momentarily silent, and Rudi could read no reaction from his face.

"What is your name, Father?"

"Ludek Zemenek."

"Do we have relatives?"

"Yes. You have a grandmother alive in Czechoslovakia and another in East Germany."

"Does Mother know?"

"She also is an agent of the KGB."

Peter thought for a while, again with no visible emotion, before saying: "Father, I am glad to know the truth. And I guess I am proud of you. I'm very happy to know that I have grandmothers. Will I be able to see them?"

"That may depend. Would you be willing to become an intelligence officer like me?"

"Father, if that is what you think I should do, I will."

"No, I cannot make the choice for you, but it would make me very happy."

"Then that is what I will do."

Rudi felt pride, triumph, joy. Knowing that his son by nature was taciturn and phlegmatic, he could have expected no more.

In Mexico City at Chapultepec Park, Rudi asked a KGB contact to inform the Center that he had unmasked himself before Peter and that his son had indicated a willingness to join the KGB. He suggested that the Center arrange for a family visit to Moscow.

"Approve family visit to Moscow. Looking forward to meeting son," said the first message Rudi received back in New York. It included complicated travel plans, which they followed after school ended in June.

Inga left Michael at a summer camp in Spain, picked up false papers from the KGB in Vienna, traveled to Budapest, then by Aeroflot to Moscow. Peter flew to Paris, Rudi to London, and they met in the night on a wharf in Copenhagen to slip aboard a Soviet freighter. A crewman hustled them into a cabin below deck and warned that they could not leave it until the ship arrived in Leningrad. The cabin was like a closet, with space only for two bunks and a toilet; there was no porthole, and the ventilation duct emitted stale, stinking odors from the galley. Locked up for three miserable days and nights, they could only sleep or sit on the bunks and eat the poor food pushed through the door. Peter did not complain, but Rudi was incensed that the KGB would introduce him to the Soviet Union and socialism in such a manner.

Inga, who landed in Moscow two days ahead of them, was waiting in the high-rise apartment they were to share. At the standard welcoming dinner there, the intelligence and maturity with which Peter answered general questions clearly impressed Pavel, the officer Rudi had met in Paris six years before.

Alone after dinner, Inga told Rudi she had been discussing their work with Andrei, one of their case officers, during the past two days. "Sweetheart, you're just going to have to cut back on your business. Work like a normal man, eight hours a day, then go out and meet people. And you must do something about the Hudson Institute."

"Spare me, Inga!" Rudi shouted. "Don't you realize they're using you as a pawn against your own husband? Remember! You are my wife first and their agent second. Go to sleep. I will hear no more."

Andrei began it all over again in the morning. "Well, tell me, what have you done about the Hudson Institute? Rather, let me tell you. You have done nothing. What have you accomplished in the last 14 months? Nothing; exactly nothing except live the *dolce vita* and add a room to your house." Andrei paused and smiled triumphantly. "You see, I know about that room. You wasted your time fattening your house so you could live the *dolce vita*." Advancing on Rudi, Andrei waved the epaulets of a full colonel in his face. "Now, if you will stop the *dolce vita* and go to work, you can earn these."

Rudi had always succeeded in retaining his poise, no matter what the duress. But now, speaking Russian so Peter would not understand, he shouted: "You asshole! You dull, miserable, peasant asshole! You are a disgrace to the Party and the KGB! You are demeaning me as an officer and father in front of my own son. And, you myopic asshole, you ask what I have done? I have delivered to you my son; that is one thing I have done. He can be a great intelligence officer unless fools like you ruin him."

Retreating beyond Rudi's reach, Andrei went on to criticize Rudi's reports as too pessimistic. "Who are you to say that for the next ten years progressive forces in Chile have no hope? Do you think you are a soothsayer? Do you not understand that the laws of history are on our side?"

"I understand that at great trouble and risk to myself and my son, I went to Chile to make an honest assessment. That I did. If you want fables, produce them yourself."

"Well, your report on détente must be revised.* It also is too negative."

"It is the duty of an intelligence officer to report what is."

"Well, your report is too harsh. You must soften it."

"I refuse to change one word."

The KGB investment of 19 years in Rudi and Inga, the illimitable opportunities Peter represented, all might have evaporated had not Pavel and other officers interceded. They dismissed Andrei, who did not appear again, and tried to mollify Rudi by appearing to accede to his demands.

To Pavel, Rudi laid down some categorical conditions: Peter must be a staff officer of the KGB, not an agent. He must be thoroughly indoctrinated in the principles of Marxism-Leninism so he would understand the purpose of his life, the kind of life he would have to lead.

"That we can do," said Pavel, "provided Peter wants to of his own accord. However, unless he chooses to join us, he cannot return to the United States with the knowledge he now has. He will have to stay here and be a Soviet citizen."

Inga, in near hysteria, trembled at the specter. Rudi was untroubled, confident that Peter would out of fidelity to his father enlist in the KGB when Pavel talked to him; and he did.

---

*Instructed to submit an assessment of American public opinion regarding détente, Rudi had written: "Détente is supported mainly by the President, the clique around him, and some intellectuals. Most Americans do not understand or care about the concept of détente. Of those who do understand, most oppose détente."

The KGB quickly postulated a glittering future for Peter—and itself. Tentatively, it decided that he should become a lawyer; as such, he would enjoy mastery of his own time, access to politicians and wider options of employment in the U.S. government. As Peter already had committed himself to enroll in McGill University in Montreal two months hence, the KGB told him to plan to transfer to a major U.S. university by his junior year and prepare to enter any one of the nation's top five or six law schools after graduation. Money, the Russians emphasized, was no factor; the KGB gladly would pay all direct and indirect costs of Peter's education. During his first year at McGill, he should concentrate upon achieving academic success while trying to identify any students or professors sympathetic toward the Soviet Union. In no circumstances should he himself evince any such sympathy. He would return to Moscow in summer 1975 to begin training and indoctrination. At a festive farewell dinner, the KGB formally baptized Peter into the cult by anointing him with his permanent code name: Erbe, the German word meaning "inheritor."

While Inga flew to Spain to pick up Michael, Rudi and Peter returned as they had come, in the same suffocating hole of the same grubby Soviet freighter. A shipboard KGB officer or agent unaccountably timed their exits so that in descending the gangway in Copenhagen, they were caught up among a group of English tourists—bona fide passengers on the freighter. Standing on the wharf, waving merrily to friends, was an "Englishman" photographing the departing passengers with a movie camera. There was no backing away; Rudi and Peter could only stride straight on toward the lens of the camera. *Incredible,* thought Rudi.

At Sunday breakfast in October, Rudi announced to Inga and Michael, "We all deserve a holiday in the sun. Let's fly down to Haiti for a few days." Inquiries in Port-au-Prince informed him that most diplomats sent their children to the American school, and he patrolled the school yard waiting to catch sight of Professor Hambleton, who was working with a Canadian foreign-aid program while on sabbatical leave. Spotting Hambleton driving away in a jeep with his son, Rudi ran through muddy side streets to intercept him on the main road to the Canadian embassy. Seeing Rudi standing in the middle of the road hailing him with both arms, Hambleton laughed and shouted, "Hop in. I'm always willing to give a vagabond a lift."

Hambleton drove some three miles up a mountainside to a palatial villa. Inside, Rudi stared speechless at the most perfectly sculpted female figure he had ever seen, a purplish-black Haitian woman, about 20, whose glistening eyes and every swaying movement proclaimed sensuality. As Rudi gawked, the professor grinned. "My housekeeper," he said.

"Our friends are worried because they have not heard from you for some time," Rudi announced, by way of explaining his visit.

"Tell our friends that I too am concerned. The address they gave me is on Karl Marx Allee in East Berlin. If I posted a letter from here to Karl Marx Allee, the Haitians would turn the island upside down to find out who's corresponding with Communists."

"Probably it is coincidence, but I've brought you a new address, a new cipher pad and radio schedule. I guess they don't understand Haiti; in fact, they would like a comprehensive report from you about conditions here."

During the Christmas holidays, as Rudi endeavored to ground Peter in the fundamentals of Marxism-Leninism, he realized how much his son had to learn and how essential it was that he learn. Having never been taught the truth, Peter could not be expected, for all his natural acuity, to see clearly through the deceitful facades of life in the West. He could not easily understand that what appeared to be freedom in America actually was an illusion; that its trappings—elections, the press, unions, courts—were artifices; that the superficial affluence was a narcotic administered to deaden the senses and control the masses; that the wealth which did exist had been amassed by war and plunder of the Third World; that everything was controlled by a tiny cabal of capitalists and militarists; that Western society represented only a transitory stage in the historically programmed march of mankind toward the genuine liberty, justice, equality and plenty that only socialism could bring. Rudi was grateful for the KGB pledge that commencing next summer in Moscow great teachers would begin to show his son the truth.

Although Peter almost never exhibited emotion, Rudi and Inga thought he was in sound spirits when he returned to McGill in early January. In February, though, he mailed them without any accompanying note a cartoon he had drawn. It showed him strangling with a rope around his neck; it was captioned "Shit." Was it a way of asking them for help? Had Peter suffered a mild nervous breakdown?

"Of course not," Rudi assured Inga. "Look at his grades. If he were sick, he wouldn't be on the dean's list. Besides, all college kids go through these phases." And besides, in the Herrmann family, as in the Zemenek family, sickness was not tolerated. There was no time for it.

On a Sunday afternoon in May, Rudi and Peter drove to Towaco, N.J., a village about 25 miles west of New York. On Indian Lane Rudi pulled to the side of the road, and Peter placed a radiator hose at the base of a giant oak tree. Stuffed into the hose were a slip of paper listing the June dates and flights on which Peter would travel to Paris, then Vienna; photographs of Peter, which the KGB needed for forged passports; and a political report from Rudi. A mile down the road, by another designated tree, Peter laid down a Coca-Cola bottle to signal that the drop had been loaded. He and Rudi drank coffee in a small coffee shop where three rather well-dressed young men were sipping soft drinks. Then they drove to a third spot on Indian Lane, and there the presence of an orange peel signified that someone from the KGB had taken away the contents of the hose.

The Center by radio confirmed Peter's itinerary: New York, Paris, Vienna, Budapest, Moscow. At one of several meeting points used by his parents in Vienna, he would receive a passport and visa identifying him as a German tourist.

In the same Moscow apartment the family had shared the previous summer, the KGB outlined Peter's future in considerable detail. Peter was to so distinguish himself in undergraduate and law schools that any department of the U.S. government would be eager to hire him. The KGB would determine where he should seek employment, according to Soviet needs at the time of his graduation; however, it most likely would point him toward the Department of State, Defense or Justice. To enhance both his job qualifications and future utility, Peter should study foreign languages, particularly Japanese and Chinese. Command of languages would increase both the likelihood of assignment to foreign policy-making areas and his ability to meet foreigners in the United States. In addition to annual summer instruction from the KGB, he would undergo on-the-job training in clandestine tradecraft from his father. Therefore, whenever his father undertook a specific clandestine task, Peter, if possible, should leave school for a few days and accompany him. He also should regard his father as his professor in ideological subjects. While in the university, every three months he was to submit through Rudi a report on his activities and contacts.

Specialists instructed Peter in countersurveillance, security procedures, the concept of drops and secret writing. A young officer, Viktor, was appointed to escort him on a three-week tour across the vast breadth of the Soviet Union, and they looked at many of the showcases reserved for the edification of foreigners—a massive hydroelectric plant, idyllic collective farms, immaculate clinics, day-care schools peopled by smiling children and devoted teachers, a new semi-automated factory producing refrigerators. But the swaggering, hard-drinking Viktor was an unhappy choice as guide. When Peter suggested a discussion of Marxism, Viktor laughed: "I've been listening to that shit all my life, and you'll be hearing it for the rest of yours. Right now, we're out for fun." In a boat on Lake Baikal, drunk at mid-afternoon, he stood up, reeled about and jeered at fishermen in a passing craft. To the astonishment of all, he whipped out a revolver and fired six rounds over their heads. As firearms are banned in the Soviet Union, their discharge is rarely heard, and the fishermen were terrified, which caused Viktor to laugh all the more.

Peter stopped at home in New York, before returning to McGill, and recounted his experience in the Soviet Union. Repressing his anger, Rudi remarked, "Obviously, the jerk is an aberration, so atypical that he signifies nothing except somebody's mistake."

"That was my conclusion," Peter replied.

"Now, tell me about your studies of Marxism-Leninism."

"They recommended a couple of books I should read."

"That's all?"

"They said you would be my professor in ideological subjects."

That night Rudi drafted a message in which he informed Moscow: Your failure to provide Erbe with comprehensive ideological training and political indoctrination violates a clear and basic understanding. Neither Erbe nor anybody else can long work successfully within any secret service without total ideological commitment. Request Center advise how it proposes to rectify this grave omission.

The Center did not reply; instead, it ordered Rudi forthwith to select two "long-term" drop sites in an area outside El Paso, Texas—"long-term" meaning the drops should be suitable for repeated use and containment of material for some time before retrieval. A map told Rudi why the Center needed the drops. The area specified was near the White Sands Proving Ground, where missiles and other advanced weaponry are tested. Obviously, the Russians now had an agent there.

Conscious of the stakes, Rudi drove around El Paso for hours, to be sure that no one was following, before he headed out into the desert, and even there he doubled back once to check for pursuing cars. He thought he heard the drone of helicopters now and then, but near a military base that was not surprising. Walking along a gas pipeline, he found a niche underneath that could hide a container for years. In a forlorn cemetery a few miles away, he picked a second site by a tombstone of a child who had died at age three. For a moment, he wondered which American secrets might be hidden at the child's grave and what the man was like who would bring them.

In early 1976, the Center ordered Rudi to select three drops within a triangle formed by the towns of Pulaski, Columbia and Fayetteville, Tenn. He studied a map again and rejoiced. The area was near the Redstone Arsenal at Huntsville, Ala., and the atomic research center at Oak Ridge, Tenn. Rudi summoned Peter from McGill to coach him in the art of selecting drops.

In the backwoods of Tennessee, Peter again made Rudi proud by picking drops at superb locations, including one near a little country church. But during their four days together, Rudi plumbed from his son's constrained words a disturbing reality: Peter was acting out of filial rather than ideological duty. He had yet to be blessed, as Rudi long ago had been, with the emancipating realization of truth, the realization of faith, the gift of a cause.

To the Center he reiterated the necessity of indoctrinating Peter ideologically that summer in Moscow, and he also made a proposal concerning his own future: Perhaps he should acquire American citizenship, for which he had been eligible since 1973, and proceed to South Africa, the Middle East or Central America, where he might be even more useful.

The Center swiftly answered: "The U.S.A. is the main enemy. All operations elsewhere are merely supportive of operations against the U.S. You will remain in the U.S."

A message, labeled "urgent," compelled Rudi to fly to Mexico City on two days' notice in May. A KGB officer named Vladimir greeted him cordially by a fountain in Chapultepec Park and handed him what appeared to be a fountain pen and lipstick. "I'm sorry, but all I can do is repeat orders from the Center. Each of these contains a metal cylinder. I have no idea what is inside; apparently, it's important, and in no circumstances are you to open either. The Center warns that would be dangerous. No later than next Sunday, find two drops in the northwest quadrant of the city of Chicago. Leave the pen in one, the lipstick in the other. Then, no later than next Monday at H.P. 1 [a hiding place in Westchester County], leave a message describing the exact locations."

With Peter, Rudi flew to Chicago on Saturday morning, rented a car, and searched throughout the afternoon for sites. Finally, he hid the pen under an expressway culvert and the lipstick beneath a rock by a telephone pole.

Soon the Center radioed: "Unable find pen. Describe location of drop in more detail. Lipstick tampered with. Explain."

It was impossible to describe the drop location in any more detail than Rudi had in his original message, but he tried. He stated that he had no reason to tamper with the lipstick or pen, that he had opened or tampered with neither.

Through Rudi, Peter had notified the Center of his acceptance by Georgetown University in Washington and his intention to enroll there as a junior in September. Expecting to spend most of the summer in the Soviet Union, he took an Icelandic Airways flight from New York to Luxembourg, then a train to Vienna, and on June 10 signaled his arrival by making a mark on a telephone booth. The next day at noon in front of a café, a KGB officer welcomed him with a hearty bear hug and informed him that he would not be going to Moscow. Instead, he would work intensively in Vienna with Max, a veteran KGB officer, then return to the United States, because the KGB wanted him to settle in Washington as soon as possible.

The following day at another café, Max repeatedly commended and congratulated him upon his choice of Georgetown. Not only was Georgetown recognized as an excellent university with an outstanding law school, it was Catholic and comparatively conservative; it was in Washington, right in the midst of everything important, and it had many ties to government. So far as the KGB was concerned, Peter's ideological instruction could wait. The Russians had concluded they could start tasting the fruits of his work at once without jeopardizing the grand future they had ordained for him. And they had readied specific assignments:

Look for students with fathers in government, fathers who because of personal problems or character flaws might be approachable.

Look for "progressive" students and professors who strongly oppose the imperialist policies of the United States.

Look for part-time employment at the Center for Strategic and International Studies at Georgetown.

Try to make friends with any Chinese students at Georgetown and learn all you can about them.

Max gave Peter an accommodation address in Mexico City to which he was to mail his reports in secret writing. He also designated rendezvous sites for future meetings in Mexico City and Vienna and required Peter to memorize code names for each, together with recognition signals. Throughout their four days together, Max treated Peter with affection, and his whole tone bespoke KGB enthusiasm about the young recruit and his prospects.

Rudi at once comprehended the import of the Vienna meeting. By equipping Peter with means to communicate directly with the Center, the KGB was maneuvering to make him an independent agent. That reflected Soviet confidence in Peter and appreciation of his potential. However, by exploiting Peter as an agent before training him as an officer, and by ignoring his ideological development, the KGB was abrogating the express understandings reached in Moscow as preconditions of his son's service. In the coldest of language, Rudi demanded a meeting at the Center to review his own status.

Belatedly, the Center in early December invited him to come to Moscow through Vienna early in January 1977. Shortly afterward, it radioed yet another urgent order commanding him to select two drops outside Fort Worth, Texas, the weekend of December 18-19. An IBM assignment obligated him to be in Chicago that weekend, so he said to Inga: "The Fatherland calls. You will have to do it." Dutiful as ever, she chose two fine sites off lightly traveled roads between the

Dallas-Fort Worth Airport and the city of Fort Worth.

As Rudi was not sure of the exact day he could land in Vienna, the KGB instructed him to announce his arrival by chalking an X mark on a door inside an apartment building, then to rendezvous at a meeting point at 6 p.m. the same day. Tired from jet lag, shivering in the fierce January cold, he walked about the city for five hours clearing his path before reaching the site, which happened to be in front of a shop selling women's lingerie. He stood there along with five or six young men waiting to pick up their girlfriends when the shop closed at six o'clock. But no KGB representative appeared.

Inside the apartment building the next morning, he found that someone, probably a diligent janitor or superintendent, had washed off the chalk mark, so he made another. The second night at the lingerie shop, he sensed that the stares of the young beaus were not entirely friendly. Again, no one from the KGB showed up; again the chalk mark was erased; again he made another and, clearing his path through the cold, went to the shop a third evening. A couple of the young men indelicately observed that perhaps he was a pervert who derived gratification from gazing at female underwear. Still unmet, he had no choice but to return a fourth night. This time, the suitors obscenely denounced him as a pervert and warned that if they caught him loitering around again, they would beat hell out of him. On the fifth night, before they could fulfill the threat, a KGB officer finally appeared.

From the moment Rudi sat down with four KGB officers in a Moscow apartment, an atmosphere of sullen hostility prevailed. A new officer named Dmitri began with accusatory remarks about the Chicago drops, interminably repeating questions Rudi had answered or tried to answer in his messages. "The fact is that we never found the pen," Dmitri shouted. "The fact is that someone tampered with the lipstick. Those are the facts. How do you explain them?"

"Nobody can explain what he does not know," Rudi yelled back. "That should be comprehensible even to someone of your limited mentality."

"We want an accounting of each of your movements in Chicago."

"You evidently trust my son, if not me. He saw me load the drops. He saw that both devices were intact when I put them in the drops. Have you thought of asking him?"

In a somewhat placating voice, Pavel said, "Douglas, we always have trusted you completely, and we trust you completely now."

"Why, then, have you failed to give me the concrete tasks you yourself promised when I was here 30 months ago?" With burgeoning anger, Rudi recited his accumulated grievances: the incessant, imbecilic orders to go to bars, to penetrate the Hudson Institute; the KGB injunction that he must become a normal American businessman and the constant criticism of him for doing just that; the dereliction in neglecting the ideological indoctrination of Peter.

"I have done literally everything you have asked which my legend allows. There are some things I cannot do because my legend has major defects."

"It is a sound legend," Max said.

"It is sound enough for the purpose you said you were sending me to America to fulfill. It is useless for other purposes which you apparently want me to fulfill."

Pavel tried to mediate. "Douglas, you are the Illegal Resident. Now let's put the past aside and speak constructively of your future."

"Perhaps I *was* the Illegal Resident, but no more. And there will be no future. I am not returning to the United States."

"Comrade!" exclaimed Viktor. "You must return to fight for peace."

"No."

A chilled silence fell upon them. Rudi folded his hands and refused to eat with them. Finally, Pavel spoke: "Comrades, our Comrade Douglas has had a long journey. He has been laboring for years under enormous pressure. So we cannot blame him for his fatigue. Let's adjourn and let him rest. We will resume our discussions at eleven o'clock in the morning."

"No, we will not," said Rudi. "I am here at my own expense on my own time from the United States. For once we will do what is convenient for me. I want to depart this city as soon as possible; to spend as little time here as possible. So if you have anything further to say to me, be here at 8 a.m."

A little after eight o'clock the next morning, Rudi heard a knock and opened the door. He looked at the man before him with surprise and gratitude, then embraced him with both arms. It was Aleks, his first teacher, the KGB officer he admired above all others.

"My dear comrade, my dear friend, come in. You are weary."

"Yes, I've been traveling all night. They called me around ten o'clock."

They talked until mid-morning about their respective experiences since their last meeting in Berlin in 1958. Aleks reminisced about his wartime years at the Residency in Mexico City and his long journey by train across the United States en route home. He was keenly curious about changes in both countries and Rudi's life in New York, and their conversation served as something of a catharsis for Rudi.

"I assume you know about last night."

"I was told it did not go well."

"And they recalled you to make me change my mind."

"That is correct."

"Well, you cannot."

"I do not intend to try. You have to make up your own mind, do what you yourself think is right."

But through his mere presence and by refraining from pressure, by leading Rudi back to his original training and reminding him of his duty, Aleks did change Rudi's mind.

Pavel and Max rejoined him the third morning and with almost embarrassing civility attempted to act as if there had been no scene, no ugliness. To emphasize their trust and his importance, they described a marvelous new radio that would vastly simplify his work. It automatically recorded burst or "squirt" messages compressed into a second and transmitted via satellite. A device within unraveled the bursts on the recording; he could listen and decipher at leisure. Never would there be any missed letters or problems with static. The radio, small and easily hidden, was extremely secret and entrusted to only a few in the field. It would be smuggled to him through a drop.

Rudi's feat in embedding himself so well in America that he could administer the entire KGB underground there, if need arose, was, they emphasized, magnificent and invaluable; the entire KGB leadership was aware of it. But in addition to his continuing responsibility as Illegal Resident, he would receive ever more important, concrete assignments, which he could execute within the confines of his legend.

As for the training and indoctrination of Peter, the KGB would indeed provide that. But at the moment, nothing was so essential as the completion of his education. And after all, who in the entire KGB was more competent to train him in either tradecraft or ideology than his own distinguished father?

For all the flattery, strain persisted between Rudi and the officers, and by mutual consent they forwent the traditional farewell dinner. As he flew out of the Soviet Union, he realized something within him had snapped. His faith and commitment to the Party, to the cause, were indestructible; but his attitude toward the KGB was irreversibly changed.

He brought with him from Moscow a new cipher pad to replace the one that he had burned in accordance with standard security procedures before he departed New York. Looking for his radio schedule, he realized it was missing and assumed he had mistakenly and stupidly burned it also. He advised the Center via secret writing that Inga would pick up a new radio schedule on May 7.

About 8 p.m. on May 2, a man who identified himself as architect Dick Martin telephoned Rudi at home. "My company has developed a new type of prefabricated sauna bath, and we need photographs for our brochure. Friends at IBM tell me you're first rate. Would you be available any time in the next few days?"

"I'm booked tomorrow, but I could do it on Wednesday."

"Fine. We've installed one on an estate about an hour away. Why don't I pick you up around ten o'clock, and we can drive up together."

Dick Martin, a big, bluff man, helped Rudi load his gear into the car, and they chatted amiably during the drive that ended on the grounds of a large estate. As they walked from the car, Rudi stopped and said, "Excuse me. I forgot my light meter."

"You won't need it. Come with me."

Rudi knew. For a moment, he tried not to admit it; but he knew.

In the living room, two men stood staring at him as Martin closed the door. One was middle-aged, heavy-set, with iron-gray hair, cold gray eyes and an unforgiving face. The other, tall, lanky, athletic, curly-haired, reminded Rudi of a young gunman in a Western movie. Neither offered to shake hands, and Rudi felt that both hated him.

"We are from the FBI," the older announced. "I am Joe. This is my partner Ed." Both displayed FBI identification cards, as did Dick.

"Rudi, we know who you are," Joe continued. "We know who you work for. We know about Inga. We know about Peter. We know everything about you. We have known for years. We have evidence: photographic evidence, documentary evidence, material evidence, all kinds of evidence. If you like, we can show much of it to you.

"Knowing your past, I know that in your life you have had to make some big decisions. Now you have to make the biggest of them all. There are two choices. We can arrest you and turn you over to the federal prosecutor. That means prison, a long time in prison—not just for you, but also for Inga and Peter, who are equally guilty. You must decide the future of your whole family. If the three of you go to prison, Michael doubtless will become a ward of the state because you have no relatives, at least none you can admit to without admitting what you are.

"Your other choice is to join us in a partnership against the KGB. If you honestly cooperate, you and your family may remain in the United States for the rest of your lives. We will relocate you, give you new identities and guarantee your security. For you the war will be over. Your sons, your wife, all of you will be able to make something of your lives."

Both outwardly and inwardly, Rudi was calm. There was no time for fear or any other emotion that would detract from intellectual concentration. He must rationally evaluate the data available and objectively decide in light of all the circumstances.

"How long do I have?" he asked.

"Until three o'clock," Joe answered. "We have teams of agents standing by outside your house in Hartsdale and on the campus at Georgetown. If by three o'clock you have not agreed to cooperate, your wife and son will be arrested for espionage."

Rudi noticed a videotape machine and movie screen. "We brought along a lot of film to show you, if necessary," Joe remarked.

"You star in them all," Ed added.

Because Rudi had gallbladder trouble, he carried with him pills for indigestion and as he suffered an attack, he started to take one. Like a leopard, Dick instantly leapt upon him and wrenched his arm away from his face.

"It's for indigestion!" Rudi protested.

"Give me that pill and all others you may have," Dick ordered.

"If you would like to walk around and think alone, you may. But don't try to run."

The two Americans who walked now with Rudi were as consecrated, as passionate, as committed to their faith as he was to his. Joe, the son of immigrants, had clawed his way out of a New York slum, earned a degree at night school while working for $2700 per year as an FBI clerk, and had then become an agent. A devout Catholic, father of six children, he had fought crime and foreign subversion for 24 years, sometimes risking his life, often separating himself for long periods from his family.

Like Joe, Ed was a New Yorker, Irish and Catholic. He worked as a night clerk in the Newark FBI office while attending college, then he waited seven years, as a clerk, to become an agent. In the FBI, his imagination, daring decisiveness and contempt for bureaucratic dodges attracted the attention of Joe, who commandeered him for the Soviet section of the New York field office.

By definition and in actuality, Rudi represented the best the KGB and the Soviet empire could send against America. Joe and Ed represented the best America could offer in its defense. They had stalked him so intently, for so long, that they understood him perhaps as well as anyone else in the world did. They understood that they were pitted against a fanatic who never could be persuaded ideologically to forsake his beliefs, any more than they could be persuaded to betray theirs. They understood that if Rudi could think only of himself, he gladly would choose martyrdom rather than surrender. So they had waited until all the data told them that KGB mistake piled on KGB mistake had built up such pressures within Rudi and his family that he was now vulnerable to other appeals.

In his solitary analysis on the estate grounds, Rudi asked himself: Are they bluffing? No, not if they know about Inga and especially Peter. How did they find out? That is irrelevant to the decision you must make. Is there any chance of escape? No.

If we all go to prison, what will be gained? We will spare the KGB the damage my cooperation with the FBI may inflict. Inga will never talk. But Peter probably will—because those goddamned bastards never indoctrinated him as they promised. But at least we won't be leading the KGB into any more traps.

What are my obligations to the KGB; what do I owe them? You owe the KGB nothing. You have given the KGB your life and family. In return, they have broken their word again and again, about your son and everything else.

But do you not owe the Party? Is not the KGB the sword and

shield of the Party? That is what the KGB says. I do not trust the KGB any more.

How can I collaborate with the American imperialists? Is that not treason to all I have lived for since I was 12 years old? But do I have the right to forfeit my son's life? I got him into this. He did it only for me. And what will happen to Michael?

Just before 3 p.m., Joe said, "Time is up."

"I accept, on two conditions."

"What are they?"

"I will not kill anybody."

"Jesus Christ!" Ed muttered.

"The KGB kills people; we don't," Joe said. "We would never ask you to kill anybody."

Rudi stipulated his second condition. "I will not give up my beliefs. I am Communist. I always will be a Communist."

"Think as you please; do as we say. All right?"

"All right."

"We have a lot of work to do, so let's begin. Eddie, make the calls."

The FBI intended the first phase of the interrogation to be professionally devastating, and it was. The questions purposely revealed that the FBI knew the exact location of all the drops—in New Jersey, outside El Paso, in Tennessee, in Chicago, in Westchester, even the drops Inga picked near Fort Worth. It knew about the trips to Moscow that Peter, Inga and he had made, about his travels to Mexico. It even knew which of his trips within the United States were made on legitimate business and which in behalf of the KGB. The scope and detail of the FBI's knowledge reinforced Rudi's conviction that it would be futile to withhold anything.

Beginning with his childhood in Czechoslovakia, Rudi spoke the truth, hour after hour, to Joe, Ed, Dick, and their tape recorders. And he spoke with the coherence, orderliness and expertise of the gifted intelligence officer he was. He himself pointed out that unless he telephoned to provide Inga an explanation of his whereabouts, she would think there was something abnormal.

"What do you propose to tell her?" Joe asked.

"I'll say that I'm at a business party which will end so late that I won't be home. That's not unusual. We're always careful on the phone." Rudi smiled. "But I guess you already know that." The agents smiled too.

While Dick listened on an extension, Rudi telephoned and Inga received the explanation with equanimity.

Narrating his story more or less chronologically, Rudi did not mention until about 2 a.m. Thursday what the FBI already knew: that Inga was scheduled to fly to Mexico City late that afternoon, May 5, 1977, to pick up a new radio schedule from the KGB. The FBI now had to make a crucial operational decision. If Inga failed to keep the rendezvous, the KGB would have just cause for concern and suspicion. If Inga were allowed to go before the FBI confronted, broke and secured control of her, then Rudi might by some sign, gesture or code word convey to her for delivery to the KGB an emergency signal that he had been caught. If Inga were confronted and not totally broken, then she might report to the KGB. So he could confer with his colleagues, Joe sent Rudi to bed at about 3 a.m.

Unable to sleep, Rudi in the tumult of his thoughts focused for the first time on one facet of the disaster. If the FBI knew the location of all the drops, then it must have been able to identify all the KGB agents and officers who serviced each drop. Why, then, had there been no arrests? Of course, he thought, the FBI is playing a game, unraveling our networks and probably purveying deceptive intelligence to the Center at the same time.

In the morning, Joe announced the FBI decision to confront Inga, and the three agents drove Rudi to Hartsdale. On the way, he asked, "Can you tell me how you found out about me?"

"That you will never know," Joe answered.

"There is one thing I have to know," Rudi persisted. "Was it because of some mistake I made?"

"No, Rudi, you were perfect. The KGB was not."

Rudi led them into the house and said to his wife: "These gentlemen are from the FBI. They know everything about us, about Peter. I have decided to cooperate with them. And I would like for you to tell them everything you know."

Inga collapsed on a sofa, sobbing and screaming. Her soulful anguish, her sense of utter ruin and catastrophe so overpowered her that she was incapable of uttering a complete sentence. Ed stepped out to the car and by radio summoned a female agent, Sheila, who had been standing by. Presently, she and Rudi calmed Inga sufficiently to extract some information, including confirmation of her imminent departure for Mexico.

"You must go," Joe said.

"No, no, I cannot. There is no way I can handle it."

"If you care anything at all about your son, you will handle it," Ed said.

Rudi added, "Inga, he is right. You must go."

Ed and Sheila drove her to Kennedy Airport, and Ed, who felt no mercy, showed none. "You have approximately 20 minutes to stop crying and compose yourself. Listen very carefully. We will be watching you in Mexico City. Our people will be all around you. And our people will be watching your husband and son back here. You are to make the meet in Chapultepec just as you always do. If you say or do anything abnormal, we will know about it."

Ed knew that no American would be watching Inga in Mexico City; there was not time to organize a sophisticated, undetectable surveillance. The FBI simply had to gamble the whole new operation on the chance that Inga's motherhood would prevail over her communism.

Upon her return, the FBI took Inga to Sheila's apartment. "Tell us all that happened," Joe ordered.

Inga stated that she met a KGB officer in Chapultepec at 10 a.m., exchanged recognition signals, then a few pleasantries, and received from him what she thought was the radio schedule. But in her hotel room she found the envelope empty. As she had no means of recontacting the KGB in Mexico, she flew back to New York. She professed to be mystified as to why the envelope was empty and adamantly denied having told the KGB officer anything about the FBI.

Disbelieving, Joe asked if she would submit to a polygraph examination. Bravely she tried; clearly, she lied. The operator noted that she exhibited pronounced emotional response to two questions: Did you inform the KGB about us? Was the envelope empty? He judged that her answers were either false or misleading. The interrogation continued, and Inga twice more flunked the polygraph test, yet obdurately refused to alter any detail of her story.

Well after midnight, Joe said, "Inga, it's futile. Don't you realize that you and I once met, long ago?"

"I never saw you before."

"Do you remember the morning before you picked the drop outside Fort Worth? You had breakfast in the motel dining room very early, and two men sat in the booth next to you. Remember when you got up, how your shoulder bag hit one of them in the head? Look at me. Am I not that man?"

For a while Inga sat slumped in silence, her face buried in her hands; then she looked up at Joe. "Yes, you are."

Finally surrendering, much against her will, she told the truth. The meeting with the KGB officer in Mexico transpired just as she had said, and she mentioned nothing about the FBI. However, the envelope did contain film of the radio schedule. Examining it in the hotel, she despaired and through the night struggled with thoughts of suicide. Desperately and illogically, she returned to Chapultepec the next morning hoping that by chance the KGB officer might be there. If she encountered him, she intended to disclose that Rudi had been caught. But of course, he was not at the site; there was no reason for him to be. Just before boarding the plane to New York, another fit of fear and frenzy seized her. If the FBI obtained the radio schedule, she reasoned, then it would read all their communications, learn about their relatives in Eastern Europe and tighten its hold on her family in the United States. To prevent that, she cut up the film and flushed it down a toilet.

While the painfully recited confession convinced Joe and Ed, as well as the polygraph operator, it confronted the FBI with a second crucial operational decision. The KGB would become suspicious unless radio communications from Moscow to Rudi now were re-established. Yet Rudi could not receive transmissions without a schedule informing him of the frequencies and times of broadcasts. And he could not request a new schedule because no explanation of Inga's failure to deliver the one given her in Mexico would be credible to the Center.

The next message from Moscow was due Saturday, May 14, 1977. At seven o'clock that morning, Joe and Ed picked Rudi up at his house, drove to the Hilton Hotel in Rye, New York, and in a room there set up a powerful radio receiver. Rudi wondered at the purpose of this exercise because he still was ignorant of the frequency and hour the Center would transmit to him. Flicking the dial, he heard a broadcast and laughed. "They're talking to another agent," he said.

At 10:21 a.m. Ed instructed him to dial a specific frequency. At 10:22 a.m. Rudi exclaimed: "That's me! That's my call sign!" With the end of the transmission and his concentration upon recording it, Rudi realized: *They had my radio schedule! They have broken into the KGB's communications!*

That was something the FBI would have preferred not to let Rudi know. But given the unexpected failure of Inga to return with the radio schedule, the FBI had to give him a copy of its own if it was to continue to involve him in the operation.

Both Rudi and Ed copied the transmission, but Ed insisted on decrypting it from a sheet from Rudi's cipher pad. The message, which requested no less than six political reports, was normal in every way, and Ed was greatly reassured. It indicated that the Center was endeavoring to assign Rudi "concrete tasks," and therefore, despite the acrimony in Moscow, the KGB still regarded him as vitally important.

"What do you think?" Joe asked Rudi.

"I think everything is all right."

At Rudi's command, Peter came from Washington by train. Introducing Joe and Ed as FBI agents, Rudi said, "We are cooperating with them. I want you to tell them truthfully all you know."

Peter appeared neither surprised nor disturbed. He suffered none of the ideological conflict his parents experienced, for he never had been a Communist, and if there had been any possibility of converting him, the KGB had forfeited it by not indoctrinating him as Rudi pleaded. Glancing somewhat condescendingly at Joe, who was puffing heavily on a cigarette, he said, "Do you *have* to smoke?"

"I don't *have* to smoke. I *choose* to smoke," Joe replied, blowing smoke at him. "Let's begin. When and how did you first become involved with the KGB?"

Peter's story, recounted over six hours, matched that of Rudi in all respects. In Lima, he had been glad to learn the truth and willing to do as his father wished. Now he seemed even more relieved to tell the truth. He agreed to work with the FBI.

Before they parted, Joe addressed father and son: "I want to be frank. All three of you will be under surveillance 24 hours a day. We have to develop a certain mutual trust among ourselves. We have not reached that point yet. Any behavior out of the ordinary will be grounds for suspicion and, maybe, action. Everything must be normal, just as it has been in the past, and that includes your relations with the KGB."

Transmitted on schedule the next morning, a message from the Center urged that Peter visit Saudi Arabia in the summer, ordered Rudi to prepare for a reconnaissance trip to El Salvador, and asked about Inga's plans for her annual summer trip to Europe. Rudi replied: "Erbe does not plan any trip abroad this summer. He will take summer courses. Gerda has severe phlebitis in leg, and for this reason will not go to Europe this summer."

Evidently, the KGB judged the message plausible, for a steady exchange of communications continued throughout 1977. In Westchester drops, Rudi deposited political reports drafted with the aid of FBI research, and they were good enough to elicit requests for more. Of course, the FBI saw who came to unload the drops. In September, the Center asked Rudi if he could "trace our man in Greenfield, Ohio." The request excited the FBI because Greenfield is near Wright Patterson Air Force Base, a site of advanced weaponry research and development. However, the Center never sent any amplifying instructions. Through the fall and early winter, the messages mirrored an ever-heightening KGB interest in Peter, his progress and future.

On January 14, 1978, the Center transmitted a two-sentence message: "You are given the high military rank of colonel for success in your work and for proper direction of Erbe. We heartily congratulate you and Gerda and wish you good health, grand success in your work, and happiness to all your family." A week later, the Center advised Rudi to come to Mexico City March 1. All indications were that the Center was exerting every effort to repair relations with Rudi, buoy his morale and guarantee his and Peter's continued services. Yet the FBI was wary.

The preceding January, a loyal American double agent had disappeared while attending a clandestine meeting in Vienna, and U.S. intelligence feared he had been forcibly abducted. The CIA, responsible for operations outside the U.S., resolved that if there was any violence in Mexico City, Rudi would not be the victim. As Rudi entered the park March 1, he was relieved to see quite a few unusually tall "Mexicans" in the area.

Nevertheless, in Rudi's position, only a fool would have been unafraid, and he wondered if he could conceal his fear. Vladimir, the same officer who had dispatched him to Chicago, approached with the prearranged recognition signal.

"Good morning, didn't we meet at the Paris Air Show?"

"It was at Farnsborough, wasn't it?"

"That's right. 1975."

"1974."

"Greetings and congratulations on your promotion," Vladimir said. "Since you now outrank me, I can't give you any orders, but I have quite a bit to tell you."

Vladimir reported how important the Center had come to regard Erbe. "They want you to make him your highest priority. Teach him every bit of tradecraft ever learned. And spend as much time as possible on his political indoctrination. Keep up your business only for appearance's sake. They sent $15,000 and said don't hesitate to ask for more whenever you need it.

"The message is: Erbe comes first. Do you think he can come to the Center or Vienna this summer?"

"If necessary, I'm sure he could. But he's just been promised an excellent job with a computer communications firm in Arlington after his graduation. The firm deals a lot with Congress, and he will have a chance to meet Congressmen and learn about computers at the same time."

"I agree it's more important for him to explore in Washington than to travel. That's what I'll report."

Glancing again at notes, Vladimir said, "They are concerned about Gerda's health. How is she?"

"Better, but her leg still bothers her."

"Take care of her and yourself. Here's your present."

In succeeding months, requests for information or action from Rudi now arrived almost weekly. The FBI fulfilled one for him by locating a farm which recently had been sold near Woodstock, N.Y. Obviously, the KGB wanted such information for the legend of an Illegal who would claim that he had worked there. If anyone in future years asked about him, the new owner would not know.

On September 8, the Center ordered him to "find five or six HPs [hiding places] convenient to Dahlgren, Va." The message disturbed Joe and Ed more than any other they had intercepted. Heretofore, the KGB had directed Rudi to select only one or two, at the most three, drop sites, even around such obviously important targets as White Sands, Redstone and Oak Ridge. Now the KGB needed five or six drops for what was obviously a major, long-term operation. But why

Dahlgren? Neither Joe nor Ed had ever heard of the place, and it appeared on none of the maps in the New York office. When Joe asked FBI headquarters to ascertain what in Dahlgren might arouse such intense Soviet interest, a senior supervisor called back four days later and ordered him to leave instantly for Washington. Dahlgren was so ringed in secrecy that it had taken the FBI that long to determine the answer to Joe's query.

In Washington, Joe's boss disclosed that Dahlgren was a hamlet situated near the Potomac estuary in the primeval wilderness of King George County, about 25 miles east of Fredericksburg. For miles around in all directions, there was little other than forests. In Dahlgren itself, beyond a couple of gas stations, a few stores and a café, there was nothing except the Naval Surface Weapons Research Center. Scientists there were developing missile guidance systems, Trident submarine weaponry, satellite surveillance systems, and electronic warfare devices.

"That's not the worst," said Joe's supervisor. "They're also working on very futuristic weapons, stuff you and I never heard of, things that could be as revolutionary as the atomic bomb. Dahlgren is one of the most sensitive installations in the United States."

"Well, the Sovs have an agent in there or think they soon will have," Joe said.

"You are to find him. You are authorized to spend any amount necessary. You can have anybody in the Bureau, whatever resources you require; there is no limit. Incidentally, we have informed the White House. Good luck."

After reconnoitering the Dahlgren area, Joe submitted an operational plan, which called for more than 100 agents and millions of dollars' worth of equipment—jeeps, pickup trucks, land rovers, field generators, miles of cable, sandbags, cameras, foul-weather gear plus secret equipment. Within three days, FBI Director William Webster approved the plan. Headquarters assured Joe that all the stated requirements as well as any more that might develop would be satisfied.

For three weeks, teams of FBI agents combed the forests, which in some areas are stately and lovely, in others dark and forbidding, searching for drop sites that met two conflicting criteria. They had to be like those an experienced professional would normally select—and yet so situated that each could be kept under surveillance 24 hours a day indefinitely.

The Center had ordered Rudi to report the locations through a drop near Irvington, N.Y., on October 14. With wartime urgency, FBI teams labored around Dahlgren from dawn to dark to meet that deadline. Over the weeks, they implanted into the forest a labyrinth of hidden equipment manned by sentries in concealed posts. On the morning of October 14, the Center radioed Rudi that because of "imperialists' provocation" he must not go near the Irvington drop. Instead, the Center told him to report the earliest date he could deliver the Dahlgren data personally in either Vienna or Mexico City.

"Instruct Rudi to report he will be free to travel any time after mid-November," Joe said. The FBI had gained a month more to prepare.

On November 25, Rudi passed all details of the five drops, plus the two signal sites accompanying each, to Vladimir in Mexico City. He also gave him a report from Peter, four political reports of his own, the name and location of the farm recently sold in upstate New York, and personal letters to Inga's mother and his mother.

With the transfer of the Dahlgren drop data, the FBI had to assume that at almost any moment the phantom agent inside the ultra-secret research center might appear in the forest. The last week in November, over 100 employees of a mythical West Coast corporation moved into a Fredericksburg motel. Anyone inquiring was told that the corporation was a private consulting firm conducting tests of microwave propagations— around the clock, in all types of weather conditions, in remote areas free from heavy electrical interference. That explained men getting up at all hours to trundle along rutty roads into the wilderness.

The agents were drawn from 26 different FBI field offices across the country, and each underwent four days of intensive training. Joe fully informed each of all that the operation meant to the security of the United States. To each he said: "Maybe you cannot adapt to the wilderness, to lying in the mud, snow and rain through the winter. Maybe you can't stand the pressure or loneliness. If so, come straight to me, and I will guarantee that you are sent back to your office without any prejudice whatsoever. But if I ever find out that you in any manner have breached security, I will devote all my energies to guaranteeing that you are fired."

Meanwhile, Moscow radioed Rudi: "Your messages received from Mexico. Information was used. Please continue to collect similar data. Erbe's penetration of company having ties with Congress approved. Tell him to continue searches for information sources, taking special precaution measures."

Through Christmas and New Year's, through snow and rain, separated from wives and children and unable to explain why, the FBI agents maintained the vigil. Then, just before noon on Friday, March 9, Joe and his deputies hurried down the motel corridors knocking on doors. "Check out! Get out of Fredericksburg immediately and go back to your field offices. If you can't make plane reservations, hide until you can. Say nothing to anybody!" Saturday morning the motel was almost empty. By Monday morning, most of the FBI equipment had disappeared from the forests. It was over, and to this day, nobody in authority will say why.

"The matter is still too sensitive to discuss," says an FBI spokesman. "I cannot imagine that it will be otherwise in our lifetimes."

Subsequently, many of the agents who had endured in the wilderness were told that the FBI abruptly terminated the operation because it feared press publicity. Still later, a leak to a Virginia newspaper—which could only have come from the FBI—depicted the whole operation as a great failure.

Rudi laughed when Joe showed him the newspaper story. "I never heard of any government bureaucracy anywhere in the world which went to so much trouble to advertise its failure."

***

The KGB informed Rudi in May that it was leaving $5000 for him in an Alpine, N.J., garbage dump. As he had not asked for money, its tender constituted further evidence of Soviet confidence in him. More such evidence was forthcoming through the summer as the Center commended his and Peter's reports and solicited additional ones. The future of both within the KGB could not have appeared brighter.

But by the end of the summer, the supply of plausible excuses as to why Peter and/or Inga could not meet the KGB outside the United States was exhausted. Given Inga's past insistence upon seeing her mother at least every two years, it was inexplicable that she should not insist upon visiting her again. Peter repeatedly had dodged a meeting with the KGB on grounds that he would not be eligible for vacation until he had completed his first year of work. That year now had ended.

The FBI incentive to continue the operation by permitting Peter and Inga to confer with the KGB abroad was great. Already Rudi had illuminated grave Soviet penetrations, and the fact that the KGB had involved him in something so transcendently important as Dahlgren indicated there were no limits to what it might involve him in during the many more years he was expected to stay in the United States. If Peter could be preserved as a double agent, he conceivably through the years could lead the FBI into the very core of KGB operations in the United States.

Yet the risks were also great. If Inga or Peter made a mistake in Vienna or Moscow, if they exposed themselves to the kind of brutal interrogation of which the KGB is capable, their chances of survival would be slight. The FBI reviewed the case in early September. Their conclusion: "Rudi gave us his word, and he kept it. We must keep our word to him."

At 5 a.m. on Sunday, September 23, 1979, an unmarked moving van took away all furnishings and belongings from the house at 5 Andover Road in Hartsdale, N.Y. Rudi Herrmann was no more. He, Inga, Peter and Michael had been reincarnated under new identities far away from Moscow and New York.

On December 1, the KGB sent its most urgent message to Rudi: "You may be under surveillance. Take precautions. Come to Vienna. We have a new assignment for you."

There was no response.

***

Some intriguing questions remain unanswered.

When and how did the FBI discover that Rudolf Herrmann was a Soviet spy? From the encyclopedic knowledge of him the FBI agents revealed, Rudi is certain it was early 1975 or even earlier. If his detection was not the result of anything he did, that means he was betrayed by a Western penetration of the KGB or by mistakes by some KGB officer servicing one of the drops through which he communicated.

Why did the FBI choose to confront Herrmann when it did, in May 1977? Herrmann himself offers the most plausible conjecture. He had just returned from Moscow in a state of rebellion and disaffection. Tensions between him and Inga mounted as she pressured him to do more for the KGB. Perhaps the FBI concluded that Herrmann now just might be vulnerable.

Why did the FBI so abruptly abandon the massive watch around the research center at Dahlgren? Some FBI agents were officially told that fear of imminent press publicity forced sudden cessation of the operation. But the only publicity that ever appeared were stories leaked by the FBI itself. They depicted the costly Dahlgren operation as a great failure. Why would the FBI want to advertise such a failure? A possible explanation is that it did identify the Soviet agent and tried by leaked accounts to persuade the KGB otherwise.

What did the United States gain from the Herrmann case?

Certainly the FBI kept constant watch on all the drops it saw Herrmann select around the country. So it must be assumed that any Soviet agent or KGB officer who came to these drops was unmasked; perhaps some were secretly converted into double agents. And doubtless, through Herrmann, the FBI added richly to its knowledge of KGB tactics.

The greatest benefit, however, derives not from what was gained but from what was prevented. If the FBI had not been able to detect Herrmann, his brilliant son Peter right now probably would be working his way upward into the highest councils of the U.S. government, sharing with the KGB all that he saw and heard.

IX

THE MAN WHO LOVED TO SPY

P RIOR TO THE 1950s, the greatest Soviet agents in the West were intellectuals who saw communism as man's best hope for universal justice or as the foremost bulwark against fascism. They served the Soviet Union selflessly and idealistically in the belief they were serving mankind. But the revelation and official Soviet confirmation of the horrors of the Soviet Union under Stalin revolted intellectuals the world over. And as the results of the Soviet experiment have become increasingly transparent, the KGB has experienced ever greater difficulty in recruiting intellectuals anywhere solely on ideological grounds. So the KGB perforce has developed other appeals and artifices to ensnare intellectuals.

In North America particularly, the KGB searches for intellectual prey from among the progeny of parents who were Communists or sympathizers of the Soviet Union. Hugh George Hambleton was such a prey.

Hambleton was born in 1922 in Ottawa, the son of an English father and Irish mother. His father was a prominent journalist, and in 1930 the Canadian Press Association chose him to be its first correspondent permanently stationed in Europe. A dashing, socially graceful man, fluent in German and French, he moved easily into the company of famous European political figures of the 1930s, including Joachim von Ribbentrop and Joseph Goebbels. Through such associations, he foresaw World War II and chronicled its approach with distinction.

While his father traveled the continent, Hambleton stayed with his mother and older sister in France. His mother possessed a photographic memory, which enabled her to store and draw upon an immense reservoir of diverse knowledge. This gift, coupled with an Irish facility for narrative, made her a scintillating conversationalist, and hostesses vied for her presence in their salons. She so beguiled a wealthy French aristocrat and his wife that they embraced her and the children as members of their family. Hence, Hambleton spent his formative childhood years in a palatial Normandy château, staffed by a small army of servants and surrounded by elegant formal gardens. And he received education from the best of tutors and in exclusive private schools.

In France, Mrs. Hambleton developed a consuming interest in Russia and the revolutionary experiment in progress there. She mastered the Russian language, studied Russian history and entered Russian émigré society which, even though composed mainly of anti-Communists, was saturated with Soviet agents. She continued for much of her life to associate closely with Russians.

Convinced that war soon would set all Europe ablaze, Hambleton's father in late 1937 sent the family back to Ottawa. There, Mrs. Hambleton attended Soviet embassy parties and reciprocated by entertaining Soviet personnel in her home and later by tutoring some of them in English. Thus, precepts of childhood and home taught Hambleton that there was nothing abnormal about friendly personal relations with

Russians or Soviet diplomats.

Graduated from high school in 1940, Hambleton familiarized himself with the United States and learned Spanish while studying at a preparatory academy in California. After the attack on Pearl Harbor, he returned to Canada, where Free French forces led by Charles de Gaulle were appealing for recruits. Drawn by the lure of adventure and his affection for France, he volunteered, and at a French training camp in Nebraska joined a heterogeneous assortment of men gathered from all parts of the world. Because he could give orders in French, English, German and Spanish, he was at age 19 made a sergeant on the spot. Upon completion of training, the French assigned him to the General Directorate of Intelligence in Algiers to translate reports from their agents in Spain. His offices seethed with intrigue as Gaullists, Vichy alumni, and Royalists plotted and connived to gain dominance over each other. Although as a young Canadian he was uninvolved in these machinations, they fascinated him and conditioned him to conspiracy.

After the liberation of Paris, Hambleton worked there in French intelligence headquarters before being assigned as a liaison officer to the U.S. Army's 103rd Division, then advancing toward Bavaria. Given the difficulty of communications and consequent absence of instructions from Paris, he took orders from American officers and performed intelligence assignments for them. In effect, he became a member of the 103rd, called the Cactus Patch Division because most of its soldiers were from the Southwest. Recalled to Paris in late 1945, he saw that the French now regarded him suspiciously because of his close collaboration with the Americans and so, with the help of his father, he obtained a transfer to the Canadian army. The Canadians posted him to Strasbourg where he interrogated prisoners and analyzed intelligence reports.

By the time he was released from the army in 1946, Hambleton had served three nations in intelligence. His duties had been neither dramatic nor unusual. But they left him with a delicious sense of adventure, of danger slight yet real, of being privy to secrets and foreknowledge of world events. Enrolled at the University of Ottawa, he sometimes found that he missed the business.

To improve his Spanish and enjoy the sun, Hambleton studied each summer at the National Autonomous University in Mexico City. He so liked the university that he spent his last academic year there and in 1950 earned a master's degree in economics. Back in Ottawa, he took a job with the National Film Board, which needed a Spanish-speaking representative to promote the distribution of Canadian motion pictures in Latin America.

By 1950, imposition of Soviet hegemony over Eastern Europe; Soviet efforts to absorb Iran, Turkey and Greece; the Berlin Blockade; revival of the Stalinist purges; and the attack by Communist North Korea upon South Korea—all had radically changed the Western perception of Russians. Canadian attitudes also had been altered by the defection from the Soviet embassy in Ottawa of cipher clerk Igor Gouzenko, who supplied evidence of how Soviet agents had stolen secrets of the atomic bomb and burrowed far into the U.S. and Canadian governments.

However, Hambleton's parents continued to socialize with Soviet diplomats at embassy functions and in their own home. And it was in their home that Mrs. Hambleton in 1951 introduced her son to First Counsel Vladimir Borodin* of the Soviet embassy. They met there again during several subsequent parties and the Russian began inviting Hambleton to dine with him at expensive restaurants.

Borodin seemed like an urbane and good-humored diplomat, earnestly interested in understanding Canada and willing to talk frankly of his homeland. He reminisced about his wartime experience, particularly in the siege of Leningrad, and thereby led Hambleton to recount his military service— all in intelligence. The mutual recollections also served subtly to remind of past Soviet-Canadian friendship in a common

*On records retained by the Canadian Office of External Affairs, the name is spelled Bourdine. Hambleton knew him as Borodin.

cause. Borodin continued the classic process of cultivation and assessment until just before his recall to Moscow in late 1953. Driving from a long luncheon, he obliquely suggested that Hambleton could help him by supplying "certain materials" from the Film Board. Nothing at the National Film Board, so far as Hambleton knew, was secret or of any special interest to any foreign power. But he recognized the overture and its implications. Wishing to be polite to a diplomat who often had been a guest of his mother and had entertained him so generously, he noncommittally changed the subject. He intended his evasion to be a negative reply. Nevertheless, Borodin showed him a site by a crossroads where he was to leave "material" if he ever elected to help his friend. As they parted, Hambleton hoped he would never see Borodin again.

Craving more intellectual challenge and adventure, he decided in 1954 to take a doctorate degree at the University of Paris and embark upon a serious career as an economist. A few months after he and his young French-Canadian wife settled into a pleasant cottage about 30 miles outside Paris, two men appeared out of the darkness of a late Saturday afternoon—Borodin and another Russian.

"I was just passing through Paris, and I could not resist looking up an old friend," Borodin announced in high spirits.

"How on earth did you run me down way out here?" asked Hambleton, whose question was real. He had given his address to no one except his parents.

"Friends always find each other. In any case, we are here! Let's celebrate!"

Over a splendid dinner at a country inn, Borodin introduced his companion Aleksei (KGB Major Aleksei Fedorovich Trichin) as an accomplished diplomat, a true and trustworthy friend. He asked about Hambleton's studies and postgraduate plans and wondered whether Hambleton could conduct some "independent research," for which, of course, the Russians would insist upon paying fair compensation.

Hambleton declined the bid by stressing that the excellence and originality of his dissertation, coupled with the recommendations of his demanding French professors, would greatly affect his professional future. He could not afford to diffuse his energies. That was true. It also was true that he understood the import of Borodin's overture and the implications of taking any money from the Russians.

Nevertheless, he could not quite bring himself to sever contact with them. Like a fascinated child flirting with the forbidden, he accepted the second or third time Aleksei invited him to dinner, and they dined together every couple of months or so during 1955. Their meetings were not exactly clandestine, but Aleksei suggested that because of the poisonous atmosphere spread by McCarthyism in America, it might be in Hambleton's interests if they chose inconspicuous restaurants and kept their friendship private. This slight connotation of harmless conspiracy appealed to Hambleton's spirit of adventure; Aleksei's serious solicitation of his views of international events flattered him; and, as a scholar above and beyond politics, he enjoyed the intellectual exercise of endeavoring now and then to look at the world from a Soviet perspective.

Hambleton possessed no secrets, and the Russian did not try to extract any from him. However, early in 1956 when they talked about what Hambleton might do after receipt of his doctoral degree in June, Aleksei began urging him to seek a position at NATO headquarters in Paris. Hambleton knew nothing of the NATO command structure and felt he had no particular qualifications to work for a military organization. But as he had prepared a form job application to submit to more than a dozen universities and institutes, he dropped a copy in the mail to NATO and forgot about it.

Soon, he forgot about all other applications also. His accomplishments at the University of Paris had so impressed the London School of Economics that it offered him a full scholarship for advanced study. At what he presumed would be his last encounter with Aleksei, Hambleton told him that the opportunity suddenly presented in London was too rewarding to refuse and that he would move to England in early summer.

But toward late spring, NATO unexpectedly called. Unbeknownst to Hambleton, a friend he met his first year in Paris had taken a job in the organization's Economic Directorate. Upon hearing of Hambleton's application, he began lobbying in his behalf. NATO officials were impressed by Hambleton's qualifications and, after an interview, made an offer even more attractive than that from London. He promptly accepted.

His job entailed analyzing the strengths and weaknesses, potential and limitations of the economies of NATO countries and Soviet Bloc nations. The most extensive and authentic data that could be obtained, covertly and overtly, were available to him and his colleagues. Their studies, often combined with political analyses, were considered by the NATO Council of Ministers in formulating plans and policies of the alliance. Hambleton experienced the gratifying feeling of working simultaneously in theoretical and practical realms, of being at the center of and a participant in world events. His peers, who emanated from different nations, diverse schools of economics, and eclectic backgrounds, were congenial and stimulating; his salary, allowances and other benefits generous. The more he immersed himself in his job, the surer he was that he had chosen well.

His satisfaction was blemished only by a fear that the Russians might reappear to jeopardize his position. Probably in consequence of wartime clearances and intelligence assignments, he easily had passed security checks and now had access to Top Secret documents and information. He knew that any further association with Soviets or even disclosure of past associations doubtless would cost him his clearance and job. Therefore, he wrote his parents and emphasized that in no circumstances should they reveal his new employment to any Russians they knew or might meet. He also moved into an apartment with a different phone number. As the summer and early autumn passed without incident, his apprehensions receded. And they were submerged entirely by the crisis that resulted in October 1956 from the armed Soviet suppression of the Hungarian uprising.

On a somber, chilly afternoon in early November, Hambleton left his office preoccupied with the necessity of finishing at home a report due the next morning. At the sight of the man waiting for him on the street, he shrank reflexively and thought fleetingly of pretending not to recognize. But Aleksei caught his eye and with a gesture of his head signaled him to follow. The gesture was not a request or an invitation; it was a command, and Hambleton obeyed.

They sat in a little café, where a second Russian, who evidently had been posted outside to watch for surveillance, joined them. By the detailed nature of his congratulations, Aleksei revealed that he knew precisely about Hambleton's NATO job and generally the type of documents routinely at his disposal. Referring to Hambleton's friendship with the Russians, sealed in their numerous dinners together in both Ottawa and Paris, and to Hambleton's natural desire for peace, he stressed that the Soviet Union could not promote peace unless it was informed. His whole casual tone assumed there was no question that Hambleton would share documents from his office. The only question was how and when he would deliver them, and Aleksei had the answer: at 12:30 p.m. the next Friday near a Metro station in a Parisian working district. "We will return them to you within an hour, and they can be back in your office by two o'clock."

Perhaps many subconscious considerations affected Hambleton's tortured deliberations in the next few days, but he was conscious principally of fear that if he did not placate the Russians, they would expose him. He decided to try to appease by supplying unclassified papers which, in his view, were harmless.

In picking the meeting point, the KGB had measured travel times and routes ably. Hambleton arrived by subway in less than 20 minutes, and Aleksei strode up, took his briefcase and said only, "Meet you here in an hour." An awaiting car driven by an operational driver sped away with him to the Residency at the Soviet embassy, where a technical team rapidly photographed the documents, and Aleksei reappeared with the briefcase in slightly less than an hour. "I left an envelope inside with money for your expenses," he said.

Hambleton snapped open the briefcase, fumbled around until he found the envelope, then shoved it into the Russian's hand. "Really, I don't need money," he said.

"As an economist, you should understand that you are not expected to subsidize the Soviet Union."

"I can afford subway fare."

"All right; two weeks from today, same time, new place." Aleksei named a café near another Metro station. "Bring what you can."

Hambleton stepped safely into his office before 2 p.m., one of the first back from lunch. It had been easy and, he had to admit, somewhat exciting.

Although the unclassified papers Hambleton first delivered were of no great importance, that did not matter. With their transfer, he crossed a threshold; he no longer was merely consorting with the enemy; he was collaborating. And for several months the KGB was content to take whatever he gave without pressuring for more, to draw and ensnare him ever more deeply into conspiracy without provoking rebellion. The pattern of bi-weekly deliveries continued, with Aleksei at the end of each fleeting meeting designating a site for the next and thanking Hambleton. Otherwise, they exchanged few words.

By the summer of 1957, however, the KGB concluded that its grip on Hambleton was sufficiently secure to begin squeezing. Aleksei matter-of-factly told him that while what he had provided thus far was valuable and appreciated, henceforth much more comprehensive and secret data would be required. "You yourself acknowledge that you work with secret data. It is just as easy to bring one document as another."

Aleksei made no threat nor was any necessary, for Hambleton understood that the only alternative to compliance was ruin. Before he began sneaking NATO papers to Aleksei, he could have immunized himself to the Russians by frankly reporting his past contacts with them. Even after the first few deliveries, he could have extricated himself by coming forward with the truth and confessing poor judgment. He might have lost his NATO job, but he would have saved his future. Now, having repeatedly and clandestinely supplied official records over eight to nine months, he would be unable to convince anybody in NATO that he was anything other than a Soviet spy. And any contentions by him that he had endeavored to limit what he stole to the innocuous would have been dismissed as fatuously false.

To the next rendezvous, Hambleton brought three Secret and one Top Secret study, the four documents together comprising some 70 pages. The KGB investment of seven years in gradually suborning Hambleton now began to yield staggering dividends, and the Center created in the Paris Residency a special detachment solely to collect and bank them. The KGB outfitted a big black truck as a mobile photography laboratory, and it parked near wherever Hambleton and Aleksei met. Sometimes garbed as a Parisian truck driver, Aleksei would disappear into the truck where technicians were able to copy as many as 100 pages in less than ten minutes.

The documents photographed or copied often reflected the highest and best Western thinking and intelligence concerning a broad spectrum of subjects—nuclear strategy, the balance of military power, political conflicts among NATO members, the affordability and capabilities of prospective weapons systems, the missile race, the space race, assessments of the outcome of war between East and West, of Soviet capabilities and intentions, of internal stresses in Western and Eastern nations, of the economic impact of new technology envisioned as being available ten, twenty years hence. In sum, there were few subjects vitally affecting Western interests that were not considered, at least tangentially, in the hundreds of documents that Hambleton spirited from NATO headquarters into the KGB truck during 1958 and 1959.

The intelligence they embodied did not consist of gossip picked up by eavesdropping in a bar or hearsay reported by a lone agent or products sold by a mercenary. The information and conclusions in the documents may or may not have been valid, but the documents themselves indisputably were authentic. From them the Russians could read what the West, correctly or incorrectly, thought was true, and sometimes what it intended to do. They could see what the West did and did not know about them and their intentions. And they could verify, augment or correct intelligence gleaned from other sources. Little wonder that Aleksei at various times told Hambleton that the documents were "pure gold" ... "extraordinarily valuable" ... "read by Politburo members."

The more precious the intelligence flowing out of NATO became to the Soviet Union, the more apprehensive the Center grew about preserving Hambleton and the penetration. His repeated refusals to accept even "expense" money had long ago persuaded the KGB that he was an ideological Marxist or an ardent admirer of the Soviet Union. The KGB also knew, as did he, that *in extremis*, it could coerce him through blackmail. But the very refusal of money, together with his undisguised intellectual independence, warned the Russians that a certain delicacy and finesse were necessary in dealing with him. The meetings between Aleksei and Hambleton, however brief and expertly arranged, always involved risk, and the longer they continued to meet, the greater the risk. Because Hambleton was married, the KGB judged it impractical to equip him with an agent radio, since he could scarcely receive transmissions in a cramped apartment without his wife's knowledge. After his marriage ended in divorce in 1958, Aleksei urged him to slip away on vacation for training in clandestine tradecraft and Morse code. Indifferently, he declined. Ciphers, like a crossword puzzle, might be amusing; dots and dashes were too tedious. So the KGB found another way.

In the spring of 1960, Aleksei instructed Hambleton to join him on a Sunday afternoon picnic in a Paris park. "Our friends will be everywhere, and if there is any danger, they will sense it. If all is well, I will stand up when I see you. If I remain seated, walk on past as if you did not know me."

All was well, and Hambleton marveled at the number of

Parisian friends the KGB could muster for a Sunday picnic. Aleksei explained a whole new set of procedures he henceforth must follow. KGB experts had designed for him a radio which could record burst transmissions on magnetic tape. The radio was an exact replica of a standard French make, and no one looking at it would think otherwise. Hambleton had merely to tune to specified frequencies at specified times, remove the tape and rub a black powder on it, whereupon code groups of five numerals would become visible. He could easily decipher these by resort to the appropriate sheet of a cipher pad, to be provided along with the radio and powder.

The KGB had concluded that it would be safer from now on for Hambleton to take documents home overnight and photograph them, then leave the film in drops designated by English Christian names. He was to acknowledge receipt of radio instructions and signal his ability or inability to comply by mailing various types of postcards to an address in Geneva. Personal meetings would be restricted to two or three a year, and if practical, these would occur outside France. However, if an emergency arose, he could dial a KGB number, ask for "Monsieur Fontaine," and Aleksei or another officer would meet him in two hours at a rendezvous point near the Père Lachaise Cemetery. Aleksei gave him keys to two lock boxes at the central Paris railroad station, where he was to pick up packages containing the equipment.

"We do all this for your own welfare," Aleksei said earnestly. "You are very important, and there is no place where you could be more important. We hope that you will plan to spend your entire career where you are. Do you think you can do that?"

"I suppose it's possible," said Hambleton.

But already he had begun to think of escape from the KGB and from the roiling conflict that increasingly rent him intellectually and spiritually.

He had found a kind of perverse enjoyment in the game, the adventure of espionage; in taking risks and slinking along dark, narrow streets; in the approbation and attentiveness of the Russians who awaited him; in being an actor on the world stage, a factor in shaping history. Yet at the same time, he believed philosophically in NATO as a necessary and constructive balancing force in international affairs. He felt an obligation and certain loyalty to the organization, his colleagues and superiors, who accorded him trust, commendation and friendship. And at times, impulses of loyalty impelled him to withhold from the KGB important documents he might just as easily have passed along with the rest.

The forced acquisition and usage of the espionage paraphernalia intensified his inner conflict. In deciphering messages, furtively photographing documents, and hiding film under rocks and in the hollows of trees, he could no longer pretend to himself that he merely was engaging in a fascinating, abstract exercise. Shorn of his delusions and sophistry, he recognized that there was one word for his collusion with the Russians: *treason*. As East-West relations deteriorated dangerously in 1961, he also recognized the deepening gravity of his subversion.

It may have been that because of this deterioration, the KGB judged the need for intelligence to be so acute that it made a considered decision to temporarily strain sources such as Hambleton beyond reasonable limits. Perhaps the officer or officers responsible for the case simply made a misjudgment. Regardless, in 1961 the KGB suddenly turned voracious in its demands upon Hambleton. Over the years, he had supplied many hundreds of documents, running to many thousands of pages. Now, the Russians frantically insisted upon more, ordering him to increase the frequency of deliveries to once a week. Worse, in his mind, they commanded him to procure specific, ultra-secret documents which they designated by exact NATO reference numbers.

Under the external pressures from the KGB and the internal pressures of his conscience, he finally elected to break, and in May he telephoned for an emergency meeting. From a rendezvous point in the Père Lachaise district, he and Aleksei ducked out of the rain into a café. "I have been fired as a security risk," Hambleton lied.

"What happened?" Aleksei asked in alarm.

"My sister in Ottawa made a secret trip to Cuba, and some Western security service spotted her," he further lied.

"Is that all?" Aleksei pressed.

"Apparently so," Hambleton said. "At least, my chief said there is nothing against me per se."

To the KGB, the dismissal as reported by Hambleton represented an outrageous abridgement of due process, the rankest form of McCarthyism, a contemptible example of guilt by assocation and a travesty of democracy. "You must hire a lawyer and fight for your rights, for your reinstatement," declared Aleksei in righteous indignation. "Find the best one in Paris. We will pay whatever he asks."

"I am afraid that would be rather futile," replied Hambleton, as if stoically resigned to his undeserved fate. "NATO is an extra-national military organization unbound by any civil codes. And even if I could manage it, I still would be suspect."

Aleksei was melancholy. The operation that had kept him in Paris for more than five years and justified his whole career suddenly had ended, and with its end one of the most productive KGB penetrations into the West was severed. At least, though, nobody could say it was his fault. "Give us a week and we will devise a plan," he said dolefully.

The plan Aleksei outlined at their next meeting mortified Hambleton. "We want you to flee to the Soviet Union and make declarations to the world over Radio Moscow exposing NATO plots against peace. It will be a sensation, a scandal to the West throughout the world. You can speak in all your languages, and people everywhere will believe you because you know; you can even quote your own documents. After you learn Russian, you can teach, study and write at one of our universities and help in many other ways."

"That's all very generous of you," said Hambleton, struggling to conceal his consternation. "I think I can do more if I stay and work quietly in the West. The London School of Economics still wants me, and I've decided to take advantage of the scholarship before they change their minds."

With Hambleton's supposed loss of his job at NATO, the KGB for the time being had lost its hold on him. No longer was any implied threat of blackmail credible, for he knew that the Russians would suffer more than they could gain should they expose him. With equanimity, he resisted the heated importunities of Aleksei to defect. Giving up, Aleksei said, "Well, we must see you one more time. We need the radio, cipher pad and camera. Put them all in a suitcase."

At their last meeting in 1961 Aleksei offered and Hambleton again refused money for his services. Out of politeness, he did take note as Aleksei explained that should he wish to communicate in the future, he could do so by appearing at noon on the third Wednesday of any month at a Parisian street corner.

In 1961 one could still live handsomely and cheaply in Spain, whose romantic coastal regions were as yet unspoiled by development and uncluttered by many tourists. As Hambleton needed to be in England only periodically, he chose to reside on the Costa Brava and commute to London via Paris by train when necessary. In the first months, he welcomed the surcease from moral turmoil and the serenity experienced in the villages, among the olive groves and on the ancient cliffs above the Mediterranean. Life was pleasant and tranquil; as it turned out, too tranquil.

The train from London was hours late, and he missed the afternoon connection from Paris to Barcelona and so stayed overnight in Paris. Over espresso and croissants in the morning, he realized it was Wednesday, the third Wednesday of May 1962. *I wonder how they're doing, if they really would be there*, he mused.

"What a happy surprise," said the KGB officer after the proper exchange of recognition signals. "Do you know I have stood on this corner every month for almost a year in hope of meeting you?"

Hambleton could not articulate to himself why he had come

back to the KGB. He did not know whether he would have been more pleased by the presence or absence of a KGB officer. But he felt he had to say something, to give something to justify his presence, so he reached back into his remembered wanderings and commenced detailing locales from which the Soviet Union could mount guerrilla warfare in Spain.

"You are a good comrade," the KGB officer interrupted. "But we need no information from Spain. We have more agents there than we can handle, and none is more important than you. Your main task is to do nothing that might attract attention. Now tell me, what are your plans?"

Hambleton explained that because he had chosen a complex and abstruse subject, he would not complete his dissertation until the spring of 1964. He was confident that with its completion his credentials would enable him to obtain a position as a professor of economics at a leading Canadian university.

"Excellent," exclaimed the Russian. "If you have any trouble with a job, we will help you."

The KGB left Hambleton alone during the next two years, allowing him to enrich his academic background and letting time diminish whatever stigma might attach to him in consequence of his presumed dismissal from NATO. And Hambleton felt no compulsion to communicate until late in the spring of 1964, when at the Paris meeting site he advised that he had accepted a professorship at Laval University in Quebec. A nervous young Russian hastily told him he must travel to Vienna, where he could confer safely. As Hambleton's savings were nearly exhausted, he took money from the KGB for the first time—$75 for his train ticket.

In a seedy section of northern Vienna, a stout Russian with a florid, pocked face led him to an outdoor Hungarian restaurant and there, under a grape arbor, introduced three other KGB officers, all baggily dressed in cheap suits. They spoke courteously, even deferentially to him, as if awed by an agent of such legendary accomplishments. They asked only that he settle unobtrusively into university life in Canada and build an academic reputation that would admit him to the highest intellectual circles. Reading from Russian notes, the heavy-set officer recited in tedious detail arrangements whereby he could meet a KGB representative in front of the main post office in Ottawa.

While visiting his mother, Hambleton met the KGB in Ottawa three times between 1964 and 1967, on each occasion talking in a car parked near the post office. At the 1967 meeting, the KGB officer exhorted him to be more resourceful and productive in spotting prospective KGB recruits among the faculty and student body of Laval University. He also urged him to commence lobbying for an appointment to the Canadian foreign office.

Hambleton had no intention of quitting his academic career nor, if he could help it, of putting himself in a position from which he would have access to Canadian secrets. Nor could he bring himself to inform on students and fellow professors, to be an instrument of their subversion. So he simply stopped reporting for the scheduled meetings in Ottawa, thereby breaking his one communications link.

His failure to appear for more than 18 months caused the Center to gamble by dispatching KGB Lieutenant Colonel Rudolf Herrmann to see him, and that decision long seemed a felicitous one. Behind Rudi's façade of affability and geniality, Hambleton saw a keenly intelligent and learned man, with whom he could convivially discuss Latin American art, Chinese applications of Marxism, the U.S. economy or the wonders of desirable women. Unaware that Rudi was a KGB staff officer, Hambleton took him to be an agent like himself, a fellow adventurer, a kindred spirit and he enjoyed visiting with him.

Following their initial contact at the university and the brief exchange on the Montreal street corner, they met in the stately old Château Frontenac in Quebec. Sitting in the mahogany-paneled bar, which looks out on the Saint Lawrence River, Rudi said, "We are making an educational film about Quebec for distribution in American schools. I am the producer. You are doing the research and writing the script." The legend blended them naturally into the executive environment of the Frontenac and allowed them to talk securely and at length, as they were to do during several subsequent meetings there.

"Do you know the Hudson Institute?" Rudi asked.

"I know of it, of course."

"One of your long-range tasks is to penetrate the Hudson Institute."

"How?"

"That's up to you. I am just the messenger, and the messages I bring are: penetrate the Hudson Institute and prepare a comprehensive report on the Chinese economy."

"And where do they expect me to gather data on China? In the Frontenac?"

"Use your imagination."

Hambleton did just that. On his university stationery he wrote the Taiwanese embassy requesting assistance in research regarding the Chinese economy. The Taiwanese promptly responded by mailing him a long and colorfully contemptuous diatribe against the Chinese Communists. However, the tract was studded with "facts," many of which probably were true. Rewriting the Taiwanese propaganda into polished English, Hambleton submitted it through Rudi as original research. Moscow pronounced the report a masterpiece, for it said what the Russians wanted to hear.

Rudi telephoned Hambleton from New York in April 1970 to ask, "Can you mail the script by Saturday?"

"I'm sure I can," Hambleton answered.

By this exchange, they agreed to meet the ensuing Sunday afternoon at the Frontenac. There, Rudi told Hambleton that if at all possible, he must meet the KGB "at the regular place" in Ottawa two weeks hence. "That's all I know," he added.

The instructions Hambleton received in Ottawa were precise, imperative and challenging. At all costs, he had to contrive reasons to conduct research in Israel during the summer. Before summer, he must learn all he could from overt sources about the processes, materials and facilities necessary to produce a nuclear weapon. He must stop in Vienna for explicit orders prior to entering Israel.

Hambleton let it be known that he would devote the summer to studying the Siege of Rhodes in the Middle East. In reply to his inquiry, the Hebrew University of Jerusalem generously offered him full use of its library and whatever additional research aid it might lend. By letter he also arranged inexpensive lodging at the Sisters of Zion Convent, which he felt no one would suspect of being a habitat for a Soviet agent. Reading technical journals and publications anyone could buy from the U.S. Government Printing Office, he learned something of the basic methodology of manufacturing nuclear weapons. Feigning interest in the economics of weaponry, he augmented his knowledge by informal talks with nuclear physicists, who were surprised by how much he knew about making bombs.

In early June, following to the letter instructions the KGB had issued in Ottawa, Hambleton strode down a Vienna street toward the Danube with a yellow book in his left hand. Unfortunately, floods had caused the river to jump its banks, and the rendezvous point was under two to three feet of water. He hesitated but, thinking orders are orders, resolved to push on to his destination. As he waded into the water, a child exclaimed, "Mommy! Look at the crazy man walking into the river!"

Standing in water above his knees with occasional waves cresting over his waist, he held the book aloft as a beacon, while a small crowd assembled on dry land to watch the spectacle. Behind the crowd, a man frantically waved to him to get out of the water, and with as much dignity and aplomb as the circumstances permitted, he waded back. As some of the bystanders clapped in approval of his decision to quit the river, the man who had gestured said, "I have some etchings for you."

Uttering what he felt was a crowning idiocy, Hambleton replied, "Thanks, I already have some from London."

"Follow me and jump into my car," the Russian whispered. Driving away, he said, "What were you doing standing in the Danube? Did you come by submarine?"

"They told me to be at the exact spot."

"Well, as soon as you dry out, we'll have something to eat. There is much to discuss."

The Russian, who introduced himself as Paula, was a pleasant-looking man with wavy gray hair and friendly blue eyes set in a strong face. Hambleton guessed his age at about 50 and noted that unlike most KGB officers he had seen, Paula was well dressed in a finely tailored dark suit and clean white shirt.

"You know, you are an unusual case, an important case," Paula said. "I expect to be working with you for many years, and I hope we will meet many times around the world. I love to travel. Austria is easiest because we don't need a visa here. But I can go anywhere if I have enough notice. You must help me by thinking up reasons for me to meet you abroad. I like Moscow, but I want to see the world while I can."

In a restaurant, Paula commended Hambleton's preparations for the mission in Israel and talked frankly about the severity of Soviet needs for intelligence about the Israelis. Whether Paula articulated only his personal views or the institutional attitudes of the KGB, Hambleton did not know. But he was appalled by the ignorance of Israel that Paula's comments revealed. In sum, they conjured up images of a gaggle of hook-nosed Jews pawing and leering over dirty money in usury parlors.

Referring to notes, Paula listed the basic questions the KGB wanted Hambleton to try to answer in Israel:

Have the Israelis produced atomic bombs? If so, would they use them in a future Middle East conflict?

How would an immigrant go about establishing a business in Israel? How much money would be required?

What is the status of the Israeli economy, and what are its future prospects?

"That's quite an order," Hambleton remarked.

"You have filled bigger ones before," Paula said. "Anything you can do will be appreciated."

Faculty and staff members at the university in Jerusalem welcomed Hambleton and graciously helped him in every way they could. Through conversations with academicians and his own observations, he answered relatively easily the questions pertaining to the economy and the founding of a small business. The intellectual detective work concerning nuclear weapons was more difficult.

By repeatedly asking which areas of Israel he should visit, he demarked locales of the small country which he *could not* visit. Through a combination of library research and casual inquiry among Israeli intellectuals, he ascertained the nature of installations in the forbidden zones, their proximity to power and transportation facilities, the identities and background of some of the scientists employed there. He also focused his disguised investigations upon intimate Israeli relations with South Africa because he believed South Africa possessed the capacity to produce nuclear weapons. By the time Hambleton departed Israel in early August for Vienna, he was sure of this.

Paula read his three reports with undisguised and unrestrained admiration. One stated that the Israeli economy was in poor condition, and for a variety of endemic reasons, it would probably not improve unless the Israelis and Arabs could cooperate with each other. But in terms of geopolitics, that did not matter very much. Israel would be artificially sustained by foreign subsidies, principally from Jewish interests in the United States.

The second report emphasized that only an authentic *Jewish* immigrant could hope to establish a business in Israel; $20,000 would suffice for a start, but supplementary funding might be required because Israeli bureaucracy, taxes and inflation militated against the success of any independent business.

The third report clearly excited Paula. In essence it stated: Abetted by secret technological cooperation from South Africa and material stolen in the United States, Israel had produced several atomic bombs. It was producing several more each year. If the Israelis during a future war determined that use of the atomic bombs would prevent their annihilation, they undoubtedly would use them as a last resort.

"Are you certain of this?" Paula asked.

Hambleton retraced the steps that led him to the conclusions reported.

"Well, it will cause a sensation in Moscow," Paula accurately prophesied.

In parting, Paula pressed Hambleton to hunt more vigorously for "progressives" at Laval University.

"To be frank," Hambleton replied, "not too many young Canadians are sympathetic toward the Soviet Union."

"But there are some. We know that from other sources." Paula ordered him to gather information about a particular male student the KGB believed to be a Marxist and to report names of especially gifted students, irrespective of their ideology. Finally he urged Hambleton anew to seek means of entering Canadian government service.

A temporary opportunity arose in 1971 when the Canadian International Development Agency asked Hambleton to take a six-month leave of absence and serve as an economic adviser to the Peruvian government. In a tense Ottawa rendezvous lasting only a minute or so, he informed a KGB officer of his plans.

In Lima, Hambleton was paid by the Canadian government, but he worked as a subordinate of Peruvian authorities. The arrangement enabled him to teach by the examples of his actions, rather than by giving orders, and he thoroughly enjoyed the assignment.

Leaving his office on a November afternoon, he suddenly experienced a sensation of *déjà vu*, of being back in Paris. It might have been Aleksei waiting for him outside of NATO headquarters; in reality, it was Paula who heartily hugged him.

They adjourned to a restaurant where Paula spoke ebulliently, obviously relishing the opportunity to see Peru and his prize agent. "Your report about the Israeli bombs received the highest evaluation," he announced proudly. "Members of the Politburo personally read it. My congratulations." He asked Hambleton to draft reports on the political situation in Peru, the stability of the government, and the political prospects of its various leaders. Most of all, though, the KGB wanted him to develop acquaintances among Americans in Lima and to look for those who might for any reason be susceptible to Soviet cultivation.

The next evening Paula gave him an accommodation address in East Berlin. He also showed him how to use a secret writing tablet by placing a page from it atop any high-quality paper and then writing on glass. "You really need professional [espionage tradecraft] training," he said. "We will schedule it whenever we can."

Hambleton was conscious of a slightly intoxicating effect the unexpected appearance of Paula in Lima had on his vanity. He was so important that Moscow was willing to send a man halfway around the world to talk to him for a few hours. What he wrote was so important that the rulers of the Soviet Union personally read his words. He possessed a direct channel of communications to the leadership of the second mightiest nation on earth. How many other professors in the world could say as much?

Having returned to Canada and the university in late 1971, Hambleton in secret writing reported on Peru and occasionally mailed brief accounts of his activities to Berlin. By his performance in Peru, Hambleton gained the professional esteem of several senior officials in the Canadian foreign-aid agency, and they approached him with another offer early in 1973. The Canadian government and the Organization of American States were sponsoring a joint project to teach Haitians how to prepare development proposals for evaluation by international aid organizations and contractors. As Hambleton was fluent in three languages spoken in Haiti—French, Spanish and English—he seemed a good candidate. With the blessings of the university, he left in May 1973 for Port-au-Prince. Although he advised the KGB in secret writing that he would be in Haiti until May 1975, once there he did not write because he feared authorities would confiscate any letter addressed to Karl Marx Allee, East Berlin. So he had no further communication with the Russians until the ubiquitous and indefatigable Rudi chased him down on a muddy Port-au-Prince street in the fall of 1974. Rudi issued him a new accommodation address in Austria and relayed a KGB order summoning him to a Vienna meeting in December.

With his exotically stunning Haitian mistress, Hambleton flew to New York, posted a letter confirming he would report in December, then flew on to Europe. The sight of a middle-aged Anglo-Saxon escorting a voluptuous 20-year-old Haitian beauty frequently drew scornful stares in Europe, but sometimes younger people conspicuously winked or smiled in endorsement. The reactions in England, France and Spain only amused him. However, their relationship abruptly ended in Spain after the young woman fell under the sway of Catholicism and deserted him to join a convent.

In Vienna, Paula displayed the same friendliness and enthusiasm he had exhibited three years before in Lima. Consulting notes, he recited a new series of requirements for Hambleton. "You must concentrate most of all on meeting and assessing Americans. It's very hard to get Americans, but we must get them. You can talk to them without causing any suspicion. You also must think about finding a replacement for yourself in Canada. We all are growing older; we all will have to be replaced eventually."

Proceeding down the checklist, Paula without the least change in inflection or manner said, "Advise us of the date of the American attack on the Soviet Union."

"What!" Hambleton blurted. "You're putting me on."

Apparently, Paula did not understand the phrase. "Yes, inform us of the measures of the American attack and the date they plan to attack."

"Actually, I doubt that the Americans are planning an attack," Hambleton said evenly, realizing that Paula was serious. "If they are, I doubt that they will notify me."

"Well, if you find out any information about the American attack on us, let us know."

"Sure, sure. I'll let you know."

The exchange amazed Hambleton. Musing about it later, he conjectured that perhaps Paula had imperfectly translated his Russian notes into English speech. "Sure, sure, I'll let you know," he laughed.

The KGB wanted Hambleton to make another expedition to Israel the next summer and afterwards to travel surreptitiously to Moscow for "high-level discussions." As instructed, Hambleton returned to Vienna in June 1975 expecting Paula to brief him about what he was to do in Israel. On four successive days he waited the maximum five minutes allowed at the meeting site, but neither Paula nor any one else came to say, "I have some etchings for you." His ticket and itinerary permitted no further delay, so he mailed a note to the Austrian accommodation address reporting that he had gone on and would be back in Vienna August 15.

Bereft of KGB guidance, Hambleton decided to make a demographic study of Israel, and again he profited from the cooperation of Israeli scholars, who had no cause to think he was anything other than a friendly Canadian academician sympathetic to their country. Tracing the pattern of immigration into Israel, he discerned that an increasing proportion of immigrants came from lands of the Middle East, rather than North America or Europe. This alteration of population composition, he predicted, would affect internal politics and force future Israeli leaders, whatever their personal judgments, to be more and more intransigent regarding the issue of Jerusalem.

To keep the August 15 appointment with Paula in Vienna, Hambleton flew to Greece and took a train from Athens. While it stopped to board passengers in Salonika, he stared at a lithe young woman coming down the aisle with her parents. Her velvety dark eyes, flowing raven hair and beautiful olive skin reminded him of a blithe gypsy. In passing, she cast him a frank, coquettish smile.

Without plan or forethought, he collected his belongings, followed her into the next coach and settled into a seat across from her. After the train pulled away from the station into the highlands of Macedonia, the mother opened a sack and spread a kind of picnic lunch. Before eating, the family held a small conference, speaking in Serbian. Then the young woman leaned toward him and asked in hesitant English, "Excuse me, are you American?"

"No, Canadian; I teach at a university in Quebec."

"I study English," she said. "I not learn very well."

"You speak very well, as prettily as you look."

"My mother asks if you would like . . ." The word *sandwich* eluded her, and she pointed.

"I would love a sandwich."

Ljiljana was 21, a student of biology at Belgrade University and a questing spirit. She had grown up in the Yugoslav mountains, the daughter of factory workers who were caring parents. The preceding summer, her older brother had worked as a waiter in an upstate New York restaurant, and he brought back not only dollars but marvelous stories of America. She eagerly asked about Canada, as if it were another world, and just as eagerly told Hambleton about life in Yugoslavia, of which she was intensely proud.

Oblivious to all else, they spoke continuously for almost three hours, and several times when their eyes met, they saw in each other the excitement and magic of spontaneous, natural attraction. At the Yugoslav border, they had to change to separate trains, and in a little shop Hambleton bought a beaded necklace for her. As he fastened it around her neck, he asked, "May I see you?"

"Yes."

"When?"

"I can meet you in Belgrade after five days."

"I will be there." They exchanged addresses, and Hambleton named the hotel where he planned to stay in Vienna. They waved to each other until her train was out of sight, and he almost missed his. The remainder of the journey to Vienna was made serene by visions of the lovely child-woman who transported him back to his youth while he led her into the future. For the first time in conscious memory, he had something personally to look forward to five days hence.

He was still thinking of Ljiljana when Paula sidled up in front of a Vienna apothecary, shook hands and shocked him with the announcement: "You're on your way to Moscow."

"What do you mean?"

"You leave tomorrow for Moscow. Are you ready to go?"

Hambleton wanted to go to Belgrade and Ljiljana, not Moscow. He feared the Russians might have found out that he lied about being fired and now planned to interrogate and punish him. But he also feared that to refuse would be to admit guilt and create suspicion if none existed, and so he agreed.

At nine o'clock in the morning he walked down a road by the Danube, and a black sedan with diplomatic license plates stopped alongside him. One of the two occupants called in clear English, "May we offer you a lift?" The two KGB officers treated him as a superior officer, respectfully requesting that he give them his passport and personal papers for safekeeping and handing him a Soviet diplomatic passport bearing his photograph. After a drive of only about 35 minutes, they reached the Czechoslovakian border, and guards waved them on without any checks. In Bratislava they enjoyed an excellent lunch at an old restaurant, then drove to a suburb.

As directed, Hambleton left the car and walked along a quiet street a few minutes before another Russian overtook him on foot. "Nice to see you," he said in English. "Come along with me."

Relaxed and companionable, the new escort alternately cursed and apologized for the sputtering Moskvitch that took them toward Prague, and he tinkered with the engine for half an hour before making it start after they had stopped for dinner. About 10:30 p.m., outside the Soviet embassy in Prague, the escort officer took Hambleton's Soviet passport, which had yet to be completed, and asked, "How old do you want to be? Any particular name you would like? Any particular place you wish to be born?"

"I'll leave it to you."

In no more than ten minutes, the Russian presented Hambleton with the finished passport and deposited him in an apartment pleasingly furnished with antiques. Falling asleep under a down quilt in a large feather bed, he longed for Ljiljana and wondered what awaited him in Moscow.

Very early the next morning, the same escort officer drove him to a military air base and put him aboard a Tupolev transport crammed with Soviet military personnel and dependents. A senior officer who seemed to be in charge of the cabin told him in broken German to ask if he needed anything. Otherwise, he was left alone until the plane landed at a Soviet base outside Berlin. There, another Russian, who apparently spoke only Russian, pointed him into a truck, which took him to an officers' mess filled with Soviet pilots. Several pilots tried to engage him in conversation over lunch until they realized he could not speak Russian; then everybody ate in silence. Following a stop in Poland, the Tupolev landed at a military base outside Moscow in the early evening.

Hambleton disembarked, and in a few minutes a black sedan sped across the field to the aircraft. A well-dressed man, about 40, ran from the car to him. "May I see your passport, please," he said in English with such a flawless American accent that Hambleton initially wondered if he might be an American. Upon comparing the passport photograph with Hambleton and a photo he had with him, he offered his hand.

"My name is Pavel. I apologize for keeping you waiting. You deserve a more auspicious reception."

As they drove in the twilight toward Moscow, the words and demeanor of Pavel assured Hambleton that the KGB had no hostile motive in bringing him to the Soviet Union. "We have prepared a very full program for you: intensive training, which you need for your own welfare; conferences about your future; and high-level discussions, the very highest level. We also want you to see something of Moscow and spend at least a day in Leningrad; it's a beautiful city. That is a lot for three weeks."

Thinking of Ljiljana waiting in vain for him in Belgrade, Hambleton said, "I cannot possibly stay three weeks. I am expected back at the university before the end of the month, and it's awkward for me to disappear even for a week."

Pavel muttered something in Russian before replying in English. "We will just have to do the best we can. Don't worry. It's not your fault."

Before entering a high-rise apartment building in the northwest section of Moscow, Pavel cautioned Hambleton not to speak English in the elevator or corridors. "This is a very secure building, and we never bring foreigners here. If anyone speaks to you, just nod. There will be no questions."

The apartment—consisting of living room, dining room, two bedrooms, bath and kitchen—was palatial by Moscow standards, and the refrigerator was full of Georgian wine, vodka, caviar, salmon, and other delicacies new to Hambleton. Pavel explained that Hambleton would stay in the apartment nightly and that Paula and various instructors would arrive each morning to work with him during the day. A car and driver were at his disposal, and he was free to explore the city whenever time allowed. If he wished, he could shop at special stores where dollars would purchase all sorts of luxuries at favorable prices. Paula gave him 100 rubles for pocket money and urged him to walk around the neighborhood on his own to derive a feeling of Moscow.

In administering tradecraft training to Hambleton, the KGB intended to equip him with multiple means of receiving communications from Moscow anywhere in the world. Hence, one technician practiced secret writing with him and taught him how to develop invisible letters with a chemical compound the KGB was to deliver to him in Canada. Another instructor reviewed the concept of drops and the use of concealment devices and gave him rudimentary lessons in how to recognize signs of surveillance when approaching drop sites.

One morning, two technicians brought to the apartment a Grundig Satellite short-wave receiver and a specially developed attachment, which they called a *luminaire*. It looked like a gray metal box approximately nine by six by two inches in size, with ten square dials on top. One of the technicians plugged the *luminaire* into the receiver, set the frequency and told Hambleton to watch. Suddenly the dials began flashing, one after the other, illuminating various numerals ranging from 0 to 9. The technician explained that particular sounds being transmitted from the Center were causing particular dials to light up. All Hambleton had to do was record the numerals as they appeared, in groups of five, then decipher them from an appropriate sheet of a cipher pad.

KGB laboratories had designed the *luminaire* for prized agents who were unwilling to master Morse code or were living in circumstances that made its reception imprudent. It offered the advantages of silence, simplicity, and virtual immunity from atmospheric interferences. However, as Hambleton instantly realized, any security service that found a *luminaire* would at once understand its origin, purposes and implications. The *luminaire* apparently was in short supply at the time, for the KGB explained that it would be some months before one could be smuggled to Canada. It would be conveyed to him personally rather than through a drop—a risky form of transfer that denoted the sensitivity of the device.

A somewhat pedantic KGB officer accompanied Hambleton on an overnight trip to Leningrad, where they toured the Hermitage, museums and standard tourist sights. The officer appeared perturbed when Hambleton showed little knowledge of the theories of Marx and Lenin and no interest in a dialogue about them. Back in Moscow, he and Paula argued animatedly in Russian, and Hambleton suspected they were quarreling about him. Paula finally dismissed the officer, and he was not seen in the apartment again.

Toward the end of the week, Pavel announced, "A very important visitor will join us for supper tonight. He is interested in your views on international topics. Just be yourself and tell him frankly what you think."

Expecting simply another debriefing by a senior KGB officer, Hambleton did not trouble to inquire who his inquisitor might be. And he was not disposed to be particularly deferent the next evening when a tall, gray, weary Russian entered the apartment in the company of three men, two of whom doubtless were bodyguards. Though quite courteous, the visitor seemed rather aloof, and he did not identify himself. He insisted upon speaking English, and Hambleton surmised he had once spoken it well, for his word selection and syntax were excellent. However, he frequently had to ask one of his subordinates for English words he desired and to clarify in Russian what Hambleton said in English.

After a brief exchange of pleasantries, they sat down to supper, and the Russian commenced questioning Hambleton about world affairs. Was it possible for the United States to sharply increase military spending beyond present levels? Hambleton replied that as an economist he was unqualified to judge whether domestic politics would permit any substantial increase in the American military budget. He also was unsure whether the United States had retained a sufficient armament industry to allow a quick increase in weapons production. But he said that the United States could easily double its defense budget without structurally changing the economy, were it willing to increase taxes and curtail nondefense programs.

The Russian meditated momentarily, then broached another subject. "Are Jews badly persecuted in the United States?"

Hambleton answered that while there doubtless were pockets of individual prejudice, Jews enjoyed equal access to education, the professions, business, housing and everything else in the United States. Anti-Semitism simply was not a significant factor in American society.

The Russian seemed surprised by the answer.

"Tell me about the attitude of American youth," he said. "Do progressive American youths look upon the Soviet Union as the hope of the future?"

Hambleton framed his reply carefully. "You know how

young people everywhere are. They're always chasing what seems new, exotic, trendy. So young American progressives are attracted by Cuba and China, whose defects have not become widely known. The Soviet Union has been around a long time, so its problems are well publicized."

"Well, the defects of China are great and glaring. They soon will be known," the Russian rejoined, showing the first trace of emotion. Sadly, he then remarked that the degeneration of Sino-Soviet relations was a "tragedy."

The conversation ranged over Western Europe, and the Russian predicted that the Common Market ultimately would fail. As Hambleton disagreed, he said nothing.

Considering Hambleton's future, the Russian said, "Your contributions in the past have been great. Do you think you could become an influence in Canadian politics? Could you be elected to Parliament as a representative of any political party?"

"Not likely," Hambleton said. "I have never been active in politics. I have no experience, no base."

"Could you work in the United States at some secret research center, at the Hudson Institute, for example?"

Hambleton said he could possibly secure such an appointment. Urging him to try, the Russian stated that meanwhile the KGB would continue to employ him in "denied areas" where it had difficulty sending agents.

An hour after his arrival, the Russian stood up rather abruptly, wished Hambleton well and departed with his aides. His last words were, "You know, you are an unusual case."

Alone in the apartment with Paula, Hambleton asked who the visitor was and learned that he had been talking to KGB Chairman Andropov.

"It was an extraordinary experience for me," Paula said.

Hambleton was incredulous. "Do you think I was impertinent?"

Paula shrugged. "You said what you believe to be the truth. That's what intelligence is supposed to be about."

Whether or not Andropov contributed to the crystallization

of plans for Hambleton is not known. But two days after their interview, Paula issued Hambleton new orders. "We want you to search for employment that will enable you to move to Washington or New York. At the same time, you should try to become associated in some manner with the Hudson Institute. We also want you to find professional reasons to travel periodically to the Middle East."

The assignment to the United States, the conversation with the chairman of the KGB, the prospect of taking custody of the *luminaire* all warned Hambleton that he was about to be projected into deadly and dangerous espionage. Once in Washington or New York, he would not be a dilettante who dabbled in spying for intellectual kicks and largely at his own discretion. He would be jeopardizing not just his career and reputation but his life and the welfare of Western civilization. Silently, in the presence of Paula, he resolved that he would never apply for any job in the United States, out of fear of being accepted.

Now he wanted only to escape the Soviet Union. He had lived in and seen only the best, but what he had seen was to him pervasive, suffocating monotony and dreariness, terrifying regimentation that crushed the very soul. He swore to himself that if he got out, he would never again touch Soviet soil. Feeling like a man trying to back away from a poised cobra without causing it to strike, he said, "Personally, I would like nothing better than to stay and explore Soviet society indefinitely. But already I have left a gap of seven days in my whereabouts and movements, and that can be dangerous. People are waiting for me in Quebec, and it seems to me it would be folly to risk everything for just a few more days. Surely there will be another opportunity. As for the assignments, I will do my best."

By military transport, Hambleton flew to Prague, then traveled in KGB cars to Bratislava and across the border to Vienna, where the same KGB pair returned his documents and with a hearty farewell dropped him near a hotel. Recovering a suitcase he had left at the hotel luggage room, he caught the first train to Belgrade, intending to ask a taxi driver to take him to the address Ljiljana gave him.

Shortly after he registered at the Slavija Hotel in Belgrade, four plainclothesmen surrounded him, and one harshly said, "We would like to ask you a few questions. Come with us." They seated him in a dingy office, bare except for wooden chairs and a table, and from all sides subjected him to grueling, hostile interrogation, again and again asking in different words five questions: Why did you come to Yugoslavia? What are you doing here? Whom do you know in Yugoslavia? What were you doing in Israel? Are you with NATO?

Determined above all else to protect Ljiljana by not mentioning her, Hambleton fended the questions with condescension and measured bellicosity born of innocence and indignation. Yes, he *was* with NATO, but he left 14 years ago. Look it up yourselves in *Who's Who*, chums. In Israel, he was gathering data about the Siege of Rhodes in 1480, a decisive engagement that made possible the spread of Christianity in the 15th century. He had hoped to consult a Yugoslav scholar who others had told him was an authority on the battle.

Which scholar?

Hambleton named an academician whose death had been reported by a scholarly journal a few months before. Ultimately, he demanded to call the Canadian embassy and warned that he would request it to notify Western journalists of his detention.

Still suspicious that Hambleton was either a Western or Zionist spy, yet lacking any evidence, the security men terminated the interrogation after some three hours, coldly suggesting that he get out of Yugoslavia forthwith. Not daring to contact Ljiljana, he departed forlornly, doubtful that he would ever see her.

In Quebec, however, a letter from Belgrade awaited him. Ljiljana was disappointed that he had not come to Belgrade as promised, and she attempted to reach him at the hotel in Vienna. Still, she hoped that he would write. Though exhausted by the flight from Europe, he composed a long and tender reply, and she promptly responded in kind. Soon they began writing to each other three or four times a week, discussing their respective universities, countries, personal lives and aspirations. Through the letters, they spoke to each other more thoughtfully, considerately and often than do many couples living together, and their words became progressively more intimate, affectionate and inviting. When Ljiljana mentioned in April 1976 that her brother planned to work again at the upstate New York restaurant in the summer, Hambleton urged them both to visit him in Quebec.

They landed aboard a Yugoslav charter flight in Montreal, and Hambleton drove them to Quebec in his new Toyota Celica. At a local shopping center, Ljiljana saw a supermarket for the first time and was as entranced as a child in fairyland. The array of products in the stores so excited her curiosity that Hambleton had to enlist her brother's help to induce her to leave. Every day in Quebec was a day of discovery, and she and Hambleton grew closer and closer as he acted as guide and tutor.

Ljiljana's brother had to report for work in late June, and Hambleton proposed that they tour New England en route. The drive through the green hills of Vermont, neat fishing towns, and resorts of Cape Cod was a romantic lark. On a moonlit night in a motel swimming pool, Ljiljana frolicked and flirted and splashed water on Hambleton until he grabbed her in self-defense. They held each other in their first embrace, and neither wished to let go.

She had planned to stay with her brother in New York until her scheduled return to Yugosolavia in mid-July, but once there, Hambleton proposed that she accompany him to Washington and watch the bicentennial observance of American independence. She looked at her brother for counsel. "It is your choice," he said. "If you wish to go, I approve."

Lowering her eyes and taking Hambleton's hand, she said, "I will go."

They found a room in a small Washington hotel overlooking a quiet park. They held hands in museums, parks, theaters, and in silent reverence before the Tomb of the Unknown Soldier at Arlington Cemetery; they drank wine and listened to folk music in sidewalk cafés; and whatever they did was ecstasy.

On the Fourth of July, they mingled with hundreds of thousands of Americans on the Mall, everywhere encountering friendliness, thrilling to the martial music and spectacular bursts of fireworks above the Lincoln Memorial. Caught up in the great celebration of freedom, Hambleton bought and she proudly wore a straw hat painted with stars and stripes. And on the Fourth of July they agreed to marry.

They stopped in New York City on the way back to Canada, and Hambleton left her alone for a couple of hours in the afternoon. When he returned, he slipped a diamond ring on her finger. During the next few days, every few minutes of her waking hours, she looked at the ring, and sometimes she held her hand up for him to look also.

Ljiljana probably would have married Hambleton immediately, had he insisted. But out of a sense of obligation to her parents, she felt she should devote some time to them and complete her studies in Belgrade before leaving Yugoslavia permanently. Placing her concerns above his desires, he agreed that they should postpone marriage until her graduation in 1978. Against the radiance of the life they anticipated together, the delay did not seem to matter. They would spend the next summer together in Canada and Mexico and until then write daily. In Canada she could do postgraduate work, then spend a life of unmitigated happiness teaching with him. On the ramp of the plane in Montreal, she paused to wave and blow kisses at him in a farewell that enriched rather than saddened.

Partially because of his happy preoccupation with Ljiljana, partially because of his reaction to the experiences in Moscow, Hambleton had ignored messages from the KGB and neglected to attend two meetings scheduled in the Ottawa area. A dispatch that he developed from secret writing in late August 1976, though, was so imperative in tone that he com-

plied with its command to withdraw "materials" from a drop
along an abandoned road near Ottawa. The "materials" turned
out to be a Parker pen containing film listing drop sites around
Montreal and future meeting places in the Ottawa area, each
labeled with a Christian name. Another message directed him
to unload one of the Montreal drops, which yielded a cipher
pad and a Grundig Satellite receiver, modified by KGB laboratories to accommodate the *luminaire*. The Center next sent
by secret writing a radio schedule and detailed instructions as
to how he would take delivery of the *luminaire*.

Following them, he drove into a Montreal parking garage in
January 1977 and waited in the area specified by the Center.
Shortly, a car parked nearby, a rotund little man got out,
opened the trunk and removed an automobile battery. Hambleton cheerfully said, "Hi, how are you?" As if about to be
contaminated by a sore-ridden leper, the KGB man dropped
the battery and ran away as fast as his pudgy legs would carry
him. Hambleton lugged the battery to his car and, upon taking
it apart in his apartment back in Quebec, saw the *luminaire*.

Having received a radio schedule in secret writing, he
turned to the frequency it stipulated on a Saturday morning,
and exactly at the prescribed time, the *luminaire* began to
light up, just as in Moscow. The first message it flashed in
code asked if he could travel to Saudi Arabia, Turkey, Egypt
or Israel in the summer. A following message asked when he
could next meet in Vienna; and a third inquired about his
progress in penetrating the Hudson Institute and securing
employment in the United States.

Interested only in a summer with Ljiljana, he replied that
because he was committed to attend a convention in Mexico,
he could not travel to the Middle East or Europe in 1977.
Doubtless he could visit any of the countries enumerated
during the summer of 1978, when he would begin a year of
sabbatical leave. He purposely made no reference to the Hudson Institute or employment in the United States.

The *luminaire* in April spelled out an assignment he considered both curious and challenging: By same methods applied

in Israel, can you ascertain status of South African program to develop nuclear weapons? The Center knew that there was no possibility in the near future of his roaming around South Africa as he had been able to do in Israel. If the legions of KGB spies, abetted by Soviet scientists and satellite photography, could not unveil South African nuclear secrets, how could he be expected to ferret them out in Quebec?

But the very improbability of solving such a puzzle made him want to try, and he was uninhibited by fears that a successful solution would cause any serious harm. He also had the advantage of having learned something in Israel about South African technological resources and capabilities. So working mainly in libraries and through correspondence with scientists and economists, he commenced an investigation under the guise of studying nuclear proliferation.

By late May he was able to draft a report showing that South Africa had amassed all the requisite resources and facilities to produce an atomic bomb exceeding in destructive force that dropped on Nagasaki. Like the Israelis, he stated, the South Africans had both the national will and a perceived need to produce nuclear weapons. And he predicted that they would detonate their first one within a few months.

Beneath a rock by a telephone pole near St. Catherines, Ontario, he left the film of his report wrapped in plastic. Having waited the standard hour, he drove down the dirt road about a mile away to another telephone pole where a chalk mark would signal that the drop had been cleared. Seeing no mark, he raced back to the drop site and retrieved the film, and as he did, a lone car drove past. He remembered the warning of a KGB instructor in Moscow: When approaching a drop, beware of the single car. Many cars are all right. A single car may mean danger. On the way home, he burned the film in a car ashtray and subsequently posted the South African report in secret writing.

When Ljiljana passed through customs in June, she looked drawn and weary, indeed five years older. The first night she was subdued and reserved, and his teasing and jokes elicited only faint smiles from her. Although she still trembled with emotion when he embraced and kissed her, she was uncharacteristically aloof. She explained only that she had been ill, declining to discuss the nature of her illness.

Hambleton was confident that the sunshine, gaiety and charm of Mexico would restore her to the irrepressible spirit he had known, and on their leisurely drive through the United States into Mexico, they did enjoy anew the intellectual communion first achieved in letters. In Mexico City he took her to the Museum of Anthropology and the Ballet Folklorico; they rode in a boat on the Floating Gardens, while in boats around them mariachis played, and mothers cooked tortillas for their families. On the Paseo de la Reforma they dined in cafés reminiscent of those in Paris, and he bought her serapes and jewelry. Yet wherever they went, a melancholy followed, and sometimes when she looked at her engagement ring, she cried. She grew paler and thinner and became so weak she could stay up only three or four hours a day. Then she confided that she had been undergoing chemotherapy treatments for cancer.

In Santille she sobbed. "I don't know whether we should be married. Mother says I cannot marry because of my cancer."

"In sickness and health, for better or worse, until death do us part. Do you know those words?"

"No."

"They are the words we will say when we are married. I love you. I want to marry you no matter what."

Never had he been more sincere.

Obsessed, incapable of serious thought about anything but Ljiljana, indifferent to all else including the KGB, Hambleton wrote to her daily. Her letters came less and less frequently and omitted any mention of her health, but she did consent to join him for a week in Spain during his Christmas holidays.

Ljiljana brought bad news. Yugoslav security police had noted the cascade of letters from Canada and brutally interrogated her for three days. "It was terrible," she said. Additionally, the physicians had pronounced the therapy a failure and advised that she must undergo major surgery as soon as possible. In Madrid, then Toledo, they lived each day as though it might be the last. When she could no longer walk or bask in the plazas, he sat on the bed talking with her until she fell asleep. For fear of inciting the police, they agreed to write only occasionally, but she promised to let him know the results of the surgery.

He heard nothing until March, when in a brief, alarmingly formal note she wrote that she had left the hospital and resumed her studies.

The Center several times had requested a meeting in Vienna at the earliest date practical. Determined to see Ljiljana at whatever risk, Hambleton scheduled a journey to Vienna in May 1978, planning to slip into Belgrade afterwards and then go on to Egypt.

He and Paula spoke for nearly three hours at the Lindmayer Restaurant on the bank of the Danube, enjoying an elegant lunch of fish and flowery Austrian wine. Glancing now and then at notes, Paula asked him to make a general assessment of the Egyptian economy and to locate investments by American companies in Egypt. Concerning Israel, the KGB wanted to know from which sources it was importing petroleum, how much oil it was producing itself, which types of strategic materials it most needed, and how international sanctions could be levied to damage the economy most effectively.

"But your main task," Paula stressed, "is to change your sabbatical plans so you can spend a year in Washington or New York. We will pay any amount of money you need for an apartment. That is where we want you. Take care of the Middle East this summer; go to the States in the fall."

"I'll see what I can do," Hambleton lied.

He bought a train ticket that indicated he would travel directly from Vienna to Athens, but jumped off in Belgrade and went to Ljiljana's room near the university without checking in at a hotel. Shrunken and emaciated, she offered him only a handshake and spoke as a stranger who scarcely recognized him. The surgery, which lasted seven hours and nearly cost her life, had not fully excised the cancer, and it was spreading.

"Listen, I am going to Egypt for a month; then I'll come back and take you to Israel. Their doctors and hospitals are excellent, and we can be together."

"I have no strength to go anywhere. I can stay up only two or three hours."

"May I see you on my way back from Cairo?"

"Yes."

He held and kissed her gently. As he turned to leave, she called in a voice that sounded disembodied, "I love you."

Staying at the Cairo Hilton, Hambleton met there a number of businessmen and military officers who talked with him freely and hospitably, as did government officials whom he interviewed. He sought to extract no secrets, only overt data pertinent to scholarship concerning economies of the Middle East; and the report he drafted for the KGB was so innocuous that he left it lying openly on a table in his hotel room.

He also sent Ljiljana innocently worded postcards, confident that they would not concern the police. But when he saw her en route back to Vienna, she was terrorized. Despite her conspicuously debilitated condition, the security police had detained and interrogated her for seven consecutive days, and she still was so frightened that she shook when talking of the ordeal. He no longer could kindle in her laughter, passion, magic or hope. The doctors offered her only the possibility of a remission, which might give her a few more tormented years. She had determined to remain in Yugoslavia to be near her family, and she told Hambleton that he must build a life independent of her.

In a Vienna hotel, he wrote an invisible note stating that he could not go to the United States in the next year because his university had refused to allow such a sudden and extreme change in his long-standing sabbatical plans. Hiding the note and his Egyptian report in a drop, he flew to Israel and arranged to do research in coming months at an Israeli university. Then he proceeded to London, where he was able to stay in the apartment of an economist friend who was away on a lengthy foreign assignment. Routinely, he notified the KGB by letter in secret writing of his address and intentions to work in England until December.

Sorting through the day's mail in mid-November 1978, he found a picture postcard bearing an emergency message: "Dear George, my wife and I are looking forward to seeing you in Vienna to celebrate our wedding anniversary in late November." The code commanded him to report for a meeting in Vienna the next Monday.

The sky was dark with black clouds, and cold winds of an impending storm moaned through the street as Hambleton, abiding by prescribed procedures, stepped into an empty car parked in front of a restaurant. In a few seconds, a huge unmarked truck rumbled to a halt and parked bumper-to-bumper behind the car, and shortly a similar truck approaching from ahead stopped about 30 yards away on the opposite side of the street. Soon men, in clusters of two or three, began to appear all around, and Hambleton realized he was surrounded by a small army of Russians doubtless backed by reserves in the trucks.

Suddenly Paula jumped into the front seat of the car, and without any of the cordial salutations he always had extended before, curtly said, "We will stay here and talk." Nervously glancing about as if any minute he might be seized or shot, he asked, "Were you followed here?"

"I don't think so. I didn't check very closely."

"That's your trouble. You never do," Paula snapped, amazing Hambleton with the harshness and anger in his voice.

"What's the matter?"

"The situation is very grave. Your letter from London was opened by a security service."

"If that's all that's bothering you, you have nothing to worry about. I opened it myself to add that I would be in London until December and resealed it with glue."

"That doesn't matter. I am telling you that it was opened professionally by a security service. You probably are under surveillance. You may not be, but you must assume that you are. We know that Western security services are combing the backgrounds of people such as yourself who have been in intelligence. They're looking up every detail of their whole lives."

"We want you to drop everything. Forget about your assignments in Israel and everything else. You can come to the East, or you can stay in the West. . . ."

"What do you mean, come to the East? How? Where?"

"It's your choice. If you come to the East, you are welcome; if you stay in the West, you're on your own. In any case, cease all activity."

Handing Hambleton a white envelope, Paula said, "Here is some money to tide you over. I must go. It's not safe to talk longer. They may be watching right now. If you're not coming to the East, get out of Vienna."

Without a word of farewell, Paula fled into the gloom. As Hambleton trudged in bewilderment toward his hotel, he heard the engines of the trucks cough and roar, and looking back he saw the little army of Russians dispersing.

In his room he opened the envelope and counted $5000 in $20 bills, and upon performing quick mental computations, he laughed. Twenty-two years times 12 divided into 5000 equaled roughly 19; since 1956 he had earned from the KGB about $19 a month.

His life lay in arid ruins, brightened only by memories of the flickering, waning spirit of Ljiljana. Resigned to his own arrest at any time and fearing that before long she would be beyond the reach of any police, he returned to Belgrade and gave her the KGB money.

Hambleton remained in Europe through the spring and summer of 1979 fulfilling his sabbatical program. Ljiljana wrote rarely, and warmth and intimacy ebbed from her letters. But Hambleton sensed no indication that he was under surveillance or suspicion, and he began to think that perhaps the KGB had been mistaken; perhaps, free of the KGB, he could during his last years put his formidable capabilities to some constructive ends.

The welcome accorded him by friends and colleagues at Laval University upon his return in September 1979 fortified his hopes, and during the first few days nothing seemed untoward. One night, however, as he proceeded along one of the many tunnels that connect campus buildings, he heard the echo of footsteps some distance behind him. He stopped, and so did the sound of the footsteps; he started walking again, and so did someone else. Then in November his doorbell rang.

"Professor Hambleton?" asked a tall man flanked by four others.

"Yes."

"We have a warrant to search these premises. May we come in please?"

The Royal Canadian Mounted Police from the Security Service soon found the *luminaire*. "Would you care to explain the purpose of this device and how it came into your possession?" one said.

Hambleton smiled. "Fellows, what are you going to believe? What I tell you or what you see with your own eyes?"

Paula was correct in telling Hambleton during their final rendezvous in Vienna that Western security services were investigating certain people with intelligence backgrounds. However, he and the KGB were mistaken in concluding that such investigation involved Hambleton. For ever since Rudolf Herrmann informed the FBI, the Canadian Security Service had known that Hambleton was a spy. But the Canadians intelligently elected to do nothing except watch him, lest they jeopardize the supremely important double-agent operation the FBI initiated through Herrmann. And not until that operation terminated did they confront him.

The evidence Herrmann provided and that subsequently collected by the Canadians proved that Hambleton was a Soviet agent. However, unless the NATO papers he betrayed to the KGB could be counted as Canadian documents, he never gave the Soviets any Canadian secrets. Nor did he ever commit any unlawful act on Canadian soil. So Canadian authorities were not at all certain that they could successfully prosecute him. Hence, they chose to forgo prosecution in return for his unreserved cooperation in reconstructing every meaningful detail of his protracted relationship with the KGB. The counterintelligence benefits of that decision were enormous, enabling the West to look deeply into hidden KGB operations of the past, present and future.

Some perceptive Canadian investigators were also aware of the remorseless punishment Hambleton inflicted upon himself by dealing with the KGB. Had he concentrated his undoubted gifts into constructive pursuits instead of diffusing his life and living constantly in wracking inner turmoil, the rewards to him and society would surely have been great. But he forfeited them all once he fell into the grip of the KGB. And in the end, he lost what was most beautiful and meaningful to him.

The last letter from Yugoslavia came in October 1979. It concluded: "I am not very well. Best regards, Ljiljana."

Throughout his life, Hambleton had been an inveterate traveler, and in the summer when he was free from teaching duties at Laval University, he enjoyed taking his son abroad. After completion of his interrogation, he asked Canadian authorities if he could safely visit the United States and United Kingdom. They advised that the FBI would probably arrest him as a foreign agent and that the British certainly would arrest him under their Official Secrets Act.

Nevertheless, Hambleton in June 1982 flew to London with his son. One can only conjecture why he did so. Perhaps he thought that the passage of time had closed his past and that the British had forgotten about him. More likely, he heard the same call of adventure that lured him back to the KGB after he broke contact back in 1961; more likely, he wanted to relive his past adventures by confessing them to the British; more likely, he wanted again to be someone important in the secret world, if only briefly.

Because Hambleton's name was on the immigration watch

list, the British began interrogating him soon after arrival. Freely and willingly, he told them the complete story of his life in espionage, just as he had told the Canadians. Thereby he doomed himself.

The Official Secrets Act makes spying against the United Kingdom anywhere at any time a crime, and there is no statute of limitations. The British felt they had no choice but to prosecute.

At the trial, which began in November, Hambleton attempted a last feeble sally into intrigue, claiming that he had been a double agent working for France and Canada. The claim soon collapsed under weight of the evidence, and on December 6, 1982, Hambleton, now haggard and spiritless, admitted his guilt in open court.

"Are you still KGB?" the prosecutor asked.

"Rather than identify with the KGB, I still tend to identify with the officer class," Hambleton replied.

That is the way he thought of himself: an intelligence officer, French, American, Canadian and finally Soviet. As a Soviet officer, Hambleton at age 60 began serving a ten-year sentence. In consequence of his ultimate act of irresponsibility, he probably will spend most, if not all, of his remaining life in an English prison.

X

FIGHTING BACK

THE KGB OF THE 1980s still abides by the dictates of Lenin, who declared in the 1920s that Communists must "thoroughly, carefully, attentively and skillfully" exploit "every 'fissure,' however small" among their enemies. As former Major Stanislav Levchenko emphasizes in his analyses of Soviet methodology, "Look where your vulnerabilities are, and there you will find the KGB."

Certain vulnerabilities of democracies cannot be eliminated without unacceptable abridgement of the freedom that is the essence, strength and purpose of democracy. Democracies are founded upon the convictions that in fair competition, truth will win out, and that given the truth, the people are the best arbiters of public policy. The functioning of democracy thus depends upon continuous criticism and clash of ideas; upon tolerance of all viewpoints and ideas, however unpopular, absurd or radical they may seem; upon the most robust debate in which each citizen may join. This democratic debate in turn depends upon the widest circulation of news, information, and opinion from all sources, and upon the presumption that until proven otherwise, all participants are people of good will and honest intent.

Nothing can debar the KGB from trying to poison democratic discourse with deceitful data or from intruding the disguised Soviet voice through Agents of Influence and front organizations. Other vulnerabilities of free societies derive from their inherent and necessary openness, from the right to travel and associate freely, from the judicial safeguards accorded all citizens. Nor can the KGB be entirely prevented from exploiting these "cracks" or vulnerabilities for purposes of espionage and subversion.

However, there is much the United States and other democratic nations can do to combat the KGB without infringing upon individual liberties. A number of practical, prudent and relatively inexpensive actions would simultaneously diminish the KGB ability to attack and strengthen American defenses against clandestine assault.

First of all, the United States should drastically reduce the KGB presence within its borders by mass expulsions. It is preposterous to allow the Soviet Union to station hordes of KGB officers in our midst; to allow them, with the impunity bestowed by diplomatic status, to wander through Congress, government offices, and universities as Soviet lobbyists; to stroll through laboratories, research centers, and factories as thieves of technology; to sneak out from their sanctuaries in the night to meet their spies; to daily intercept the telephone conversations of hundreds of thousands of Americans.

The Soviet consulate in San Francisco, which looks down upon one of the greatest seats of scientific research and development in the world, is a nest of spies and little else. The consulate should be closed forthwith and its entire staff sent home. Additionally, the United States should reassert sovereignty and inform the United Nations that it may no longer employ legions of Soviet Bloc spies on American territory, that it must insist employees obey the law of the host country. If the United Nations finds such conditions too onerous, then it can relocate its headquarters to a more hospitable land. Perhaps after 37 years in America, U.N. delegates would enjoy the achievements of socialism in Moscow, or life in East Germany behind the security of the Berlin Wall.

By reducing the number of Soviet intelligence personnel from hundreds to relatively few, the United States would force the KGB to rely primarily upon Illegals and officers bereft of diplomatic immunity. Such operatives are far more restricted in movement and access than are "diplomats," and they are further inhibited by awareness that if caught they will be imprisoned, rather than merely put on a plane to Moscow. And with far fewer threats to watch, U.S. counterintelligence could concentrate much more effectively upon those remaining.

The Soviet Union and sympathizers doubtless would greet mass expulsions with a barrage of bombast and rhetoric— "fanning the flames of the Cold War," "jeopardizing détente," "threatening peace," etc. But all the shouting would soon prove to be hollow, as it did in 1971 when Great Britain summarily ousted 105 Soviet "diplomats." Since then, the British have continued to expel intelligence officers detected violating their laws and have not permitted the Soviets to replace them. But this resolute action has not in the least impaired normal diplomatic relations between the United Kingdom and the Soviet Union.

Next, the United States, in concert with its allies, should revise prohibitions against export of advanced technology and should stringently enforce them. During the Carter Administration, the Commerce Department's Compliance Division, which was responsible for preventing the loss of embargoed technology, had a staff of only about 25 people. By contrast, the Bureau of East-West Trade, created to encourage exports to the Soviet Bloc, had a staff of nearly 90. In the heady days of détente, the Compliance Division ignored hard evidence of major violations of export laws. After one Commerce Department official, Lawrence J. Brady, truthfully testified to Congress about some of the violations, he was pressured into leaving.*

Through an organization called COCOM, the United States, NATO countries and Japan maintain a list of items whose sale to the Soviet Bloc is forbidden. The U.S. complains that allies have disregarded the proscriptions as well as allowed American technology shared with them to be transferred to the Communists. However, during the 1970s the United States was the leader in requesting exemptions to the COCOM list, that is, in asking to sell the Russians items everyone had agreed should not be sold.

Manifestly, the United States must define and enunciate for itself a coherent policy governing technology transfer, then scrupulously abide by it. Most American corporations do not wish to sell the Soviets anything the government does not want sold; much of the evidence of violations of the export laws has come and will continue to come from private firms that volunteer it. The few violators who seek short-term profit for themselves at national expense should be swiftly prosecuted and severely punished.

United States intelligence and security services, particularly the Central Intelligence Agency and Federal Bureau of Investigation, must be reinvigorated. In poll after poll of public opinion, the American people have asserted their will and readiness to maintain armed forces sufficiently powerful to defend the nation against any combination of enemies.** But the mightiest military forces ever amassed, the most devastating weapons ever devised are of little avail in the kind of warfare the KGB wages. The Americans best equipped to

---

*Brady was subsequently named an Assistant Secretary of Commerce in the Reagan Administration.

**A Gallup Organization poll conducted in 1981 showed that 83 percent of Americans would prefer to go to war rather than submit to Communist domination. Of those polled, 11 percent had no opinion. Only 6 percent were willing to surrender without a fight.

A Gallup Organization poll conducted in 1961 showed that 81 percent of Americans would choose all-out nuclear war rather than live under Communist rule.

combat the KGB on the "invisible front" are a few thousand men and women in the CIA and FBI. Both agencies, however, still suffer from ravages visited upon them in the 1970s.

The one element of American intelligence that duels with the KGB around the world is the Operations Division or Clandestine Service of the CIA. Officer for officer, the Clandestine Service is the equal of the KGB or any other service in the world. But between 1971 and 1975, the personnel complement of the Clandestine Service was cut approximately in half. In retrospect and in light of contemporary needs, the reduction was too large. Mainly, though, it was accomplished by attrition, with personal consideration for those affected and thus without serious harm to morale. The Congressional attacks and often false defamation of the CIA during the mid-1970s also did less injury to morale than might be expected. Men and women do not volunteer for the Clandestine Service in quest of a comfortable, safe life of repose, and officers had long been inured to fabrications and slander inspired by the KGB.

The real unraveling began with the so-called Halloween Massacre in October 1977, when CIA Director Stansfield Turner ordered the summary elimination of 820 positions throughout the Clandestine Service. Though there is dispute about how many personnel were fired, there is no doubt that some officers in mid-career or a few years from retirement were dismissed without regard to their well-being or that of the agency. The consequent bitterness set in motion a train of resignations by gifted officers, who were able to earn higher incomes in private business. At least two chiefs of station abroad quit on the spot, one with an obscene message of contempt to headquarters. Another officer wrote in his resignation letter: "I fear we have turned a dark corner and that the service never will be the same. We could withstand all the attacks from without; we cannot withstand attack from within."

Collectively, the hundreds of officers—2800, according to one authoritative report—who departed in the late 1970s took with them irreplaceable operational experience, linguistic skills and highly specialized knowledge of areas of the world. The effects were soon felt, if not publicly known.

While Ayatollah Khomeini prepared in Paris to take over Iran, his deputy, Sadegh Ghotbzadeh, twice attempted to establish private communications with the CIA. Twice the CIA witlessly ignored the pleas from this future Iranian Foreign Minister, who with Western help might have spared Iran the tragedy that has befallen it. When the CIA finally did recognize the desperate American need for intelligence about Iran, it found that its foremost authority on the country, an officer capable of comprehending every nuance of Iranian life, was gone.

The CIA retains many outstanding officers, particularly in the field, and, as will be seen further in this chapter, some of their accomplishments have been spectacular. But the Clandestine Service is undermanned, and the wealth of expertise lost in recent years cannot soon be recouped.

The overall counterintelligence capabilities of the FBI have also eroded, largely in consequence of Congressional attacks and political reaction to them. While the threat to U.S. security from drug traffic, organized crime and foreign subversion dramatically increased, the number of agents available to the FBI declined from 8619 in 1976 to 7844 in 1980. For 40 years the FBI gathered intelligence about demonstrably subversive organizations, including the kind through which the KGB conducts Active Measures. It also collected intelligence about individuals committed to subversion, terrorism or other political violence. Numerous court decisions upheld the legality of such investigations, and in 1973 the FBI had more than 21,000 domestic security cases under investigation. However, in April 1976, Attorney General Edward Levi decreed that henceforth the FBI could not investigate any domestic organization or citizen in the absence of evidence that a crime had been committed or was about to be committed. Moreover, he precluded the FBI from even keeping any records of members of subversive or terrorist organizations. Consequently, in 1982 the FBI investigated fewer than 100 domestic security cases.

In purely counterespionage operations against the KGB and Soviet-controlled organizations it is allowed to investigate, the FBI continues to perform well, even brilliantly. But here, too, repairs are needed. Traditionally, young agents entering counterintelligence learned on the job from veterans who had fought the KGB on the streets for many years. As a result of wholesale retirements and inadequate emphasis upon counterintelligence in the 1970s, relatively few veterans remain, and the experience level has dropped to an appallingly low level. And on any given day, the Soviet Bloc can send into the streets of Washington and New York more professional intelligence officers than the FBI can deploy against them.

To rejuvenate the CIA and FBI, the United States must reaffirm a national commitment to maintain permanently strong intelligence and security services as an indispensable component of national defense. That reaffirmation can be made through a Congressionally approved charter defining the missions of both services and the latitudes of their operations. Such a charter will make clear, once and for all, to the public, press, courts, politicians, and to intelligence personnel themselves what must be done and what may not be done. Next, the Congress should appropriate funds to augment the manpower of both services. The CIA Clandestine Service and FBI counterintelligence annually cost the nation less than do the purchase and maintenance of two modern fighter squadrons. Money invested in the CIA and FBI will buy more security for the U.S. than any comparable investment. From all sociological sectors of America, exceptionally qualified young people will volunteer to serve. But in the next few crucial years, experienced professionals are needed. That need cannot be entirely fulfilled except by reenlisting, in one form or another, a good many of the accomplished veterans who have recently left.

To the extent that Soviet subterfuges are exposed, their continuation becomes more difficult, and their effects are lessened. To the extent that the American people are denied knowledge of Soviet machinations, their ability to form enlightened judgments about national policy and international affairs is diminished. So there are compelling reasons why the public should be kept informed about what the Soviet Union is doing secretly. There is no reason the United States should keep secrets for the Soviets, unless their disclosure would betray American sources.

However, the main American repositories of data about secret Soviet operations against the United States and the world are the CIA and FBI. Were they to release data on their own, many would suspect them or the Administration in power of acting out of ulterior or partisan political motives. Always, intelligence services, like the armed forces, must remain scrupulously aloof from politics; if ever they involve themselves, they will lose the credibility and popular support essential to their effectiveness.

Therefore, Congress should establish in the form of a joint bipartisan committee a mechanism to annually brief the American people about developments in the ongoing underground war against them. By law, the CIA and FBI should be required at the end of each year to submit reports as comprehensive as can be compiled without compromising intelligence methods and sources. Having satisfied itself as to the validity of the data, and having excised parts that should still be classified, the committee could then release the reports under its own bipartisan imprimatur. The fact that such a summary is mandated by law and issued annually under bipartisan Congressional authority, no matter what, would strip it of any political stigma. And it would forewarn the Soviets that their clandestine depredations may entail unfavorable public consequences in America.

Finally, the United States henceforth must disregard the double standard the Soviet Union has succeeded to an astonishing degree in persuading the world to accept. Under this standard, the Soviets consider themselves at liberty to steal, lie, cheat, subvert, intrude into the affairs of nations, foment terrorism, incite and support wars throughout the world. All such actions, by Soviet definition, are in furtherance of "peace." Protests against Russian violations of the Helsinki Accords, psychiatric torture of peace advocates and dissidents, and persecution of religious believers, or efforts to propagate news and Western views inside the U.S.S.R. constitute provocative and intolerable interference in internal Soviet affairs. Such action, by Soviet definition, menaces "détente" and "peace" and pushes the world toward nuclear war.

But the world does not have to obey Soviet rules and definitions. Repeatedly, the Soviet Union has declared that in relations with the West, it is committed, as Andropov himself put it, to a "bitter and stubborn struggle on all fronts—economic, political and ideological." If so, then the West must transform the Soviet Union itself into a battleground, a battleground of ideas.

The West should flood the Soviet Union with books by great Russian authors who bear persuasive witness to Soviet realities and articulate the primordial longing of the people for restoration of the greatness of Russian culture. As factually and objectively as human competence allows, it should broadcast day and night to the Soviet people news of events in their country. The self-published writings and appeals of Soviet intellectuals and artists should be circulated and broadcast back into the Soviet Union so that their authors will know they are not spiritually isolated, alone, and helpless against the overwhelming might of the state.

The Soviet oligarchy fears nothing so much as the subversive effects of the ideas of truth and freedom, especially when the ideas are voiced by Russians themselves. That is why the greatest living Russian authors have been deported as lepers, and their works banned, as if they were germs of a fearful plague.

So long as the Soviet Union persists in attacking, then the West must seek and accept confidential alliances with individual Soviet citizens who offer them. In the judgment of Levchenko, never have so many Russians in the intelligence and foreign policy establishments, even in the Party hierarchy itself, been willing to enter into such alliances. From briefings received in the KGB, he cites three remarkable examples.

While stationed in Algiers during the mid-1970's, senior GRU Colonel Anatoli Nikolaevich Filatov approached the CIA and proposed to collaborate with the United States. As a professional intelligence officer, he well knew what he was risking. He also well knew how best to hurt the Party.

Rendezvousing with the CIA in Algiers over a span of some 14 months, Colonel Filatov passed volumes of Soviet intelligence and military secrets. Among the more important data were details of Soviet involvement in terrorism and guerrilla warfare in many parts of the world.

Reassigned to Moscow, Filatov continued to give the CIA operational secrets collected in GRU headquarters. He survived nearly a year before KGB surveillants caught him filling a drop, which they probably had located in consequence of following an American agent. After months of interrogation, the Soviets sentenced Filatov to death.*

The KGB also briefed Levchenko about the dramatic case of Aleksandr Dmitrevich Ogorodnik, a Ministry of Foreign Affairs officer who changed from an idealistic Communist into a passionate anti-Communist. Serving at the Soviet embassy in Bogotá, Colombia, Ogorodnik made contact with the CIA sometime in 1974, and by the time his tour ended in 1975, he was thoroughly trained in espionage tradecraft.

Back in Moscow, Ogorodnik maneuvered himself into the Global Affairs Department of the Ministry of Foreign Affairs, one of the few MFA sections the KGB trusts with sensitive intelligence. The Global Affairs Department is also the repository of other exceedingly secret and revealing data. Each Soviet ambassador must annually submit a comprehensive report analyzing the political situation, likely developments, and Soviet standing in the country where he is stationed. The KGB Residency is required to assist by contributing information and judgments derived from its agent network. If person-

*As part of a deal resulting in repatriation of two KGB officers arrested *in flagrante delicto* in New Jersey in 1978, they promised to commute the sentence to 15 years' imprisonment.

al relations between the Resident and Ambassador are good, the Residency usually makes available virtually all it knows. An astute analyst reading these annual reports could look at the world as the Kremlin views it, ascertain Soviet strengths and weaknesses in given nations, infer much about Soviet intentions and, in some cases, gauge the nature and extent of KGB penetrations.

For 20 months, Ogorodnik conveyed to the CIA microfilm of hundreds of secret Soviet documents, including many ambassadorial reports. The CIA circulated their essence to the White House, the National Security Council and the State Department, and by the summer of 1977 the KGB became aware that the Soviet Union was suffering a hemorrhage of political secrets. Initially, KGB investigators could glean no indication of where the puncture might have occurred, but as they more precisely defined the intelligence being discussed in Washington, they focused upon the Department of Global Affairs. Analyses and surveillances of personnel yielded nothing; strict controls seemingly precluded removal of documents, and inventories showed none missing. Sure that no one would dare photograph documents except when few people were in the offices, the KGB installed concealed television cameras, which continuously monitored the spaces at night and on weekends. On a Saturday night, one of the cameras photographed Ogorodnik photographing documents with a tiny camera made in America.

Upon being arrested, Ogorodnik capitulated immediately, in effect telling his inquisitors: My beliefs and yours are different. When I began, I knew exactly what I was doing, and I knew the price I would pay if you caught me. I am prepared now to pay. I bear you no ill will personally; I understand that you must do your job. I see no reason to obstruct your work and I will cooperate fully. In fact, if you like, I will be glad to write down everything that happened from the first day I met the CIA. Then you can ask whatever you want.

After preliminary questioning, interrogators led Ogorodnik to a cell and gave him desk, pen and paper.

"By the way, for many years I have written with the same pen, a Mont Blanc," Ogorodnik said. "I think it's on the top of my desk. If one of your people happens to go near my apartment in the next few days, I'd like to have it."

Soon the KGB delivered the Mont Blanc pen, which contained poison so cleverly hidden that only an expert in concealment could have discovered it. Ogorodnik opened it, swallowed a pill, and died within ten seconds. The KGB, so Levchenko was told, never ascertained just how he communicated with the CIA in Moscow, or all that he communicated, or whether he had confederates.

The case which affected Levchenko most was that of Arkadi Shevchenko. On any authoritative 1978 list of the 100 most important Party figures, the name of Shevchenko would surely have appeared. Graduated from the Institute of International Relations with a doctoral degree in 1954, he rose almost magically in the Ministry of Foreign Affairs, wafted ever upward by his own abilities and the patronage of his friend and mentor, Soviet Foreign Minister Andrei Gromyko. The Party awarded him full ambassadorial rank when he was 40, allowed him to become Under-Secretary General of the United Nations in 1973, and regarded him as one of its foremost experts on disarmament. Beyond Gromyko, Shevchenko knew and conferred with Politburo members, including Brezhnev and the leading ideologues of the International Department, Suslov and Ponomarev. Soviet rulers so trusted and relied upon Shevchenko that as his five-year term at the United Nations neared expiration in 1978, they decided to keep him there two more years.

According to the Line X colonel who first told Levchenko the story of Shevchenko, in early 1977 the Soviets were surprised by how well the Americans comprehended and even anticipated their positions regarding arms-limitation issues. As American prescience continued, Soviet suspicions grew, and the KGB began to investigate. By 1978, the KGB reached an appalling conclusion: In all likelihood, the amazing foreknowledge the Americans seemed to possess could be provided by one of only three persons—Soviet Ambassador to the United States Anatoli Dobrynin, Soviet Ambassador to the United Nations Oleg Troyanovsky, or Shevchenko. Andropov requested and obtained from a mortified Politburo special dispensation to investigate these three illustrious suspects.* The KGB caused each to receive an authentic, undoctored Top Secret document stating new Soviet positions concerning arms limitations, and then put each under surveillance. Only Shevchenko escaped his watchers. When the Russians and Americans next chatted informally, the Soviets surmised that the contents of the document were known.

Moscow soon sent Shevchenko a cheerful cable: He was doing a grand job. Everyone was pleased he had consented to soldier on in New York two more years. As he would be there longer than expected, however, there were a few matters that ought to be discussed in Moscow at his convenience. No great rush. Any time in the next few weeks would be fine.

The first week in April 1978, Shevchenko told his staff that illness of his mother-in-law necessitated a trip to Moscow, and doubtless he would have returned to Moscow had not a friend alighted in New York on temporary duty. "I don't know what's going on in Moscow, but the KGB is after your ass," he confided. "If you go back, you'll never get out again." Thereupon, Arkadi Shevchenko, Under-Secretary General of the United Nations, intimate of the Soviet Foreign Minister and confidant of the Politburo, announced his defection.

Continuing the investigation, KGB agents traced the travels and activities of Shevchenko in the United States during preceding years. They found that beginning about 30 months before his defection, he often ran up daily hotel bills in excess of $500 and otherwise spent money far more lavishly than his salary would permit. Ultimately, they also found that for about 30 months he had been working as a controlled agent of the FBI and CIA. If the Americans wanted to know something about Soviet policy or intentions, Shevchenko simply asked

*The KGB is strictly forbidden to investigate ranking Party personages without express Politburo authorization.

Moscow or his benefactor Gromyko. Which of the 450 or so
Soviet nationals employed by or assigned to the United Nations in New York belonged to the KGB or GRU? Shevchenko,
as the second ranking Russian at the U.N., could easily point
out most. Who in the Party hierarchy in Moscow and the
Soviet foreign service around the world might be amenable to
future American recruitment? Shevchenko had some good
ideas. Were the Russians earnest about achieving meaningful
reductions in strategic and conventional arms, and would they
honor agreements negotiated? As a leading Soviet strategist
on disarmament, Shevchenko could supply not just authoritative judgments but evidentiary answers.

For the KGB, the whole mess was too horrific to sort out,
and it eventually gave up trying. That was the Party's problem: Shevchenko was above all else the Party's man. The
Party preferred passivity to embarrassment, and thus hushed
up the affair.

The presence of Levchenko himself in the United States
further attests to the growing vulnerabilities of the Soviet
Union and the KGB. The fact that such an accomplished
officer, who was trusted with the most sensitive duties in one
of the four or five most important Residencies in the world,
would cast away his whole career and all he had for nothing
except freedom suggests the difficulties the KGB faces within
its own ranks. And Levchenko is not alone.

Sometime in the summer of 1982, a young Russian, very
much like Levchenko in background, intellect and ideals,
defected to the British from Tehran. He was Vladimir Andreevich Kuzichkin, an attaché from the Soviet consulate. Born in
1947 in Moscow, Kuzichkin attended good secondary schools
and served three compulsory years in the army, part of them in
East Germany. Upon discharge, he entered Moscow University
and mastered Farsi while concentrating upon Oriental studies.

Kuzichkin's exemplary military and academic record, combined with his personal urbanity and popularity, made him an
ideal candidate for the KGB, and the First Chief Directorate
drafted him when he was graduated in 1975. After he complet-

ed the basic foreign intelligence course, the KGB assigned him to Directorate S, where he underwent highly specialized training.

Aside from Department 16, which tries to subvert foreign cipher and communications personnel, Directorate S is probably the most secret component of the KGB. In addition to harboring the department responsible for assassinations and sabotage, it selects, trains and directs illegal agents throughout the world. So far as is known, prior to 1982 no foreign intelligence service had ever succeeded in recruiting or securing the defection of a staff officer from Directorate S.

Having impressed his superiors at the Center, Kuzichkin was posted to the KGB Residency in Tehran in 1977 as an Illegals Support officer. There he watched and participated in KGB machinations during the last days of the Shah and the subsequent rise of Khomeini. Initially, he confined himself largely to his own duties, which entailed slipping out alone at night to remote drops, where he left instructions for agents or recovered their reports for transmission to the Center. But as his professionalism gained him the confidence of the Resident and as Khomeini expelled more and more KGB officers from Tehran, he was drawn into the Residency brain trust and thus came to know about a much wider range of operations, including those in Afghanistan. Twice Kuzichkin was promoted in the field, and by 1982 he had attained the rank of major.

But in 1982, Kuzichkin, for virtually the same reasons as Levchenko, had decided that he could no longer tolerate life within the Soviet system—or the KGB. It is unclear whether he was long in touch with the British before his flight, or whether he made his own way to the West. In any case, during the summer of 1982 Kuzichkin disappeared. The Illegals Directorate was devastated and large numbers of its officers and networks identified.

The flights of Arkadi Shevchenko, Stanislav Levchenko and Vladimir Kuzichkin each confronted Soviet oligarchs with a clear if difficult choice. They could thoroughly and objectively investigate and question in search of answers: How did this happen? What was the cause? How can we prevent a recurrence of such catastrophe? The other alternative was to pretend that nothing of consequence had happened, to cover up and thereby avoid the embarrassment, the trauma of wholesale dismissals and bureaucratic cataclysms that the truth would dictate.

In each instance, the oligarchy chose the latter alternative. The KGB was so afraid of the truth about Kuzichkin that it behaved almost as if it did not want to ascertain his fate. The Soviets were so desultory in their inquiries about him that they did not learn where he was until October 1982, when, to scotch press rumors and end speculation, the British decided to inform them.

Few people in the West will now work for the Soviets unless they are trapped, ensnared, bribed—or duped into thinking they are working for something else. In the Soviet Union, there is a small yet growing band of idealists—some well placed—willing to war secretly against a system that smothers the spirit of Russia and strangles the lives and hopes of its people. They are motivated not by greed, vanity or fear, but by patriotism, claustrophobia, and resolve to strike back, to liberate and rebuild their native land.

The KGB serves a corrupt oligarchy, and in operations abroad it is circumscribed only by what the oligarchy thinks it can get away with. Inside the Soviet Union, the KGB is constrained not at all, except by the innate strength and character of the Russian people, which more than 60 years of tyranny has failed to extirpate. Western intelligence agencies serve democratically elected governments, which can ignore only at their peril the conscience of their people, the norms of civilized behavior and the laws of their society.

Because of these fundamental differences, there is an imbalance in the secret war, an imbalance that is both real and illusory. The real imbalance results from the unequal resources and restraints each side applies or does not apply. The erroneously perceived imbalance is between the respective vulnerabilities of democratic and totalitarian political systems.

Because democracy does not ultimately depend upon secrecy, there is a limit to the damage a spy can inflict, grave though that damage may be. Because democracy depends upon a continuing contest of divergent ideas, there is a limit to the damage subversive ideas can inflict, for they inevitably will be countered in free debate.

The Soviet system, relying as it must upon secrecy and stealth, can tolerate no penetration or leakage, for when penetration or leakage occurs, the consequences can be catastrophic. Because the Soviet system can tolerate no contest of conflicting ideas, an idea subversive to the system can travel with exceeding force and velocity, once let loose.

As the Soviet Party bureaucracy blunders on, growing first more arthritic and then more wily, it becomes increasingly vulnerable to the KGB officer or the Party *apparatchik* who rips off the veil—and to ideas of human liberty.

Ignored, the conditions that catapulted Levchenko and Kuzichkin into the West persist, and their persistence guarantees future calamities. It is the same with all Soviet society. Until Andropov and the men from the KGB he has elevated to pivotal positions of power dare to initiate radical internal changes, the economic and social malignancies, of which they themselves are acutely aware, will persist and grow. Without substantive reforms, the world during the 1980s can only expect more of what it received from the Soviet Union in the 1970s—more and greater Active Measures, more and greater clandestine assault.

Until visible changes in the Soviet Union occur, the world will do well to remember some of Andropov's words: "The arena of historic confrontation between socialism and capitalism is the whole world, all spheres of social life, economics, ideology, politics." And, "Cheka authorities [the KGB] operate in an area where there are not, nor can there be, truces and breathing spaces."

The world might also bear in mind that Andropov's occasional smiles are not always benign. While Andropov was Ambassador to Hungary, the Budapest police had a gypsy band, and Andropov sometimes called Police Chief Sandor Kopacsi to ask that it play at the Soviet embassy. On November 5, 1956, as Soviet tanks prowled the city, Kopacsi and his wife were captured while fleeing toward refuge in the Yugoslav embassy. The captors took them to the Soviet embassy and Andropov. "He met us, and was rather cordial and friendly," Kopacsi recalled long afterward. One might have thought all was well, but suddenly the KGB dragged the couple away to prison. Kopacsi can still vividly recall looking back and seeing Andropov standing at the embassy gate, waving to him and smiling.

APPENDIX A

SOVIET OFFICIALS EXPELLED OR WITHDRAWN BECAUSE OF INVOLVEMENT IN ESPIONAGE OR SUBVERSIVE ACTIVITIES 1974 TO 1983

Unless otherwise stated, all those named in this list are officers of the KGB. Since publication of the first edition this list has been revised to include the most recent expulsions of Soviet officials.

Abramov, Mikhail Nikolaevich: Canada, March 1982
Aleksandrov, Leonid Nikolaevich: Switzerland, February 1981
Aleksanyan, Eduard Ivanovich (GRU): Canada, January 1980
Alekseyev, Vladimir Ilich: USA, February 1977
Andreyev, Anatoli Viktorovich: USA, January 1975
Androsov, Andrei Stanislavovich: France, April 1983
Andrusov, Eduard Valentinovich: Sudan, May 1977
Arutyunov, Malkas Levonovich: Iran, May 1983
Asadullayev, Allakhverdi Mibulai Ogli: Iran, May 1983
Averin, Yuri Dmitrevich (GRU): Sweden, December 1982
Babayants, Yuri Arkhamovich (GRU): Portugal, January 1982
Barabanov, Leonid Andreevich (GRU): Switzerland, August 1982
Baratov, Nikolai Andreevich: North Yemen, August 1977
Bardeyev, Igor Aleksandrovich (GRU): Canada, January 1980
Barmyantsev, Yevgenni Nikolaevich (GRU): USA, April 1983
Baryshev, Viktor Ivanovich (GRU): Thailand, May 1983
Bashmashnikov, Yevgenni Ivanovich: West Germany, June 1979
Baykov, Vladilen Vasilevich: Pakistan, July 1981
Belik, Gennadi Sergeevich: France, April 1983
Besedin, Timor Anatolevich: Norway, April 1981
Bibikov, Valeri Ivanovich: Italy, December 1982
Bobin, Oleg Georgevich: France, April 1983
Bochkov, Viktor Alekseevich: France, April 1983
Bogomolov, Yevgenni Vasilevich: Switzerland, September 1976
Bondarev, Aleksandr Aleksandrovich: Singapore, February 1982
Borishpolets, Vadim Anatolevich: Canada, February 1978
Bryantsev, Igor Nikolaevich: West Germany, March 1977
Burmistrov, Gennadi Makarovich: Netherlands, April 1976
Bychkov, Anatoli Yefimovich: Ghana, August 1978
Bychkov, Yuri Ivanovich: Spain, March 1981
Bykov, Yuri Georgevich: France, April 1983
Charchyan, Eduard Babkenovich: USA, June 1975
Chekmasov, Valeri Viktorovich (GRU): France, April 1983
Chelyag, Ivan Mikhailovich (GRU): Italy, December 1982
Chernov, Vladimir Aleksandrovich: UK, January 1983
Chernov, Yuri Viktorovich: France, April 1983
Chernyayev, Rudolf Petrovich: USA, May 1978
Chernyayev, Sergei Viktorovich (GRU): Netherlands, March 1978
Chernysh, Yuri Stepanovich: Costa Rica, August 1979
Chetverikov, Nikolai Nikolaevich: France, April 1983
Chistyakov, Aleksei Fedorovich: Egypt, September 1981
Churanov, Oleg Viktorovich: Spain, February 1980
Churyanov, Yuri Dmitrevich: France, April 1983
Dementyev, Aleksandr Vladimirovich: Norway, January 1977

Dmitriev, Igor Ivanovich: Malaysia, June 1976
Dokudovsky, Oleg Dmitrevich (GRU): Norway, February 1982
Druzhinin, Vadim: Bangladesh, June 1976
Dubas, Oleg Konstantinovich (GRU): Portugal, March 1982
*Dumov, Aleksei Nikolaevich: Switzerland, May 1983
Dzhashi, Enriko Avksentevich: USA, July 1977
Enger, Valdik Aleksandrovich: USA, May 1978
Fedorin, Vasili Nikolaevich: Spain, April 1982
Filippov, Boris Anatolevich (GRU): France, June 1978
Finenko, Aleksandr Pavlovich (GRU): Indonesia, February 1982
Fomenko, Valentin Petrovich (GRU): Ghana, January 1974
Frolov, Vyacheslav Ivanovich: France, February 1980
Gadzhiyev, Abdulkhalik Magomedovich: USA, June 1975
Gerasimov, Gennadi Borisovich: France, April 1983
Geyvandov, Konstantin Yervendovich: Canada, January 1974
Golovanov, Vladimir Vladimirovich: Iran, July 1980
Golovatenko, Yuri Vasilevich: Spain, March 1981
Gordeyev, Vladimir A.: Portugal, March 1982
Goryachev, Yuri Vasilevich: France, April 1983
Govorukhin, Valeri Nikolaevich: France, April 1983
Grenkov, Vladimir Fedorovich: France, April 1983
Gromov, Sergei Zakharovich: Norway, January 1977
Guliyev, Gusein Abasgulievich (GRU): Iran, May 1983
Isayev, Yuri Nikolaevich (GRU): Spain, April 1978
Ivanov, Sergei Vladimirovich (GRU): UK, March 1983
Ivanov, Valeri Nikolaevich: Australia, April 1983
Ivanov, Yevgenni Fedorovich: France, March 1976
Ivashkevich, Gennadi Vladimirovich: Canada, February 1978
Kabanov, Boris Nikolaevich: Iran, September 1977
Kamensky, Aleksandr Vasilevich: France, April 1983
Kanavsky, Vadim Ivanovich (GRU): India, December 1974
Kapitonov, Konstantin: Egypt, September 1981
Karelin, Vadim Vasilevich (GRU): West Germany, May 1976
Karpov, Yevgenni Petrovich: USA, February 1977
Kartavtsev, Valeri Vasilevich: France, April 1983
Kedrov, Viktor Nikolaevich: Denmark, August 1975
Khamidulin, Zavdat Lutfulovich: Malaysia, July 1981
Khlystov, Vladimir Timofeevich: Netherlands, April 1976
Khrisanov, Yevgenni Nikolaevich (GRU): Iran, May 1983
Khvostantsev, Lev Grigorevich: Canada, February 1977
Kinyapin, Andrei Leonidovich: Italy, May 1980
Kisayev, Yuri: Equatorial Guinea, February 1981
Kiselev, Anatoli Aleksandrovich (GRU): Netherlands, August 1975
Klimanov, Yevgenni Aleksandrovich: Norway, January 1977
Koblov, Yevgenni Konstantinovich: Canada, February 1978

*Dumov used his position as Novosti Bureau Chief for interference in internal affairs, subversion and to infiltrate the peace movement.

Kocheshkov, Anatoli Nikolaevich: Iran, May 1983
Kochev, Anatoli Kazimovich: Sweden, December 1982
Kolosov, A. A. (GRU): China, January 1974
Konoval, Aleksandr Fedorovich (GRU): Netherlands, February 1983
Konstantinov, Oleg Vadimovich: USA, April 1983
Konyayev, Vladimir Vasilevich (GRU): Portugal, August 1980
Korepanov, Gennadi Varlamovich: France, April 1983
Korniyenko, Anatoli Fedorovich (GRU): Bangladesh, May 1976
Kotov, Yuri Mikhailovich: France, April 1983
Kovalev, Aleksei Gavrilovich (GRU): Canada, December 1974
Kovalev, Nikolai Grigorevich: Nigeria, March 1981
Kozyrev, Nikolai Ivanovich: Iran, May 1983
Kozyrev, Vitali Stepanovich (GRU): France, April 1983
Krasilnikov, Anatoli Ivanovich: Spain, February 1980
Krepkogorsky, Valeri Viktorovich: France, April 1983
Krivtsov, Yuri Ivanovich: France, April 1983
Krysin, Andrei Vladimirovich: Canada, February 1978
Kryuchkov, Sergei Vladimirovich: France, April 1983
Kukhar, Aleksandr Afanaseevich: USA, October 1979
Kulagin, Aleksandr S. (GRU): Portugal, August 1980
Kulemekov, Vladimir Yanovich (GRU): France, November 1981
Kulik, Vladimir Yevgennevich (GRU): France, October 1979
Kulikovskikh, Vladimir Kirillovich (GRU): France, April 1983
Kuznetsov, Anatoli Vasilevich: Italy, August 1981
Lapshin, Anatoli Konstantinovich (GRU): Iran, May 1983
Larkin, Anatoli Alekseevich: Singapore, February 1982
Lazarev, Vladimir Vladimirovich: Bangladesh, August 1981
Lazin, Viktor Nikolaevich: UK, August 1981
Leonov, Vadim Vasilevich: Netherlands, April 1981
Leonov, Yuri Petrovich (GRU): USA, September 1981
Lesiovsky, Viktor Mechislavovich: Spain, June 1977
Lezin, Oleg Sergeevich: Switzerland, April 1975
Lilenurm, Petr Rudolfovich: Canada, February 1978
Lisin, Yuri Viktorovich: USA, November 1977
Liyepa, Albert Andreevich: Sweden, April 1982
Lobanov, Vladislav Sergeevich: Sudan, May 1977
Lopukhov, Roman Mikhailovich (GRU): Netherlands, March 1978
Lovchikov, Vasili Dmitrevich (GRU): Switzerland, April 1979
Lugovoy, Vladimir Vasilevich (GRU): Switzerland, February 1983
Lyko, Anatoli Alekseevich (GRU): Malaysia, May 1975
Machekhin, Aleksandr Yegorovich: Japan, May 1976
Manukyan, Ashot Babkenovich: France, April 1983
Marakhovsky, Yuri Nikolaevich: USA, October 1981
Marchenko, Vladimir Ivanovich: China, January 1974
Marchenko, Yuri Fedorovich: Egypt, January 1981
Markelov, Aleksandr Pavlovich: India, August 1980
Markov, Valeri Aleksandrovich (GRU): Iran, May 1983
Matveyev, Albert Alekseévich: Portugal, August 1980

Matveyev, Yuri Gennadevich: France, April 1983
Mayorov, Vladimir Mikhailovich: France, April 1983
Merkulov, Vladimir Dmitrevich: Denmark, October 1981
Mikhalin, Anatoli Aleksandrovich: Canada, February 1978
Mikhaylov, Yevgenni Nikolaevich: Belgium, May 1983
Mikheyev, Aleksandr Nikolaevich: USA, April 1983
Minkov, Yuri (GRU): Egypt, July 1976
Mironenko, Sergei Vladimirovich: Singapore, February 1982
Mironenko, Yevgenni Sergeevich: Norway, April 1981
Mizin, Viktor Vladimirovich: India, March 1976
Mordovets, Aleksandr Leonidovich: Costa Rica, August 1979
Morozov, Mikhail M.: Portugal, January 1982
Motorov, Yevgenni Leonidovich: Denmark, February 1983
Muerner, Igor Ivanovich: Switzerland, October 1974
Mukhin, Yevgenni Nikolaevich: France, April 1983
Muravyev, Aleksei Alekseevich: France, April 1983
Mushchinin, Sergei Yefimovich: Brazil, January 1975
Muzykin, Ivan Ivanovich: Liberia, March 1981
Myagkov, Grigori Petrovich: Switzerland, June 1978
Nagornoy, Yevgenni Dmitrevich: France, April 1983
Nesterov, Aleksandr Ivanovich: France, April 1983
Nesytykh, Vladislav Leonidovich: Liberia, June 1981
Nikiforov, Oleg Nikolaevich: West Germany, June 1979
Nilov, Viktor Prokopevich: Ghana, August 1978
Nurutdinov, Bakhtiar Sirodshevich: France, April 1983
Obidin, Vyacheslav Aleksandrovich: Portugal, March 1982
Ogurtsov, Aleksandr Viktorovich: France, April 1983
Oshkaderov, Vladimir Ivanovich: Canada, February 1978
Osipov, Aleksei Nikolaevich: Denmark, August 1975
Oslikovsky, Sergei Nikolaevich: Spain, April 1983
Pagonets, Anatoli Ivanovich: France, April 1983
Panchenko, Aleksei Yakovlevich: Iran, October 1981
Panfilov, Aleksandr Leonidovich (GRU): Iran, May 1983
Pape, Andrei Aleksandrovich: France, April 1983
Pashukov, Aleksandr Alekseevich (GRU): Denmark, October
    1977
Penkov, Viktor Aleksandrovich (GRU): France, July 1978
Pereversev, Yuri V. (GRU): Egypt, April 1979
Petrakov, Igor V.: Egypt, September 1981
Petrosyan, Petros Artachesovich: USA, June 1975
Petrov, Georgi Georgevich: Norway, April 1981
Petrov, Valentin Mikhailovich: Liberia, March 1981
Pivovarov, Yuri Sergeevich (GRU): Spain, March 1977
Plakhtiy, Vladimir Vasilevich (GRU): Iran, May 1983
Pokrovsky, Sergei Georgevich: Switzerland, March 1982
Poleshchuk, Anatoli Ivanovich (GRU): Netherlands, March 1978
Polomarchuk, Valeri Vladimirovich: Sudan, May 1977
Polyakov, Vladimir Porfirevich: Egypt, September 1981

†Poperechny, Vladimir Ivanovich: Liberia, April 1979
Popov, Yuri Pavlovich (GRU): Spain, May 1978
Primakov, Gennadi Alekseevich (GRU): UK, March 1983
Printsipalov, Aleksandr Kirillovich: Norway, January 1977
Pugin, Sergei Yakovlevich: France, April 1983
Reztsov, Oleg Dmitrevich: Canada, February 1978
Romanov, Vladislav Petrovich: Malaysia, July 1981
Rostovsky, Grigori Grigorevich (GRU): France, March 1976
Rybachenko, Vladimir Ivanovich (GRU): France, February 1977
Samoylenko, Nikolai Aleksandrovich (GRU): Denmark, June 1977
Samunin, Valeri Ivanovich: Iran, May 1983
Sarychev, Mikhail Ivanovich: Iran, May 1983
Semenov, Yuri A.: China, January 1974
Semenychev, Yuri Konstantinovich: Portugal, August 1980
Sepelev, Yuri Fedeevich: Yugoslavia, March 1976
Shamirov, Elman Ibragim-Ogli: Iran, April 1978
Sharov, Anatoli Vasilevich: Denmark, August 1975
Shebanov, Yuri Konstantinovich: Egypt, September 1981
Shelenkov, Aleksandr Ivanovich: Egypt, October 1978
Shelepin, Vladimir Leonidovich: Egypt, October 1980
Shepelev, Viktor Pavlovich (GRU): West Germany, July 1981
Shipilov, Viktor Dmitrevich (GRU): France, April 1983
Shirokov, Oleg Alekseevich: France, April 1983
Shiroky, Petr Ivanovich (GRU): Sweden, December 1982
Shishkov, Viktor Ivanovich: France, April 1983
Shitov, Vasili Ivanovich (GRU): USA, February 1982
Shulikov, Lev Aleksandrovich: France, April 1983
Sidak, Valentin Antonovich: France, April 1983
Smirnov, Igor Petrovich (GRU): Switzerland, February 1981
Smirnov, Valeri Nikolaevich (GRU): Canada, July 1977
Smolin, Aleksandr Mikhailovich (GRU): Belgium, June 1982
Sofinsky, Vsevolod Nikolaevich: New Zealand, January 1980
Sokolov, Eduard Alekseevich (GRU): France, April 1983
Sokolov, Vladimir Ivanovich (GRU): Canada, January 1980
Solomonov, Yuri Aleksandrovich (GRU): France, June 1982
Solovyev, Mikhail Matveevich: France, October 1976
Stankevich, Nikolai Vasilevich (GRU): Denmark, October 1977
Stepanov, Gennadi Ivanovich: Malaysia, July 1981
Stepanov, Svyatoslav Alekseevich: USA, September 1976
Stolbunov, Vyacheslav Ivanovich (GRU): Switzerland, March 1982
Suchkov, Vitali Ivanovich: Spain, May 1981
Suntsov, Vladimir Gennadevich: Egypt, January 1981
Suvorov, Vladimir Leonidovich: Canada, February 1978
Sveshnikov, Gennadi Vasilevich (GRU): Spain, July 1977

†Although not identified as KGB Poperechny, Timoshkin and Trekhlebov were involved, probably on behalf of the International Department of the Central Committee of the CPSU, in organising anti-government demonstrations.

Syzdykov, Ased: Egypt, September 1981
Talanov, Nikolai Mikhailovich: Canada, February 1978
Telezhnikov, Viktor Andreevich: Egypt, April 1976
Tertishnikov, Vladimir Lukich: Spain, April 1982
Timoshek, Vladimir Vladimirovich: Mexico, May 1976
†Timoshkin, Mikhail Yevgennevich: Liberia, April 1979
Titov, Gennadi Fedorovich: Norway, February 1977
Titov, Igor Viktorovich: UK, March 1983
Titov, Sergei Nikolaevich: India, March 1976
Travkov, Gennadi Yakovlevich (GRU): France, February 1980
†Trekhlebov, Igor Gavrilovich: Liberia, April 1979
Trofimov, Vitali Konstantinovich: Canada, February 1980
Trushenko, Yuri: Egypt, January 1981
Tyurenkov, Aleksandr Ivanovich: Switzerland, March 1981
Vartanyan, Igor Paruirovich: Canada, February 1978
Vasilyev, Vladimir Mikhailovich (GRU): Canada, December 1976
Veber, Voldemar Pavlovich: Canada, February 1978
Vinogradov, Arkadiy Arkadyevich: Japan, June 1983
Vitebsky, Viktor Vasilevich (GRU): France, April 1983
Vlasov, Valeri Pavlovich: Egypt, September 1981
Vopelovsky, Yevgenni Konstantinovich (GRU): Norway, February 1982
Vorontsov, Oleg Sviatislavovich: France, April 1983
Vyatkin, Sergei Lazarevich: West Germany, October 1975
Yadroshnikov, Lev Konstantinovich (GRU): Egypt, August 1976
Yakubenko, Stanislav Aleksandrovich: France, April 1983
Yefremenkov, Vladimir Ilich: Spain, March 1981
Yefremov, Albert Dmitrevich (GRU): Ghana, September 1978
Yegorov, Sergei Petrovich (GRU): Indonesia, February 1982
Yemelianov, Igor Konstantinovich: Switzerland, January 1983
Yermakov, Oleg Vyacheslavovich: Denmark, September 1975
Yerokhin, Vyacheslav (GRU): Belgium, June 1982
Yudenkov, Vitali Sergeevich: France, April 1983
Zadneprovsky, Vadim Fedorovich (GRU): UK, February 1982
Zagrebnev, Vladimir Fedorovich (GRU): Norway, June 1983
Zarkich, Yuri Grigorevich: India, March 1976
Zarya, Vyacheslav Ivanovich: Iran, May 1983
Zashchirinsky, Igor Ivanovich: Norway, January 1977
Zaytsev, Aleksandr Fedorovich: France, April 1983
Zazulin, Anatoli Gerasimovich: Italy, January 1981
Zevakin, Yuri Fedorovich: France, April 1983
Zhadin, Boris Vasilevich: France, April 1983
Zinyakin, Vladimir Petrovich: USA, May 1978
Zolotukhin, Aleksei Nikiforovich: Bangladesh, August 1981
Zotin, Yevgenni Georgevich (GRU): Norway, January 1977
Zotov, Anatoli Pavlovich (GRU): UK, December 1982
Zuyenko, Oleg Sergeevich (GRU): Iran, January 1983

APPENDIX B

ORGANIZATION OF THE KGB

Author's note:

The basic mission of the KGB is, as it has always been, to preserve and expand the power of the Communist Party oligarchy throughout the world by essentially clandestine means. Within the past ten years or so, however, the KGB has undergone some organizational changes. They reflect shifts in operational emphasis, a quest for efficiency, reaction to past reversals, and an effort to repair conspicuous deficiencies. Doubtless there will be more changes in the future. But examination of the present structure affords another perspective of all the KGB will continue to be and do.

Most of the fresh data herein offered pertains to KGB elements involved in operations against foreigners and other nations. Brief descriptions of units that work against the Soviet people are included for reference purposes. In delineating the organization of the KGB, I have relied upon data reported by former Major Stanislav Aleksandrovich Levchenko as well as Western intelligence officers.

KGB headquarters are organized into five Chief Directorates, which are divided into Services and Departments. The First Chief Directorate conducts KGB operations abroad; the Second Chief Directorate is responsible for counterintelligence and control of the civilian population within the Soviet Union; the unnumbered Border Guards Directorate administers the KGB troops who patrol the frontiers and form an elite military force; the Fifth Chief Directorate is charged with suppression of ideological dissidence; the Eighth Chief Directorate monitors and tries to decipher foreign communications.

Additionally, there are lesser, independent directorates assigned specialized duties.

First Chief Directorate

There are three separate Directorates within the First Chief Directorate.

Directorate S, the largest, is in charge of KGB Illegals throughout the world and functions independently of other elements. One division recruits and trains Soviet citizens to be Illegals. Another prepares the stories or legends and false documentation that will enable them to assume fictitious identities in foreign societies. A third manages the agents already deployed, and a fourth administers the Illegal Support Officers stationed in foreign Residencies.

When practical, the KGB prefers to send out husband-wife teams, so it tries to select young couples or arrange marriages. A prospective Illegal normally undergoes at least three years of individual training in safe apartments around Moscow. Illegals additionally may spend several years in one foreign country orienting themselves to life abroad and building their legend before infiltrating the nation that is the ultimate target.

To forge documents and weave legends, the Directorate gathers minutiae about other nations—tourist brochures; street maps; telephone directories; records of births, deaths, and construction projects that demolish houses and buildings; old bus schedules; handwriting samples; copies of immigration, labor and alien registration laws. If a consular official who has been signing visas in Taiwan retires or resigns, the KGB wants to know, for his successor's handwriting will be different.

Illegal Support Officers, known in the Residencies as members of Line N, collect such data themselves and recruit low-level support agents to add more. But the main duty of the support officers is maintenance of communications between the Center and Illegals. They select sites for drops, caches of equipment, and meetings between officers from the Center and the agents, and frequently they load and unload the drops. Usually the support officer has a cover job in the consular section of the embassy, where he can examine foreign passports and amass information about current immigration procedures.

Directorate S in the 1970s absorbed the formerly independent Department V, charged with assassination and sabotage. After Oleg Lyalin defected in 1971 and was later found to have been a British agent, the KGB ravaged Department V, firing or demoting its senior officers and recalling all its representatives from Residencies abroad. The deputy director of the Department, a particularly distinguished and suave officer, was reduced to practicing agent meetings on the streets with students from the Foreign Intelligence School, and the Department, in effect, was disbanded.

Soon, though, it was reconstituted and gradually rebuilt as Department Eight of Directorate S. To reform support networks abroad, the KGB allowed Department Eight to take over agents of marginal utility from foreign Residencies and to reactivate agents who had been dropped because they no longer had access. By 1982, Department Eight appeared to be flourishing, and the upsurge in terrorism and sabotage training at its Balshikha complex suggests that the KGB envisions a busy future for it.

Directorate T, the second largest in the First Chief Directorate, is responsible for collection of scientific and technological intelligence, including the theft of high technology of all types. In addition to having been trained in clandestine tradecraft and languages, many, perhaps a majority, of Directorate T officers are qualified scientists or engineers, and a large number hold advanced degrees. A Directorate T research institute, near the Belyoruski railroad station in Moscow, employs hundreds of scientists, analysts and translators, who process the voluminous data flooding in from Residencies in the industrialized democracies. Directorate T officers and a veritable army of co-optees are positioned in all Ministries and Soviet organizations concerned with science and technology, and in those that have any regular dealings with foreign scientists. Soviet delegations to scientific symposia abroad invariably include Directorate T officers or trusted co-optees. If any continuing, overt relationship between Soviet and foreign scientists is not exploited by the KGB, that is the result of oversight.

In close consultation with the State Committee on Science and Technology (GKNT) and the Academy of Sciences, Directorate T defines national needs and undertakes to fulfill them in accordance with a master collection plan. Officers in Japan are instructed to answer one set of questions, those in America another set, and those in France still another. Combined at the Center, the collective answers often yield solutions to problems the Soviets have been unable to solve themselves. Similarly, equipment or even whole factories are assembled by procuring components separately—some from one place, some from another.

Officers from Directorate T, which in the field is called Line X, comprise a large percentage of the Residency staffs in industrialized countries. They tend to be less recognizable than other KGB officers because they actually are scientists and engineers who can live their cover as scientific counselors, trade mission members or Aeroflot employees.

Directorate K, known in the field as Line KR, is responsible for penetration of foreign intelligence and security services and for enforcement of ideological conformity among Soviet citizens abroad. It also assists the Ministry of Foreign Affairs in maintaining the physical security of Soviet embassies.

The Directorate is divided into both geographical and functional sections. Some sections try continuously to recruit foreign intelligence and security officers in different geographic sectors of the world. By all covert and overt means available, they collect information about individual personnel, organizational structure, operational methods and new tactics.

One section is charged with penetration of terrorist organizations abroad and another with control of Soviet merchant seamen, Aeroflot crews, and civilians allowed to travel abroad.

The most secret section, once authorized by the vice chairman of the First Chief Directorate, can investigate any officer in the Directorate and in so doing appropriate the resources of any element in the entire KGB.

A large number of Directorate K officers have come from the Second Chief Directorate and the provinces, where they acquired the mentality of internal repression. Their linguistic skills and general education tend to be poorer than those of the average First Chief Directorate officer. Accustomed to the ease of working inside the Soviet Union, many shrink from hazardous operations against foreign services and plead that they must concentrate upon the security of Soviet colonies abroad. As they preside over the eternal networks of informants within any colony, they as a group are distrusted and often disliked, especially by GRU officers, upon whom they also spy. There are, of course, exceptions, and Levchenko knew several excellent, honest officers in Line KR at the Tokyo Residency.

There are three important Services within the First Chief Directorate.

Service I, sometimes referred to in the KGB as Service 1, analyzes and disseminates the intelligence clandestinely collected by all elements of the First Chief Directorate. It also publishes a daily summary of current events for the Politburo and regularly submits forecasts of future world developments. (Agent reports adjudged particularly important are still sent directly to the Politburo in raw form and evaluated by Politburo members themselves.) Although Service I during the 1970s grew to be the third largest in the Foreign Directorate, it nevertheless lacks the manpower to digest the huge glut of intelligence gathered overtly. And occasionally it is not even able to absorb all the intelligence from agents.

Twice a month, Service I transmits to foreign Residencies an evaluation of all reports they have forwarded during the preceding two weeks, and it provides an annual evaluation of the overall reporting of each Residency. Upon request from a Residency, the Service reviews and assesses intelligence supplied by a given agent or contact during a defined period.

On the basis of his personal observations and the experience of the Tokyo Residency, Stanislav Levchenko believes that Service I makes a conscientious, scholarly effort to give the Politburo and other clients objective and accurate analyses. It does shade or doctor intelligence personally unflattering to Politburo members but eventually finds means to subtly communicate the facts. And Levchenko is convinced that regarding any important issue, the analysts would report the facts as they saw them, regardless of personal sensitivities.

Service I tends to be cautious in its long-range forecasts because it is upbraided whenever these prove to be wrong. However, in the mid-

1970s it did venture to predict a resurgence of political conservatism in the United States and Western Europe during the early 1980s.

Service A (Sluzhba Aktivnykh Meropriyatiyi, or Active Measures Service) evolved during the 1970s out of the former Department A, which was long known as the Disinformation Department. Its growth into one of the most important divisions in the KGB manifests greater reliance upon Active Measures as means of projecting Soviet influence.

The Service works closely with the International Department, the Department of Socialist Countries, and the Propaganda and Information Department of the Central Committee. It is staffed with some of the most gifted officers in the KGB, who are chosen on the basis of creativity, writing and analytical ability, or authoritative knowledge of a given nation or issue. The KGB bends the rules and tolerates a certain amount of eccentricity among these officers, who are notoriously heavy drinkers. It is said that in consequence of weekend imbibing, Service A accomplishes little work on Monday mornings, and its spaces are rife with the fumes of virtually every form of alcohol known to man.

Foreigners who have been forced to flee to the Soviet Union advise the Service about nuances of language and life-styles in other nations. It has its own facilities for production of forgeries, fabrications, and literature of disguised origin. An entire section of the Novosti press agency is reserved for the Service's personnel, and the Academy of Sciences accommodates a goodly number of them in its humanities divisions.

The idea of a new Active Measure or Active Measures campaign may originate anywhere—within Service A itself, a Residency abroad, the International Department or even the Politburo. Once approved by the Politburo, the idea is referred to Service A, which drafts a plan and supervises its implementation, often in cooperation with the International Department.

Service A presently has no officers permanently stationed abroad, and execution of Active Measures is left to the Residencies, the foreign Communist Parties and Soviet front organizations. In each major Residency an Active Measures officer, who belongs to Line PR, receives instructions from Service A and parcels out assignments to officers handling agents best suited to do what needs to be done.

Periodically, Service A publishes a Top Secret bulletin for the Politburo, charting the progress or successes of the most important Active Measures, and these accounts are read avidly by the Soviet leadership, which itself participates in the bigger campaigns.

Service R continuously analyzes in detail KGB operations abroad, with a view toward improving them. By the late 1960s, the worldwide networks of KGB agents had become so huge and unwieldy that they were impervious to centralized control, planning and coordination. In some countries, the networks had grown old and were peopled with agents who had lost access or could report on subjects no longer of interest. In other countries, priority targets had not been penetrated, and Residencies were occupying themselves with matters of peripheral interest. And in still others, carelessness and poor planning had resulted in the unraveling of networks or disruptive expulsions of KGB officers.

The KGB believed that the CIA had a division that, with the aid of computers, constantly monitored the performance of all agents and could quickly determine which were the most valuable or promising in terms of global requirements. Intending to duplicate, it established an Operational Analysis and Planning unit, which during the 1970s became Service R. Initially a sinecure for compromised or worn-out officers, this Service now is staffed with first-rate men, many of whom have been Residents or Group Chiefs abroad.

Granted broad authority to examine files at the Center, Service R personnel record and analyze details and results of each officer's every meeting with an agent throughout the world. They submit to the director of the First Chief Directorate statistical reports and analyses of each foreign Residency's network, including level and quality of penetrations as well as number and potential of newly recruited agents. They also try to keep a record of each reported contact between a Soviet citizen and a foreigner abroad.

Levchenko heard that as of 1979 Service R was still using cardotacks to maintain records, having been unable to acquire computers appropriate to its endeavors. But Residencies around the world still had to reckon with Service R, and they increasingly feared an unfavorable evaluation from it.

Important as the respective Services are, the operational core of the Foreign Directorate lies in its eleven geographic Departments. These departments send out and administer the officers who form Line PR in each Residency, and generally they are the most able the KGB has in the field. Although the letters "PR" stand for the Russian words meaning Political Intelligence, officers from the geographic Departments are unrestricted in their hunting. While managing Agents of Influence and executing Active Measures. they also try to penetrate the government, press, political factions, and labor and religious movements of their target country—to steal its most guarded secrets. If they have an opportunity to suborn an intelligence or military officer or a scientist, they will do so.

The eleven Departments and their attack areas are:

First Department—United States and Canada;

Second Department—Latin America;

Third Department—United Kingdom, Australia, New Zealand and Scandinavia;

Fourth Department—Federal Republic of Germany and Austria;

Fifth Department—France, Italy, Spain, the Netherlands, Belgium, Luxembourg and Ireland;

Sixth Department—China, Vietnam, Korea, Kampuchea (Cambodia);

Seventh Department—Japan, Indonesia, the Philippines, Thailand, Singapore;

Eighth Department—the Arab nations, Turkey, Greece, Iran, Afghanistan, Albania;

Ninth Department—African nations wherein English is the predominant foreign language;

Tenth Department—African nations wherein French is the predominant foreign language;

Seventeenth Department—India, Pakistan, Bangladesh, Sri Lanka. (These nations were formerly the responsiblity of the Seventh Department. To intensify operations against both Japan and India, the KGB divided responsibility among two Departments. The new Department was numbered Seventeen because existing Departments had claim to lower numbers.)

Each geographic Department is subdivided into Desks, which oversee particular countries or individual Residencies within a country. The First Department, for example, has a Washington Desk, New York Desk, San Francisco Desk, Canadian Desk, and a Desk that coordinates operations against U.S. citizens abroad. Generally, the typical officer may expect to spend his entire career in the geographic Department that he joins upon entering the Foreign Directorate. However, each Residency, wherever located, has a Main Enemy or American Group that tries to recruit U.S. citizens and undermine U.S. interests in its area of operations. And an officer who has worked in a Main Enemy Group in, say, Cairo or New Delhi, might well be transferred to the First Department and duty in the United States.

There are also functional Departments in the First Chief Directorate.

The *Eleventh Department* conducts liaison with and penetrates the intelligence services of Soviet satellite nations, all of which in their foreign operations are required to serve the KGB. Soviet control of these services is effected primarily through the relationships between the Moscow oligarchy and the oligarchies of the satellite state. But the KGB also influences the services by developing its own agents within them and through liaison officers stationed at their headquarters. The KGB most trusts the Bulgarians, East Germans and Cubans. The Bulgarians are good at terrorism, drug and arms smuggling, and the rougher forms of clandestine operations. The East Germans excel in espionage against West Germany and have shown themselves in Africa to be more effective subversives than the Russians. The Cubans are best at influence operations, both in the United States and Third World, and their analyses of the United States are outstanding. All of the satellite services, however, contribute to the Soviet causes. None of the satellite states, including Cuba, is allowed to pursue a foreign policy of its own. Yet, at onerous expense to their people, they support large clandestine services, which benefit the Soviet Union.

The *Twelfth Department*, described in Chapter I, represents an imaginative innovation and perhaps grows out of Yuri Andropov's conviction that "all spheres" of the world are part of the combat arena. The concept underlying it is that senior officers who have proven themselves abroad should be free to chase and capture quarry anywhere in the world. The Department is composed mainly of veterans who, in consequence of long service overseas, well understand foreign languages, mores, and mind sets, and who are accustomed to mingling among different nationalities. From cover positions in the Academy of Sciences, the Institute for USA and Canada, and other prestigious-sounding "research institutes," they naturally can meet foreigners visiting the Soviet Union. Just as naturally, they can travel abroad to engage in "research" at Western universities or attend sundry international conferences. Thus, they can spot and follow prospects almost anywhere. Department Twelve has been so successful that it is likely to be expanded into a full-fledged Service.

(Apparently, there currently is no Department Thirteen. For many years, the assassination and sabotage unit was designated Department Thirteen, before it became Department V, then Department Eight of Directorate S. If a Department Thirteen now exists, its functions are unknown to the sources available to the author.)

Department Fourteen develops and supplies the technical tools of clandestine operations—concealment devices, self-destruct containers for transporting secret documents and film, disguised audio and radio equipment, incapacitating chemicals, special cameras, secret writing, etc. Its laboratory produces the special poisons and assassination devices for Department Eight of Directorate S. The Department trains technicians from Soviet Bloc intelligence and security services and, on occasion, important KGB agents. The Technical Operations officers, who guard the audio security of the Residencies and monitor police and counterintelligence frequencies, are from Department Fourteen.

Department Fifteen maintains the archives of the First Chief Directorate.

Department Sixteen, one of the most secretive of all, directs operations against foreign cipher personnel of all nationalities. Each officer supervises only one case from an office of his own. Generally, but not always, the Department allows an experienced officer from Line PR to handle a recruited code clerk or cryptographer in the field. Every detail of the operation, though, is supervised by the Department in Moscow. Levchenko reports that Department Sixteen grew in size during the 1970s.

The *Personnel Department*, which is unnumbered, recruits new officers for the First Chief Directorate, seeking bright graduates from the ranking universities and institutes. While the KGB can coerce most people into serving as co-optees or informants, it cannot risk forcing unwilling young men to become staff officers. Qualified candidates increasingly decline appointment, and as a result, for the first time in the past two decades, the KGB has begun to suffer some shortages of area specialists.

A *Party Committee* endeavors to enforce ideological conformity, discipline and "socialist morals" among officers of the Directorate. Through subsidiary committees in all echelons of the Directorate, both in Moscow and the field, it arranges and supervises regular party meetings, where political as well as operational matters are discussed. The Committee oversees indoctrination of new officers, and no officer is permitted to go abroad without its clearance. The meetings, at which dogma heard since childhood is repeated interminably, are one of the banes of KGB life. Nevertheless, the Party Committee and its network form one of the effective means by which the oligarchy controls the KGB.

A *Secretariat* functions as an administrative clearinghouse, issuing orders regarding assignments, promotions, and training, and conducting annual inspections in Moscow and the foreign Residencies. The Secretariat also processes administrative correspondence between the Residencies and headquarters and oversees the couriers who transmit classified documents on Soviet territory.

Second Chief Directorate

The Directorate administers the vast apparatus of internal repression that reaches into every city, town, village and farm of the Soviet Union. Local KGB offices throughout the nation are under its jurisdiction.

Special divisions called "Directions" *(Napravleniye)* are supposed to investigate major corruption and economic crimes, maintain security in industry, and determine which Soviet citizens may travel abroad.

In Moscow, geographic Departments concentrate upon subversion of foreigners residing in the Soviet Union and upon counterintelligence. Other Departments devote themselves to suborning foreign journalists, students and tourists.

Border Guards Directorate

The Directorate actually constitutes a special military force, equipped with artillery, armor, and patrol ships. Its personnel, estimated to number between 300,000 and 400,000, are deployed along Soviet frontiers, where they are concerned equally with keeping foreign intruders out and with keeping Soviet citizens from escaping.

Third Directorate

Officers and agents of the *Third Directorate* work in every unit of the Soviet armed forces down to the company level. They even spy on the General Staff and the GRU. Together with Political officers, they are responsible for purging the military of any dissidence and guaranteeing its obedience to the oligarchy.

Fifth Chief Directorate

Known as the "dissident" or "ideological" Directorate, the Fifth was created under Andropov especially to harass, intimidate and ultimately eliminate nonconformists. It is widely despised among KGB officers because of its methods, which include beatings and the mailing of threatening letters signed by criminals or terrorists. The Fifth Directorate, however, has been effective.

Seventh Directorate

During the 1970s, the Seventh or Surveillance Directorate was grant-ed a measure of autonomy, empowered to instigate surveillances on its own initiative and allowed to establish its own analytical group. It employs more than 3000 personnel, most of whom have undergone two years of professional training at the Surveillance College in Leningrad. They are well equipped with infra-red binoculars, long-range cameras, miniature radios and endless disguises. The standard Seventh Director-ate car looks like an ordinary Volga but has a powerful engine from a Chaika and ballast in the trunk. It can outpace any other vehicle in Moscow. The Directorate is one of the few in the entire KGB that employs large numbers of females in an operational capacity. Because of frequent accidents, assignment to the Directorate is classified as hazardous duty, and one year of service counts as two for retirement purposes.

All major embassies in Moscow, but particularly the American, are continuously watched by disguised surveillants, as is anyone suspected of being a foreign intelligence officer. On very short notice, numer-ous teams can be summoned to form an invisible cordon around a suspect. It is difficult to imagine a more accomplished surveillance outfit than the Seventh Directorate. Yet, to the consternation of the KGB leadership, Western agents still succeed in eluding it for protracted periods.

The Eighth Chief Directorate

The Directorate has two primary functions. It develops cipher and cryptographic systems for the KGB and Ministry of Foreign Affairs and maintains the security of government communications within the Soviet Union. Directorate personnel additionally monitor, intercept and try to decipher foreign communications, using satellites, ships, and equip-ment inside Soviet embassies.

The Ninth Directorate

The Ninth Directorate safeguards the personal security of Party lead-ers as well as the physical security of important installations, including those of the KGB.

The Sixteenth Directorate

Existence of such a Directorate has not been verified by sources available to the author, nor, if it exists, is its purpose known. At a resort in 1974, Levchenko became friendly with another KGB officer, who eventually confided that he worked for the Sixteenth Directorate. When Levchenko remarked that he had never heard of such an outfit, the officer said, "We work underground, literally, digging tunnels."

CHAPTER NOTES

Abbreviations:

FBIS—Foreign Broadcast Information Service
HCIS—House Committee on Internal Security hearings
HPSCI—House Permanent Select Committee on Intelligence hearings
SPSI—Senate Permanent Subcommittee on Investigations, Committee
    on Governmental Affairs, hearings

CHAPTER I

Hambleton's reception by Andropov: author's interviews with Hambleton; intelligence sources; Washington *Post*, November 30, 1982; *Daily
Telegraph* (London), December 8, 1982; *Times* (London), December
8, 1982.

Plot to assassinate the president of Afghanistan: former KGB Major
Vladimir Kuzichkin; intelligence sources; New York *Times*, December 28, 1979; *Time*, November 22, 1982.

Forgery of President Reagan's signature on a bogus letter to the king of

Spain: *Soviet Active Measures: An Update,* Special Report, no. 101, Bureau of Public Affairs, U.S. State Department, July 1982; HPSCI, July 13, 14, 1982.

Soviet dependence upon clandestine action: Georg Von Rauch, *A History of Soviet Russia,* 5th rev. ed., trans. Peter and Annette Jacobson (New York: Praeger, 1967); Hedrick Smith, *The Russians* (New York: Quadrangle, New York Times Book Co., 1976).

Stories flattering Andropov that appeared in Western press: Washington *Post,* May 25, 30, 1982; Baltimore *Sun,* September 28, 1982; others cited by Edward J. Epstein in "The Andropov Files," *The New Republic,* February 7, 1983.

Andropov biographical details: Official Soviet Biography broadcast in Moscow, Domestic Service, in FBIS, November 12, 1982; U.S. State Department biography of Andropov, November 1976; *Congressional Record,* January 3, 1983, pp. S 16–S 21; Miklos K. Radvanyi, *Soviet Leaders and The Americas,* Council for Inter-American Studies, Washington, 1980; *Problems of Communism,* September/October 1982; *Prominent Personalities in U.S.S.R.* (Metuchen, N. J.: Scarecrow Press, 1968).

Kuusinen quotation: "Report of the Commission for Work Among the Masses," *International Press Correspondence,* vol. VI, no. 28, April 1926.

Andropov during Hungarian Revolution: Noel Barber, *Seven Days of Freedom* (Briarcliff Manor, N.Y.: Stein and Day, 1974); *United Nations Report of the Special Committee on the Problem of Hungary,* 1957; *Hungary's Fight for Freedom,* a special issue of *Life,* 1956; New York *Times,* December 18, 1982; Professor Endre Marton, Georgetown University.

Internal repression under Andropov's KGB: Peter Reddaway, *Uncensored Russia* (New York: American Heritage Press, 1972); New York *Times,* November 16, 1982; Andrea Lee, "An English Lesson for Moscow Jews," *New York Times Magazine,* September 7, 1980; New York *Times,* January 20, 1983, account of warning given Roy Medvedev, the dissident Marxist historian; New York *Times,* September 8, 1982, report that Soviets who monitor human rights have been forced to break up their group; Washington *Post,* November 5, 1982, report on tightening controls in U.S.S.R.; Rudolf Tökes, ed., *Dissent in the U.S.S.R.* (Baltimore: Johns Hopkins University Press, 1975).

Andropov quotation, "we try to help . . .": *Yu. V. Andropov: Izbranniye Rechi I Stat'i* (Moscow: Politizdat, 1979), in *U.S.S.R Report: Collection of Speeches and Articles by Yu. V. Andropov,* Joint Publications Research Service, Washington, D.C., November 29, 1982, p. 79.

Soviet withdrawal from the World Psychiatric Association: New York *Times*, February 11, 1983.

Perversion of psychiatry: Diary of Major General Petr Grigorevich Grigorenko, as translated by David Floyd, *Sunday Telegraph* (London), April 5, 1970; Sidney Bloch and Peter Reddaway, *Psychiatric Terror* (New York: Basic Books, 1977); Zhores and Roy Medvedev, *A Question of Madness* (New York: Knopf, 1971); Ludmilla Thorne, "Inside Russia's Psychiatric Jails," *New York Times Magazine*, June 12, 1977; Walter Reich, "The World of Soviet Psychiatry," *New York Times Magazine*, January 30, 1983; Washington *Post*, March 1, 1983; *Matchbox*, February 1983, Amnesty International, U.S.A.; New York *Times*, February 11, 1983.

KGB involvement in terrorism: The complex known as Balashikha was described by former KGB Majors Vladimir Kuzichkin and Stanislav Levchenko.

Technological theft by U.S.S.R. under Andropov: *Transfer of United States High Technology to the Soviet Union and Soviet Bloc Nations*, SPSI, May 4, 5, 6, 11, 12, 1982.

Andropov·quotations: "Peaceful coexistence . . .": *Pravda*, December 21, 1967; "The arena of the historic confrontation . . .": in *Soviet Watch*, Advanced International Studies Institute, Bethesda, Md., November 30, 1982; "Cheka authorities operate . . .": in *U.S.S.R. Report*, p. 65.

Appointments of Fedorchuk, Aliev and Chebrikov: Washington *Post*, May 26, 27, October 3, November 25, 1982; Adrian Karatnycky, "The KGB Hetman," *American Spectator*, August 1982; *Soviet Analyst*, June 2, 1982; New York *Times*, December 18, 1982; *The Wall Street Journal*, January 6, 1983.

Twenty-Second Party Congress 1961 promised true Communism by 1980: *Current Digest of the Soviet Press*, vol. 13, no. 45, December 6, 1961; *Area Handbook for the Soviet Union* (Washington, D.C.: U.S. Government Printing Office, 1971); John Barron, *MiG Pilot* (New York: Reader's Digest Press/McGraw Hill, 1980), pp. 53–54.

Feshbach: Murray Feshbach, *The Soviet Union: Population Trends and Dilemmas*, Population Reference Bureau, Inc., vol. 37, no. 3, August 1982.

Brezhnev admits medical system is deficient: speech February 23, 1981, opening 26th Party Congress, in *Current Soviet Policies VIII: Documentary Record of the 26th Congress of the Communist Party* (Columbus, Ohio: The Current Digest of the Soviet Press, 1981).

Average pay in health-care and other economic fields: *Narodnoye kho-zyaystvo SSSR* (National Economy of the U.S.S.R.), 1922-1982 (Moscow: Central Statistical Directorate, 1982).

Knaus: William A. Knaus, *Inside Russian Medicine* (Boston: Beacon Press, 1981).

Alcoholism as a cause of increased mortality: *The Wall Street Journal,* November 10, 1981; Vladimir G. Treml, *Alcohol in the U.S.S.R.: A Statistical Study* (Durham, N. C.: Duke University Press, 1982); Feshbach, *The Soviet Union: Population Trends and Dilemmas;* Merton Hyman, et al., *Drinkers, Drinking and Alcohol-Related Mortality and Hospitalization* (New Brunswick, N. J.: Rutgers University, Center for Alcohol Studies, 1980).

Reduction of budget allotted to health: Feshbach, *The Soviet Union: Population Trends and Dilemmas.*

It costs 53.5 hours of work to feed four in U.S.S.R. for one week: 1982 study of work time required to fill food baskets in Washington, London, Paris, Moscow and Munich, by the National Federation of Independent Business Research and Education Foundation, San Mateo, California.

American agriculture engages 3.4% of work force: U.S. Agriculture Department.

Inefficiency of Soviet agriculture: U.S.S.R. Central Statistical Administration's 1981 Economic Report, as reported in the New York *Times,* January 24, 1982; report of Worldwatch Institute in Washington *Post,* October 3, 1982; *Pravda,* June 19, 1981.

Agriculture is greatest problem: Brezhnev's speech to Central Committee, November 1981, as reported in the New York *Times,* January 15, 1982.

Size of Soviet agricultural work force: U.S. Agriculture Department; Feshbach says there are eight times more farm workers in the U.S.S.R. than in the United States..

Shops often empty of food: New York *Times,* January 15, 1982; Lev-'chenko; former MiG pilot Viktor Belenko.

Importance of tiny private farm plots: *Narodnoye khozyaystvo, SSSR 1980,* in Feshbach, *The Soviet Union: Population Trends and Dilemmas; Izvestiya,* January 18, 1981, reported measures to increase production on these plots, indicating how great is concern over food shortage.

Predominance of Russians in Soviet officer corps: S. Enders Wimbush and Alex Alexiev, *The Ethnic Factor in the Soviet Armed Forces,* The Rand Corporation, Santa Monica, California, March 1982.

Wheeler: Geoffrey Wheeler, "The Study of Soviet Central Asia Today," *Middle Eastern Studies,* May 1976.

Fifty million people in the Ukraine: *Demographic Trends in U.S.S.R., 1950-2000,* June 3, 1982, Foreign Demographic Analysis Division, U.S. Census Bureau, Washington, D.C.

Armed resistance in the Ukraine after World War II: Roman Rakhmanny, *In Defense of the Ukrainian Cause* (North Quincy, Mass.: Christopher Publishing House, 1979); Yaroslav Bilinsky, *The Second Soviet Republic: The Ukraine after World War II* (New Brunswick, N.J.: Rutgers University Press, 1964); *The Ukrainian Encyclopedia* (Toronto: University of Toronto Press, 1963).

Muslim birth rate: Feshbach, *The Soviet Union: Population Trends and Dilemmas.*

Andropov quotation: ". . . large scale and speedy introduction . . .": in FBIS, November 23, 1982.

U.S.S.R. lags behind West except in some areas of military technology: see Chapter V.

Semi-conductor and silicon chip technology and uses: J. Fred Bucy, president and director, Texas Instruments, Dallas, Texas, in numerous conversations with the author.

Soviet labor productivity: Richard Pipes, "The Soviet Union in Crisis," address delivered before the French Institute of International Relations, Paris, October 5, 1982. (Pipes—former director, East European and Soviet Affairs, National Security Council—generously made available to the author a copy of the text.)

Andropov quotation, "it must be confessed . . .": Andropov election speech, February 11, 1980, in *Soviet Watch,* November 30, 1982, p. 27.

Pipes quotations: Pipes, "The Soviet Union in Crisis."

Corruption in U.S.S.R.: Konstantin Simis, *U.S.S.R.: The Corrupt Society* (New York: Simon and Schuster, 1982); Levchenko; Barron, *MiG Pilot.* Execution of Ritov—*Pravda,* April 27, 1982. Payments to "ghost workers"—*Boston Globe,* January 14, 1983. Brezhnev calls for crackdown on corruption—Baltimore *News-American,* September 29, 1982. Deputy aviation minister fired for corruption—Washington *Post,* February 20, 1983.

Defection of young Soviet from United Nations job: New York *Times*, March 31, 1981; intelligence sources.

Andropov speaks of problems but does not face causes: Andropov election speech, February 11, 1980, in *Soviet Watch*, November 30, 1982, p. 20.

Aristotle: *Politics*, Book 5, Chapter 11, Paragraph 5.

Police use of terror and spies: Robert Conquest, *The Great Terror* (London: Macmillan and Company Ltd., 1968); Smith, *The Russians;* New York *Times*, November 20, 1982, report in which dissident Roy Medvedev says he was warned by Soviet officials, including KGB, to stop critical writing. Medvedev says he took the warning as a symbol of what could be expected from Andropov. "At first when people asked me about the new leadership I said it would be strict but intelligently so. Now that we have seen the new leadership at work we can say without question it is going to be strict, but still not intelligent."

Dissidents off to labor camps or mental hospitals: Sixteen members of the Soviet human rights group that monitored human rights violations are now in labor camps or internal exile and the group has been forced to disband, New York *Times*, September 8, 1982.

Rusk quotation: verified by Dean Rusk in telephone interview, December 31, 1982.

Brezhnev quotation: Baltimore *Sun* and Washington *Post*, June 28, 1972.

Chandra quotation: Georgetown (Guyana) *Sunday Chronicle*, December 19, 1976.

Lenin quotation: David Shub, *Lenin, A Biography* (New York: The New American Library, 1948), p. 189.

Pravda quotation: *Pravda*, August 22, 1973.

Lubyanka on Dzherzhinsky Square: Conquest, *The Great Terror;* Peter Deriabin and Frank Gibney, *The Secret World* (New York: Doubleday, 1959).

Lubyanka remodeled: Levchenko.

Organizational changes in KGB: Levchenko; Kuzichkin; intelligence sources.

Bogdanov: State Department Biographical Sketch; John Barron, *KGB* (New York: Reader's Digest Press, 1974), p. 382; Nora Beloff, "Escape

From Boredom: A Defector's Story," *Atlantic*, November 1980.

Description of First Chief Directorate building: Levchenko; intelligence sources.

Expulsion of Soviets from Egypt, Norway, Pakistan, Spain, Costa Rica, Canada, Malaysia, Bangladesh, U.S., Liberia: Foreign Affairs Notes, February 1982 and January 1983, U.S. State Department; intelligence sources.

Geoffrey Prime case: Washington *Post*, October 25, 31, November 11, 1982.

Seizure of embargoed material: Christine Frazer, U.S. Customs Service, Treasury Department, Washington, D.C.

Lenin quotation: *Collected Works*, vol. 12 (Moscow: Foreign Languages Publishing House, 1962), p. 424.

CHAPTER II

Chapters II, III and IV are based primarily on interviews the author conducted with Stanislav Aleksandrovich Levchenko over a period of more than two years.

The CIA, FBI and other elements of the U.S. intelligence community have determined that Levchenko is a competent, authoritative and honest source, and have so certified to Congress. FBI Director William H. Webster sent Levchenko a personal letter of gratitude in 1982. Martin C. Portman, of the CIA Clandestine Service, testifying before the House of Representatives Permanent Select Committee on Intelligence, on July 13, 1982, stated: "We did a very thorough investigation of Mr. Levchenko after he defected, which included the polygraph. He gave us very extensive information not only on the Soviet system, but also on the activities of the KGB Residency in Japan. He personally identified to us those agents and assets that he knew about. In many cases he did not know the names of these individuals, but by the identification that he provided us we have been able to identify a large number. The information that he gave us we have been able to check out through various other means, and we are satisfied not only that he told the truth, but also that the extent of information that he gave us was so damaging to the Soviet cause that it would be inconceivable that he might be under Soviet KGB control. Some of the most damaging information to the Soviet cause which he has provided concerns the detailed information about the KGB's operations and activities in the Japanese area."

In agreeing to share with the author all his knowledge about KGB operations, Levchenko stipulated a condition: with few exceptions, the Japanese he recruited as agents of the KGB could not be identified by their true names. He recognized that they would have to be quietly neutralized. But he said that because it was his fault that they were lured into subversion, he did not want to bring down public opprobrium upon them and their families.

In other cases, true names are omitted because Levchenko knew only the KGB code names. (As the CIA testimony suggests, all agents to whom Levchenko referred, even if only by code name, have probably been identified.)

National security interests of both the United States and Japan prevent identification of still other agents, at least for the present. Again, however, their identities are known to non-Communist intelligence services.

Levchenko is the sole source of details relating to his years in the Soviet Union and to his personal experiences there. He is also the sole source of descriptions of the Tokyo Residency and happenings within it, although the presence in Japan of the KGB officers he names has been verified by diplomatic directories and other public source data.

Efforts have been made to verify those facts that could be independently checked. The results follow.

Information on Levchenko's trial and the verdict comes to Levchenko indirectly, from his wife, who is still in Moscow. Under Soviet law, she was apprised of the court's decisions, even though not allowed to participate in the proceedings. As a result of this verdict, even though under current Soviet law she should not have been prosecuted for the alleged failings of her husband, she has been persecuted. Source: transcripts of Levchenko's telephone conversations with his wife.

Methods of execution: Levchenko; intelligence sources. Soviet assassinations of defectors: Karl Anders, *Murder To Order* (New York: Devin-Adair Company, 1967); Nikolai Khokhlov, *In the Name of Conscience* (New York: McKay, 1959); Barron, *KGB*.

Information on Agents of Influence: *The CIA and the Media—CIA Report on Soviet Propaganda Operations*, HPSCI, April 20, 1978; *Soviet Covert Action (The Forgery Offensive)*, HPSCI, February 6, 19, 1980; *Soviet Active Measures*, HPSCI, July 1982.

Levchenko's employment by *New Times:* Japanese Foreign Ministry press credentials; Levchenko's articles, numerous issues of *New Times*, 1974 to 1979.

Beria and Stalin purges: Conquest, *The Great Terror; Area Handbook for the Soviet Union* (Washington, D.C.: U.S. Government Printing Office, 1971).

Tukhachevsky and the German plot against the Soviet military: *Area Handbook for the Soviet Union;* Anthony Brown and C. B. MacDonald, *On a Field of Red* (New York: Putnam, 1981); *Encyclopaedia Britannica;* James McSherry, *Stalin, Hitler and Europe,* vol. 2 (Arlington: Open-Door Press, 1970); Walter Schellenberg, *The Labyrinth* (New York: Harper & Row, 1956).

Soviet penetration of the Manhattan Project: H. M. Hyde, *The Atom Bomb Spies* (New York: Atheneum, 1980); Brown and MacDonald, *On a Field of Red.*

Philby: Andrew Boyle, *The Fourth Man* (New York: Dial Press, 1979); Brown and MacDonald, *On a Field of Red; Encyclopaedia Britannica.*

Sorge: F. W. Deakin and G. R. Storry, *The Case of Richard Sorge* (New York: Harper & Row, 1966).

Abel (William Fisher): Los Angeles *Times*, August 22, 1972; New York *Times*, August 27, 1972; *Encyclopaedia Britannica.*

Molodoy: *Encyclopaedia Britannica.*

Nosenko: New York *Times*, February 10, 11, 12, 1964.

Lyalin: (London) *Times*, August 31, September 30, October 1, 19, 1971.

Ishida's meetings with Soviet leaders and release of Japanese fishermen: *Asahi Shimbun*, September 4, 1973, June 15, 1977; Information Section, Ministry of Foreign Affairs, Tokyo; Information Office, Japanese Maritime Safety Board, Tokyo.

New Times journalist cover for KGB agents: Levchenko testimony, HSPCI, July 1982.

Cinema Club (Dom Kino): Fodor's *Soviet Union* (New York: David McKay, 1979); Press Office, Embassy of the Soviet Union, Washington, D.C.

CHAPTER III

Soviet embassy in Tokyo: photograph of the compound; embassy inspected by a researcher from the Japanese *Reader's Digest;* Japanese Desk, U.S. State Department.

Japanese antipathy toward Russians: A 1981 public opinion poll conducted by the Research Office of the Japanese Cabinet showed that 84.4 percent of the Japanese people felt "no desire for friendship" with the Soviet Union or "not friendly at all" toward it. A poll sponsored by the monthly magazine *Gekkan Pen* showed that among Japanese the Soviet Union is the least popular foreign country.

Soviet diplomats in Tokyo: list of Soviet embassy personnel in Japan for the years 1975-1980, as published by the Japanese Foreign Office.

Levchenko's first *New Times* article published from Japan: *New Times*, no. 14, April 1975.

Levchenko first Soviet admitted to National Press Club: confirmed by club to Japanese *Digest* researcher, January 1983.

Levchenko's former apartment: examined by Japanese *Digest* researcher.

Russian Orthodox Church: Japanese Section, Library of Congress; *Area Handbook for Japan* (Washington, D.C.: U.S. Government Printing Office, 1974); visited by Japanese *Digest* researcher.

Machekin: *Asahi Shimbun*, May 14, 17, 1976; Public Security Division, Metropolitan Police Board, Tokyo.

Lockheed bribes: New York *Times*, February 4, 5, 6, 1976.

Belenko: New York *Times*, September 7, 1976; Barron, *MiG Pilot*.

Forged letter from Belenko's wife: Los Angeles *Times*, September 11, 1976.

Buraku Kaiho Domei (*Burakumin* Liberation League) and the *eta:* Japanese section, Library of Congress.

Brezhnev's purge of Podgorny: *Newsweek*, June 6, 1977; Soviet Desk, U.S. State Department; Levchenko.

CHAPTER IV

Lenin "testament": *Encyclopaedia Britannica; Collier's Encyclopedia.*

"Last Will of Zhou Enlai": HPSCI, July 1982; *Sankei Shimbun*, January 23, 1976.

Colby quote: *U.S. News & World Report*, December 2, 1974.

Helsinki agreements: Press Office, U.S. State Department; New York *Times*, July 30, 31, 1975.

Soviet emigration: Soviet Desk, U.S. State Department.

Agence France-Presse quoting TASS: Washington *Post*, January 12, 1982.

Assault forces on Okinawa: Public Affairs Office, U.S. Defense Department; *U.S. News & World Report*, December 27, 1982.

Sihanouk and the Khmer Rouge: *Area Handbook for the Khmer Republic* (Washington, D.C.: U.S. Government Printing Office, 1973); *Cambodia/Kampuchea*, Fact Sheet, 1979; "Kampuchea: Growing Humanitarian Crisis," *Current Policy*, no. 95; *Cambodia*, Background Notes, April 1977—Bureau of Public Affairs, U.S. State Department; New York *Times*, January 9, 1979; John Barron and Anthony Paul, *Murder of a Gentle Land* (New York: Reader's Digest Press, 1978).

Story in Japanese press about tanker rescue: *Shukan Gendai*, August 23, 1979.

Ambassador Dobrynin's demand to Vance: confirmed by Cyrus Vance in telephone interview February 10, 1983.

Bessmertnykh, Minister Counselor at Soviet Embassy: Protocol Section, U.S. State Department; Levchenko's copy of minutes of meeting.

CHAPTER V

Numbers of Soviet and Soviet-Bloc officials in the United States: official lists and directories published by the U.S. State Department and by the United Nations, as well as testimony before Congressional committees by FBI Director William H. Webster. U.S. intelligence officials estimate that from 30% to 40% of Soviet-Bloc officials in the United States have some type of intelligence-gathering responsibilities.

Value of technology stolen by Soviet Agents: Levchenko; SPSI, May 1982.

William Holden Bell and Marian W. Zacharski: transcript of trial of Marian Zacharski in U.S. District Court, Los Angeles, California; SPSI, May 1982; John L. Martin, Chief of the Internal Security Section, Criminal Division, U.S. Justice Department; intelligence sources.

Walter J. Spawr and Frances A. Spawr: statement concerning the Spawr case prepared by Assistant United States Attorney Theodore Wai Wu, May 1982, for the SPSI. (Mr. Wu, now a Deputy Assistant Secretary of Commerce, generously agreed to review and offer comments upon an early version of the author's presentation of the Spawr case.) Ehud Yonay, "Mirrors for Moscow," *New West*, September 1981; Los Angeles *Times*, September 5, December 13, 1980; Washington *Post*, April 4, 1980.

Soviet difficulties in building and operating microcomputer and integrated circuit factories: testimony of Dr. Lara H. Baker, Jr., of Los Alamos National Laboratory, before the SPSI, May 1982; Soviet engineer (alias Joseph Arkov), SPSI, May 1982.

Illegal activities of the CTC syndicate: statements and testimony of Fred Asselin, investigator; Theodore Wai Wu, then Assistant United States Attorney; Dr. Baker; SPSI, May 1982; Christopher Simpson, "Electronics Underworld," *Computerworld*, August 31, 1981.

Inadequacies of the Compliance Division, Office of Export Administration, U.S. Commerce Department: testimony of Fred Asselin, SPSI, May 1982.

Jacob Kelmer case: R. Jeffrey Smith, "Eastern Bloc Evades Technology Embargo," *Science*, January 23, 1981; Office of Export Administration Annual Report FY 1980, pp. 68–69, U.S. Commerce Department; Christopher Simpson, "High Tech Smugglers: 60% of Those Caught Try Again," *Computerworld*, September 14, 1981.

CIA analysis: exhibit entitled "Soviet Acquisition of Western Technology," SPSI, May 1982.

DeGeyter case: statement of Assistant United States Attorney Theodore S. Greenberg and testimony of John Maguire, president of Software AG, SPSI, May 1982; Washington *Post*, July 8, August 2, 1980.

"Gennadi Popov" is used as a pseudonym for a Soviet whose background and presence in the United States were brought to the author's attention by a genuinely concerned industrial executive. This individual's true identity is known to United States intelligence authorities.

CIA study, "Soviet Acquisition of Western Technology": SPSI, May 1982.

Soviet misuse of technology obtained from the United States: "Kama River Truck Factory: Best and Worst of Tech Export," *Industrial Research & Development*, July 1980; SPSI, May 1982; intelligence sources.

Soviet interception of telephone calls: intelligence sources; John Barron, "Espionage: The Dark Side of Détente," *Reader's Digest*, January 1978; San Francisco *Chronicle*, May 1978; *Forbes*, September 15, 1980; New York *Times*, December 21, 1981; *Washington Post Magazine*, February 20, 1983. Moynihan quotation: news release from office of Senator Moynihan, July 27, 1977.

Kampiles case: John L. Martin, U.S. Justice Department; intelligence sources; New York *Times*, August 24, November 6, 7, 8, 12, 15, 18, 1978; *Newsweek*, September 4, 1978.

Barnett: A 25-page "Statements of Facts" was made public by the U.S. Justice Department; intelligence sources.

Efforts to assert influence and gather intelligence in Washington, D.C. by personnel of the Soviet embassy: Washington *Post*, March 28, 1982; testimony of FBI Assistant Director Edward J. O'Malley, HPSCI, July 1982.

United Nations budget data: U.S. State Department annual reports to Congress entitled "United States Contributions to International Organizations," 1979 through 1981.

Identification of KGB officers in United Nations and Washington: intelligence sources; for more data regarding Boris Davidov, see John Barron, *KGB* (New York: Reader's Digest Press, 1974), pp. 3–4.

Report critical of Western press: New York *Times*, October 15, 1982; Washington *Post*, October 16, 1982.

Women's International League for Peace and Freedom: *Soviet Active Measures: An Update*, Special Report, no. 101, Bureau of Public Affairs, U.S. State Department, July 1982.

Carol Pendell statements: interviews with Pendell by phone, January 28, 1983.

Use of KGB to furnish funds to the Communist Party, USA, and KGB monitoring and guidance of CPUSA: FBI Assistant Director Edward J. O'Malley, HPSCI, July 1982; intelligence sources.

Trip report by Farid Handel: HPSCI, July 1982.

Membership of CISPES Steering Committee: Memorandum of the Institute on Religion and Democracy, Washington, D.C., May 1, 1981. Membership verified January 1982 by Washington offices of CISPES.

Fabricated "Dissent Paper on El Salvador . . .": HPSCI, July 1982.

CISPES demonstration in Washington: Washington *Post*, March 28, 1982.

Data concerning El Salvador elections March 1982: Peter Romero, U.S. State Department.

CHAPTER VI

Russians mail protests to NATO: transcript of a speech by the chairman of the Soviet Committee for Defense of Peace, May 22, 1982, in FBIS, May 25, 1982.

Ponomarev quotation: TASS, March 26, 1982, in FBIS, March 29, 1982.

Zhurkin quotation: Moscow Domestic Service (television), March 28, 1982, in FBIS, March 29, 1982.

Zamiatin's quotation: *Literaturnaya Gazeta*, September 29, 1982, in FBIS, October 1, 1982.

Brezhnev's quotation: New York *Times*, October 28, 1982; TASS, October 27, 1982, in FBIS, October 27, 1982.

Greenpeace exploits: New York *Times*, June 4, 1982.

Soviets arrested for peace activity: New York *Times*, June 14, August 7, 1982; Washington *Times*, June 15, 1982; Los Angeles *Times*, June 13, 1982.

Pravda quotations: *Pravda*, April 30, 1982; *Pravda* editorial, November 30, 1981, in FBIS, December 7, 1981.

Ogarkov quotation: *Kommunist*, no. 10, July 1981, in Joint Publications Research Service, Washington, D.C., September 1981.

Milovidov quotation: *Voprosi Filosofii (Questions of Philosophy)*, no. 10, October 1980, Institute of Philosophy, U.S.S.R. Academy of Sciences.

Active Measures, definition and general use of: *Soviet Active Measures: An Update*, Special Report, no. 101, Bureau of Public Affairs, U.S. State Department, July 1982; *Forgery Disinformation, Political Operations, Soviet Active Measures*, Special Report, no. 88, U.S. State Department, October 1981; Levchenko interviews.

Threat of KGB theft: Levchenko; HPSCI, July 1982; SPSCI, May 1982.

Carr quotation: E. H. Carr, *The Bolshevik Revolution*, vol. 1 (New York: Macmillan, 1951).

Comintern and Disinformation: *Encyclopaedia Britannica;* David Caute, *The Fellow Travellers* (London: Weidenfeld & Nicolson Ltd., 1973); Leonard Schapiro, *Communist Party of the Soviet Union* (London: Eyre & Spottiswoode Ltd., 1960).

"Human regeneration" and "social correction": Conquest, *The Great Terror.*

George Bernard Shaw: Conquest, *The Great Terror;* Caute, *The Fellow Travellers.*

Stalin not a dictator: Hewlett Johnson, *The Socialist Sixth of the World* (London: Victor Gollancz Ltd., 1939).

Dean of Canterbury: Johnson, *The Socialist Sixth of the World.*

Duranty: Conquest, *The Great Terror;* Caute, *The Fellow Travellers.*

Malraux: Caute, *The Fellow Travellers.*

Present-day Active Measures: HPSCI, February 1980, July 1982; Levchenko; *Soviet Active Measures: An Update; Forgery, Disinformation, Political Operations, Soviet Active Measures.*

Weather Underground, Felt and Miller: Trial—*U.S. v. W. Mark Felt, et al.,* U.S. District Court for the District of Columbia, November–December, 1980.

More than 150 forgeries: HPSCI, February 1980.

Service A's speciality: HPSCI, July 1982, February 1980; Levchenko.

Forgeries aimed at Sadat: HPSCI, February 1980.

U.S. Army Field Manual ignored: HPSCI, February 1980; Levchenko.

Field Manual and Moro: HPSCI, April 1978, February 1980; *El Triunfo,* Madrid, September 23, 1978.

Soviet journalists as intelligence officers: HPSCI, April 1978, February 1980, July 1982; Levchenko.

Pierre-Charles Pathé as Agent of Influence: HPSCI, July 1982, February 1980; *Time,* October 6, 1980; *Le Figaro,* edition de 5 heures, July 4, 1981; *Forgery, Disinformation, Political Operations, Soviet Active Measures.*

Münzenberg's "Innocents' Clubs": Ruth Fischer, *Stalin and German*

Communism (New Brunswick, N.J.: Transaction Books, 1982).

"Solar system" quotation: O. V. Kuusinen, "Report of the Commission for Work Among the Masses," *International Press Correspondence*, vol. VI, no. 28, April 1926.

World Peace Council: HPSCI April 1978, February 1980, July 1982; Levchenko; *Moscow and the Peace Offensive*, Heritage Foundation, Washington, D.C., May 14, 1981; *World Peace Council: Instrument of Soviet Foreign Policy*, Foreign Affairs Note, U.S. State Department, April 1982; "U.S. visa policy toward the World Peace Council and other organizations attending the Second U.N. Special Session on Disarmament," Press Statement, Bureau of Consular Affairs, U.S. State Department, June 4, 1982.

Afro-Asian People's Solidarity Organization: Levchenko; intelligence sources; HPSCI, April 1978.

Institute for U.S.A. and Canada: Levchenko; *Moscow and the Peace Offensive;* U.S. State Department background information on Georgi A. Arbatov, April 8, 1972; HPSCI, July 1982; Nora Beloff, "Escape From Boredom: A Defector's Story," *Atlantic,* November 1980; intelligence sources.

Orionova quote on Bogdanov: Beloff, "Escape From Boredom: A Defector's Story."

KGB and foreign Communist Parties and the Soviet Active Measures apparatus: HPSCI, April 1978, February 1980, July 1982; Levchenko; *Soviet Active Measures: An Update.*

Soviet peace campaign beginning in 1977: HPSCI, April 1978, February 1980; Levchenko; *Forgery, Disinformation, Political Operations, Soviet Active Measures.*

Destruction capabilities of weapons in Europe: Public Affairs Office, U.S. Defense Department; National Security Council Memorandum, July 13, 1977; *Bulletin of the International Civil Defense Organization*, Geneva, July 1980; *Air Force Magazine*, November 1977; *Time,* July 25, 1977, April 17, 1978; *U.S. News & World Report*, October 18, 1976, June 14, 1982.

Soviet "rationale" for West Germany: HPSCI, April 1978, February 1980; *U.S. News & World Report*, June 14, 1982.

Gerald Ford's approval of ERW: *Air Force Magazine*, November 1977; Washington *Post*, June 7, 1977.

Jimmy Carter's delay: *Air Force Magazine*, November 1977; Washington *Post*, June 7, 1977; *Time*, April 17, 1978.

KGB press campaign: Levchenko; HPSCI, April 1978, February 1980; *Moscow and the Peace Offensive*.

Pravda quotation: *Pravda* editorial, November 30, 1981, in FBIS, December 7, 1981.

Soviet press and radio blitz: HPSCI, April 1978, February 1980; Washington *Post*, July 10, 1977, July 31, 1977; New York *Times*, July 10, 1977; *Time*, April 17, 1978.

Reuters August 8 report: New York *Times*, August 9, 1977.

Demonstrations in Soviet Union: Los Angeles *Times*, August 10, 1977.

Harold Brown's announcement and effect: HPSCI, April 1978; *Moscow and the Peace Offensive*; *Time*, April 17, 24, 1978.

TASS Baptist dispatch: Washington *Post*, August 12, 1977.

Carters in church: former pastor of First Baptist Church, Washington D.C.; Washington *Post*, October 17, 1977, December 5, 1977; Minneapolis *Star*, November 16, 1977.

Brezhnev's 1978 newsletters: HPSCI, April 1978, February 1980; *Forgery, Disinformation, Political Operations, Soviet Active Measures*.

Chandra operating in Congress in 1978: "WPC Call From Washington," World Peace Council, Helsinki, 1978; *Moscow and the Peace Offensive; Daily World*, February 25, 1978.

Multi-national peace meeting in Geneva and Vienna symposium: HPSCI, April 1978.

March 19, 1978, Amsterdam rally: HPSCI, April 1978; *Moscow and the Peace Offensive*.

Production of ERW urged in U.S. by Foreign Policy Advisors and the press: Washington *Post*, April 10, 1978; Washington *Post* editorial, April 6, 1978; New York *Times* editorial, March 30, 1978.

Carter announces cancellation of ERW: Washington *Post*, March 4, 1982; "Presidential Statement on Enhanced Radiation Weapons," Office of the White House Press Secretary, April 7, 1978.

Janos Berecz quote: HPSCI, February 1980.

Brezhnev confers award: HPSCI, February 1980; *Newsweek*, August 24, 1981; *Intelligence Requirements for the 1980s: Counterintelligence* (Washington, D.C.: National Strategy Information Center, 1981).

KGB–NATO journalist letter: HPSCI, February 1980.

Soviet's SS-20 missiles: Public Information Office, U.S. Defense Department; *Soviet Military Power*, U.S. Defense Department, 1981, 1983; New York *Times*, December 31, 1977.

U.S.–NATO plan for deployment of missiles: *Time*, November 16, 30, 1981; New York *Times*, December 12, 1981; Washington *Post*, November 16, 1981; *Moscow and the Peace Offensive*.

Soviets stepped-up campaign after Reagan takes office: *Time*, November 16, 30, 1981. Chandra cable—"Cable to Reagan," *Peace Courier*, publication of the World Peace Council, vol. 12, September 1981. More marches in Europe—*Washington Report*, June 1982; *The American Sentinel*, June 28, 1982; *Human Events*, April 17, 1982; *Time*, November 16, 30, 1981. Communist marshals—*Time*, November 30, 1981. Amsterdam—New York *Times*, November 22, 1981. Madrid—Washington *Post*, November 16, 1981. Athens—Washington *Post*, November 16, 1981; New York *Times*, December 7, 1981. West Germany—*Time*, November 30, 1981.

Michel Meyer quote: John Vinocur, "The German Malaise," *New York Times Magazine*, November 15, 1981.

Vadim Leonov expelled by Dutch authorities: intelligence sources; *Moscow and the Peace Offensive;* Washington *Post*, April 16, 1981; *Washington Report*, June 1981; *Expulsion of Soviet Representatives from Foreign Countries*, Foreign Affairs Note, U.S. State Department, February 1982, January 1983.

Yuri Babayants and Mikhail Morozov expelled from Portugal: intelligence sources; *Expulsion of Soviet Representatives from Foreign Countries*, January 1983.

Lisbon march, Socialist Party statement, Rep. Gus Savage participation: Washington *Post*, January 17, 1982; office of Savage.

Savage quotation on the World Peace Council: "Your Congressman Gus Savage Reports to You from Washington," vol. 1, no. 4, December 6, 1981.

Forged documents, U.S. plans to blow up Europe, based on Robert Lee Johnson: HPSCI, July 1982; *Forgery, Disinformation, Political Operations, Soviet Active Measures;* intelligence sources. Plans to destroy

Austria, HPSCI, July 1982; intelligence sources; *Moscow and the Peace Offensive.*

Arne Herløv Petersen and Vladimir Merkulov: *Soviet Active Measures: An Update; Expulsion of Soviet Representatives from Foreign Countries, 1970-1981,* February 1982; intelligence sources; HPSCI, July 1982; *Moscow and the Peace Offensive;* New York *Times,* December 11, 1981; Baltimore *Sun,* November 6, 1981.

Brezhnev, February 23, 1981, calls for a nuclear freeze: Brezhnev, "Report of the CPSU Central Committee and the Current Basis of the Party in Home and Foreign Policy," February 23, 1981, in *Current Soviet Policies VIII: Documentary Record of the 26th Congress of the Communist Party* (Columbus, Ohio: The Current Digest of the Soviet Press, 1981).

Zhukov quotation: *Pravda,* November 30, 1982, in FBIS, November 30, 1982.

Soviet and U.S. weaponry: Public Information Office, U.S. Defense Department.

Launching of the U.S. freeze movement, March 20, 1981: *Daily World,* April 2, 1981; *The Mobilizer,* April/May, 1981, p.6.

Terry Provance: *Washington Report,* June 1982; *Science,* vol. 197, August 5, 1977; *Report,* Nuclear Weapons Facilities Task Force National Conference, October 23-25, 1981, Nyack, N.Y.; Agenda of the U.S. Peace Council meeting, founding conference, November 9-11, 1979, Philadelphia; "NATO-*Beschluss erhoht Kriegsgefahr*" ("NATO Meeting Increases War Danger"), *Neues Deutschland,* April 6, 1981; "National Task Forces of the Nuclear Weapons Freeze," Freeze Newsletter, vol. 2, no. 4, April 1982; "World Conference to End the Arms Race, for Disarmament and Détente," booklet of the meeting held in Helsinki, September 23-26, 1976. The last two World Peace Council official membership rosters, for the years 1977–1980 and 1980–1983, list Terry Provance as a WPC member. The official "U.S. Peace Council Founding Conference" agenda (November 9–11, 1979, Philadelphia) lists Provance as a "Workshop" leader on the subject of "New Weapons." The other "Leaders" listed in this "Workshop" were "James Jackson, Member of Presidential Committee, World Peace Council" and "William Hogan, Chicago Clergy & Laity Concerned; Chicago Peace Council."

Topics discussed at Georgetown: Agenda, "Call for a bilateral nuclear freeze—first national strategy meeting," Reiss Science Center, Georgetown University, Washington, D.C.

Mobilizer quotation: *The Mobilizer*, April/May 1981; telephone interview with *Mobilizer* reporter Maxine Alper, August 5, 1982.

Oleg Bogdanov and Yuri Kapralov: Involvement in "peace" movement—*Daily World*, April 2, 1981; Agenda—"Call for a bilateral nuclear freeze—first national strategy meeting" Reiss Science Center; *The Mobilizer*, April/May 1981. Kapralov at the Riverside Church—Jane Rockman, ed., *Peace in Search of Makers*, Riverside Church Reverse the Arms Race Convocation (Valley Forge: Judson Press, 1979); the January 24, 1979, issue of *Carillon*, a Riverside Church publication, reported and pictured Kapralov as present at the founding conference of the Riverside Church Disarmament Program. Kapralov assuring American audiences and at Harvard—New York *Times*, November 12, 1981; Boston *Globe*, November 15, 1981.

Identification of Bogdanov as International Department representative and Kapralov as KGB officer: intelligence sources.

Georgi Arbatov, International Department: "Summary Proceedings of the first Congress of International Physicians for the Prevention of Nuclear War,". Airlie House, March 20-25, 1981; Washington *Post*, March 24, 1981; Toronto *Star*, March 29, 1981; intelligence sources.

International Physicians Conference, Cambridge, England: "Preliminary Documents of the Second Congress of the International Physicians for the Prevention of Nuclear War," including workshop summaries, April 3-7, 1982.

Chandra and Congress in May 1981: *Washington Report*, June 1982; "Dear Colleague" letter, from Congressional members, on the stationery of Rep. John Conyers, Jr., May 1, 1981.

Mobilization for Survival Strategy Conference, Nyack, N.Y., October 1981: "Report: Nuclear Weapons Facilities Task Force, National Conference, October 23-25, 1981, Nyack, N.Y.," minutes of the meeting.

Chandra and Achim Maske: *Peace and Solidarity*, U.S. Peace Council newsletter, January/February 1982.

Gus Savage and John Conyers speak about inducting minorities into the disarmament drive and the transfer of funds from the defense budget to welfare programs, respectively, and their participation: *The War Called Peace*, Western Goals, Alexandria, Virginia, 1982; "Second National Conference Sets Direction for New Year," *Peace and Solidarity*, U.S. Peace Council newsletter, January/February 1982; information booklet, U.S. Peace Council Second National Conference, November 13-15, 1981; telephone interviews with legislative aides to Savage and Conyers.

Myerson's statement: "The New War Danger: The Peace Movement's Challenge for the 1980s," report to the U.S. Peace Council Second National Conference by Michael Myerson, Executive Director, November 13-15, 1981.

Identification of Myerson as Communist functionary: *Subversive Involvement in the Origin, Leadership, and Activities of the New Mobilization Committee to End the War in Vietnam and Its Predecessor Organizations,* Staff Study by the Committee on Internal Security, House of Representatives, 1970, pp. 16, 61; intelligence sources. The Communist *Daily World* on November 13, 1979 quoted Myerson, who is Executive Director of the U.S. Peace Council and a member of the World Peace Council, as saying: "There has been great pressure on the peace movement not to affiliate with the World Peace Council because it has Communists in its leadership and at its base."

November 15, 1981, conference at the Riverside Church: *The Arms Race and Us,* publication of the Riverside Church Disarmament Program, November 15-16, 1981.

Weiss background: HCIS Staff Study, 1970; New York *Times,* July 10, 16, 1968, December 23, 24, 25, 1969, December 17, 1976, December 20, 1977; *July 4th Bulletin,* publication of the July 4th Coalition, April 1976; Tenth Anniversary booklet, Center for Cuban Studies, 1982; "National Conference on Cuba," Center for Cuban Studies, New York, N.Y., November 2-4, 1979; Letter from Fidel Castro to the Directors, Center for Cuban Studies, April 30, 1982; booklet on Cuba, *In Concert with Cuba 78—End the Blockade, A Salute to the XIth World Festival of Youth and Students.*

Caldicott statements: *The Arms Race and Us.*

Kapralov at Riverside: Rockman, ed., *Peace in Search of Makers;* "Riverside's Disarmament Convocation Reviewed," *Carillon,* January 24, 1979.

Cagan statement: In a telephone interview August 10, 1982, Cagan confirmed she made the statements this book attributes to her.

King statement: In a telephone interview August 12, 1982, King confirmed he made the statement attributed to him and that he is active in the World Peace Council and U.S. Peace Council.

Account of other proceedings and statements at MFS meeting: verified in telephone interviews August 10, 1982, with two participants—Paul Mayer, Religious Task Force, Brooklyn, N.Y., and Mark Pickett, Coalition for Nuclear Disarmament, Princeton, N.J.

Peace Courier report: *Peace Courier*, December 1981.

Kennedy and Hatfield resolution: *Congressional Record*, Senate and House, March 10, 1982.

KGB officers Paramonov, Shustov and Divilkovsky, involvement in peace movement: intelligence sources; *Carillon*, January 24, 1979.

Soviet delegation visiting campaign leaders: Boston *Globe*, June 23, 1980; telephone interview with the *Globe* reporter, August 5, 1982; intelligence sources.

Mostovets: *Canadian Tribune*, January 14, 1980; intelligence sources.

National Academy of Sciences meeting: Public Affairs Office, National Academy of Sciences, Washington, D.C.; intelligence sources.

Soviets rehearse a surprise nuclear attack on the United States: Washington *Post*, June 20, 21, 1982; Public Information Office, U.S. Defense Department.

Attempt at disarmament rally in the Soviet Union quickly squelched: Washington *Post*, April 20, 1982.

Associated Press dispatch on psychiatric abuse in the Soviet Union: New York *Times*, August 9, 1982.

Edward O'Malley and John McMahon testimony: HPSCI, July 1982.

Rep. Edward Boland quote: New York *Times*, December 10, 1982.

CHAPTERS VII and VIII

These chapters are based primarily upon interviews the author conducted with Rudolf Herrmann. The first interviews occurred in November 1980 at Williamsburg, Va., and Associate Editor William Gunn participated in some of them. Further interviews took place in Washington, D.C., during December 1981, when Herrmann laboriously corrected the chapter drafts, working with the author, Gunn, and David Pacholczyk. In the opinion of the researchers, Herrmann regarded the story as the testament of his life and wanted it correct, to the last detail.

Although Herrmann remained an ideological Marxist even after he became an American double-agent, the FBI apparently came to trust him.

Herrmann is the sole source of details relating to his childhood and adolescence in Czechoslovakia, introduction into the KGB, meetings with KGB officers, and family life prior to the mid-1970s. Efforts have been made to check other aspects of his story, with the following results.

The Gathering Storm by Winston Churchill recounts the events pertaining to the Munich conference that so influenced Herrmann.

Data concerning Herrmann's homeland: *Encyclopaedia Britannica; Collier's Encyclopedia;* Press Office, Embassy of Czechoslovakia; European Division, Library of Congress; U.S. State Department Background Notes.

Facts about the late Otto Seefelder: checked with his sister-in-law in Ichenhausen, West Germany.

Harold's Famous Delicatessen: Toronto tax records.

Confirmation of Herrmann's employment with the Canadian Broadcasting Company: personnel office at CBC in Toronto.

Confirmation of Herrmann's naturalization in Canada: Canadian citizenship records, Department of the Secretary of State, Ottawa.

The meetings and relationship between Herrmann and Hambleton were described to the author by both men. (Confirmation of Hambleton's background and activities comes from several sources. See Chapter Notes, Chapter IX).

Herrmann's house in Hartsdale: Tax Assessor's Office in Greenburgh, N.Y.

Herrmann's film company was listed in the Manhattan Telephone Directory Yellow Pages.

Information on the Hudson Institute: *Research Centers Directory*, 5th ed. (Detroit: Gale Research Co., 1975); Public Affairs Office, Hudson Institute, Croton-on-Hudson, N.Y.

Confirmation of "crank letters" written to NASA prior to the space flight: NASA News Service, Washington, D.C.

Information on Gen. Drozdov: Arkadi Shevchenko in *Intelligence Report*, Standing Committee on Law and National Security, American Bar Association, Chicago, 1980; Protocol Office, U.S. State Department; intelligence sources.

Peter Herrmann's attendance at Georgetown University: confirmed by the university's Registrar's Office in Washington, D.C.

The Dahlgren operation: Fredericksburg *Free Lance Star*, July 15, 1980; Washington *Post*, July 12, 1980; intelligence sources.

Published reports of Herrmann's story: New York *Times*, Washington *Post*, Washington *Star*, New York *Daily News*, Chicago *Tribune*, Los Angeles *Times*, *Newsday*—all March 4, 1980; *Newsweek*, March 17, 1980.

CHAPTER IX

In writing this chapter, the author relied chiefly upon his conversations with Hugh George Hambleton at the Château Frontenac and Laval University, in Quebec, during December 1980. Subsequent correspondence between the author and Hambleton indicates to researchers that an amicable relation between the two existed, and that they planned further interviews.

All published accounts of Hambleton's testimony at his trial in London are basically consistent with what he told the author, except in one area. At the time of their conversations, Hambleton was convinced that his Yugoslav girlfriend had died of cancer. However, in December 1982, British newspapers published photographs of a young woman in Belgrade identified as the girlfriend. Efforts to verify aspects of Hambleton's story yielded the following results.

For information on Communist agents and sympathizers, see David Caute, *The Fellow Travellers* (London: Weidenfeld and Nicolson, 1973); Leonard Schapiro, *Communist Party of the Soviet Union* (London: Eyre & Spottiswoode, 1960); Hewlett Johnson, *The Socialist Sixth of the World* (London: Victor Gollancz, 1939).

Various aspects of the story of Hugh Hambleton have come out in press reports over the past few years. See Montreal *Gazette*, November 12, 14, 1979; March 4, 12, May 8, 24, 1980; July 3, 7, 21, 23, 1982; Washington *Post*, November 30, December 8, 1982; New York *Times*, December 1, 8, 1982; Toronto *Globe and Mail*, August 21, 1982; New York *Post*, November 30, 1982; Ottawa *Citizen*, December 4, 1982.

Information on Hambleton's father: Ottawa *Citizen*, December 4, 1982, and the Canadian Press Association.

Hugh Hambleton's background, education and experience are detailed in *Who's Who in Canada*, vol. 16 (Toronto: University of Toronto Press, 1981) and in his personnel file at Laval University in Quebec.

Information on the Free French Forces: *Encyclopaedia Britannica.*

Hambleton's World War II military service: verified by his official service record.

French training camp in Nebraska: Nebraska State Historical Society, Lincoln; Center for Air Force History, Washington, D.C.

The 103rd Division: U.S. Army Center for Military History, Washington, D.C.

Hambleton's employment by the National Film Board of Canada: confirmed by that group's personnel office in Ottawa.

For information on Soviet penetration of the Manhattan Project, see Montgomery H. Hyde, *The Atom Bomb Spies* (New York: Atheneum, 1979); *Encyclopaedia Britannica.*

Vladimir Borodin's presence in Canada: Canadian Office of External Affairs, Ottawa.

Hambleton's professorial position and duties: the Faculty of Economic Sciences at Laval University.

Information on Herrmann and his dealings and relationship with Hambleton was told to author by both men.

The Defense Programs area of the Department of Energy confirms that it was possible to get an idea of the workings of an atomic bomb from reading readily available literature.

The Canadian International Development Agency confirms that Hambleton worked for them in the early 1970s.

Information on Hambleton's arrest, trial and conviction come from several previously mentioned newspaper sources, and his sentence was confirmed by the Office of the Clerk, Central Criminal Court, London.

Chapter X

Lenin quotation: V.I. Lenin, *"Left-Wing" Communism: An Infantile Disorder* (New York: International Publishers, 1921), p. 52.

Soviet activities in the U.S.: HPSCI, July 1982; SPSI, May 1982.

Great Britain's diplomatic relations with Soviet Union after expulsion: Press Office, British Embassy, Washington, D.C.

Commerce Department's Compliance Division: SPSI, May 1982; Press Office, U.S. Commerce Department, Washington, D.C.

Bureau of East-West Trade: J. Mishell George, Bureau of East-West Trade; Press Office, U.S. Commerce Department.

COCOM (Coordinating Committee) and U.S. requests for exemptions: SPSI, May 1982; Subcommittee on International Finance of the Banking, Housing and Urban Affairs Committee, U.S. Senate, hearings, March 22, 23, 1976.

Public opinion polls regarding armed forces: The American Security Council, Washington, D.C., stated in January 1983 that its polls consistently have shown willingness by a majority of Americans to maintain powerful armed forces; a CBS News/New York *Times* poll conducted in May 1982 asked subjects: "What if a nuclear freeze would result in the Soviet Union having somewhat greater nuclear strength than the United States—would you favor or oppose such a freeze?" Sixty-seven percent of the respondents said they would oppose such a freeze, Poll cited in *Public Opinion*, August/September 1982, p. 39.

Operations Division of CIA: Theodore Shackley, *The Third Option* (New York: Reader's Digest Press, 1981).

Turner's Halloween Massacre: Shackley, *The Third Option*.

Data concerning departing officers from CIA: These data were reported to the author by a number of former CIA personnel, including one of the station chiefs mentioned.

Ghotbzadeh approach to CIA: intelligence and Congressional sources.

Statistics on FBI agent strength and case load: FBI Annual Reports, 1973 through 1982; FBI Appropriations Requests, 1977 through 1983.

Ogorodnik: Levchenko; intelligence sources.

Filatov: New York *Times*, September 10, 23, 1980, and Los Angeles *Times*, November 3, 1982, report deal regarding Filatov; other data are from Levchenko.

Shevchenko: New York *Times*, April 4, 1973; November 3, 1975; April 13, 18, 23, 24, 27, 29, May 2, 5, 11, October 10, 12, 1978; September 23, 1980; *Newsweek*, November 6, 1978; Levchenko.

Kuzichkin: New York *Times*, Washington *Post*, October 24, 1982; *Time*, November 22, 1982; (London) *Daily Telegraph*, January 23, 1982.

Andropov quotation: "The arena of historic confrontation . . ." in *Soviet Watch*, Advanced International Studies Institute, Bethesda, Md., November 30, 1982.

Andropov quotation: "Cheka authorities . . ." in *U.S.S.R. Report*, November 29, 1982, p. 65.

Kopocsi and Andropov: *The Wall Street Journal*, November 15, 1982; confirmed by Mrs. Kopocsi, by phone January 1983.

INDEX

DONALD JAMES

A SPY AT EVENING

'Nothing that I have read from the school of Le Carré is as good as A SPY AT EVENING ... Every detail of its twilit world is beautifully realised, all the characters, just slightly larger than life, are superbly etched and all in all this is the most exciting espionage debut since Le Carré himself'
SPECTATOR

Was Tom Hart dismissed from the Secret Intelligence Service a victim of office in-fighting or because he was too drunk and unstable to continue?

Of course Hart has his own answer and in an attempt to reinstate himself he accepts freelance work from a King-and-Country General and his *Action England* movement. But as he fights for his future, he is dogged by the past: a disastrous error of judgement in New York, his unsatisfactory relationships with women, even the historical past that constantly absorbs his imagination. Salving his disappointments with sex and alcohol, Tom Hart is personally engaging but potentially dangerous. Is his attempt to destroy the *Action England* movement, therefore, just further evidence of his instability ...

Post·A·Book

A Royal Mail service in association with the Book Marketing Council & The Booksellers Association.

Post-A-Book is a Post Office trademark.

ANTHONY OLCOTT

MURDER AT THE RED OCTOBER

Vanya Duvakin, night security officer at the Red October Hotel in Moscow finds a foreign guest murdered in one of the rooms. The dead man, Miller, is 'the worst kind' – American – and when the police are called in a grand cover-up is quickly set in motion.

Duvakin looks on puzzled but dismisses it as CIA and KGB games, until by chance he finds himself involved in it up to his neck. The *matryoshka*, a set of nesting dolls, which he picked up from Miller's bedroom floor turns out to contain 100 grams of heroin. When he reports this to the KGB he is 'persuaded' to let himself be drawn into a ring suspected of smuggling heroin and black-marketeering.

Given a short briefing and a bundle of foreign currency, a reluctant Duvakin sets off to try and penetrate the organisation. A night-shift Sherlock, he has to do his sleuthing in his spare time. Even in moments of high danger, he struggles to stay awake. Taken for a ride, all he can think about is his poor bursting bladder. Trapped in dire straits, his main worry is that his only winter coat has been destroyed. Matching wits with thugs far smarter than he, he learns to bluff his way through and develops a happy talent for mendacity, but soon he wants out: only a security guard after all, he feels unable to cope with these machinations, but he is caught in a trap from which there is no escape.

CORONET BOOKS

ANDREW BOYLE

THE CLIMATE OF TREASON

THE CLIMATE OF TREASON is the sensational book on the background to the Burgess, Maclean and Philby affair that led to the exposure of Anthony Blunt as the 'fourth' man. Brilliantly researched and compulsively readable, it shows how four upper-class Cambridge-educated Englishmen could work for Russia and consistently betray their country.

CORONET BOOKS

NIGEL WEST

A MATTER OF TRUST

MI5
1945–72

For the first time Britain's most secret government department is described in painstaking detail. Never before have its successes – and failures – been so well researched and so completely presented.

Was the former Director-General of the Security Service, Sir Roger Hollis, a traitor? Who was the defector whose memory of files in Moscow led to the identification of more than a dozen Russian spies in the West? These are just two of the questions posed in this unique and highly readable account of Britain's premier counter-intelligence organization. The answers are stranger than fiction, and yet thoroughly documented with names, dates and places.

CORONET BOOKS

ALSO AVAILABLE FROM CORONET BOOKS

☐ 25390 8   **DONALD JAMES**
            A Spy At Evening   £1.25

☐ 33782 6   **ANTHONY OLCOTT**
            Murder At The Red October   £1.75

☐ 25572 2   **ANDREW BOYLE**
            The Climate Of Treason   £1.95

☐ 33781 8   **NIGEL WEST**
            A Matter Of Trust   £1.95

All these books are available at your local bookshop or newsagent, or can be ordered direct from the publisher. Just tick the titles you want and fill in the form below.

Prices and availability subject to change without notice.

CORONET BOOKS, P.O. Box 11, Falmouth, Cornwall.

Please send cheque or postal order, and allow the following for postage and packing:

U.K. – 55p for one book, plus 22p for the second book, and 14p for each additional book ordered up to a £1.75 maximum.

B.F.P.O. and EIRE – 55p for the first book, plus 22p for the second book, and 14p per copy for the next 7 books, 8p per book thereafter.

OTHER OVERSEAS CUSTOMERS – £1.00 for the first book, plus 25p per copy for each additional book.

Name ....

Address ....

....